MW01200658

ALL PROCEEDS RECEIVED FROM THE SALE OF THIS BOOK WILL BE CONTRIBUTED TO THE GUIDE DOG FOUNDATION FOR THE BLIND. IT IS MY HOPE THAT THOSE PERSONS RECEIVING THIS BOOK AS A GIFT WOULD BE INCLINED TO SEND A GENEROUS CONTRIBUTION TO THE ADDRESS LISTED BELOW. ALL SUCH GIFTS WILL BE APPRECIATED AND ACKNOWLEDGED TO YOU DIRECTLY BY THE FOUNDATION.

Please make check payable to:
Guide Dog Foundation for the Blind, Inc.
and send to:
John C. Ostlund
318 West Second Avenue
Cheyenne, WY 82001

For additional information about the Guide Dog Foundation,
please contact them at:
Guide Dog Foundation for the Blind, Inc.
371 East Jericho Turnpike
Smithtown, NY 11787
1-800-548-4337
www.guidedog.org

QUITE A LIFE
John C. Ostlund

ELTON-WOLF PUBLISHING

Seattle • Los Angeles

QUITE A LIFE

ISBN: 1-58783-003-5
Library of Congress Catalog Card Number: 00-105633

First Printing December 2000
Printed in Canada

Published by Elton-Wolf Publishing
Seattle, Washington

ELTON-WOLF PUBLISHING

2505 Second Avenue Suite 515   Seattle Washington 98121 (206) 748-0345
e-mail: info@elton-wolf.com   Internet: http://www.elton-wolf.com
Seattle • Los Angeles

To My Grandchildren

Acknowledgments

THIS PAGE OF MY BOOK GIVES ME THE OPPORTUNITY TO EXPRESS MY DEEP APPRECIATION TO JUST A FEW OF THE MANY PEOPLE WHO ASSISTED ME IN BRINGING MY LONG EFFORTS AT WRITING TO COMPLETION.

For more than a decade, while listening to the monotonous drone of the artifical voice from my computer, I have written and edited every page of this text. Although I am unable to see photographs or documents, to those who have done this for me, I express thanks.

Major assistance came from my wife, Mary, who carefully examined hundreds of photographs, selecting and captioning many of those finally chosen for this book.

Thanks to our daughter, Peg, for suggesting the title of my book, *Quite a Life*. Peg also found numerous historical photos appropriate for my book. We thank the Wyoming Cultural Resources Division for permitting us to use these photographs.

Both Peg and Karin deserve thanks for embellishing my book with additional photos and other documents placed throughout my manuscript. Their diligence was a real assist in the final organization of this book. Our sons, John and Scott, were of utmost help in the final editing of the book.

Thanks to my USNA 1949 classmates for giving Mary the correct names of friends shown in my Navy photos from long ago. These friends include Jack Rupe, John Greene, Bill Jones, Zeke Roland, Chuck Swanson, and Fred Wilder. It was great visiting with them again.

Thanks to our son, Tom, for converting my entire text from an older program to the new Microsoft Word. His technical skills have been invaluable.

A million thanks go to all of my family who have always been lovingly supportive. Without them, this publication would never have been considered.

John C. Ostlund, 2000

Contents

Prologue

JULY 4, 1986, WAS A DAY OF GREAT CELEBRATION BECAUSE IT MARKED THE unveiling of a newly refurbished Statue of Liberty. It also marked the 100th Anniversary of the original Statue of Liberty which was dedicated on October 28, 1886. A huge flotilla of ships was assembled in New York Harbor, as well as a huge number of dignitaries headed by President Ronald Reagan. The entire Country seemed to be caught up in a renewed patriotic fever that we had not experienced for a long time.

Among the people who were interviewed on television and radio were many who had actually immigrated to the United States. They were describing the wonderful feelings they experienced on first sighting the beautiful Statue of Liberty. Some told of their remembrances of being processed through Ellis Island. Unfortunately, some were turned back, while the more fortunate ones were passed through.

As I listened to the events it occurred to me that both my paternal grandparents as well as my maternal ones had immigrated to the United States in the late 1800s. I was aware of this, but I never knew the stories behind their immigrations. As I dwelt on this, it also occurred to me that I really had very little firsthand knowledge of my grandparents. Most of what I knew came from stories I heard my parents recall. How sad, I thought. Now that my parents were no longer living there was no opportunity left to capture anymore of their facts or anecdotes.

On impulse, I called my mother's brother, C. D. "Scotchie" Roberts. At this writing, Scotchie is eighty-two and in fair health. He and his wife, Frances, now live in Spearfish, South Dakota. He seemed both surprised and pleased to hear from me.

"Scotchie," I opened, "I am going to attempt to write a bit about my life and my family for my own grandchildren, and it occurs to me that I missed a great opportunity to know a lot about my own grandfather. For example, why did your father decide to immigrate from Scotland?"

Scotchie thought he had probably forgotten, but he did know that my grandfather, M.C. Roberts, first went from Scotland to Canada. From Canada, he then came to the United States, and on to Sturgis, South Dakota. Scotchie said my grandfather sent for his future wife, Elizabeth Bain Spence, to come from Scotland and they were married in Sturgis on July 9, 1901.

Next I called my Aunt Rose Carlson in Paxton, Illinois. Aunt Rose was my father's youngest sister and the only family member still living from the eight children born to my paternal grandparents. I always remember her as such a happy lady. Aunt Rose is now widowed and her only son, Ron, died recently of cancer. Aunt Rose is now about eighty-eight years of age. I told Aunt Rose I wanted to know about my grandparents and the reason for their immigrating to the United States from Sweden.

Rose told me her father just decided to do it—left his wife and their first child, Hartwick, in Sweden while he came and found a job. He went directly to a Swedish community called Paxton and became a laborer. After he saved money, he sent for his wife and child along with his sister, Minnie. My Ostlund grandparents raised four boys and four girls—a feat that Mary and I later duplicated in our own married life.

From this short introduction I shall attempt to write about my own life. My book, which at this time is nameless, will be dedicated to my grandchildren. Although I want my book to be factual, I certainly hope it will not be thought boring! I shall endeavor to bring a smile to the faces of my grandchildren from time to time. That is not my promise, but rather my hope!

Our daughter, Peg, suggested the idea that I write about my life and she worked steadily trying to convince me to make a start. I even tried to use the excuse of being blind since 1985, and how that would frustrate my attempts to write.

Peg would counter by saying, "You are a good typist and since you installed the new software which reads your typing back to you, your letters are very good! Don't think of writing a book; just begin by writing whatever comes into your mind. At least try it!"

It is with this acknowledgment that I recognize Peg who has been instrumental in getting me started. With her gentle persuasion I kept on writing. Peg, I thank you for your encouragement!

John C. Ostlund, 1986

1

The First Days

Burlington Lake, Gillette, Wyoming. *Wyoming Division of Cultural Resources*

THE YEAR WAS 1927 AND SEPTEMBER WAS DRAWING TO A CLOSE. THE FALL breeze put a chill in the air. As a pair of cowboys rode their horses toward the grazing cattle, they buttoned their denim jackets tighter at the throat. This was the kind of morning when a good neckerchief was welcome, and they snugged their red bandanas around their necks to keep out the chill air.

The two cowboys worked for the Chicago, Burlington, and Quincy Railroad. This time of year they were busy each day loading and unloading cattle for shipment heading east toward Omaha and Chicago.

Livestock production was flourishing in the Powder River Basin of northeast Wyoming. However, water was always the critical element. To help resolve this problem, the railroad had undertaken a big project. During the early 1920s, the railroad hired men along with teams of draft horses to build a ditch to carry water. This ditch would divert water from Donkey Creek, south of Gillette, to a man-made lake north of town. This was to become known as the Burlington Lake. It was essential to the transport of cattle and sheep because the livestock had to be fed and watered.

With the availability of both grass and water, along with its rail location, Gillette, Wyoming, was becoming the largest livestock shipping point on the Burlington system. During the fall, cattle arrived daily. The long trains of livestock cars were filled with cattle or sheep. Huge black, coal-burning steam locomotives, with smoke belching from the stack, and white steam escaping from the driver pistons, powered these livestock trains. Some days the sparks flying from the smokestack could ignite dry range grass. Then the fire bell would ring in the town and volunteers would rush to the scene. Equipped with sacks and shovels, the men would attempt to beat out and control the grass fires.

By necessity livestock trains arriving from the north would often unload their stock for overnight feed and water. Producers were concerned for their stock and shrinkage due to transportation could amount to lost dollars. Railroaders were well aware of this and grass and water were afforded at intervals to keep shrinkage to a minimum.

Gillette, Wyoming, had tamed some. After all it was now thirty-seven years since Frank Gillette originally had surveyed it as a rail site. In those early days, like all new railroad towns, Gillette was a wild place: saloons, card games, hard drinking, and fighting were commonplace. But now, thirty-seven years later, Gillette was maturing—surrendering its wildness.

On this particular day a couple of teams harnessed to wagons were at the hitching rail in front of Daly's store. The wagons were being loaded with supplies which ranchers and homesteaders needed for the coming winter. The main dirt street was dry and dusty. The sidewalks were made of wooden boards. Several cottonwood trees could be seen growing along the wide main street.

The old Buffalo Hump Saloon had recently been replaced by the new Montgomery Hotel. It was a brick two-story building with sleeping rooms on the second floor. On the ground floor was a café with a long partition dividing and separating the café from the saloon.

The saloon belonged to a gray-haired man affectionately called "Jew Jake." Jake Kauffman was his real name and cards were his game. Round tables covered with green felt were at the back of the saloon and even during the day there were usually a few fellows wagering their money at the tables.

Jake's place was unique in that all the walls were covered with wild animal heads. Most were native to Wyoming such as the deer, antelope, elk, and moose. In addition, a few eagles, bear, coyote, and wolf lined the walls. But the most unusual head on the wall was that of an elephant.

The origin of this elephant head was unknown to me until in later years my pal, Dick Hall, told me the story. Dick's father, Otis Hall, was working for the railroad out of Sheridan when there was a circus train derailment. The elephant had died in the wreck and a local taxidermist immediately went to work. Jake was proud to acquire this unusual trophy and thus it claimed its spot on the wall of the Montgomery Bar.

Jake's place was the first saloon to be reached after a person stepped off the train in Gillette. It was popular with railroaders as well as with local folks.

Axel W. Ostlund, age thirty-six, walked in the front door of Jake's place with a smile on his face. He wore a bigger smile than usual and he ordered a prohibition approved "near beer."

"Well," he raised his glass, "I've got a new son, just born early this morning. He weighed nine and a half pounds."

Red, the bartender, offered his congratulations by buying the first drink.

Jake, seated at a table, spoke. "So you've got another plumber, huh Axel?" He glanced up at the daily calendar and noted that it was September 29. "How's the Missus?"

Axel responded by saying that both his wife and the baby were doing fine.

Meanwhile, several blocks away, up on a hill, was a house that served as the hospital. Dr. James Hunter was talking with Axel's wife, Mary S. Ostlund, who was known to all her friends as Polly. "What are you going to name the boy, Polly?"

Polly said, "We are going to name him after both his grandfathers, John Chapman Ostlund. Axel's father spelled his name Jon, but we are going to spell the baby's name John. The Chapman is my father's middle name."

With that information Dr. Hunter dutifully filled out the birth certificate showing that the mother was twenty-five years old and this was her second baby. Their first son was named Axel Roberts Ostlund, born March 28, 1925.

Having finished his beer, Axel began the two-and-a-half-block walk back to his plumbing shop. As he walked the wooden sidewalks he contemplated the coming antelope season. Axel was also assistant game warden; a job that supplied much needed extra income. Just this year the Wyoming legislature had passed a law that provided for the first antelope season ever held. Up to one thousand licenses were to be sold in Wyoming and Campbell County was sure to issue many of these licenses. Resident permits were $2.80 each and nonresident permits were set at an exorbitant $50 to discourage people from coming in to hunt.

The short walk ended when Axel reached the small two-room plumbing shop. Since chilly weather had returned, he built a fire in the wood and coal stove in the back room where the single stove provided heat for the two rooms. He noticed Lou Gilbert sitting in a chair close to the stove reading the weekly paper.

Lou spoke, "Congratulations, Axel, I understand you have a new son."

"Yeah, that's right, just born this morning," Axel said. "Both Polly and the baby are doing fine."

"That's good," said Lou, not taking his eyes off the newspaper. The *News Record* came out every Thursday afternoon and Lou had picked up his copy at the paper office just down the alley from Axel's shop.

Frank George, a local carpenter and wagon builder, walked in the front door and said, "Axel, I need a couple of roof jacks for sheep wagons."

Axel smiled and told Frank he could have them in an hour if he wanted to wait. Axel would make them from galvanized steel sheets that he kept in stock under the workbench.

The conversation immediately switched to the Tunney-Dempsey fight, the World Heavyweight Championship that had just been won by Tunney the previous Thursday. A special Atwater Kent radio had been set up at the Dick Stone hardware store as well as radios at the two local pool halls.

Gene Tunney had retained his title that he had previously taken from Jack Dempsey, the Manassa Mauler. The fight had been staged at Soldiers Field in Chicago. The purse of three million dollars was the largest in history. During the seventh round, Dempsey knocked Tunney to the canvas and this became a bitter point of argument to continue for years. It became known as the "long count." The referee refused to begin the count until Dempsey went to a neutral corner. So when the count commenced, Tunney had regained his feet before the count of ten. At the end of the final round, the tenth, the judges awarded the decision to Tunney. Fans all over the country were listening to the radios that Thursday night in September. Gillette sport fans took advantage of the three radios that delivered the broadcast from Chicago. The arguments over the "long count" went on and on. Although the decision was awarded to Tunney, the public arguments were never resolved.

Lou Gilbert was a sheep rancher and had put a good-sized ranch together in the process. He liked Axel, as did a lot of people. It was always interesting to watch Axel make things from sheet metal and Axel took pride in doing his job well. The King Oak coal stove provided plenty of heat and on cold days it was quite enjoyable to spend time in Axel's shop. The coal scuttle beside the stove also served as a spittoon and, consequently, the shiny lumps of coal not only appeared wet, they actually were wet.

Whenever business slowed down at the shop, Axel was willing to start a game of cribbage or perhaps a game of pitch. Axel loved card games and a game usually was played for small monetary stakes. Today, as different people came and went, the local news of the day gradually unfolded.

Major League Baseball had just concluded its season and the leading home-run hitter in 1927 was George Herman "Babe" Ruth with sixty home runs!

The first solo flight across the Atlantic had been made ninety days ago. Charles Lindbergh became a renowned world hero when he accomplished that mission in his *Spirit of St. Louis.* News stories of Lindbergh continued to take space in every paper.

Typical news items appearing in the newspaper being read by Lou Gilbert were: McGrew's Garage had received a carload of Chevrolet automobiles yesterday and they were already all sold and delivered. Prices for cattle, sheep, and wool were all good and the threshing harvests were showing plenty of grain production. All in all, business was excellent and the economics of 1927 were considered very favorable. Predictions of increased land values were being made. As these predictions were being forecast, certainly no one was expecting that in less than twenty-five months we would witness the greatest market crash in the history of the United States. And then the thirties were to bring years of drought and depression.

Axel told Lou Gilbert he was going to buy a lot and probably build a house the following year. The lot was later to be described as the corner of Fifth Street and Warren Avenue. At that time there were only four buildings in the entire block. Facing Gillette Avenue, the main street, was the County Courthouse, which was the former Daly residence. Adjacent to the courthouse, and to the north, was a small wooden building that served as the county library.

The lot Axel bought was across the alley and west from the courthouse. Two small wooden houses were adjacent and to the north of Axel's lot. One of the houses belonged to Lou Gilbert. Lou said, "That sounds like a good idea, and besides, we would then be neighbors."

During the year of 1928, Axel and Polly began building the house they were to live in until their deaths in 1980 and 1982. It was a very nice house for its time. The house had a full basement, one bedroom on the main floor, and two small bedrooms on the second floor. Axel installed metal shingles that were always painted red. There was no doubt that Axel's favorite color was red. By 1929 he had also built a two-car garage detached from the house. It was all finished just in time for the terrible market crash of October 29, 1929.

Main Street, Gillette, Wyoming, 1902. *Wyoming Division of Cultural Resources*

The Buffalo Hump Saloon, Gillette, Wyoming. *Wyoming Division of Cultural Resources*
Left to right: Roy Montgomery, #5 Bob Tantum, #8 Ote Spielman, John T. Daly. Others unidentified.

Ostlund Plumbing Shop, Gillette, Wyoming, 1927. Henry Ostlund, Axel's brother, standing in the doorway.

Campbell County Library. *Wyoming Division of Cultural Resources*

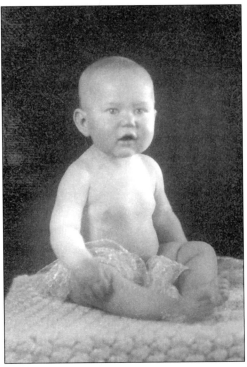

John Chapman Ostlund, 8 months, May 1928.

2

My Parents and Grandparents

AXEL WILLIAM OSTLUND, MY FATHER, ARRIVED IN GILLETTE IN 1919. WITH the signing of the armistice on November 11, 1918, he had ended his army service as part of the American Expeditionary forces in France. From his hometown of Paxton, Illinois, he joined the army at the beginning of World War I and trained at Fort Riley, Kansas. He was sent to France and served with the signal corps during the "great war to end all wars."

Coming home from the army and returning to a farm town in Illinois must have been a bit dull for a young man just back from France. I recall a very popular song written at that time named, "How You Gonna Keep Them Down on the Farm, After They've Seen Paree?" Jobs were scarce for discharged soldiers. With the spirit of adventure, Axel and three of his army buddies decided to go west. After all, the federal government was offering 640 acres of free land in the west if you took up a homestead. What a deal!

The four of them loaded their meager belongings into a Ford Model T touring car with a canvas top and headed west for their new adventure. The trip across country was long and undoubtedly arduous. Roads were not good and pushing out of mud holes was commonplace. Sometimes they had major mishaps, like breaking an axle. Although they carried spare parts, it was the long hours of repair that consumed their time and their money. Often they stopped to pick up small jobs along the way. This was a necessity to not only stay liquid, but also to stay alive.

The government land office was probably in Buffalo, Wyoming. I recall meeting Theodore Warnus who ran the land office at the time my father applied. I never did know for certain how my father ended up on his homestead around the north butte of the famous Pumpkin Buttes. It must have been forty to fifty miles south from Gillette. To be set down on a piece of this rugged country and be expected to make a new home on it was hard to imagine. In the year or two that was required, he "proved up" on his homestead and ultimately received the deed from the government.

My dad was doing the same as thousands of others at that time and the 640-acre homesteads were carving large chunks out of an otherwise unfenced rangeland. Over time most of these places were sold to larger ranchers. Making a living on 640 rugged acres proved to be a pretty desperate gamble. During the drought of the 1930s, many of these homesteaders literally dried out and walked away from their homesteads forever.

Axel was young and strong. He prided himself on being a wrestler while growing up in Paxton. Occasionally he would wrestle in Gillette when a match was offered. My mother kept a news clipping about Axel winning a match from a guy named Nelson by getting a toehold on his opponent. We kids thought that was great!

To earn money to live on, Axel took a job with the railroad. He worked as a brakeman on freight trains between Gillette and Billings, Montana. Axel liked to tell about how cranky railroaders were, especially to new employees.

We used to laugh at his story about the first time he rode to Billings on the freight. According to Axel, the conductor ordered him to jump off the train at the outskirts of Billings and run ahead of the moving steam engine so that the train would not have to stop to allow time for Axel to throw the switch to put the train on the proper track. Of course it was dark and when given the 'go' sign, Axel took off at high speed. Running desperately ahead of the engine, he stared at the red signal light glowing from the switch that he was supposed to throw. Unfortunately for Axel, those switches had long steel rods that ran horizontal to the ground and were about ten inches above it. Axel found this out when his shins connected with the first undisclosed steel bar from an unlighted switch. He went head over heels and was in terrible pain. (Axel always said, "I went ass over appetite!")

But the warning from the train crew was still ringing in his ears as he rose to his feet and raced forward, determined to throw the switch. Still leading the oncoming locomotive, he was desperate to reach the switch in time when—"Oh my God!"—he hit a second steel bar that was the same as the first. Axel always said that the train crew laughed their heads off at his pain and suffering, while he carried shin scars the rest of his life.

Axel also worked at odd jobs, including helping the sheriff at times. Growing up in Paxton, he had apprenticed at a local shop called Nordgren's, where he learned the plumbing trade. He was also a very good tinsmith. About 1922 or 1923 he learned of a new school that was to be built in Sundance, Wyoming, and he put in a bid on the plumbing and heating and was awarded the contract. That began his Wyoming career as a plumber, a trade he was to practice until his retirement.

The logistics of building a school in Sundance were severe. Material that came by rail was off-loaded in Moorcroft and had to be hauled to Sundance by truck, or more likely by horses and wagons. Winter weather, and sometimes spending the night on the trail, made the job a rough one for a young plumber from Gillette, especially since Axel had very little money saved to begin his business.

Axel was destined to meet a young lady in Sundance who was to become his wife on June 18, 1924. Her name was Mary Spence Roberts, eldest child of Matthew Chapman and Elizabeth Bain Spence Roberts. Mary Roberts was known to everyone as Polly, a nickname she carried all her life.

Polly's father, Matthew Chapman Roberts, was born September 18, 1870, in Avonbridge, Scotland. He was educated in the public schools at Avonbridge, the University of Glasgow, and the Congregational Theological Hall at Edinburg, Scotland. In 1898 he came to Canada. Soon afterward he visited Sturgis, South Dakota, to call on a former classmate.

Deciding to remain in the United States, Matthew affiliated that fall with the Black Hills Mission Conference and served as pastor of the Methodist Episcopal Churches of Terriville and Central City, South Dakota, until 1903.

On July 9, 1901, Matthew married his fiancée, Elizabeth Bain Spence, in Sturgis, South Dakota. The Reverend Willey, who was a college chum of Mr. Roberts while attending Glasgow University, performed the service.

Elizabeth was born in Paisley, Scotland, March 27, 1870. After leaving high school she devoted her time to the study of music. She graduated from the Athenaeum of Music, Glasgow, Scotland. Then she graduated from Trinity College of Music, London, England.

At the age of fifteen she joined the Congregational Church. She taught Sunday school and was organist of the church for many years until she came to America. She became engaged to Matthew C. Roberts, then a student of the Congregational Church in Scotland, and after Matthew located in Sturgis, he sent for Elizabeth so they could be married.

Unfortunately, I have only a vague recollection of my Grandmother Elizabeth Roberts. She died following an illness on June 7, 1930. At that time I was almost three years old. From all I have been told, she was an accomplished musician and a wonderful wife and mother. In 1947, I felt lucky when I had the good fortune to visit her sister, Polly Spence Orr, in Scotland. What a dear lady!

My mother, Polly, was born in Terriville, South Dakota, on April 19, 1902. Later, the family moved to Sundance where three more children were born. Clyde Dunsmore, "Scotchie", was the only son, born in 1904. Jessie Mable was born in 1906 and Elizabeth Lucille was born in 1908.

Matthew Roberts, taking advantage of any opportunity that might help him make a living, opened a mortuary in Sundance. Later he added a mercantile store as well. When Matthew moved to Newcastle in 1922, he left his eldest daughter in charge. Matthew became receiver of the U.S. Land Office. Five years later he entered business in Newcastle and became an organizer and director of the First State Bank. From 1933 until his death in 1943, he also served as president of this bank.

Following the marriage of Polly to Axel in 1924, Clyde Roberts took charge of the Sundance business. Clyde greatly expanded his operations and later added a flourmill, an implement business, a furniture store, a sand and gravel operation, and also a motel. "Scotchie" was always recognized as an astute businessman. On April 26, 1926, Clyde married Frances Ruth Barr and two children were born. Elizabeth Janice was born April 26, 1932, and Clyde Alan was born September 13, 1934.

Lucille Roberts was the youngest. In Newcastle she married George Culver. Gerald

George was born on January 29, 1932, and Elizabeth Jean was born on June 24, 1933.

As a small child Jessie Mable Roberts suffered from scarlet fever that caused some brain damage. In 1934 her widower father had her confined to the Wyoming State Training School at Lander, Wyoming. At the time of this writing, Jesse is the sole survivor of that immediate family and now is living at a nursing home in Casper.

In 1922, following graduation from high school, Polly and her mother made a voyage to Scotland to visit her mother's sister. Her name was Polly Orr. Polly Orr's aunt, Jane Steel, also lived there. The grand trip was extended for three months.

As a small boy growing up, I used to love to hear my mother tell me about crossing the ocean in a great liner. Unfortunately, my mother became seasick on the crossing. For that reason both coming and going were not a particularly happy time for her. To travel in Scotland and England seemed like a magic fairy tale and I could not imagine that my very own mother actually traveled so far away.

Twenty-five years later, in 1947, when I was a midshipman attending the United States Naval Academy, I was aboard the aircraft carrier USS *Kearsarge*. We were on a Scandinavian cruise. While our ship was anchored at Edinburgh, Scotland, I put in for three days' leave to visit "bona fide" relatives. I visited Great Aunt Polly Orr and Great-Great Aunt Jane Steel in Ardrossan, Scotland, where my mother had been in 1922. I took many pictures and loved every minute of my visit.

Polly Roberts then went to the University of Wyoming for a year. She studied music and earned her teaching certificate. Polly returned to Sundance and taught school. During the summer of 1923, when Polly was in charge of the Roberts Mercantile, Axel Ostlund came in to purchase items he needed for the school job. Polly's father had moved to Newcastle by then. Although he was a partner in a mortuary and furniture business in Newcastle, he was also appointed by the President to be Receiver and Disburser of Public Monies at the Federal Land Office.

When Axel and Polly decided to get married, the wedding took place at the Roberts' residence in Newcastle, with her father, M. C. Roberts, performing the ceremony. The date was June 18, 1924. The following news item appeared in the Newcastle newspaper. I found the news clipping in one of my mother's scrapbooks.

OSTLUND-ROBERTS
by Joe Lytle

In the presence of more than two score relatives and close friends of the principals, a pretty wedding was solemnized at the home of Mr. and Mrs. M. C. Roberts in Newcastle, at high noon, June 18, 1924, when their daughter, Miss Mary Spence, became the bride of Axel W. Ostlund, of Gillette, Wyoming.

Misses Jessie and Lucille Roberts, sisters of the bride and Lyle E. Poole of Gillette attended the couple. To the soft, sweet strains of the wedding march Lohengrin, delightfully executed by the mother of the bride, the latter entered the bridal chamber upon the arm of her father, who, with the assistance of Rev. Lewis Weary of the Newcastle Methodist Church, officiated in the beautiful ring ceremony which united the lives and fortunes of the happy, hopeful young couple.

The bride was handsome in white Baronet satin done in pearls, with a veil of tulle ornamented with orange blossoms and white Scotch heather from the cher-

The wedding of Axel William Ostlund and Mary Spence Roberts in Newcastle, Wyoming, June 18, 1924.

ished land of her parents' nativity. She carried a bouquet of white roses and sweet peas. The groom made a fine appearance in conventional attire. Soft strains of music during the ceremony and the inspiring Mendelssohn march during the felicitations were especially pleasing.

Always a model of pleasing and refreshing taste and architectural simplicity, the pretty Roberts home was especially attractive for the occasion. Interior arrangement and decorations were particularly appropriate, while the verdant lawn, with large American flags promiscuous among the pleasing effects, presented a splendid setting for the photographic reproduction of the assemblage.

Immediately following the ceremony the bridal party repaired by auto to the spacious banquet room of the State Armory, where a finely appointed four-course wedding breakfast was served by the Ladies Aid Society of the Methodist Church. The wedding cake was a large and palatable culinary production, a gift of Captain and Mrs. Orr, Uncle and Aunt of the bride, of Ardrossan, Scotland.

Judge Harry P. Ilsley, from Sundance, in his usual easy manner, presided as toastmaster, prefacing his remarks with a brief but well-received eulogistic reference to the bride and groom and eliciting cheery responses from the members of the festal board addressed. Among the latter were the touching remarks of Mr. Roberts, father of the bride, who recounted how, as a young man a quarter of a century ago, he sailed from the rugged shores of Scotland, ultimately arriving in the Black Hills of South Dakota, and forthwith happily adopting the great, free, United States of America as his permanent home.

Mrs. Ostlund is the eldest daughter of Matthew C. and Elizabeth Spence Roberts, born and reared in the shadow of the Black Hills and has spent the greater part of her life in the Sundance community. Her father was educated for the ministry and occupied Methodist pulpits in his native land and in the United States for many years. He has also discharged with distinguished honor and ability many positions of public trust and is at present receiver of public monies and special disbursing agent of the Government Land Office at Newcastle, a position to which the late President Harding appointed him in 1922. Reared under the enduring environments of a Christian home, Polly Roberts, the pretty June bride of yesterday, became a gem and a jewel in that happy home and a power for all that is good and desirable in splendid young womanhood. She has been especially helpful in church, social and educational activities in her home community; is an accomplished musician; a popular and successful instructor in the schoolroom; and for the last two years has had charge of her father's mercantile business in Sundance. This latter responsibility now devolves upon her only brother, Clyde D. Roberts, a student at the State University at Laramie. In company with her mother, two years ago Miss Polly spent several months abroad, visiting in London, Glasgow, and other points in Great Britain, returning by way of Canada.

Mr. Ostlund is a worthy veteran of the World War, a young man of sterling qualities and business ability, and conducts an extensive and expanding plumbing enterprise with headquarters at Gillette, where the happy couple will make their home following their auto wedding trip to Illinois and other eastern states.

Among the guests present at the wedding were: Judge Harry P. Ilsley and Mrs. Ilsley, William Roberts and son William and daughter Mary, Mr. and Mrs. A. L. Dickinson, Mr. and Mrs. J. T. Farrell, Mr. and Mrs. O. D. Ticknor, Mr. and Mrs. Fred Schloredt, Mr. and Mrs. Edwin Rounds, Mr. and Mrs. Ben Justice, Mrs. J. C. Hurtt, Mr. and Mrs. Richard Champ, Sundance; Mrs. and Mrs. L. E. Poole, Attorney and Mrs. Dolezal, Dr. O'Farrell and Mrs. O'Farrell, Mr. and Mrs. W. R. Fox, Gillette; Mrs. Russell, Moorcroft; Rev. Weary and Mrs. Weary, Mr. and Mrs. H. M. Brown, L. A. Weeks, Mr. and Mrs. Joe Lytle, Newcastle.

While reading the long newspaper account of the wedding, I imagined the editor must have said to Joe Lytle, "Cover that wedding for us, Joe! Give us a good account and a lot of copy. There is not much other news this week!"

Although there were many wedding guests, none of Axel's family was present for the ceremony. Paxton, Illinois, was a faraway place from Newcastle, Wyoming. Polly had never met any of Axel's family. The wedding trip to Paxton was the first time Polly would meet Axel's four sisters, three brothers, and his parents who were called "Ma" and "Pa."

Per Jon Ostlund, my grandfather, was born on January 1, 1859, and raised in Mulseryd, Jonkoping, Sweden. He married Emma Justine Faust, on October 31, 1886. Emma was born at Kavsjo, Jonkoping, Sweden on September 11, 1862. Their first son, Hartwick, was born in Sweden in 1887.

I don't really know what inspired my grandfather to come to the United States, but he must have been looking for better times. When he was a young man in Sweden, like other young men, he had to take compulsory military training and was in a cavalry unit. Opportunities in Sweden must have been meager and I assume that was the reason for his emigration. He left his wife and son in Sweden and worked his passage to New York. He traveled to Paxton because he knew there were other immigrants from Sweden residing there. He worked as a day laborer and frugally saved his money. When he had enough money for passage for his wife, son, and sister, they took a ship to the United States also. They must have arrived about the time the Statue of Liberty was constructed.

Living in Paxton, the first daughter was born in 1890 and named Ellen. Axel was born on August 28, 1891. It was humorous to me in later years that my father kept his age from my mother for a long time— he was more than eleven years her senior. Polly learned the truth about Axel's age when she met her new mother-in-law in Paxton. Polly never cared about it, but Axel seemed sensitive about his age throughout his life.

Hartwick, Axel's eldest brother, was the first to marry. He and his wife, Esther, had moved to a farm in Michigan. They raised one daughter, Ruth. Hartwick was a tenant farmer, as were many in those days. During my first year at the Naval Academy in 1945, my cousin, Ruth Ostlund, came to visit me. Ruth was a WAVE in the Navy at that time. Unfortunately, that was the first and only visit I ever had with Ruth.

Ellen married a man named Parker and they had two sons, Bill and Dick, and one daughter, Mary. Ellen's husband was killed at a train crossing in the late twenties or early 1930s. In 1951, Ellen visited us in Gillette. I remember driving her back to Paxton while I was making a trip to New York to visit Mary. Rarely a slow driver, I was ticketed for speeding. Ellen and I had a very nice time on that trip. I always hoped my driving did not frighten her. Ellen's daughter, Mary, married Bill Purcell and in 1964 they also visited us in Gillette.

Axel's sister, Olga, married a man named Carr who suffered an early death. They had three daughters. His sister, Nellie, married Ray Paulson and they had a son, Kenneth, and one daughter named Pauline.

Axel's youngest sister, Rose, married Walter Carlson, a farmer, and they lived at

Paxton. During the times I used to drive between the east coast and Wyoming, I always tried to stay with Aunt Rose and Uncle Walter. They had one son, Ron, who once visited us with his wife, Pat. Unfortunately, Ron suffered with cancer and died at a relatively early age.

Axel's other two brothers were John Albert and Henry. As far as I know, Henry never married, but Albert finally married later in life.

Polly was to learn that Albert and Henry, along with Axel, had a fondness for moonshine whiskey. The three brothers knew how to procure a jug and would nip on it from time to time. This was Polly's first knowledge that Axel and his brothers liked to drink and coming from her strict religious upbringing, this was quite a shock!

Axel's mother was a kind woman and she dearly loved Polly. As I recall, Emma seemed short and almost frail in stature. But when you think of the years of raising eight children, doing all the laundry on a scrub board, raising a garden, baking daily bread, and more, it is no wonder she looked a bit frail. Axel's parents always spoke Swedish to each other and their neighbors. All of their children spoke Swedish when growing up at home and then spoke English in school. Emma and Polly understood each other and shared their love for each other.

My memories of my Grandfather Jon are few. I remember him carrying me on top of his shoulders when I was young. I also recall, clearly, how my grandparents used to teach me how to count in Swedish.

I also recall an incident when my Grandpa Jon had a terrible toothache. He insisted that my father tie a string around the offensive tooth and yank it out. The first jerk on the string was too timid and Grandpa only moaned louder. My dad then tied the string to a doorknob and violently slammed the heavy door. That did the trick!

During the early thirties when my Ostlund grandparents came to Gillette to visit, they were ticketed on the train, but somehow only to Edgemont, South Dakota. My dad and I drove to Edgemont in the Studebaker to meet them. They marveled at the long and seemingly wonderful trip. I believe it was during this time when Grandpa lost the tooth referred to previously.

Beginning in 1920 and lasting until the election of 1932, the country had voted in prohibition by constitutional amendment. All through the twenties bootlegging and the making of illegal whiskey flourished. Those were the days of Al Capone and others who made millions through the sale of illegal whiskey. Nightclubs that sold whiskey were called speakeasies. J. Edgar Hoover first organized a government force known officially as the Federal Bureau of Investigation. The public and the underworld called them G-men. Sale of beverages with alcoholic content was limited to 3.5 per cent alcohol. Even in Gillette, Wyoming, people made their own whiskey and Axel, a good sheet metal man and plumber, made a few copper stills for some of his customers.

When I was about five or six years old, I can recall my dad decided to make his own beer. I believe that a very limited amount of home brew was not considered illegal. Axel bought big crocks, some as large as ten gallons. He carefully made the beer in the basement and would peek into the crock every day trying to decide when it was ready for bottling.

By mail he had ordered a bottle capper and caps from Henkel & Joice Hardware Company. Beer bottles were easy to pick up because low-alcoholic beer, referred to as "near beer", was allowed to be sold in the bars. When the decision was finally made to bottle the beer, the family assembled to carry out Dad's orders. He had a long red rubber hose to be used to siphon the beer from the crock into the bottles. The hose was at least a quarter inch in diameter. When the bottle was properly filled, the hose was pinched off and an empty was substituted for the full one. The full bottle was then placed under the bottle capper, which was operated by Dad. Of course, before this process took place, my mother had to wash and clean the bottles with a special bottle-brush that was forced through the neck of the brown-colored bottle. The brush had a handle on the end so that it could be rotated inside the bottle. Clean bottles were essential to good beer, according to the brew master, my father.

Finally, all was completed and the bottles were neatly placed on an empty shelf in a special room under the porch that was always known as the "dark place." It was a dark place until a few years later when someone put an electric light bulb in it. Even with an electric light, it still retained the same name. The room had a dirt floor. My mother used this room to store all of the jars of produce that she canned every summer. She was especially famous for her wonderful variety of pickles. Now she had to provide space for beer storage.

After a couple of weeks, we occasionally heard a small explosion in the basement that seemed to be coming from the dark place. Sure enough, it was the bottled beer exploding. Axel was torn between drinking it all first or thinking perhaps that no more would explode. I don't recall how that tough decision was resolved.

When I was born there were no street signs in Gillette and not for a very long time afterward. But based on today's locations, the house we lived in at my birth was on the east side of Gillette Avenue between Fifth and Sixth Street. The Carter Mining Company has built an office building over the very site that was our home for my first year. Dr. Marshall Hannum, a chiropractor, lived in the house on the north side and the Catholic Church was on the corner to the south. The coal shed, woodshed and outdoor toilet were located by the alley. While living there, a most unusual thing occurred that was to make the newspapers countrywide some years afterward. My mother had a diamond ring which was a gift from her mother. The ring was misplaced and lost. Years later, Jerry Hannum, who lived next door, was playing football in the yard of our former home. When the football hit the ground it uncovered a ring that he took to his mother. Mrs. Hannum remembered Polly Ostlund losing a ring about twelve years earlier. When Mrs. Hannum called my mother, who now lived a block and a half away, my mother identified the ring and it once more was in her possession. Papers from all over picked up the story and even relatives from Paxton sent her clippings. Young Jerry Hannum, who found the ring, later became a medical doctor. Jerry was a year older than I. His younger brother, Tom, also became a medical doctor. Jerry was the doctor who delivered three of our children, Patrick, Jane, and Scott. Unfortunately, Jerry Hannum died in the late 1960s during heart surgery.

It had to be a great day in early 1929 when the Ostlund family moved into their new house at the corner of Fifth Street and Warren Avenue. Imagine enjoying the benefits of indoor plumbing. I was told that our dog, Spot, had a difficult time understanding that we no longer lived on Gillette Avenue. Going back and forth between the two houses, Spot just disappeared one day, never to be seen again.

My parents lived in this house for the rest of their lives. My mother died in 1980 and my father died in 1982. By that time the County had built a three story parking garage on the other side of Fifth Street across from their residence. The County had also built a new courthouse, which closed off Fifth Street and was built over the top of a small park area that memorialized Korean War casualties. My brother and I offered the residential property that belonged to our parents to the County for a park area. In addition to our home on the corner, my parents had also acquired the old house next door to the north. The County bought the property and removed the two houses. Today, as I write these words on January 31, 1998, the area is a beautiful park that is certainly enjoyed by the citizens of Gillette.

I have a special feeling about this park because our parents planted the majority of the trees that still remain on the property. I still smile when I think of my mother's pride when planting a catalpa tree. It was probably the only tree of its kind in Gillette. The last I knew, it was still there and doing well! I believe my parents must still be smiling down upon it.

Mary Spence "Polly" Roberts, 1920.

Axel W. Ostlund, 1917.

New school building, Sundance, Wyoming. *Wyoming Division of Cultural Resources*

John's maternal grandparents at home in Sundance, Wyoming, in 1909. Matthew Chapman Roberts and Elizabeth Bain Roberts with Clyde Dunsmore, Jessie Mable, Elizabeth Lucille, and Mary Spence (Polly).

Shooting crickets off the wires in front of C. D. Roberts Hardware, Sundance, Wyoming, during the cricket infestation, 1938.

John's paternal grandparents at home in Paxton, Illinois, in 1917.
Seated: Ellen, Jon, Olga, Emma, and Rose.
Standing: Albert, Axel, Nellie, Hartwick, and Henry.

3

Early School Days

My entry to kindergarten would not be in accordance with the regulations that exist at the date of this writing. I began at the age of four. Of course my birthday was September 29, at which time I would be five like most of the rest of the kids. Consider me an early beginner.

The kindergarten classroom was at Campbell County High School. Kindergarten was held there for a very practical purpose. Persons who had graduated from high school could enroll for an additional year to take classes known as normal training. The successful completion of one year of normal training entitled the person to teach in the country school system and the kindergarten class was used as a training school for these students who desired to become teachers.

This high school facility was certainly the largest building in town and it occupied a space at the south end of Gillette Avenue. To me it was awesome.

It was only three blocks from my home. On the first day of kindergarten my mother walked me to school. After that it was presumed that I could walk alone. However, when my first report card was sent home, my parents could not understand why I was tardy so many times. My mother knew I was leaving home plenty early. The second report card showed that I was tardy thirteen times. I declared I had no idea why I was reported late so many times. Unknown to me, my father decided to park his pickup so he could observe my three-block walk to school. The truth of the matter was that in my kindergarten class there was a blonde girl with long curls named Rosemary Rohan. She lived in a white house that I had to walk by on the way to school. The house, no longer existing, was on the west side of Gillette Avenue and the north side of Sixth Street. I walked very slowly past Rosemary's house in the hopes that she would just happen to come out and we could walk to school together. On this day, I evidently dawdled by Rosemary's front steps at the time my father drove up. He yelled out of his window, "What are you standing there for?" He used to laugh when he told that story. He said, "John took off like a streak of light and he didn't stop until he was inside the school." I was never reported late again!

A teacher named Miss Clements was in charge of normal training. I also recall one of my kindergarten teachers named Mr. Johnson. In later years he was better known for his nickname, "Bones" Johnson. Bones later became county clerk of Campbell County long after I became an adult.

It was 1932 and the Depression was felt by everyone while I was attending kindergarten. My father, in an effort to save money, decided he would give haircuts to my brother and me. Professional haircuts were twenty-five cents at that time. He would sit me down on a stool with a towel wrapped around me. I never liked these sessions and I never believed he really did a very good job. The worst thing about it was the clippers. They were not electric, but hand powered. I always thought he pulled the clippers away too soon and yelled that he was pulling out my hair when he did that. His retort was, "Sit still! How do you expect me to cut your hair if you move all the time?" It was a no-win situation.

In school one day, one of my classmates, a boy named L. D. Lane, said that he was going to get a haircut soon. I told him that I could cut his hair if he would come to my house. So I put L. D. Lane on a stool and draped a towel around him. After all, I knew how from experience. So I gave L. D. Lane a haircut that his mother never forgot. When the kids in school asked him who cut his hair, he proudly announced, "John the barber cut it."

As boys will do, I recall the cold day when I walked home from the Saturday afternoon movies. I was in the habit of taking a shortcut up the alley, which caused me to walk across the bridge over the Burlington ditch. Looking over the edge of the bridge, I noticed the nice icy surface. Carefully, I went down the bank and slid on the ice. What fun! Then, to my surprise, the ice broke, and I found myself standing chest deep in the icy water. I scrambled out and ran the short distance to our home. Now clad in very cold and wet clothes, I was worried about what my mother would say. Trying to think of something to save the moment and prevent the expected scolding, I offered, "But my bow tie is dry!" My mother laughed about that in later years, but not at the time of the incident.

The following year I began first grade in a two-room, wooden structure that was the original courthouse in Gillette. The building lot is now occupied by the drive-in facilities of the First National Bank. This was the northwest corner of Fourth Street and Kendrick Avenue. After beginning the school year, since first grade was crowded, they picked about three kids who appeared to be doing well and promoted them to the second grade. My pals, Dick Hall, Hazel Underwood, and I were in that group. So having skipped the first grade, I was now in the second grade and still would not be six until the end of the month. The promotion evidently did not hurt me, because in the third grade I was the honor boy student who also received an award for never being tardy. My father should have been proud about the award for never being tardy. After all, he was responsible for putting the fear in me during kindergarten.

During the fourth grade year I missed about six weeks of school. Because I had been sick with scarlet fever when I was about two years old, that early sickness was blamed for problems that occurred during my fourth grade. My mother took me to the Mayo Clinic where it was presumed that I had some kind of heart trouble. I believe this presumption was made because both my mother and maternal grandfather were also considered to have "heart trouble." When doctors of that time did not know what to diagnose, then heart trouble sounded good. To this day I still don't believe that diagnosis, but until I started high school it was presumed that I had a weak heart.

When I returned to classes, my teacher, Miss Harnish, really embarrassed me in front of the class. I seemed to be having trouble catching up and one day she gave a test. After she collected and reviewed the papers, she announced to the class in a loud voice that just because I had been absent was no excuse for me not doing better. I can still recall the embarrassment that I felt and I lost my enthusiasm for trying to get good grades.

In spite of tough economic times, my mother was always concerned that her two sons should know music. Of course both Bob and I took piano lessons from my mother, as did a lot of other kids. About this time she also decided we should take dancing lessons. This was not ballroom dancing, but rather tap dancing.

Fred Astaire and Ginger Rogers were the current rage at the movies. They danced in a way that caused every mother to wish for the same talents to show up in their own children. Gillette was hardly the tops in talent, but there was a lady named Sylvia Lipman who gave tap dance lessons.

Lessons were one thing, but it had to be a public performance to really demonstrate talent. Sylvia Lipman volunteered that my brother and I were ready to perform at a dinner to be held in honor of Wyoming's Governor Leslie A. Miller. We were to perform the "Shadow Dance"!

I was to wear a white suit with a white top hat, while my brother, the shadow, was wearing the same thing but in black. Of course, in good Fred Astaire fashion, we also had canes. Sylvia Lipman played the piano. Our outfits were undoubtedly rented from a costume place in Denver.

The big dance performance took place where all dinner events were held, at the Odd Fellows Hall. This two-story building was located at the northeast corner of Third Street and Kendrick Avenue. It was undoubtedly the largest hall in town. Unfortunately, the hall was located on the second floor and everyone had to climb creaky wooden stairs. We used to say that during dances held in this hall you could feel the building sway. However, back to our dancing! It would be most kind of me to say that on the night of our performance I can only recall receiving what might be termed a nice hand of polite applause. Courtesy demanded no less.

Those early school years were Depression years and I now marvel at how my parents kept us kids in food and clothing. School facilities and even supplies were meager. However, we all thought that it was very normal, so there were no complaints. My fourth grade building was an old yellow brick facility that stood where the present post office now stands. The school playground was at the southwest corner of Kendrick Avenue and Fourth Street. The playground equipment consisted of some teeter-totters and swings. My absolute favorite equipment was something we might strain to call a merry-go-round. Further description is not warranted.

During wintertime an empty lot was found and flooded for a skating rink. Usually, an old shack would be moved to the skating rink and a wood-burning stove would be placed inside. On cold days the heat from that stove felt wonderful.

My ice skates were simple clamp-ons. Shoe skates, as we know them today, were out of the question for most kids. The problem was two-fold. First, how to keep the skates fastened to your shoes and secondly, how to keep your feet warm. To clamp the skates on your shoes, you had to use leather shoes with a sole and that meant taking off your overshoes. It was no wonder we liked to go in by the stove in the shack frequently. I will always remember an old bum that was warming up by the stove one day. He told us that he had been to China. That was beyond my comprehension. Whether or not the bum was ever there, I never knew, but I did recall this incident when I traveled to China in 1977.

One summer day an unusual event occurred that I thought was the answer to my dreams. I looked out the window toward the alley and there were two horses standing by our ash can. I had always dreamed of owning a horse and there were two of them. I found an old rope and tied them to a shed. One was so old and bony that he was probably ready for the glue factory, but I certainly overlooked those small details. I just prayed that no one would come along and claim them. It never occurred to me that I would have to feed the animals and pasture was out of the question. I finally got on the oldest one and I recall feeling momentarily like the Lone Ranger! Great disappointment came later that day when the owner found them. They had escaped from his fenced pasture about a mile to the north during the night. He came about the time when I was dreaming of ordering a saddle from the Montgomery Ward catalog, although paying for it was an impossibility—my dream was shattered before the day ended.

Children today would find it difficult to grow up without electronic games, radios, and especially TV. Since such things did not trouble us. We made up our own ways to enjoy outside activities. Sandlot baseball was one way. Kids from the neighborhood would gather in a backyard and with a bat and a ball we had some exciting play. Kids like Hazel Underwood, Gordon McKenzie, Pete Lucas, Jack and Arnold Duca, Jerry Hannum, and the two Ostlund kids were always anxious to play. Many other names could be added, but those are the ones who come easily to mind.

Gordon McKenzie lived only a couple of doors north of the house where Hazel Underwood lived. Nothing seemed too ambitious, if only someone came up with the idea. At the backyard of the McKenzie house we made an underground place to use for some reason and that reason was probably just because someone thought it would be a great idea. How long it took for us to dig a large hole in the ground is not remembered, but the enthusiasm for the project kept us digging. We accumulated old discarded boards to use for the ceiling and once the boards were in place, more dirt was used to cover the boards. This became a very "secret" place to hide.

Then someone came up with the idea of stringing an electric wire overhead between the Ostlund house and the McKenzie house. We not only had to cross Warren Avenue with this wire, but the McKenzie house was also several doors north of our home. Undaunted by such small details, we set about acquiring the cheapest wire we could find. It was very small and thinly insulated; connections were simply made by twisting the wire together. What were we planning to transmit over this wire? Why Morse code by telegraph key of course! All we needed were a few batteries, a couple of sending keys, and a way to keep the wires high enough so that cars could pass underneath it. The wires extended out of our attic window and somehow ended up at the McKenzie house. Strangely enough I don't believe we were ever successful in transmitting a coded message, but it certainly kept us busy.

Other games were easier to devise and also much fun. Games like kick the can and different versions of outdoor hide-and-seek were favorites.

Another was played by two people with one on either side of our peaked roof garage. Throwing a ball up the roof so that it went down the opposite side, while at the same time calling "andy-over", was a fun game. The object was for the person on the other side to actually catch the ball and if he did, then he became the short-term winner. I cannot recall the benefit to the winner, but it was a simple game, which actually gave us good exercise.

Our neighbors were Lou and Emma Gilbert. Lou subscribed to the Denver Post. Consequently, when they were finished reading the Saturday comic pages, they offered them to us kids. Saturday afternoons I could hardly wait to get what we called the "funny papers". Often I would knock on their backdoor too early and they had not yet read them.

On these occasions, I was invited inside while Lou read the funnies to Emma. Emma was losing her eyesight. This was the very reason that the Gilberts decided to drive to Kanasota, South Dakota, to see a faith healer there who was curing people of all sorts of maladies. Since my mother was concerned about my health, they invited Mother and me to accompany them. We did.

We departed in Lou Gilbert's automobile, either a DeSoto or a Hudson. It was a cold winter day. Car heaters hardly circulated heat to the front seat occupants and mother and I rode in the back seat. We had been traveling perhaps an hour when Emma kindly passed her lovely fur coat back to my mother to use over our laps as a comforter. That was really a nice gesture.

However, my stomach was telling me that I was getting carsick and I could not bring myself to interrupt Lou Gilbert while he was driving. Despite his kindness, I was afraid of him and I suppose I had some trepidation about interrupting an elder. We had already planned to stop in Newcastle to see my grandfather for a few minutes. I prayed I could hold on until we reached his house. We did not reach there in time. Here it came! I vomited straight out and all over that lovely black fur coat. I was so embarrassed! So was my mother. Emma was nonplused as she exclaimed, "We'll just wipe it off, don't worry!"

At Kanasota we stayed in the hotel where the healer practiced. The lobby was full of distressed people and patients. Most were in wheelchairs or on crutches. The healer placed his hands on the sick and suffering. There were times when a poor patient would struggle out of his wheelchair and stand. "It's a miracle!" people shouted.

After returning from Kanasota, Emma slowly continued going blind. I never noticed any difference in my own health, but I never felt there was anything wrong with me anyway!

Kids did not have a place to swim in Gillette. About once every week or two in the summer, Mr. Byrd, a high school teacher and scoutmaster, would borrow a truck. He would announce that at one o'clock on a certain day he would take kids to the Spaith reservoir to swim. We would all show up, usually carrying an old inner tube for flotation. It was a pretty small water hole, but kids would jump off a high bank with a big splash and have a grand time.

Finally, during the middle thirties under the WPA (Works Progress Administration) program, Gillette received its very first swimming pool. It was a rectangular concrete box without amenities. It was deeper in one end to allow for diving. There was not a circulation system. In other words, there was no filter, no chlorination, nor a heater. About once a month someone would drain and flush it for safety's sake. The water was so murky you could not see someone beneath the surface. It was fun anyway and no one knew the difference about what a swimming pool should be. We all knew it was so much better than the Spaith reservoir.

In 1933 the government was trying to get the "New Deal" started to get the country out of the Depression. Livestock prices were at an all-time low. The government finally began paying farmers to kill their litters of pigs instead of raising them to market. People could hardly believe what was next coming out of Washington! However, thanks to the WPA program, Gillette had a swimming pool and the American Legion Hall was built at Rockpile and Second Street.

In January of 1934, my dad took me with him to feed his cows. He hardly had money for feed, but the snow was so bad he had to take them hay. He borrowed a team of horses to pull the borrowed sled. We gave the hay to his few cows and I felt pretty frozen as we headed back for the homesteader's shack.

I cannot remember the name of the homesteader who provided the team and sled that day, but I do remember something else! This fellow offered us sourdough pancakes. Both cold and hungry, how I loved those big thick pancakes into which he also put raisins! Those pancakes stayed in my mind for the rest of my life. Finally, as an adult, I learned to make my own sourdough and, sure enough, I placed raisins in the pancake batter. I loved to serve those wonderful cakes to our family and guests.

My dad had been hoping and planning to go to Illinois during the summer of 1934. Dad was an avid baseball fan and especially loyal to both the Chicago Cubs as well as the Chicago White Sox.

Dad had acquired a few cows, which he was pasturing on the Bob Johnson place. In 1934 cows were unbelievably cheap. In order to make the trip to Illinois, Dad sold his cows. He received about seventeen dollars per head. A friend of his, who had just returned from a trip, told him he should figure out an amount to cover gas and oil, food, lodging, and all other expenses. Dad's goal was to have twenty dollars available for expenses each day that we were gone, which is the amount advised by his friend.

There were no motels in 1934 as we know them today. There were cabin camps. Usually the cheaper ones were without indoor plumbing. Some allowed cooking and some did not. Buying a few groceries along the way and staying in cabin camps was how we made the journey. I believe we had a 1928 Studebaker and it was dependable.

By plan, my dad first headed west. He heard there was a healer in Ogden, Utah, who could cure hay fever and asthma. My dad and I both suffered from hay fever and I also had attacks of asthma. My brother had only slight hay fever as a boy.

We found the healer's house in Ogden. You could not miss the location, because the line of people waiting to go inside was over a block long. The healer did not make appointments. We stood by the hour, slowly advancing toward the front door. After getting inside, the line continued up the stairs. Finally we were admitted to see the healer.

In those days everything was paid with cash. Credit cards were unheard of. The price was one dollar per treatment. My dad and I both had treatments, which only took about a minute. My parents were most impressed when the healer placed his hands on my brother, Bob, and said, "I can't give this boy a treatment!"

"Why not?" my folks inquired.

"I can tell by my hands that a treatment on this boy could do considerable harm," responded the healer.

In awe, my parents were further convinced that the healer was trustworthy. Strangely enough, I never was bothered with either hay fever or asthma again. However, all the people were impressed when the healer turned down a dollar or two so easily. It really added to his reputation and mystique.

Leaving Ogden, my dad was determined to drive to St. Louis to catch a game with the Cardinals at their stadium. My mother was distressed by the speed he was driving. Although tired, I believe my dad was smiling when we were sitting in our seats during the game.

After visiting in Paxton, we headed 100 miles north for Chicago. In fact, we arrived in Chicago just a day or two after the notorious fugitive John Dillinger had been shot and killed as he left a movie theatre. The White Sox were playing the New York Yankees. That was the time when I watched my heroes, Babe Ruth and Lou Gehrig, play. No ballplayer before or since has commanded the national respect of those two famous fellows. As I recall, "The Babe" disappointed me because he failed to get a home run that day. But just to have seen him left me in awe!

We attended the Chicago World's Fair. It was called the Century of Progress. It was impressive to everyone, but to me, not yet seven, it was fantastic!

At the fair we men took a fun ride. Our mother never considered it and I could not imagine any lady doing what we did. In the first place, ladies wore dresses or skirts, but never slacks or shorts. For this reason this particular ride was out of the question for women. To take this ride you first had to get to the top of a tower. You did this by walking up a spiral ramp. Reaching the top, you sat on something like gunnysacks. The slide was curved, waxed wood, and spiraled downward. We all thought it was terrific fun. However, my dad had an accident. He was the last one to come down and he fell over from his sitting position, landing on his elbow. He stayed on his elbow the rest of the way to the finish line, unable to regain his upright position. I was impressed as they took him to the first-aid station to bandage his suffering elbow.

As nighttime drew on I can remember getting so tired my dad sometimes carried me as we returned to the car. What a big day!

In those days law enforcement was performed by the county sheriff and his single deputy. In the town of Gillette, there was a single city marshal who also ran the road grader. I recall at one time, Mayor Hibler also ran the road grader. The streets were either dirt or dirt with a gravel topping. The road grader was used to keep the ruts to a minimum. The marshal was also responsible for dog control and I remember most vividly what would happen when too many dogs ran loose; the marshal would simply shoot them. I saw this happen to three dogs one day and I felt so badly for them. I don't believe I had ever seen anything shot before and the impression was one of real pity. I walked over to the side of the street and just stared down at those poor dead dogs. With blood running out of their mouths and their wounds, I experienced the shock of sudden, violent death.

A somewhat similar incident happened in front of the courthouse one day, however, this day no guns were fired. There was a small bounty paid on coyotes and in the spring coyote dens would be dug out and the pups would be brought in by the sackful. The sheriff would certify the claim for bounty and then take the sackful of cute and cuddly coyote pups outside to the curb. I wanted one in the worst way, but I stood in amazement as the sheriff took them one at a time, and cracked their skulls on the curb. This was another shocking fact of life.

There were no paved streets in Gillette. In fact, it was not until my father was mayor in the 1950s when Gillette got its first paved streets other than the two blocks of Main Street. The streets were sometimes covered with the local red scoria that quickly ground to red dust and for the most part, the streets were either mud or dust and seldom in between.

One day in the 1930s, I was playing in our backyard. Our garage was adjacent to the alley and there was a suitable play area between the garage and the house. On this particular day someone had vacated an automobile up the hill on Fifth Street and the brake came loose. Fortunately, I looked up in time to see this car charging straight for me at great speed and I merely stepped out of the way. The car tore across the yard where I had been playing and crashed right into the side of our garage. My father did not have his pickup in the first stall of the garage, but our Studebaker in the second stall sustained minor damage and the side of the garage had a car sticking through it. In today's world that would probably have invoked a million-dollar damage suit, but at that time I doubt if insurance even was spoken about.

The Fourth of July was always an exciting celebration. My father enjoyed it as much as we kids. Supposedly unknown to us, Dad would order fireworks from Henkle & Joice Hardware Company. Sometimes we would discover the box well in advance of the Fourth, but we never let it be known. The night of the Fourth my dad would light the skyrockets. What a thrill!

We always got to light sparklers and my mother also liked to hold them. However, my appetite for the "big stuff" was growing every year. I recall watching our neighbor across the street, Roy Underwood, light their fireworks. I was absolutely certain that one of the explosives did not go off. The next day I set out trying to find it. Find it I did!

The fuse had gone out before reaching the powder. There was perhaps a quarter of an inch of fuse still left. With some apprehension I put a match to the firecracker. I was holding the cracker in my left hand as I applied the match. Boom! It went off so suddenly I almost wet my pants. However, my left hand was totally numb and also discolored from powder burns. I was scared that my mother would find out. I feared that more than the thought of losing my hand. Until this day, no one else has ever known of this accident that could have been much more of a disaster than it actually was.

My best recollection of fifth grade was my teacher, Geneva Morrison. She had beautiful penmanship and was determined to teach the Palmer Method to her students. She made me aware and appreciative of fine handwriting and I have always marveled at excellence in that art. That probably had something to do with my taking a class in calligraphy during the early 1980s.

In 1936 the school district approved a bond issue to construct a new school building for grades one through eight. My last year in the ancient yellow brick facility was sixth grade. How proud we all were to enter the brand new school as we began seventh grade. That was the year I first met Floyd Hart, coach and history teacher.

While I write, Floyd Hart is still living in Riverton, Wyoming, as far as I know. Unknown to him was the fact that he was quite an influence on my life in those days. At that time I had found and collected a few arrowheads. Floyd Hart admired my very best one that was a perfect red flint specimen. I gave it to him. I used to wonder if he still had it. In all my travels around this state, I have never happened to see Floyd Hart. That has certainly been my misfortune.

As I look back on my early school days, I remember entering the declamation events each year. My pals, Dick Hall, Hazel Underwood, and Jack Nicholas, were among others competing.

Discouraged from playing sports, I had to content myself with being student manager of basketball and football. Our friend, Lawrence Hunter, got rheumatic fever while in junior high school that kept him confined to bed for several weeks during that year. Unfortunately, it also restricted him from athletics. My memory of L. J. Hunter in seventh grade was that he was very good at basketball.

We had lived through the worst of the depression by this time and life seemed good. I don't recall ever showing concern about what Adolph Hitler was doing in Germany as we sailed through the junior high years. At the movies, newsreels showed pictures of Nazi banners in the background as Adolph Hitler ranted to huge crowds in Germany. At that time, the United States seemed blissfully content to be separated from wars or possible wars by two huge oceans. How the changing times were about to change our world as we knew it!

Young Bob and John in front of their house.

Gillette's main street with the high school at the end, 1923. *Wyoming Division of Cultural Resources*

Neighborhood picture of Gillette. 7th Street high school looking east from Wagner's house.
Wyoming Division of Cultural Resources

The "Shadow Dancers", John and Bob.

Bob with "Queen" and John with "King", 1935.

Cowboy John on the bronc, 1936.

John's first grade school (original courthouse). *Wyoming Division of Cultural Resources*

Junior high basketball team with John as manager.

4

First Working Days

AT AN EARLY AGE I LEARNED THERE WAS NO SHORTAGE OF CHORES THAT needed to be done. On cold days our furnace needed coal that, of course, was shoveled by hand. The ashes and clinkers had to be removed and taken out to the ash can by the alley each day. Our hot water came from a small "monkey" stove that was also hand fired, first with kindling and then with coal. In summer the grass needed mowing and there was always errands and sweeping.

My father was a great one for neatness. His plumbing shop was a very old building with a lot of sheds for storage, however his tools were always well cared for and neatly stored. That is the way my brother and I were brought up. I used to think it was almost impossible to please my father when it came to doing a job, but in retrospect I'm sure it was probably good training.

In our alley there was an old shed next to our ash can. Across the alley was the county jail. This shed was actually on the property next door, but those people said I could use it for a chicken house. I raised a couple of chickens that turned out to be hens. I cleaned up the shed and built a couple of nests out of old boxes. We used to scour the grocery stores for old apple and orange crates when we needed wood to build anything. I was soon providing our family with one or two fresh eggs every day. When winter came, I found I then needed to take warm water out for the chickens and also learned that taking care of chickens was a rather monotonous daily task, rain or shine. Surely there must be something less boring and with perhaps a little excitement for me!

Ahah! Rabbits! I decided to raise rabbits, thinking I could sell the meat to the butcher shop. My wise mother questioned how I could ever do that after raising them, but with a great deal of bravado, I assured my family I could without hesitation. I daydreamed I would be supplying rabbits to customers as far as Moorcroft and perhaps even Newcastle.

My ideas for raising rabbits came from Mr. Morgan, who owned the Rex Movie Theatre and had a lot of rabbits. In order to get a free ticket for the movie on Saturday afternoon, I would cut a gunnysack full of fresh alfalfa and deliver it to his house. I found alfalfa growing in the alley. Otherwise, a movie ticket cost ten cents. I was determined to pattern myself after Mr. Morgan and become the biggest rabbit-raiser in town.

When my white doe rabbit gave birth to a litter, I was really excited. As they grew, I began talking to the butcher shop about furnishing them with fresh rabbit. I even obtained a sample of a carton which said "fresh rabbit" on the box. I had mailed a request for this package to Purina Feed and it was most impressive. I knew the butcher shop had to take me seriously now.

Secretly, I was worried about butchering one of my rabbits. I would never admit this and I kept convincing myself that I must be brave. The butcher shop had told me they would only accept them already butchered. I now believe they were in cahoots with my mother and father. The butcher shop was just next door to Dad's plumbing shop. I was determined to prove them wrong and I talked with anyone who could give me pointers on butchering rabbits. At the county agent's office I learned that it was best to strike the rabbit on the neck, behind the ears, with a club, like a piece of pipe. After much searching I ultimately settled on a piece of steel shaft which was the axle from an old windmill. I had confidence that it was heavy enough to deliver a fatal blow.

Finally, it could be put off no longer. I took one rabbit down to the plumbing shop and put him behind the coal shed. I must have raised the steel club at least two dozen times trying to summon the courage to actually strike. I just could not find the strength to deliver the necessary blow. Someone saw me and began to taunt me. Rather than suffer the embarrassment of failing, I hauled off and delivered the fatal blow. It was with heavy heart when I finished the job. I skinned it, gutted it, and cut it up. The butcher shop told me they needed more than one and I really did not want to do anymore. I went to my mother and asked if she would cook it for the family. She did, but I don't believe I ate any of it. After that traumatic experience I decided I had better make my fortune in a different line of endeavor, preferably one which did not require me to kill anything.

By nailing three orange crates together, a person could make an ideal lemonade stand. The countertop was almost three feet high and the inside had a shelf. The lemonade business was pretty good in the summer. I sold two glasses for a nickel. When the new grade school building was being constructed in 1936 and I viewed all the construction workers as potential customers, I decided to forgo the lemonade stand and sell only to the construction workers. Toting a large thermos jug, my lemonade was freshly brewed each afternoon. Lugging my jug with one arm and toting my sack containing paper cups and small change with the other arm, I slowly worked my way through these three floors of ongoing construction. Workers became accustomed to my afternoon visits and liked to keep asking me the price. I took a lot of kidding. "Is it two for a nickel or three for a dime?" Frankly, it depended on the time of day. If my inventory was heavy, I would reduce from three for a dime, to two for a nickel. I spent a lot of time trying to figure out if I was making any money. As I recall, the amount of sugar was the toughest thing to account for in my calculations.

In 1935 I took a job at the *Gillette Daily Journal*. There were two papers in town at that time and the *Daily Journal* decided to print both a morning and an evening edition. Harmon Rice was the publisher and editor. He was, in my opinion, a flamboyant crusader with zeal to become an influential citizen in the community. Roy Montgomery was the mayor and Harmon Rice was unforgiving in his constant attacks on the Montgomery administration.

One day Harmon Rice was beaten. He looked awful. To make it more newsworthy, he had his picture taken with his head wrapped in layers of bandages. He further blackened his eyes and his lips were swollen. His headline ran: "Victim of Mayor Montgomery's Political Machine". The story told of his being beaten by two of Montgomery's hired thugs. Some teeth were knocked out and the story added, "It is believed that some teeth were knocked down the victim's throat!" For the record, Roy Montgomery lasted a lot longer than Harmon Rice. When Harmon finally left town, he probably owed a lot of people, including me.

A guy named Joe ran both the linotype and the press. There were two or three of us who delivered the papers, including Bill Carroll and Bob Wagner. After a page went through the press twice, we also folded them. The page was placed in the press by hand and following it being applied to the inked format, resulted in one large page, printed on both sides, and folded into a paper which was numbered page one to page four. I gradually picked up additional duties at the paper office. The chore that seemed to be my least favorite was having to swamp out Harmon Rice's office. I only did that about once a week. By that time the paper would be about six inches deep on the floor—finding anything in his office was impossible.

The big problem with this job was that you were never sure of getting paid. Harmon Rice only operated with the cash in his pocket. In fact, with banks going bust, a lot of people did business this way. These were years before such regulations as minimum wage, social security, and withholding taxes. There were no child labor laws or minimum working age either. Life was much simpler compared to the overregulated life of today!

I remember how interesting it was to watch the linotype make printed slugs out of molten lead. These slugs then became a column of print. Ads and job printing were all set by hand. Harmon Rice lived hand-to-mouth and it seemed there was little money or security in newspapers. I believe this finally came home to me when I had to quit my job because we just did not get paid.

With the Depression in full-swing there was terrible unemployment. The federal government began the WPA. After the new swimming pool was built, and having left the newspaper business, I undertook a new venture. Again I utilized nailed orange crates, but this time I had a crowd to work with. I set up my stand at the new swimming pool. Instead of lemonade, I bought soda pop by the case. I had to take the pop in bottles, with a deposit on the bottles. I also had to buy it warm and finding enough ice to cool the pop was a major problem. Transportation was another obstacle that was difficult to overcome. There must have been ten blocks of dusty road from the Bury Mercantile, where I bought the pop, to the swimming pool. My transportation was a four-wheel wagon, which I pulled myself. I also began to get orders for candy bars, but it did not take long to learn that chocolate bars lose their appeal in the hot sun.

Also I began to get requests to hold watches and rings for the people who swam. I did this without charge and it became my undoing. One day a guy named Tommy White asked me to hold his towel. He also said he had his class ring wrapped up inside the towel. I did not open it to check. When he came for the towel he said the ring was missing and he had wrapped the ring in the towel. I never did discover whether or not he was telling me the truth, but I felt so badly about being responsible for his loss that I decided to sell my business. I sold cheap!

My best working summer was 1940. My pal, Burt K. Reno, was my age and he lived on a ranch in southern Campbell County. His father and mother, Everett and Pauline, were building an addition to their house. They also had a lot of hay to put up. There was plenty of work to do. I never received any money, nor was I expecting any, but I did get a great place to sleep plus all of the wonderful food I could eat. After a big breakfast early in the morning, we would harness the teams of horses for mowing, raking, buck raking, and stacking. I loved it. Best of all I was learning how to do so many new and exciting tasks. Before the summer ended I had harnessed teams of horses, driven the sulky rake, the buck rake, and even the stacker team—working experiences every young man should have the opportunity to do.

We had not been to town for more than a month and I well remember the ominous feeling I got when I saw the headline in the local newspaper in Gillette. "FRANCE FALLS!" The story related how Nazi Germany had conquered France on June 17, 1940. Of course there was conversation that the United States would end up going to war before long.

To me, working on a sheep ranch like Reno's was wonderful and I thought I would like to be a rancher. At that time in my life I had thought about many things that I would like to do as a career, but in less than eighteen months, with the United States going to war, all career thoughts then turned to the military.

Living at Reno's that summer laid the foundation for many things I was to do in later life. I had never worked so much with horses before and my later love for ranch life originated at Reno's. During off-hours, Burt and I made boats and rafts to use on the reservoirs as well as hunted and fished. We carried .22 caliber rifles in saddle holsters and Burt and I fired many hundreds of rounds that year. Fortunately, Everett Reno paid for the ammunition. Later, in 1944–45, Burt and I were both on the varsity rifle team at Kemper Military School—all the hours of practice we did at the ranch made both of us experts. In fact, our Kemper team of five boys won one of the top three trophies in the William Randolph Hearst national competition and I personally was the third highest national individual scorer. It was one of my many lucky days!

The fall of 1940 I entered Campbell County High School as a twelve-year-old ninth grader. My birthday was at the end of September. I had been playing the alto saxophone and became a member of a dance band in which my brother was a trombone player. We had a seven-piece band known as the "Loud Shirts." This provided a great way to make spending money for the balance of my high school career. We played most every country dance hall within a hundred miles and there were many country halls in those days.

The spring of 1942 I went to work for Bill Edelman at the Edelman Drugstore on the corner of Gillette Avenue and Second Street. It was originally built as the First State Bank. During the period following the crash of 1929, the bank failed and closed like so many others. In 1932 I was told my savings account at that bank was lost forever. I recall having trouble understanding what they had done with my money. It was probably less than five dollars, but it was all the precious money I had saved.

Bill Edelman had originally opened a drugstore at the corner of Gillette Avenue and Third Street. The First Interstate Bank, previously the Stockmen's Bank, is now located there. Bill took a bold step forward and decided to move his drugstore to this location, formerly occupied by the First State Bank. He removed the front steps so that people could walk into his store at street level. This also meant that he had to lower the floor inside the building—his basement had the lowest ceiling I had ever experienced.

At this new modern store he sold package liquors. I applied for and received my five-dollars-per-week job before school was out that spring. The new social security law had gone into effect by then, so ten cents was deducted from every paycheck for my retirement. At fourteen years of age that seemed like never-never time. During school hours I worked after school and until eight thirty at night, on Saturdays until we closed at eleven at night, and every other Sunday.

Bill started by having me dust the entire store and every item of inventory. I'm sure that Bill used this method to insure we knew where everything was. He carried a huge amount of stock and after this initial and rather tiresome phase, I was assigned other jobs.

Bottling mineral oil was one of those odd jobs. Bill bought mineral oil in large drums and then put his own label on various sizes of bottles. I also sometimes bottled formaldehyde and fumes used to gag me in that low ceiling basement. Walking around in the basement was only accomplished by bending at the waist. To forget for even a moment gave you a head cracking on the low ceiling.

Working the soda fountain was best and we had a big lunch business as well. My mentor at the soda fountain was Loree Cates, formerly Loree Barnes. In later years Loree was our neighbor while we resided at 410 West Fifth Street in Gillette.

Bill Edelman's father-in-law was Harry W. Keeline who liked to sit in the drugstore and watch people go by. Every time I walked by, he would ask me the same question. "Johnny, do you think you are ever going to amount to anything?"

"Yes sir, Mr. Keeline, you can count on it," would always be my response.

Besides Loree Cates, some of the people I worked with that year included Kelly Swenson, Chet Haley, and George Hunter. George Hunter was attending pharmacy school and only worked at Edelman's during the summer months.

Bill Edelman's oldest son, Bill Edelman III, was about the same age as Kelly Swenson's son, Jimmy. Both boys liked to sit on the floor in front of the magazine sections and read comic books. At the time of this writing, undoubtedly Jim Swenson, and probably Bill Edelman, both now have grandchildren of their own.

While working at the drugstore I would know most everyone who came there except for the tourists. One day I was surprised to see Chuck Appel walk in wearing his army uniform and wearing the wings signifying that he had become an Air Corps pilot. Anyway, I was happy to see Chuck and he still comes to reunions in Gillette. Chuck became a fighter pilot and was shot down over Europe. I am uncertain, but I believe he was a prisoner of war for a time.

My mother's birthday was on April 19. I wanted to buy her an outstanding birthday present. I chose carefully and settled on an Evening in Paris bottle of perfume. It came in a lovely box and was priced at $4.95. I carried it to Kelly Swenson and told him I was buying it as a gift for my mother's birthday. Kelly advised me to take it to Bill. I believe he thought perhaps Bill might give me a little break on the price. After all, my paycheck was for only $4.90 and there would be sales tax on top of the $4.95. I recall Bill looking at both the gift and my extended paycheck and just called it an even exchange!

When summer arrived, I worked full-time and my wages were doubled to ten dollars per week. Of course $9.80 was my take-home pay. Bill had me doing all kinds of jobs. When the weather warmed and it was time to start air-conditioning, Bill took me to the roof. In those days, air-conditioning consisted of what we now refer to as swamp coolers. I outfitted the cooler with new pads and cleaned the circulating pump. In fact, I was surprised just how well it worked when I started it.

One Saturday night, Bill told me he wanted me to stay after the regular 10:00 P.M. closing. We covered and refrigerated all the food items behind the soda fountain in order to fumigate. This was my first experience at using sulfur candles. Once they were lit, it was necessary to leave the building. During the night, the stubby candles burned out. The following morning the store was ready for business, however any roaches or other bugs were expected to be quite dead.

During the next school year I chose not to work, but Bill did offer my job back when school was out for the summer. He also offered to pay me fifteen dollars per week. After all, I was experienced.

However, my friend, Jack Ripley, tipped me off to the news of Gulf Oil Company sending a seismograph crew to Gillette and I applied for a job with them. They were paying the incredible amount of seventy-five cents per hour. They offered me the job and I took it; in fact, you could say that I snapped it up quickly. First I called Bill Edelman to tell him I was taking a different job that summer. He asked what wages I would be making. When I told him seventy-five cents per hour, he said rather sadly, "I can't imagine what the country is coming to."

I almost lost my new job with Gulf before the first week was over. I began work on a Monday morning, but it was not until Wednesday when they asked for my social security number and birth date and they learned I was not yet sixteen. Their age requirement seemed insignificant as I would be sixteen in September. However, since I had already been working for a few days, they kept me anyway. At my first and only interview with Gulf, I had acknowledged I would be a senior in high school that fall; it was their wrong assumption that I would be at least sixteen. Thankfully, I was able to keep my job!

Working for Gulf meant I had to carry a lunch pail. I began work at seven in the morning with a survey team. Wyoming did not require a driver's license and in my job I got to drive a pickup. I would drop the surveyor off at a certain point and then drive down the road and stop. By following his hand signals I would give him shots on the stadia rod which was attached to the side of the pickup. On this job I learned to become adept at driving backward to pick up my surveyor—it was often easier to reverse directions on some of the narrow roads than it was to turn around.

One day I was driving to work on the Jim Daly ranch with my surveyor, Penn Iles, riding on the passenger side. There had been a violent rainstorm during the night. I was too casual as we drove along and was looking at Penn more than the road as we talked. Suddenly Penn hollered and as I looked immediately ahead, I saw a small bridge had been washed out. There was no stopping as we were traveling at a pretty good clip; then there was the sound of a terrible crash and, like a miracle, thank God, we ended up on the other side of the stream bank. How we kept from dropping the nose of the pickup into the opposite bank and then crashing through the windshield, I will never know. The good news: we were not injured. The bad news, unfortunately, was that this new pickup's frame and front axles were bent. Luckily, I did not lose my job—the second miracle of that day!

That summer we covered a lot of country. We even worked around Moorcroft and the Devil's Tower area. Most of the country we worked would later become oil-producing fields. However, as far as I know, I don't believe Gulf ever retained a lease that eventually turned into production. In fact, Gulf did not retain any of the lands we worked that summer, but my knowledge of this was miniscule.

One day we stopped to eat our lunch at a closeout sale on a farm. We took it in as a matter of simple fact. I recall the deeded land sold last for a total bid of six dollars per acre which included the mineral. Old-timers shook their heads muttering, "He'll never make it on six-dollar-land. It just ain't in the cards!" And that land turned out to be one of the major oil-producing areas.

During the war, in an effort to save precious rubber and gasoline, the national speed limit was reduced to a mandatory thirty-five miles per hour. Consequently, we always drove carefully on the way to the job. Sometimes we would crowd that on the way back home. One day we had been working forty miles west of Gillette and both of us were anxious to return home. I was stepping on my older black Ford pickup gas pedal along a dirt and lightly graveled road. As I came around this rather sharp curve, there were sheep standing in the road. They scattered, but one leaped across the road right in front of my pickup and was caught in the right front fender. In those days, headlights were not recessed into the fender, but separately mounted. This old ewe tore off the headlamp and most of the fender. We had to find out the name of the owner so that Gulf could properly reimburse him. I was the sheepish one again, for that was the second time that summer I had banged up a Gulf vehicle, and with the war on, they could not be replaced, only repaired.

As I recall, a standard workweek was then forty-eight hours. My gross pay came to thirty-six dollars per week. I even signed up for war bond savings deductions. And when we were given the opportunity to work over forty-eight hours each week, we received one and a half times the regular rate. This was the incredible sum of $1.25 per hour. Pretty heady stuff as I prepared for entering my senior year at Campbell County High School.

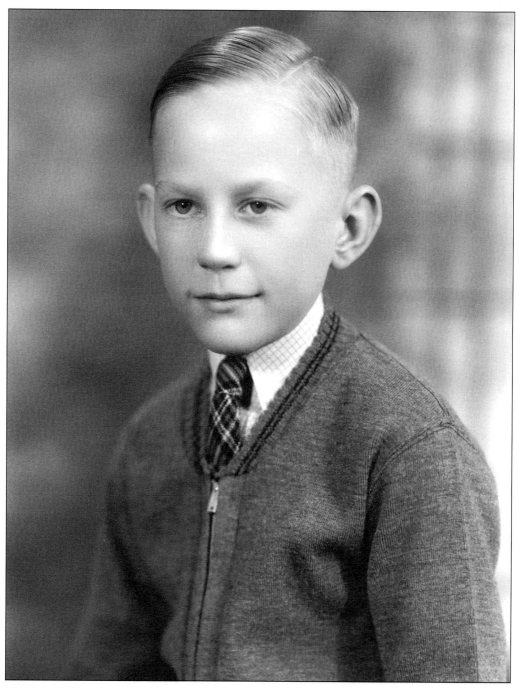

John C. Ostlund

John holding the birthday cake his mother made for him, 1937.

John and Burt rafting at the Reno Ranch.

John with his rabbits, 1939.

Gillette Graded Schools

SCHOOL BOARD
MR. ALLEN HUNTER, PRES.
MRS. A. W. OSTLUND, SEC.
MR. J. C. McGEE, TREAS.

ACCREDITED JUNIOR HIGH SCHOOL
SCHOOL DISTRICT NO. 1
J. M. CHAPPELL, SUPERINTENDENT

GILLETTE, WYOMING
June 11, 1939

Jerry,

I guess you are tired of your rabbitt so don't let any body else byy it because I well give a dollar and a half (for th black). Ask George if he sees those people again to ask if they have a black buck and I well give a dollar for it. Talk to Claybath becaus its a big chance to make some mon. Shes only worth a dollar but I'll give a dollar and a half to be sure you gets some profit

Thanks,

John Ostlund

P. S Don't let anybody else have her for any price because I'll bid more.

John's business letter to cousin Jerry Culver, 1939.

Edelman's drugstore, Gillette, Wyoming. *Wyoming Division of Cultural Resources*

5

School Days During War Years

ON DECEMBER 7, 1941, WITH THE ADVENT OF THE UNITED STATES ENTERING the World War, life as I knew it changed suddenly and dramatically. While some young men were enlisting to fight, others were drafted. The CCHS marching band gathered at the bus depot and played martial music, while the contingent of men said farewell to their loved ones before departing. Unfortunately, some said good-bye for the last time. And many others returned wounded or missing body parts. To me, the First World War seemed ages ago because my father had served in it. Looking back, the First World War had only ended twenty-three years before the United States entered World War II. Hardly any time at all.

Before the fall of 1942, we still had a great group of fellow band members: Howard Hardy on drums, Bob Ostlund on trombone, Warren Taft on trumpet, Bob Wagner on clarinet, Donovan Riley on tenor sax, Ava Brambelette on piano, and I played alto saxophone.

Although we played dances on Saturday nights, there was one occasion when we had our plans changed suddenly. We were to play at Moorcroft, but for some reason now unknown, the job was canceled. So we found ourselves together, but no job to play. Instead, Gordon McKenzie mentioned there was a dance at Upton and why not go there! I do remember Howard Hardy and Ava Brambelette had better sense, or maybe it was just because they had something better to do.

Go we did—in Gordon McKenzie's car. I believe Gordon had recently obtained this car which had already seen its best days. This must have been around the summer of 1941 because gas rationing evidently had not yet presented us with a problem. Indeed we were a lighthearted bunch driving the forty-eight miles to Upton. There were at least four of us who made this outing including my brother, Bob Wagner, Gordon McKenzie, and me. If I have overlooked another person I can only apologize for having a bad memory.

In Upton, we found no dance, however, we were told that there was a dance south of Upton several miles at a country clubhouse. Off we went again and this time the dance was found! We began dancing with available girls and having a great time, stayed until the dance was over and then decided to return home. It was at this time when things not only went bad, but also went from bad to worse!

Returning to Upton, it was necessary to make a railroad crossing on the south edge of town. We had previously made this same crossing on our way to the dance, but now the driver experienced too much enthusiasm and unfortunately missed the regular crossing and instead took off across several sets of railroad tracks! Inside the car we experienced the same violence I presumed to be similar to being inside a cement mixer.

The car halted as the front bumper finally contacted the familiar railroad-crossing sign that says: STOP! LOOK! LISTEN! At that time, with three blown-out tires and smashed rims, to my best recollection, the badly worn spare tire was placed on the front along with the only other tire still holding air.

"What about the rear wheels?" you might ask. We just continued to drive on the flat rear tires, what else could we do? Although driving slowly, the rear tires threw off chunks of hot rubber. Of course there is a limit to what a man-made implement can take and we soon found out what happens.

The reader must understand we were still driving in the dark of night. Soon we were shaken by visible sparks thrown from one rear wheel and then the other and we correctly reasoned the brake drums must be creating friction while being dragged on the ground! Finally the friction overcame the ability of the engine to move the car forward and we came to a grinding halt!

Leaving the car, though only Gordon McKenzie cared, we began hiking north toward Gillette. I cannot recall where the abandoned vehicle was left, but it was probably somewhere just north of Moorcroft. The sunrise was breaking in the east and the summer sun would be shining down upon us. The fellows did not maintain good order; one couple walked ahead of the next three. It turned out to be my lucky day when we were picked up by a nice person who recognized fellow travelers in obvious distress. It also was evident that he only had room enough for two.

According to my brother, I was picked up because it was obvious I was the youngest. Why should I ever doubt my brother? To answer would only deter me from my story.

The important fact was that I was the first to reach home, although it was already past noon. Of course it became my responsibility to explain to anxious parents where I had been, what I had been doing, and why I did not let them know, plus many other questions. It was no wonder my brother shrewdly wanted me to be the first to arrive home—by his plan, his later entrance was anticlimactic!

After the end of 1941, our dance band still played for both country and town dances on Saturday nights. However, more and more uniformed men showed up at these affairs. Our own conversations always turned to what branch of the service we thought we would be entering. During intermissions, there were often sales of war bonds. Scrap drives were constantly being pushed. The focus of every event was on helping the war effort.

Before long, our dance band was beginning to be decimated by fellows going to the service. It was increasingly difficult to replace a member. We not only witnessed our band shrinking, but also the high school enrollment as well.

Our high school coach was Chet Bowen who also was a terrific trumpet player. For about a year the band consisted of Chet Bowen and Warren Taft playing trumpet, John Ostlund on sax and clarinet, Ray Stimson on drums, and old Ava Brambelette on piano. She seemed old to me, but she was only in her sixties. Then Chet Bowen was drafted and later badly wounded in Germany. With Chet gone the school was missing a coach. In those days a single coach handled all athletics, including teaching duties as well.

During my senior year I played football. Shortly after the season began, we lost our coach to the draft. Ray Ritter, local druggist, and owner of Gillette Pharmacy, volunteered to coach football. He should have been given a medal for heroism, because we actually won one game against Newcastle. The only other games we won were the two we played against Midwest. They probably could not get eleven boys to play against us—even Upton, Sundance, and Lusk beat us. Now I also recall playing Buffalo to a 6 to 6 tie.

Toward the end of the season, we received a new coach named Ben Dobbs. Ben had played professional football with the New York Giants. His football injuries left him with a 4F draft classification. Although new at coaching, he could intimidate the team members into performing beyond their expectations. I suppose we salvaged something out of the season, however, the good news must have been so meager that I can't recall it.

Our final game was scheduled against Lusk. Unknown to me at that time was their quarterback, Jim Griffith. In later years we became good friends. However, the day of the game we knew we were up against one of the toughest teams in the state. Their fullback was named Jim Fagan. He was named All State fullback that year. I claimed to have his cleat marks all over my body following that game, which we lost. In fact Lusk went on to win the State Championship!

As all sporting activities should be, we had a lot of fun. Bill Lamb was elected team captain and I still see both Bill and his wife, Dee, on occasion. They still live in Dubois, Wyoming. They have been successful in the telephone business and have been recognized as a family who has accomplished so much for their community as well as for the state of Wyoming. They emulate what I consider to be the very best of Wyoming!

During both my junior and senior years I acted in the class plays. As a junior we performed Robert Brome's play *Quiet Please*. We did not have to pay the usual ten dollar royalty because Robert Brome was not only our director, but also on the faculty at CCHS.

Jiggs (Louis Dean) Wright was the male star and Bonnie Lynde (later Marquiss) was the female lead. I played Jodwillow, the English butler, and attempted to bring some humor to the part. My English accent, although humorous, must have been outrageous.

During my senior year, I played the male lead opposite Hazel Underwood (later

Smith). Toward the end of the play, my part called for me to take Hazel into my arms and plant a kiss. Hazel's mother lived across the street from our house and always thought that Hazel and I made a cute couple. During the 1950s when I had returned to Gillette, Hazel's mother saw me in the post office. She was hard of hearing and consequently talked very, very loudly. As I recall, the place was crowded when she began shouting, "I remember when you kissed Hazel in high school! That was the cutest thing I ever did see!"

I felt some embarrassment thinking that everyone might believe this just happened last night, but there was never a better, more thoughtful lady in the world than Beulah Underwood. Hazel was our class president when we graduated and also class salutatorian.

The home economics teacher, Lorraine Green, decided to expand her classes and offered one for boys called "bachelor survival". She filled the class that included me. Miss Green informed us that before we commenced working in the kitchen, we first had to learn other tasks. The first chore was to cut, fit, and sew an apron. We also had to make chef hats to wear. Naturally, this required certain equipment: a thimble, needles, and thread. We also went to the V & R Store to buy a few yards of designated white cotton material suitable for a man's apron. The ultimate test came when we were taught to man the sewing machines. Sometimes high speed stitching seemed to replace better judgment. All in all, this seemed to go rather slowly, but finally we were ready for the kitchen. However, I never felt that the kitchen was ready for us!

All of us had a lot of fun. There were a few times when we got a bit out of hand though. One of those times came while making pies. We learned that the secret to a good pie was in the proper making of the crust. About the time we rolled out our pie dough, unfortunately, Miss Green was called to the front office.

During her absence, some guy playfully tossed a hunk of pie dough to someone else. Before anyone realized it, there were large chunks of pie dough being hurled at one another. I recall having a fistful of dough made into a ball just as my intended victim was running out the door and I fired at him like a professional pitcher. Even now I wince as the sound of that dough splattering on the door casing comes back to my memory. The reason I cannot forget it is because Miss Green stepped into the doorway just as that ball of dough smacked right beside her face. My! My!

It was 1940 when I entered high school and I was admittedly bashful around girls. School dances were held in the gym, but I would not go. Why not? Because I didn't know how to dance! On top of that, I was too bashful to tell anyone!

My pal, Jiggs Wright, was from a ranching family who lived about twenty miles south of Gillette. Jiggs went to country schools like all ranch kids, however, when it was time for high school, all country kids came to town. Jiggs had a grandmother, Laura Wright, a widow, who lived at Sixth Street and Warren Avenue, only a block south of my house. During the week Jiggs lived with his grandmother and usually, on weekends, he returned home to the ranch. As a country kid who went with his family to country dances for a main social event, Jiggs knew all about dancing. Naturally, Jiggs went to the high school dances and kept after me to join him.

"Big deal!" he said. "Everyone learns to dance there. Besides a lot of girls would be glad to teach you."

Before the first year was over, I gave in. I was scared to death. Jiggs brought a girl over, probably Marianne Hart, and she not only told me how easy it was, but also showed me. First thing I knew I was actually dancing and I never stopped.

That was only the beginning of my education with girls. As the dance was about to end, Jiggs said, "You better get a date to take one of these girls home!"

"Really?" I asked with certain incredulity. "Which one?"

To my surprise, a girl did agree. I found myself in a car with a girl named Billie Setterland, plus two other couples. More than likely L. J. Hunter was driving his father's four-door Chevrolet. Was I ever surprised when he parked on dump hilltop. I had been there many times in the daylight and knew we were surrounded by garbage and ash pits. After all, I had been in the ash-hauling business myself at one time.

L. J. picked this spot because there was no traffic or other noises. The lights were turned off and he began kissing his date in the front seat while the four of us were crowded together in the back seat. I looked over and saw Jiggs kissing his date. I just couldn't believe this girl, whom I hardly knew, would want to kiss me. Instead I thought I would be better advised to just try and carry on some kind of casual conversation. We had no radio or music as is available today—the perfect quiet was only interrupted by the sounds of lips parting. Not believing I should do the same as was going on around me, I sat and talked. What a great beginning! Following that night I don't recall ever being bashful again.

Early in the school year of 1941, a local tragedy occurred. A ranch family named O'Neal had rented a house for their freshman son, Robert, to occupy during the week while attending high school. As with most country kids, he would return to the ranch when school was over on Friday night. This particular Sunday night he drove into town and built a fire in the cookstove in the kitchen. For some reason the fire did not start. His fatal mistake, which occurs often, happened when he decided to pour kerosene onto the coals. The resultant explosion and fire left him badly burned over most of his body. However, he was still alive and placed in the McHenry Hospital. Little was really known in those days on how to care for burn cases. Skin grafting was only experimental, at best, and never tried locally. Doc McHenry decided that skin graft was his only chance for survival.

Doc McHenry asked for volunteers from the high school to offer skin for this unfortunate classmate. There was good response from most of the boys. As a matter of procedure, Doc had one boy at a time report to the hospital. On the operating table, Doc injected Novocain into his back, then clipped off a patch of skin with surgical scissors, placing pieces of skin like patchwork on the bare flesh of Robert O'Neal. The new skin grew with some success. At first, McHenry only took about twenty pieces off a volunteer. I was not surprised to have them call me one day to report to the hospital and I shall never forget that day.

I lay facedown on the operating table and McHenry began injecting Novocaine into my back. I felt the tug and sounds of snipping and it seemed as though there was no stopping. When he finished with one side, he began on the other and did not tell me how much he was taking. When he was finally done, the nurses bandaged both sides of my back and said to return in a few days for new bandages. As I stepped off the operating table I started to faint, much to my surprise. It was days later when I found out McHenry had taken a total of two hundred pieces from each side of my back. For years to come, every time I was in a public shower, the same question always came, "What are those scars?" I got tired of responding. Unfortunately, my many scars had developed red keloids that were not pretty. This would not have mattered except that, unfortunately, Robert's body finally rejected all of the new skin. Following a long and very painful time, death mercifully came to him.

At that time in my life I was certainly no different from a young man of today. There never seemed to be enough money to do all the things I felt were necessary. For that reason I was always on the lookout for a job opportunity. It also occurred to me that opportunity was staring me in the face! I had found a good market demand and I certainly had the ability to handle the challenge. The discovery was garbage! Everyone had garbage!

All households in Gillette burned coal for heat, which leaves a good deal of ash to haul away. Everyone I knew had an ash can at the alley behind their house. Often there was an opportunity to haul away people's ashes and other garbage as well. Some folks hauled their own, but not everyone.

My father owned a 1929 Model A Ford pickup. It burned white gasoline, which was the very cheapest kind. As I recall, it was less than fifteen cents per gallon. I bought white gas from the Gilstrap garage which was just down the alley from the plumbing shop. This pickup resembled a roadster because it no longer had a top; the original top had been rubberized canvas. My dad let me use it on Saturdays. Jerry Hannum volunteered to help me and, after expenses, we split the profits. We developed a fine clientele and business was good. We charged about $1.50 for the big cans, which were four feet in diameter, and one dollar for lesser units. You can't imagine how absolutely filthy we got during a long Saturday, but it felt good to have a few extra dollars in our pockets. Jerry Hannum went on to become a physician and surgeon. Unfortunately, he died during the sixties at an early age following heart surgery. In my old black-and-white movies I know I have pictures of the two of us shoveling garbage into old "Leaping Lena," as we affectionately called the Model A pickup.

During 1943, my grandfather, Matthew Chapman Roberts, became very ill. Two years previously he had married Bessie Oats, who had taken care of him for some time and took him to Denver where he died in a hospital at the age of seventy-three. He was buried in Newcastle following the services at the Methodist Church. I was so impressed with all the nice things that were said about my grandfather during the service. As I recall, people always said good things about my grandfather who left a wonderful reputation and heritage for his family. At the time of his death, Grandfather Roberts was president of the First State Bank of Newcastle. In retrospect, I would loved to have known him better—in many ways I hardly knew him at all. I suppose this is the way with many grandfathers and this is exactly the reason I have labored to write this book!

My grandfather gave me five shares of Cerro de Pasco Copper stock during the 1930s. Those five shares germinated my continued interest in the stock exchange from that time and probably for the rest of my life.

I rarely considered that I got into a lot of trouble, though there were times when trouble seemed to be peeking over my shoulder. One of those times happened during a music festival held in Rapid City, South Dakota.

CCHS did not own a school bus and all school trips, including athletic events, depended upon parents or friends to furnish necessary transportation. With strict wartime gas rationing in effect, you needed a parent with a "C" ration book, like most ranchers had. Charlie Marshall, a rancher who was well liked by everyone, offered to haul five band kids to Rapid for this event. He probably hauled five kids plus himself. We stayed at the old Harney Hotel because they had the cheapest rate. The new Alex Johnson Hotel looked beautiful, but was expensive. I only got to see their lobby area.

The musical events are not worthy of mention in this narrative. However, the return trip back home was momentous as well as memorable. Charlie decided to drive by Mount Rushmore. We thought that was a great idea. It was not tourist season and there were few cars on the road in wartime to cause traffic. When we arrived at Mount Rushmore, there were only two or three other cars there.

Kids in groups can get the craziest ideas. Believe me! Discontented with just viewing the great heads carved into the Rushmore granite, four of us began exploring how the workmen got there. We found the way!

Walking through the trees, we discovered this wooden staircase that appeared to head onward and upward. Fascinated in the same way that Jack looked upon the beanstalk, "Let's go up there!" I called out. And we did exactly that!

We had reached a lofty level when we saw an obstacle, a definite threat to our moving onward. A steel-cable suspension bridge was strung to provide a way to cross a deep chasm. To prevent people from crossing, a barred gate was set in the middle of the swinging bridge. It was built in such a way as to discourage anyone from attempting further progress—the type of thing that we always looked upon as a challenge. Four of us, including Jiggs Wright, scaled our way over the gate. From then on it was duck soup to make it to the top. What a fascinating place to visit!

All around the top of Mount Rushmore there were catwalks and a huge storage hall that was carved by drilling into the side of a granite hill, which we explored. And for a souvenir, I pocketed the end of a rusty drill bit. The best was yet to come.

We actually walked out and stood on the granite head of George Washington. It was magnificent. I can vividly remember looking over at the Abe Lincoln face that seemed so incredibly huge! Momentarily, I found myself looking at what appeared to be a small crack developing across Lincoln's nose. I also recall the large granite post left sticking out from the top of Washington's head. Obviously this was to anchor the suspended scaffolding used to enable the workers to be lowered to the desired height as they carved on the face of Washington. From the ground, no person could be aware of this massive post protruding from the head.

One of our party was more intent upon looking down than looking outward. "Look down there!" someone cried. "I think they are shouting at us!"

Far, far below, at the ranger station and museum, a small crowd was gathering. We could hear someone shouting through a megaphone like a cheerleader would use. "Come down from there!" We heard faintly but plainly. There was no doubt their demands were directed at us. We had been discovered!

We immediately removed ourselves from the top of the mountain. As we descended the wooden stairway, the chief ranger met us. To say that his face was beet red would be a serious understatement.

We marched silently behind the chief ranger as he took us into his office. I felt badly that Charlie Marshall had to listen to the invective and tirade that we had to endure from the chief ranger. Among a few of his remarks were such things as:

"I'll have you barred from every national park in the United States."

"Never in my twenty-two years of service have I ever seen such disgraceful conduct! You will be forever blackballed from this park for the rest of your lives! In fact, if I ever hear of you again being on national park land, I'll try to have you put behind bars!"

Later, on the way home, Charlie Marshall dryly observed, "That feller was kind of sore, wasn't he?"

Looking back, I think old Charlie was trying to raise our spirits. Charlie was like that! Jiggs Wright was one of my pals who went to the top with me and I believe Warren Taft was also with us. But I cannot recall the other fellow. Someday, when I speak with Jiggs, I'll get his recollection.

During the first three years of high school, I was a member of the debate team. Jiggs Wright was my debating partner. The first debating question that we had for the year 1940–41 was, "Resolved, the United States Should Have Compulsory Military Training!" Now, looking back, we actually had it for more than forty years!

There were other years and other questions, but it was resolved that we had some great times on debate trips. Our coach and mentor was J. J. Cline who really was an excellent coach and a fine speaker in his own right. I believe he was drafted during our junior year, as were so many other male teachers.

Warren Taft and Bill Hays were also a debate team. They were a year ahead of us, very accomplished, and won a number of awards. Dick Hall and Hazel Underwood were good debaters, too, as well as terrific cheerleaders. Hazel was class president our senior year, and my pal, Dick, was also class treasurer.

Having been diagnosed as having a "weak heart" early in life, I began to believe that was all hooey. As I neared my senior year, I determined that I was going to play football and worked hard, giving it everything I had in me. I recall carrying scabs for months during the football season and beyond. We carried scabs because we played on sand and gravel—a grass field was unheard of in our area. In retrospect, I am glad I played, even though it was for only one year and I gave up debate for that year. It had to be one or the other and football won out.

My senior year was the last of the "Loud Shirts" band. Nerb Crossman, coach and superintendent of Rozet School, booked me to play the Rozet prom. We booked well in advance of the event and I agreed to have a quartet. As the date approached, I became increasingly worried—my drummer and trumpet player got drafted and Ava Brambelette was sick in bed. It dawned on me that I was the only one left in the band. Never daunted, I began to recruit players for the prom. Rozet was thirteen miles east from Gillette toward Moorcroft. The prom was hardly different from a regular Saturday night dance, except that the girls would be wearing long dresses. Otherwise the usual families, friends, and neighbors would all show up like any other dance.

I was disappointed when Ava Brambelette refused to get out of her sickbed. Every dance drummer I knew was either in the army or just left town to join the war. In desperation, I called my pal, Jiggs Wright, who played snare drum in the high school marching band—not exactly the right qualification to play a set of dance rhythm drums, but I was in no position to do it alone. Fortunately, I owned the set of dance band drums which I had purchased from the last drummer when he was drafted. Reluctantly, Jiggs agreed to give it a try and for piano, my mother told me she thought Anna Lee Pines was as good as any of her students. I called Anna Lee. She politely thanked me for thinking of her, but said, "No!"

Within a couple of days, in desperation, I called her back and pleaded. My pleadings evidently could not be refused a second time. Thank goodness, I had a trio! We had never played together and two of the trio had never even played dance music. Perhaps it was my youthful optimistic outlook that was momentarily giving me that false sense of security. "I know perfectly well, Mr. Crossman," I said on the telephone. "I can hardly keep band members with the draft taking them. But I do have a trio and we'll do you a good job!"

With that promise I felt like calling it quits with my music career—I was going to Kemper in the fall and a new life was ahead of me. Those thoughts gave me the courage to show up at Rozet for the prom. The short rehearsal was cut even shorter because people gathered to listen. I realized it was not only sad, but also sick! This is by no means to run down my friends, Jiggs and Anna Lee. However, everyone needs practice time and there was none available for the three of us. We had to begin.

We opened with the usual standbys—tunes like "The Darktown Strutters Ball" and "The Sheik of Araby" were popular. But on this night, people had difficulty finding the beat . . . the proper pace . . . perhaps even the tune! For the benefit of the dancing crowd, we took a relieving break. An old-timer came up to me and asked, "Would you like for me to sit in on the drums?"

"Bless your heart, old friend!" I soothed. Please help me out of this!"

He did. Not wanting to appear ungrateful to my pal Jiggs, I said, "Jiggs, why don't you go dance a few, and give this old fellow a chance to drum some!" Jiggs seemed relieved as well as grateful. But then, he was an extraordinary pal.

No one volunteered to play piano, but then, I believed Anna Lee was doing better all the time. However, I knew in my heart and by glancing at Nerb Crossman, that was only wishful thinking in a quite hopeless situation which I had gotten myself into. At midnight, during intermission, Nerb Crossman approached me. He had been glaring daggers all night without speaking a word.

"Let's get this contract settled while intermission is going on," he said. "However, you only gave me a trio instead of the quartet you promised!"

"Mr. Crossman, it is really getting tough out there. Most of the musicians are in the service. I had to pay extra just to get the people I have," I answered lamely.

"You mean you aren't going to knock off anything?" he barked.

"Oh yes I am," I answered. "I think taking off five bucks will make things all right with the others."

Under protest Nerb Crossman paid and I swore this was to be my last dance contract. I couldn't take it any longer. I felt I had really aged that night!

On June 3, 1944, the big news was the Allied invasion of Europe. In the meantime, the Pacific War seemed to be going well for the United States and their Allies. Many of my classmates were already in the service. Gene Hole, a friend I had met in second grade, was killed during the invasion of Tarawa Islands in the Pacific. Thomas Wolf, another classmate, had enlisted in the Navy. During a typhoon in the Pacific, his destroyer turned over and sank with all hands lost. Bob Birdsal, who lived next door to us when I was young, died as a captive of the Japanese during the Bataan Death March from the Bataan Peninsula across the water from Corregidor. There were many others that I would hate to slight by omission, but that is not my intention.

I played in the band the day we sent off a few fellows from the bus depot. Earl Stopher was one who was killed a year or two later. Some find glory in war! Others find heartaches and often death. That is the way we have been since the beginning of time. Will we ever find another way?

In the fall of 1944, I was to turn seventeen years old and was eagerly looking forward to going to Kemper Military School. I had ordered their catalogs when I was in junior high and studied them carefully—I loved looking at all the pictures. Yet, I had never been there. My pal, Burt Reno, had started at Kemper when he was a freshman in high school; he would graduate as a senior this year and was also the Battalion Commander at Kemper, their highest position.

Leaving for Kemper was a big day. Never accused of lacking imagination, I planned a trip that was something of an excursion for me. I decided to visit the Army Air Base at Sioux Falls, South Dakota, where my brother was taking radio training. Bob had been drafted into the army in June of 1943. I had not seen him for a while. After getting off the train, I checked into a hotel. Bob and his buddy, Dean Orvis, came as soon as they were off duty and we had a great visit and dinner that evening. I told them I was thinking about flying to Kansas City the next day, which surprised them and surprised me, too, but I felt adventurous.

I booked a Mid Continent DC3 and flew to Kansas City and felt grown-up. The Hotel Continental in Kansas City was new back then. I was so proud of my brand new brown suitcase. Before leaving Gillette, I had carefully placed a Kemper decal on the side of my bag so that it looked absolutely perfect. I could not have felt better about life at that moment!

That night after supper, I walked around the streets. Imagine my surprise when I passed a burlesque house. I had heard about burlesque, but now, I was standing right in front of temptation. You might say that I was intrigued. I bought a ticket and went in.

Those days of burlesque are gone forever, but to a young kid from Gillette, I thought it was the greatest show on earth. Funny comedy routines, a few jugglers, an animal act, and those exotic striptease numbers left me goggle-eyed! My God! If my mother could have seen me! Thankfully she couldn't!

The next day I boarded a Greyhound bus for Boonville, Missouri. It was a ninety-mile trip. I sat next to an "old boy," as the returning students were known. I learned that my new status was to be known as a "new boy." Kemper was both high school years plus junior college. I was enrolled as a junior college freshman. Probably the majority of students were high school seniors.

My new bus friend, Jack, showed me how to get to the school. It was exactly like I had pictured it. He suggested we stop first at the PMS&T office (which stood for Professor of Military Science and Tactics). I approached the desk in my usual casual manner and leaned on the desk as I spoke to the officer. After Jack and I checked in, we turned and left for our assigned barracks. On the way out Jack said to me, "That is the last time you will ever stand in the PMS&T office slouched over and leaning on the desk." He was certainly correct!

I was assigned to D Barracks as a member of "A" Company. My only roommate was a junior college freshman named Ed Potgeter from Steamboat Rock, Iowa. I thought someone might be kidding me. When tall, blond, Ed Potgeter walked in, I knew he was for real. A good friendship was easily developed. That school year we got along famously except for when Ed decided to take up smoking. During the war, cigarettes were almost impossible and at the least very difficult to find in the stores. Ed Potgeter decided to roll his own. He bought canned tobacco, papers, and being unable to roll with his fingers, he also acquired a simple rolling machine. At night, while we were all supposed to be studying, sometimes I would see Ed trying to roll cigarettes with tobacco all over the desk, as well as the floor. I would get exasperated! However, everyone has to have some disagreements sometime and ours were only trifles.

We each had a desk and chair, as well as a twin-sized bed. The closet was adequate. The lavatories, stools, and showers were down the hall a short way. We lived on the second floor and the cadet dining room was on the ground floor of our barracks.

We went through procedure to get uniforms, textbooks, mailbox assignments, health check, library usage, and generally getting to know where everything was located. We also received our government issue items: a set of army issue wool pants, shirt, and cap, canteen, ammunition belt, and Enfield rifle. At that time the army was using the new Garand rifle, but after all, we had to begin somewhere. Because of out ROTC training, we began with this particular army gear on Saturday and every Saturday thereafter.

Our Saturday hikes began with formation in the courtyard in full army regalia and packs. We proceeded to the Kemper Farm and like proper infantry soldiers, we marched about five miles. These Saturday maneuvers convinced me that the infantry was not my cup of tea. We did infantry exercises every Saturday. My platoon was scouting, deploying as skirmishers, digging foxholes, and rolling in the dirt and brush just as though we loved it. The best part of Saturday came when we lined up with our mess kits and got a hot lunch. We learned early on that we had better scrub those mess kits carefully, or else we could spend the next night sitting on the toilet. To top it off, we finally returned to the school for a hot shower.

The social life at Kemper was another new experience. Instead of dances, we had "military balls." First we were given formal dancing instructions; you received them whether you wanted it or not. The local community furnished partners for our lessons which were held at the Johnson Field House. This was probably done to make us feel at home when the actual ball took place on the same floor.

I was already acquainted with a girl who was attending Stephens College for Women in Columbia. Her name was Ann Napier and she was in my high school class in Gillette. I sent her a letter inviting her to the next ball and she accepted.

Several buses were required to bring girls from Columbia; from Stephens, Christian College, and the University of Missouri. The buses arrived about fifteen minutes before the ball and departed about fifteen minutes after the ball. I suppose, at that time, I took all this personal control over our lives for granted—we were chaperoned all the time, everywhere we went. Getting into trouble, as we know it today, was impossible even if you wanted to. There were a few rumors about some cadet quietly taking his date to the lower level of the Johnson Field House, where supposedly, undetected, he had his girl alone at the swimming pool. I never had a confirmation of that activity, but sometimes it was pleasant to think about.

Academic life was just what I needed. Tough! The classes were small and there was no sliding by as I had sometimes done in high school. I should have been under this strict academic routine years before. If I could ever do it over again, which I can't, I would have studied harder in high school.

My pal, Burt Reno, was now in his fourth year at Kemper and was given command of the battalion and proved to be a splendid leader as a Cadet Major, the highest-ranking cadet. On occasion, Burt would come by. Ed Potgeter would simply excuse himself and leave the room, while Burt and I visited like old friends should. However, for good appearances that could not happen too frequently.

Sometime during the fall my mother and my Aunt Lucille Culver came to visit. Somewhere I have pictures of that visit and it was good to see them. Otherwise, I had no visits from anyone from home until school was over.

While at Kemper something occurred which caused my parents to decide to have me return home for a short visit. This had to be something important, but I can't remember the circumstances today. Probably it was because of my brother getting a short furlough from the army. I do remember the trip.

My parents wired me money to buy a train ticket home. It was when I tried to pick up my money from Western Union that I ran into a frustrating problem. A taxi dropped me off, along with my suitcase, at Western Union. I was to take the bus to Kansas City and from Kansas City, a train home. I walked up to the counter dressed in my Kemper uniform and imagine my surprise when I was asked to present identification. I had a billfold with my name in it.

"That's not satisfactory!" commented the lethargic operator. I took off my uniform cap and showed him my name imprinted in that. "Not satisfactory!" he repeated.

"I can call Kemper and they will verify who I am to you," I pleaded.

"We can't take phone calls as a means of identification!" came his pious response.

"Well, what can I do to satisfy you?" I cried out. As I recall the operator only grunted about needing a driver's license or a draft card.

"Wyoming does not issue driver's licenses!" I croaked. "And since I am only seventeen, I don't yet have a draft card!" Finally, in desperation, I called my parents collect. My dad stormed, "Let me talk to that guy!"

The Western Union operator did not dare hold the receiver too close to his ear. I had no problem hearing my dad yell at him, "Give the kid the money!" The operator attempted to explain the rules, but he was cut off by my dad interrupting with, "By God give him the money or I'll come down there and make you wish you had!"

I was not used to hearing my father threaten people. However it worked! The telegraph operator grudgingly handed me the money along with a receipt to sign, just in the nick of time to board the last possible bus, for I had already missed the bus I originally intended to take.

Now it was going to be nip and tuck to make my train out of Kansas City. As it turned out, I ran into the station and without daring to stop to buy a ticket, I headed for the tracks. The call-board showed the track number and when I raced down to the track and the train came into view, it was already moving. I caught the last car, the observation and club car, and swung aboard. Made it! Once aboard the train I paid the conductor for a ticket, being thankful for the cash received from Western Union. Other than that, I had a nice and uneventful trip home.

At Kemper I made many great friends. Jack Stapleton was from Saint Joe, Missouri, and his father was in the newspaper business. We still get a Christmas card every year from Jack and Pat Stapleton. I met my future Naval Academy roommate at Kemper. His name was Dave Gunckel from Tulsa. Tom Nymchek went to the Naval Academy from Kemper also. I almost overlooked the fact that a third Gillette boy came to Kemper. His name was Paul Kirby. I have no idea where Paul Kirby is today.

Another good longtime friend was Alan Poe. He was from Peabody, Kansas. I was intrigued to hear Alan tell about how his father raised turkeys—not small flocks, but rather thousands. Alan Poe is now retired and with his wife, Polly, is living in St. Louis. They visited us in Gillette a few years ago. Recently, during the summer of 1995, Alan phoned from the Buford Store. What a surprise! We told Alan and Polly how easy it was to get to our Remount Ranch and they came for dinner. We sent our regards to the Stapletons along with them on their return trip to St. Louis.

Burt Reno and I were both on the varsity rifle team, as was Alan Poe. Kemper had an excellent team and a long history of good marksmanship. The library was the place where all of the William Randolph Hearst trophies won by previous Kemper rifle teams were displayed. When Mary and I took our daughter, Peg, to enroll at Stephens College, we stopped at Kemper. I recall proudly pointing out the trophy with our five team members' names inscribed on it. Of course two of the five were Burt Reno and John Ostlund.

Kemper had four honor societies: scholastic, athletic, military, and general. I wanted to make all four. I did make three, but lacked the scholastic honor. I was proud of Burt Reno for making all four. In order to win the general honor I availed myself of an opportunity open to the entire Corps of Cadets. They offered a prize for the winner of an annual original oratory contest. I decided to enter. By the time you went through the elimination process, only two finalists remained who had to present their orations to the assembled Corps and Faculty at an assembly program. The other finalist was first to present by draw of the cards. When my turn came, I remember approaching the podium in the auditorium and looking down at the front row where I saw Colonel A. M. Hitch, the superintendent. Sitting beside him was Burt Reno, who slyly gave me a wink and a smile as I began speaking. When finished I was elated to receive first prize.

The name of my original oratory was "Peace Everlasting." I had worked hard on my paper. Lights were out and taps were played every night at ten, however, I would take my portable Smith Corona typewriter and go down the hall to the bathroom where lights burned all night. I placed my typewriter on a lavatory and pulled a folding chair up to it. That extra effort gave me the paper I needed to win the contest which also gave me my General Honor award. I hope I still have that paper somewhere. It is just as appropriate today as it was in 1945.

In 1944, while attending Kemper, I was inspired to try to get an appointment to the United States Naval Academy at Annapolis, Maryland. In retrospect I believe my attraction to the Naval Academy, rather than West Point, came from the fact that I had never seen one of the oceans. I had been reading constantly about sea stories and the war in the Pacific going on at that time could only be sustained and won by a strong navy; also, Kemper taught me the reasons why I did not want to be in the infantry.

It was during the fall of 1944 when I talked with my parents about trying to get an appointment. My grandfather Roberts was respected in political circles. My mother and father asked a friend of theirs in Newcastle for help in obtaining an appointment. They spoke with an old friend of my grandfather's by the name of Harry Ilsley, a district judge living in Newcastle. Wyoming had only one congressman since it became a State and the congressman at that time was Frank A. Barrett, who later became governor and then United States Senator. In 1944, he gave me a first alternate appointment. Within several weeks, I was fortunate to be advised that I was now his principal appointment and I was thrilled.

It was not until about thirty-five years later when I learned that my good friend, Jim Griffith from Lusk, was my first alternate. During my senior year in high school, I had played against the Lusk football team when Jim Griffith was quarterback. They had demolished us. Jim Griffith went on to become publisher of the *Lusk Herald* and then Wyoming State Treasurer and State Auditor. Best of all, we became good friends!

During the fall of 1944, the Navy advised the several of us holding Naval Academy appointments to go to St. Louis to take our first Navy physical. My friend, Alan Poe, who also had an appointment, traveled with me. We both passed without any problem, but I was certainly apprehensive about the approaching mental exams to be held soon after the beginning of the new year of 1945.

This was the greatest incentive to study and learn that I had ever experienced. I lacked confidence in math and the math exam was extensive. When the time arrived to take the tests, I recall being worried. The math exam was first and lasted all morning and when the test was finished, I felt as though I might have passed. I was not so worried about the English, history, and government, but I still knew that it would be weeks before I learned the results. In fact, the last day of school, when I went to my post office box for the last time, there was an envelope from the United States Navy. I was afraid to open it. When I tore it open and it showed that I had passed the tests, I felt that the weight of the world had been lifted from my shoulders. I did not just ride home to Wyoming, I might have flown I felt so high. I felt badly for my friends who did not pass the tests, but two of my other friends, Dave Gunckel from Tulsa, and Tom Nymcheck both passed. The three of us were all soon to be heading for the Naval Academy to be in the Class of 1949!

At the conclusion of our Kemper experience, instead of going immediately to Gillette, my good friend, Alan Poe from Kansas, and I went to Saint Joseph, Missouri, to visit our friend Jack Stapleton, also a Kemper cadet. We more than enjoyed a few days of visiting before we both returned to our own homes.

My parents had accepted an invitation from Everett and Pauline Reno to go to the Kemper graduation. There was a lot of fanfare, including parades. I was pleased my parents could be there for all these activities and also to be able to tell them in person about passing the Naval Academy tests!

Arriving back in Gillette, I was expecting to receive word to report to the Naval Academy in June. June came and went and I was disappointed when I did not receive orders. Meanwhile, my friend, Dave Gunckel, was ordered to report. Finally, toward the end of July, a telegram arrived from the Naval Academy. I was shocked to read the message that said in effect, if I expected to be in the entering class this year I must see that my secondary education credits and grades were immediately sent to the Academy. I was angry when I contacted the Campbell County High School superintendent by the name of N. D. Morgan. I had mailed the request to him from Kemper months before and assumed that he had performed. Years later I always recalled an admonition from my father, "Assume! Never assume anything."

Campbell Count High School football team, 1943. John is in the back row, fourth from left.

Polly visiting John at Kemper.

Visiting in "E" Barracks at Kemper on Sunday afternoon. John standing at far left.

In the prone position at the Kemper firing range.
Left to right: J.C. Ostlund, R.F. Johnson, B.P. Waggener, B.K. Reno.

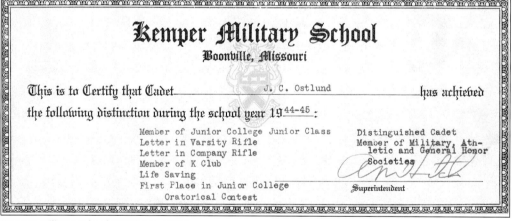

Kemper Military School Certificate, 1945.

6

Lost!

Sunset had occurred about a half hour ago. Total darkness soon would replace those last vestiges of sunset that still lingered along the western horizon. A kind of lonesome feeling was coming on me as I rode a bay horse mile after mile. I figured that I must have been in the saddle for at least thirteen hours straight and it was at least twelve hours since I last saw my two companions. How could there be so much open rangeland without ever seeing another human being? How badly I wished for someone to talk with.

Earlier that morning, after gathering cows out of Reno's winter pasture, I was supposed to meet Burt Reno and his friend, Larry Smith, from Saint Louis. Since I was presumed to be familiar with the country, Burt had me work a different part of the big pasture from my friends. I had chased cows through scrub cedar hills and canyons until I had gathered perhaps a dozen that had been left behind from an earlier gathering. We had agreed to meet at the Jennings reservoir and I had readily acknowledged that, "Sure! I know where that is!"

To my surprise, I was there first. The longer I waited the more uneasy I became and finally the awful truth began to dawn. Was this really the Jennings reservoir?

About a mile away, I could see a high hill that would undoubtedly provide a good vantage point. Leaving my cows at the reservoir and after viewing the situation from atop the hill, I still could not recognize anything that was really familiar and began to regret my overconfidence that I assumed when we left the ranch. Had I been more cautious I would have noted the directions we traversed more carefully, but then, chasing cows in and out of draws had really turned me around.

From atop that high hill, I made a decision. Holding to the truth that the horse will always take you home, I urged him forward. The horse seemed bewildered to not receive guidance. After first turning to the left, he swung to the right and went steadily down the hill.

"How strange!" I thought. My own instincts would have made me go to the left like the horse started to, but then, I may as well admit that I was lost!

By late afternoon, I also was convinced that the horse was lost. My stomach kept reminding me that lunch was long past. The sunrise breakfast we had at the ranch that morning lingered in my mind. How good another plate of eggs, pancakes, and mutton slices would be right now!

Traveling mile after lonesome mile, a great discovery was about to dawn upon me. My horse came to a water hole and began drinking. I bailed off and muzzled right in beside him. Although the water was certainly not clear in color, it was wet and that was what counted. Then as I stood there beside my horse, I finally saw something that had been silently staring at me all day. I should have noted this when saddling up. This horse did not wear the familiar Heart Spear brand of Reno horses. Instead this horse carried the Hog Eye brand of the huge Keeline Ranch. "My God! I'm riding a Keeline horse!" I realized I was only talking to the horse and he didn't have the courtesy to answer.

Instead I felt him saying, "Well, it took you long enough to figure that out! You Greenhorn!"

From that first enlightening moment, until my remaining confidence was completely stripped away by the surrounding darkness, I had felt full of hope that this horse was carrying me to the Keeline Ranch—but when do we ever reach there?

Just as the stars appeared in the sky, we topped another hill and lo and behold, lights came from windows in the distance. Sure enough, this horse that I had been cursing and sarcastically questioning his ancestry, was now suddenly transformed into the smartest and most faithful horse in the world!

As I rode into the yard, the dogs were barking. I recognized George Keeline stepping out on the porch—how good it was to see another human. Although George Keeline was quite good natured, at that time I was always somewhat intimidated by the profane way he usually expressed himself.

"This is a hell of a time to come calling, but I sure do thank you for bringing that horse home for me!" George added, "I've been wondering how the hell I was going to get that son-of-a-bitch home. Maybe you would like to come in and have something to eat! Are you hungry?"

I recall trying not to overreact to my good fortune of finding the Keeline Ranch. I casually allowed that a bite to eat would go really well with me, but first I had to take my horse to the barn for a few oats.

George said, "If you put that saddle in my pickup, I might drive you back to Reno's after you eat. Unless you would rather ride that damn horse!" He added his final comment with a sly grin.

That all sounded perfect to me and I ate Elaine's cooking like a famished hobo.

George grilled me at length and insisted that I describe my entire day. I told him about seeing a fence late in the afternoon and how I almost succumbed to the idea of going through it.

"Damn good thing you didn't!" George said, "There's close to a hundred square miles in that pasture without a cross fence or a shack of any kind. We would have had a hell of a time finding you in there!"

There was a very rudimentary private telephone line strung between the Keelines and Renos. It worked perhaps half the time and then only by shouting into the wall unit. I learned that Renos had called George Keeline about my disappearance and, of course, since Burt explained I was riding a Keeline horse they were hoping that I would end up with George. By hand-cranking the telephone, a call to Renos relieved their minds as to my whereabouts.

As we climbed into the pickup and left George Keeline's that night, I could never have dreamed that it would be approximately twenty-eight years before I would again set foot on the Keeline Ranch. And when I did return, in 1971, it was to buy that very ranch from Joe J. Keeline, Jr. But in 1943, that thought was too lofty for a boy who had not yet turned sixteen!

The events leading to the acquisition of the Keeline Ranch are contained in the chapter entitled, "Recollections."

John riding the Keeline range.

7

1945–46 USNA Plebe Year

As soon as the required paperwork reached the Academy, the Navy sent a telegram ordering me to report at once. This was during the second week of August 1945. Before I reached Annapolis, the atomic bombs were being dropped on Nagasaki and Hiroshima! Everyone on the train was hopeful the Japanese were going to capitulate!

I had boarded the train out of Gillette for Washington, D.C. Troop travel was by train in those days, and the trains were both busy and crowded. Most of the passengers were some branch of military. As I recall, I took an overnight trip from Gillette to Omaha and the second night we traveled out of Chicago. The next day I arrived at the huge Union Station in Washington.

For a kid from Gillette it was inspiring to walk out the front door of Union Station and look at the beautiful Capitol building in the distance. I took a cab to the Greyhound bus terminal and bought a ticket for Annapolis. It was east coast hot and muggy, but my appreciation, coupled with awe, did not allow a little discomfort to interfere. The twenty-eight-mile trip was on a two-lane highway with little traffic due to gas rationing. When the bus brought me to Annapolis, the bus driver directed me to the nearest gate, Gate Number Two, which was known as the "Second Class Gate." The privilege of using this gate would not come to me again for two more years.

Having read so many books and seen so many pictures of the Naval Academy, I was walking on a cloud as I entered. Striding up to the main entrance of Bancroft Hall was a powerful experience. My eighteenth birthday was about six weeks away and to my young mind I could not have been placed in a more inspirational setting.

At that time most of the upper classes were on cruise. The class of 1949, of which I was to become a member, was the first class to enter as a four-year class since the outbreak of World War II. To make this transition and break the three-year wartime schedule, the class of 1948 had just been cleaved in half by academic standing. There was to be a Class of '48A and a Class of '48B. This left some bitter tastes in the mouths of the '48B midshipmen.

On my first big day of entering Bancroft Hall, someone pointed out the direction to the Main Office. I walked in carrying my suitcase and the midshipman Officer of the Watch told me to follow him. I almost made my first bad goof at that time. The Officer of the Watch was named John Geary, Class of '47, who later became my company commander. As I followed him, I thought that his black suspender on the right side had inadvertently not been placed over his shoulder. He was wearing the formal white service uniform and I felt embarrassed for him to think that he had forgotten to properly dispose of his right suspender before putting on his jacket. Fortunately for me, I kept my mouth shut. Later, I learned that Officers of the Watch carried a sword and the sword belt was worn under the white service jacket. There was a small slit on the right-hand side at the waist of the jacket, and the hanging piece was also hooked to the side of the sword scabbard to hold it in place. John Geary was not wearing his sword at that time, but he was wearing the proper sword belt. I was later thankful for my silence.

It took a few days to go through the necessary physicals and other procedures. Finally, the rather small group who were among the last to enter the class, were called to Memorial Hall, a special room at the top of the marble stairs that ascend from the Bancroft Hall rotunda. There, under the original "Don't Give up the Ship" flag carried by Commodore Perry, we took the oath and were sworn in as midshipmen in the United States Navy. From that moment until graduation four years later, we were very busy people.

Immediately, we went to the Midshipmen Store for supplies and uniforms; prior to that, we went to the barbershop. The haircut took less than a minute—our hair was shorn off with electric clippers. I don't suppose my hair was over a quarter-inch long. But then, we were not going anywhere until Christmas, so what difference did it make?

From that moment forward, everything we did was totally new and exciting. We rowed whaleboats, fired carbines on the rifle range, sailed the knockabouts, marched, learned semaphore, and the obstacle course, to mention only a few drills. All the time we plebes, as we were known, were apprehensive about the return of the Brigade. That was when the upperclassmen returned, and the fall academic year would begin. I was happy to know that for the academic year I would be rooming with my old Kemper pal, Dave Gunckel, and also a boy from New York City named Dick Mergl. We were to live in a three-man room. All rooms were conveniently equipped with a shower and lavatory and there was ample room for each of us, as well as our gear. All of our civilian clothes were required to be sent home.

Organizationally, as I recall, there was one Brigade and under that two regiments; under that six battalions; and under that thirty-six companies. All of us plebes who were in the same company were assigned that way because we had all chosen the same foreign language, which was Spanish. At that time, foreign language was the only elective at the Naval Academy. This program has changed immensely over the years, with wide choices of academic curriculum at the present time.

The big day arrived and the upper classes returned to form the Brigade. For the balance of plebe year, we fourth classmen were under strict and severe discipline. At all mealtimes, the entire Brigade would form and march to the midshipmen dining room. The dining room at the Naval Academy is a huge long room and the entire Brigade takes their meals together at a single seating. I always felt that the food was good, but sitting at the table as a plebe and often responding to questions by the upper classes was somewhat unsettling. You were never allowed to respond that you did not know the answer. If you did not know, the proper response was, "I'll find out, sir!"

During one of the first meals, I was told, along with another plebe named Bill O'Flaherty, that we would be responsible for furnishing "happy hour" at the evening meal on Sunday night. Bill was from Richmond, Virginia, and throughout our years at the Academy we were the greatest of friends. However, this occasion was our first opportunity to get acquainted. We sweated on our happy-hour performance. As I recall, we told jokes and I believe I recited some lewd poem that I had picked up during high school. We received no plaudits, but whatever we did evidently turned out to be satisfactory.

Class sections were relatively small and since only first classmen were allowed the special privilege of walking, the rest of us marched to classes. I recall the average class consisted of about ten students, which meant each person was required to recite during each class. Since we were taking engineering courses, there was a heavy load of mathematics.

At that time in my life, math was not my best subject. I later determined that this was because I had been allowed to slide by math in high school. In retrospect, my high school teachers' leniency was certainly no favor. I paid for this mistake at the Naval Academy when I was forced to relearn high school math while trying to keep up with the standard heavy load. What really saved me in this regard was the year I spent at Kemper Military School. I will always thankfully remember an instructor named Captain Anderson. The first day in college algebra class he gave a test to see how much we knew. He later interviewed each of us about our test. He asked me what my future plans were and I told him that I wanted to go to the Naval Academy. His response was very frank and honest. "You will never pass the math test." So under his guidance I not only took college algebra, but relearned high school algebra and trigonometry. That is how I passed the Naval Academy entrance exams and that is how I stayed in the Naval Academy.

Plebe life was restrictive. We could not date during our plebe year. We could not attend dances and could only leave the Yard on Saturday and Sunday afternoons to go to Annapolis to see a movie. On those great weekends, before the winter weather began, I took advantage of learning to sail. I qualified in knockabouts, and then got to crew on the yawls. Later I earned handling qualifications that certified me to check out a yawl in my name. Sometimes I was given the chance to crew on the yachts, although I preferred the smaller yawls. Sailing on the Chesapeake Bay was a happy and memorable experience that will remain with me for my lifetime. I suppose it was special coming from Wyoming as I did. Probably it came from never having seen the open water before. A whole new world opened for me and I loved it!

With most of the able-bodied young men in the Country serving in the armed forces, there was no wonder that both Army and Navy had the best football teams in the nation. With the advent of the football season we had something new to look forward to. Our first away football game, scheduled to be played in Baltimore, meant that the Brigade of Midshipmen could go. Gas rationing and troop movements by rail had precluded the movement of the Brigade, as we know it today. We went to Baltimore by ferryboat; another new experience for me. After the game, we did not have to report back to the boats until ten o'clock that night.

On one of these first trips, and before I had the opportunity to meet any young ladies, I was sitting in a tavern with another midshipman. We were invited to join a table occupied by someone connected with the Baltimore Port Authority who introduced us to a Swedish ship captain. The captain wanted to meet an American midshipman and we had a nice visit. I told him that my grandfather had emigrated from Sweden. He asked me if I would like to visit his ship and since we were already at the waterfront I said that I surely would. Frankly, I was disappointed when I first saw it. He was hauling coal and the outside of the ship looked dirty. But what a nice surprise I had when we went into the officer's lounge. It was clean and neat as a pin. They served us liquors and I developed a whole new image and respect for the merchant fleet.

Early in December came the Army-Navy football game. Wartime transportation was still in effect so the Brigade was to make the trip to Philadelphia by boat. It was an overnight trip on large ferryboats and now, in my later life, it seems rather incredible. We put on our best uniforms and carried wool blankets for warmth. We boarded the boats at the Academy and went to Philly via the inland waterways. The next morning we lined up to use the bathroom and shave and I do recall that we ate from box lunches. When we off-loaded, we formed and marched from the docks to Municipal Stadium, which I believe has been renamed the Kennedy Stadium. I will never forget the impact that I felt when we marched into the stadium with over one hundred thousand people there—the sight awed this country kid. I was so proud to be in formation on that beautiful grass playing field. Little did it matter that Navy lost to Army; the experience was unforgettable.

After the game we had dates, which was accomplished by my roommate, Dave Gunckel. He knew a girl who agreed to bring two of her friends. Our other roommate, Dick Mergl, was the third person, and the six of us got together following the game. We had to be back at the waterfront to board the ferries at about eleven o'clock. The plan was to take the girls to dinner at one of Philly's prominent hotel dining rooms. The first thing I noticed when I looked at the menu was the prices, which were shocking to me. I seemed to be the only one who was surprised.

Following a great dinner that included wine, the girls all adjourned to the powder room. That was the moment when Dave Gunckel admitted that he was short of funds and asked to borrow some money. The girls returned about the same time the waiter brought the ticket. Dave Gunckel asked the waiter to give it to me. I suggested that we gentlemen adjourn to the men's room. We pooled all our money and together we still were short a considerable amount of dollars. The only thing that saved our bacon was the fact that I was still prudently carrying a few travelers' checks from my journey from home last August. What an uncomfortable evening. We hardly had time to pay the bill before returning the girls to their train. We barely reported in to the ferryboats before departure time. What a weird evening!

During the fall of 1945, the Naval Academy celebrated its 100th anniversary. On the principal day of celebration, the Brigade stood in formation while they fired a 100-gun salute with the cannons. The previous year at Kemper, we had done the identical exercise. I was impressed to know that Kemper was a year older than the Naval Academy. The event was formally recognized and we did much parading. Vice Admiral Aubrey W. Fitch was superintendent and Rear Admiral Ingersoll was commandant. Admiral Fitch carried the nickname of Jake and kidding about that one day earned the same nickname for me. It is hard to recall how those things get started, but I responded to the name of Jake not only through the Academy, but during our reunions.

There were many parade occasions during my years at the Academy. When Fleet Admiral Chester Nimitz returned from the Pacific, he was accorded a proper parade in Washington, D. C. The same was done for Admiral "Bull" Halsey. Halsey presented his silver-mounted saddle to the Naval Academy museum where it is still on display. I also enjoyed the opportunity to meet and visit and be taught by so many naval heroes of World War II.

Just before commencing Christmas leave, I was surprised when the entire Brigade of Midshipmen were awarded the World War II Victory medal. Many of my classmates had actually been in action during the war, but the majority of us had not. At that time I envisioned the medal to be the very first of the many more medals I would earn during my naval career.

Through all of this, I was counting the days until Christmas vacation would begin. We were allowed nine days off and instead of the slower train, I had reserved a seat on a United Airlines plane to fly to Denver. A few days before the vacation, the weather turned bad and no planes departed. However the day before we were turned loose, the weather became beautiful. I took my suitcase and boarded a bus for Washington, as happy as could be. My first disappointment came when I was told that all the planes were bottled up in Chicago, due to bad weather. However, United Airlines had reserved train space for us as far as Chicago if we wanted to take it. I was reserved on the Pennsylvania Railroad, which turned out to be eight hours late reaching Chicago the next day. I was grumbling about this turn of events, especially when I learned that the Baltimore and Ohio railroad ran the same distance on time. I missed the chance to catch the available train to Omaha. There was an all-reserved train called the Rock Island Rocket preparing to leave Chicago for Omaha, but the line of people waiting to get tickets seemed to be at least a block long. Imagine my surprise when a railroad person came and took several of us uniformed service men to the head of the line. I was told there were no seats left on this reserved train, but if I would sit in the lounge of the men's bathroom they would let me on. I took it!

That train was due to make Lincoln about twelve thirty that night. There was only one train each day that left Lincoln for Gillette, and it was scheduled to leave at eleven thirty. I hoped that it would be late, as usual. Unfortunately, I had to change stations in Lincoln. When the taxi got me to the Burlington station, I was about forty-five minutes late to catch my train. That meant I had to spend twenty-four hours in Lincoln,

Nebraska, before another train would be available. The cabdriver had come into the station with me to see if I caught my train. He seemed disappointed, also, because business was terribly slow. If I would let him pick up his girlfriend for the ride, he would try to catch the train at a town sixty miles away. He agreed to do this for a reasonable amount and we made a deal. I forget the name of the Nebraska town where we conspired to catch the train, but when we arrived at the station there was no train on the track. Entering the depot, I asked the operator if train #42 was in yet. The man said, "If you look out that window toward the west you can still see the taillight going down the track!"

Both the cabdriver and I asked, "Where does it stop next?" We were told York, Nebraska, was the next stop. Even though it was one o'clock in the morning and those Nebraska plains were cold and snowy, I agreed to pay another five dollars to try and make York before the train arrived there.

When we arrived in York, we were disappointed for a third and last time. We had missed the train by five minutes. The next stop was Grand Island, and the cab driver figured he could not get to the station in time. I gave up. I asked the cabbie to try to find a rooming house and he dropped me off in front of a place where I woke the lady and booked a room that cost two dollars. Frankly, my resources were being rapidly depleted.

Early the next morning I arose after a short night in bed, dressed in my uniform and was determined to hitchhike home. I recall getting a ride to Grand Island and then a second ride, which took me to the outskirts of another small Nebraska town. Instead of going into town, I chose to remain on the highway where I felt I was more likely to get another ride. Then a most unusual event occurred. A car passed me, slowed, and stopped, then reversed. I observed two older women in the front seat of a four-door sedan. They looked me over and evidently decided that I passed their examination. I was invited to ride in the backseat along with their bags of groceries and I was de-lighted to get in out of the cold December weather. They drove westerly about thirty miles down the highway when they stopped, and said, "Well, this is where we turn off to go to the ranch. We hope we helped you out!"

I gazed out at the bleak snow-covered panorama, with the wind blowing snow across the highway. I was speechless to believe that I was being turned loose on this forsaken empty road. Remember, with gas rationing, there was little traffic, especially on Highway #2 across Nebraska going toward Alliance. They started to drive away, then stopped and backed up. The lady in the passenger side rolled down her window and reached into one of the sacks of groceries in the backseat. She jerked a banana off a bunch and handed it to me. "You better take this in case you get hungry!"

In their hearts I knew they really thought they had done me a good turn, but as I stood alone on that cold prairie, I was deeply apprehensive. Wearing my heavy navy bridge coat with no overshoes or anything to protect my ears and attempting to keep my feet warm by stomping on the cold pavement; I determined after a half-hour I would stop the first vehicle that came along, regardless of which direction it was travel-ing. Just then, an old dump truck came from the east heading west. It went by a good distance before reaching a squealing stop. There were no new vehicles in those days because none other than military necessities had been manufactured since the war began in 1941. A Mexican and his wife drove this old dump truck. They unwired the door to let me in and then wired it closed again. The wind blew in through the cracks and there was no heater. But I was so happy to get the ride, I probably would have been glad to have ridden in the dump box if necessary, for I had been having visions someone would find me frozen to death on that lonesome road. They took me all the way to Alliance and I was grateful. Once out of the truck, I found a place where I ate a bowl of good hot soup and went back to thumbing rides. I finally arrived in Crawford, Nebraska, before giving up.

It was nighttime again and I could go no farther. I checked into a hotel and called my parents. My brother, Bob, was home from the University of Wyoming and he volunteered to drive to Crawford and get me. He and his friend, Alva Wilson, arrived just after midnight and we returned to Gillette before morning. What a relief!

From this experience, I thought perhaps I should remain at the Naval Academy the next Christmas. With so few days of leave to spend, I hated to use so many of them traveling. And what a rough way to travel. The return trip was another three days by train and again I could only get the Pennsy from Chicago to Washington and was certain that my assigned car on the Pennsy had been resurrected from the Civil War days. The chair car was heated by a coal stove, but with little effect and the snow and ice on the floor never melted. Returning to Bancroft Hall was almost a relief after almost four thousand miles of rough travel.

At the Naval Academy everyone had to participate in athletics at some level. I had delayed signing up for fall sports. My failure to sign on time only meant someone else did it for me. Imagine my surprise when one day I was told I was on the company cross-country team for the fall season; what an experience. I thought surely I would die on those runs and with my legs turning to rubber and my chest on fire, I was usually among the last group to cross the finish line. Another lesson was learned, the hard way!

For winter sports I anticipated ahead and signed for the rifle team. This was really my thing and I did excel in varsity rifle at Kemper. I made the plebe team at the Naval Academy and earned my only "letter" in the form of a '49 for my bathrobe. At the Naval Academy all sports awards were sewn to your bathrobe. There was no opportunity to ever wear letter sweaters, so bathrobes were the fashion.

In retrospect one of the many benefits of attending the Naval Academy was the physical fitness push. I believe this great fitness program, beginning at this early time, was to pay dividends for the balance of my life. Not only were there formal programs in physical training, but also voluntary fitness programs were sought-after by most of us. The physical training curriculum covered everything imaginable to me: boxing, gymnastics, fencing, swimming, handball, rowing, track, squash, basketball, and on and on. The availability of facilities seemed to be incentive enough for pursuing these activities with our free time, which there was little of anyway. For that reason, the Brigade of Midshipmen was in excellent physical condition.

Every plebe has a first classman. The first day we plebes joined the Brigade, a first classman walked into my room and asked my name. He took me on as one of his plebes and from that time on he was like a big brother to me. We never got too familiar, but maintained a certain reserve. He taught me to tie a necktie in a very unique manner that he called the "reverse Windsor." The tie is actually tied inside out so as not to wear out so rapidly. I still use this method today and have taught all my sons to tie a necktie that way. The name of my first classman was C. G. Batt and he hailed from the state of Washington. I have never heard from him or about him again since he graduated in June of 1946. He was actually in the class of '47, but that was still a three years and out class.

When June Week of 1946 finally arrived, I was more than ready. I was doing all right in my academic work except for math. I worried over my math classes and during plebe year we covered college algebra, spherical geometry, differential calculus, and integral calculus, among others. I prayed I would pass the final examinations. We were scheduled to go on a thirty day leave right after June Week and then return to the Academy to begin summer cruise. My worrying about the math finals caused me too much anxiety and when the grades were posted, I was down in math. I was sick at heart when I learned this.

Since my other grades were good and my record was clean, I was given an opportunity to take a second exam in math. I studied every day and took special classes to prepare. I also went to the chapel every day and prayed for success. I did have success and though I was a week late, it was one happy guy who took off for Wyoming and I never again failed a test at the Academy.

Although I enjoyed being in Wyoming for about two weeks, I was really looking forward to going on cruise. As plebes, we were assigned to battleships and our task force included two battleships; the sister ships, the *Washington* and the *North Carolina*. Also in the task force were two aircraft carriers, some cruisers, and many destroyers. We embarked at Norfolk Naval Station, a place I was to become very familiar with.

Officially we were no longer plebes because we had been elevated to third classmen, or in Academy terms called "youngsters." Nevertheless we were assigned the lowest duties on the ship. Starting at the bottom of the ladder was probably the best way toward eventually becoming a good naval officer.

The battleship *Washington* carried over three thousand men. We were to be gone for more than two months, so you can imagine all of the supplies it took for provisions. Of course we resented that most of these supplies were carried aboard on the backs of us "youngsters."

Railcars of supplies were lined up alongside the ship to be unloaded. At the time it seemed incredible that we would need all of the provisions being off-loaded from the railcars. Those days of preparations for sea were very exciting for me.

I stood in awe of the main battery of sixteen-inch guns mounted three to a turret with two turrets forward and one turret aft. Before returning to Norfolk, I was to know a great deal about the operation of these nine sixteen-inch guns, as well as learn a great deal about the operation of the entire ship.

Everything about this ship was impressive. The ship's own war record was like a history book. The *Washington* had the proud record of engaging a Japanese battle group and succeeded in sinking a Japanese battleship in the process. In addition to the nine sixteen inch guns, it also carried many twin five-inch guns, twin 40-millimeter guns, 20-millimeter machine guns, and so on. The main armor deck and the belt of steel at the torpedo line was at least sixteen-inch steel plate. I was assigned to a sleeping compartment that must have been on the fifth level below the main deck. I slept on a canvas which was stretched on a pipe frame to make a bunk. There were four bunks stacked one above the other and the amount of space between bunks was less than generous.

The oddest thing to me was our toilet room, known in Navy terms as the "head." With so many men using the toilet rooms, they were pretty basic. The crew's toilet rooms were equipped with long stainless steel troughs with toilet seats hinged down over the top of the troughs. Seawater was pumped into one end of the trough and the continuous torrent of water kept flushing everything out the other end and back into the sea. Certainly nothing fancy, but it was effective. On those infrequent occasions when the flushing pump would break, the powerful odor emanating from that room was pretty bad. One whiff of the odor would remind me of the days before plumbing when outhouses were the substitutes. We made our own potable water from the ship's evaporators. As long as they were all performing correctly, we had sufficient water for washing and showering. If there was a problem making water, we went on water hours with restricted usage, which led to some griping from most of the hands.

Our task force was on a Caribbean cruise with Panama as our farthest destination. But first we had to go to Guantanamo Bay in Cuba. Never having been out of the United States, I thought this was very exciting. That trip was the first of many times I would be in Cuba during my naval career. The palm trees and the clear bay water impressed me. When we were anchored, I could actually see fish, including shark and barracuda, off the side of the ship.

We would leave the naval base for the little Cuban town of Culebra, where the favorite pastime was drinking Cuban beer. As I recall, the label on the Hatui bottle was a picture of a one-eyed Indian. Cerveza freo was what we asked for and I thought how fortunate I was to have learned Spanish at the Academy.

Being in Panama was an adventure and we spent time on both the Atlantic and Pacific sides. The Caribbean side featured Colon and Cristobal as the nearest port for sailors going ashore. Trying to remember these two towns, thinking back to 1946, my recollections are of a main street with countless gin joints and places full of cheap souvenirs. That is probably an unfair assessment, but after all these years those are the thoughts that seem to stick in my mind.

One day Jack Rupe, Bill O'Flaherty, and a couple more of us decided to take a bus to Panama City on the west coast. We had a great day and actually took in a few historic sites, such as a place that Pirate Henry Morgan once occupied. Panama City was not only much larger, but also had a certain charm about it. We enjoyed a long day in Panama City and then had a fine dinner at a local restaurant. Finally the day ended when we boarded another bus to return to our ship at Colon.

Years later, in 1976 and again in 1980, Mary and I were to transit the canal on passenger liners. I could not get over the proliferation of tall buildings in Panama City. In 1946 they were mostly single-story buildings and, of course, back at that time air-conditioning was unheard of.

While at sea, we were constantly doing ship drills and exercises. The second classmen were flying off the carriers and the first classmen were mostly on destroyers. Some, of course, were on the battleships to supervise us youngsters. We had to stand regular four-hour watches with eight hours off. Watch assignments changed weekly to give us the broadest experience in the shortest time. In my opinion, we did everything that no one else wanted to do. When I was assigned to a watch station, I first had to learn how to get there. Standing engine room and fire room watches in the warm tropical climate was a new experience. The temperatures in the engine and fire rooms could reach at least 105 to 110 degrees Fahrenheit, and while we were there we did various duties. I can recall painting the bilge and a boiler from midnight to four in the morning. I consoled myself by trying to believe it was important to be on the receiving end of orders if you were to learn how to give them. At times that thought was a small consolation!

The most monotonous watch I can recall was in shaft alley. Each huge shaft that turned one of the four giant propellers went through special compartments. It was necessary to have a man on watch in these areas to check the bearings, but it did get tiresome. My favorite watch was on the bridge, where the real decisions were made. We rotated stations frequently, both during watch and also during general quarters or battle stations. My first station during general quarters was in a five-inch gun mount. Later I was in a sixteen-inch gun turret and I was awed by the size of everything. A sixteen-inch armor piercing shell weighs about one ton and stands about six-feet tall. Depending on how far you are going to fire it, it takes many bags of gunpowder behind each projectile. When all three guns in a turret were fired simultaneously, or sometimes all nine guns in a salvo, you could actually see the projectiles going through the air, provided you had a proper vantage point. We could fire those projectiles for about twenty miles, as I recall.

Both the *Washington* and the *North Carolina* had teak decks. To keep these decks clean and spotless was the job of the deck division. Like most youngsters, I was a member of the deck division. Traditionally, the teak decks were scrubbed with a stone which had a hole partway through the middle similar to pumice . The hole served to enable a deckhand to place a round stick, similar to a broomstick, into this hole. The proper cleaning of the decks was called, in Navy terms, "holy stoning." Of course the proper dress for this occasion was barefooted with pants rolled up to the knees. On this wet deck we all moved with practiced precision, a method probably in use since the days of sailing ships.

Destroyers were required to fuel by pulling alongside one of the battleships. These were great performances to watch. We all admired the excellent ship-handling techniques required to do these maneuvers without coming to a stop. The sea is too rough to perform this refueling operation slowly and it must be done while traveling at good speed. This became a fairly routine matter until one day we witnessed an accident.

It was necessary to keep both ships traveling on a straight course so that the destroyer would gradually come into proper position alongside the battleship. Then a line was shot across from our ship to the destroyer. Finally, lines would be properly rigged, hoses attached, and pumping would commence. However, this time a fuel line was parted while pumping was ongoing and the heavy black oil began pumping all over our clean and beautiful teak deck. Can you imagine the extra work the deck division was required to perform for the next week to clean that mess?

At night the portion of the crew who did not have watch duty would assemble on the fantail for boxing and, later, after dusk, for movies. This is how I earned another nickname that was to stay with me during the rest of my Academy career. Usually they pitted one of the midshipmen against one of the crew and this was done by weight. Frank "Zeke" Roland, a classmate of mine, signed me up for a bout without telling me! He had been saying that he was going to do this, but I did not take him seriously. According to Frank, we needed a good ring name for me, so he put up a notice that Gunboat Ostlund, better known as "Guns", was boxing on Thursday. Those three round matches did not amount to much, but I was also known as Guns or "The Gunner" until after I graduated.

In those days, each battleship carried two observation planes, which were floatplanes that were launched from their own catapults carried at the stern of the ship. Their purpose was to observe our sixteen-inch gunfire and radio corrections back to the Combat Information Center. When these planes returned to the ship, our ship would make a gradual continuous turn to provide smooth water for landing the plane. Then the plane would power its way close to the stern of the ship to be recovered by a crane. Most all of these practices were soon to become obsolete with the introduction of jet aircraft and better radar.

During the cruise, I picked up small gifts for my family and friends. At Guantanamo Bay, I discovered I could buy Chanel No. 5 perfume without duty, so I bought small bottles for my mother and my aunts, Lucille and Frances. I remember buying carved wooden horse heads from Haiti for my friend, Burt Reno, and my mother. It was indeed fun to visit and see the various island places that summer.

Before the cruise ended we went to New York City. Our battleship anchored at Sheepshead Bay. In those days the raw sewage was piped from the city directly into the bay. I was flabbergasted at the sight of all the things, especially hundreds of condoms, floating by the ship as the current carried all of it out into the ocean. I always hoped we were not taking in seawater for our evaporators while in harbor.

Since Dick Mergl came from Flushing, New York, we three roommates arranged to stay overnight at his home. Dick Mergl's father, Anton, had been a New York cop until he was badly injured in a motorcycle accident and was forced to retire. We enjoyed the visit and we had a night out on the town. Dick arranged dates for all of us and the six of us took the subway to Manhattan. I recall going to a dinner and show at a nightclub called the Carnival. The master of ceremonies was unknown to me; a comedian named Milton Berle. He also introduced a celebrity in the audience named Lucille Ball. Both of these people became very famous in the years to follow.

How amazed I was to see New York. The liberty boats would take us to the Battery Park area. I remember well how one of our first stops was at a Battery bar. Big glasses or mugs of beer were only a nickel. Times Square was unbelievable. What a life!

We next put in at Newport, Rhode Island, for a few days. Since that was my first visit there, I also found Newport to be interesting as well. For some reason I recall spending some time in Falls River, Massachusetts, at an amusement park. Later we went ocean swimming.

Our first cruise ended when we returned to Norfolk Naval Base. When I disembarked from the *Washington* I carried many exciting memories of the new adventures we had all experienced, but I never saw the battleship *Washington* again—it was mothballed or scrapped a few years later. I was most anxious to return to the Academy because I was now to be a third classman. With this elevated status came new privileges. We could now date girls! We could also be left alone while the upper classes had a new bunch of plebes to work over. Besides, my monthly cash allowance was raised from a meager two dollars per month to three or four dollars per month. That was indeed progress. Pay for midshipmen in those days was about seventy-eight dollars per month, however, your money was handled for you. Uniforms and supplies were purchased through the Midshipmen Store and you were never allowed to be overdrawn, other than initially. The only cash you ever saw was dispensed once each month, known as the monthly insult. We lined up in the steerage to receive our two dollars' plebe pay while the disbursing officer would peel off a two dollar bill. Your name was checked off as you were handed the cash. The Navy thought the appearance of all of these two dollar bills would show the town of Annapolis where their income was coming from. Since we seldom had an opportunity to spend money and could never have a date, it did not take much in the way of funds.

With the completion of my first year at the Academy, there was a certain feeling of relief. This was accompanied by the anticipation of new experiences to come. As third classmen our blue service uniforms now carried a single gold diagonal stripe across one forearm and our shoulder boards showed the same insignia. It was a great relief to carry this outward sign that we were no longer plebes. We felt elevated and we loved it!

Cuba, 1946.
Seated: Mills, O'Flaherty, and Roland.
Standing: Ostlund, MacMurray, Rogers, and Reiher.

Four Handsome Gentlemen. Left to Right: Rupe, Reiher, Ostlund, and Gunckel, 1946.
Photo provided by Jack Rupe

Ship's deck—"holy stoning".

Cuba 1946—much shopping and Hatui beer.
Left to right: Ostlund, Swanson, Reiher, Wilder, Kneale, McCullough, and Sprague.

8

1946–47 USNA Youngster Year

DURING MY FIRST YEAR AT THE NAVAL ACADEMY I DEVELOPED SOME GREAT friendships. While on Youngster cruise, for the first time I was with class-mates from other battalions which gave us a new opportunity to expand our acquaintances and friendships. Some of these bonds have lasted through-out my lifetime.

The two roommates whom I had for the first two years at the Academy now come to mind. I first met Dave Gunckel at Kemper Military School during the 1944–45 school year. We applied to room together during plebe summer and the request was granted. Dick Mergl also became our roommate and the three of us became very close friends. Following graduation I never saw either one of them again. Dave Gunckel died of a heart attack while stationed in Washington, D.C. Dave was a Commander when he passed away. Dick Mergl was killed while instructing students in dive-bombing tech-niques off the coast of Florida. He was a Lt. Commander when their dive-bomber went straight into the ocean. What great friends these two were!

During my final two years at the Academy, I roomed with John L. Greene of Atlanta, Georgia. We had a four-man room and Herman W. "Bill" Jones of Newcastle, Indiana, and Edgerton Ten Eycke "Tenny" Sprague of Michigan City, Indiana, were also my roommates. John Greene already had two years at Georgia Tech to his credit, while Sprague and Jones each had two years at Purdue. They had received their college work under the Navy V-12 programs. Dick Mergl came directly from high school to the Academy and he worked hard and did very well. My honest conclusion has to be that your academic success depends on your preparation and study habits.

The attrition in our class was the worst during the first year. Approximately 1,200 of us entered during the summer of 1945, but only about 770 were left at graduation. Grading on the curve caused some to fail by planned attrition, but it also caused terrific academic competition.

Other close friendships were Bill O'Flaherty of Richmond, Virginia, Chuck Swanson of Delta, Colorado, Fred Wilder from Clearwater, Florida, Bill McMurray from Evanston, Illinois, Jim Kneale of Texas, Frank "Zeke" Roland, Tom Rogers, and Clint Josey all from Texas, and many, many more who will always be remembered by me.

Returning from a leave, a few of us found it wonderfully convenient to arrive at Bill O'Flaherty's house in Richmond a day or two before we were expected at Annapolis. The O'Flaherty home at 3603 Moss Side Avenue was the essence of southern hospitality. Bill's parents were so gracious and understanding.

Since the distance between Richmond and Annapolis was not great, I began to arrange dates with Richmond girls to come to the Academy dances. These were called "hops" in the vernacular of the midshipmen. Hops were held in Dahlgren Hall, which had the official designation of the Armory. This setting was not what you might call romantic for dancing, but we had no choice in the matter. Mounted on the deck in one corner was a twin mount of five-inch guns. In another corner were a cluster of five torpedo tubes. Perhaps four thousand rifles, carried by midshipmen at parades, were racked on the walls around the room.

My first hop was another experience which I now look back upon with fondness. At the time I was worried. I don't even remember the name of the girl whom I invited. The preparations were enormous. After having a girl accept a weekend invitation, you had to arrange a place for her to stay. There were countless private homes in Annapolis which rented spare bedrooms for that purpose. The girls would arrive on Saturday afternoon by bus, or perhaps by train from Baltimore. You tried to meet them on arrival, if possible. At that time midshipmen were not allowed to ride in autos, therefore it was necessary for you to carry her baggage and walk her to the accommodations you had previously reserved. Annapolis streets and sidewalks were invariably cobblestone as well as quite narrow. You quickly learned the tremendous advantage of finding a home which was close to the Academy Yard. If you had not learned this in advance, you certainly learned it after your first dating weekend.

The hops were officially over at midnight and at that time they played "Sleepy Time Gal," the final dance tune. No midshipman with a date could leave a hop early and not before the last dance tune was just a memory. At the stroke of midnight the rush began! Probably many young ladies, at the Academy for the first time, sustained mild shock. As youngsters we had exactly thirty minutes to escort our lady to her home and return. Youngsters were required to sign in at Bancroft Hall within thirty minutes following the end of the dance. This meant that any Youngster who arrived past twelve-thirty was automatically placed on report. Second Classmen had forty-five minutes and the privileged First Classmen were allowed a generous hour for check-in. It was indeed a thundering herd who poured through the main gate every fifteen minutes. I remember running all the way from the house where my date was residing to Bancroft Hall. I used to think that my cross-country experience was finally being put to good use. In later years it seems incredible that young men and women could be put in such extreme situations, but at the time, you accepted it as something completely normal. Such limitations on your time certainly insured that no couples got into trouble—it was nearly impossible.

Many a young lady must have collapsed on the bed when she finally reached her temporary quarters. She had been dancing for the past several hours and probably enjoying the activity, but then to race homeward over the cobblestone streets in her dancing slippers must have been a trying experience. Perhaps a quick smooch at the door was followed by watching her dancing partner transform into a long-distance runner as he headed toward Bancroft Hall. Unfortunately, some young ladies might be staying a mile from the Academy.

Alcoholic beverages were absolutely prohibited. At the hops fruit punch was served. We were required to wear both black bow ties as well as white gloves and it was awkward to learn to handle your punch cup and your dance card while wearing gloves. The formality of the occasion required you to fill out your dance card by trading dances with your friends. Of course, you always danced with the girl you brought for the first and last dance numbers—additional dances you reserved for yourself sometimes depended on how much you cared for the girl.

Blind dates were most often the way midshipmen met girls. Sometimes, if a blind date turned out to be a real turkey, you were treated to a "bricking" party by your classmates. It was a good-natured way to roast a guy and after much speech-making he was usually formally presented with a brick. One of my roommates and I were the recipients of a bricking party one Sunday night. John Greene had arranged for a couple of blind dates. We met the bus and when there were only two girls left unclaimed, we correctly figured they were our dates. They were wearing the largest hats I had ever seen, except for someone on stage in a comedy play. Without the hats they had no claim to fame, but with the hats I could hardly believe they were not embarrassed to appear in public. Acting like the gentlemen we tried to be, we escorted them to a rooming house. I will state that midshipmen were only allowed to be in the parlor at the rooming house, but if this rule had not been in force, I absolutely had no inclination to do otherwise with either of these two.

It was a rough weekend. When we marched to chapel on Sunday, people lined the sidewalk to watch us march by. There was a second shock. Each of our dates had a second large and colorful hat which was at least as prominent as the hats they wore the previous day. It took a lot of courage to claim them after chapel service and I was so relieved when they finally took the bus on Sunday afternoon. We certainly deserved the bricking party which we received!

As I previously stated in another chapter, many of the naval officer instructors and Executive Department officers were indeed naval heroes. Two of them especially remain in my memory. Both fellows were Motor Torpedo Boat skippers and had served together in the same PT boat squadron. One was Commander John D. Bulkeley, who had won the Medal of Honor while he was squadron commander during the early stages of World War II. The other was Commander Robert S. Kelly. This squadron also evacuated General Douglas McArthur and his staff off the Bataan Peninsula and the Corregidor area. They successfully evaded the Japanese naval forces trying to trap MacArthur during the spring of 1942. Bulkeley took the General to the southern Philippines where he then flew out to Australia. Kelly received the Navy Cross for attacking and sinking a Japanese cruiser with his motor torpedo boat. However, Bulkely was the most highly decorated Navy person during the whole of World War II.

Returning from cruise, I was surprised to learn that Commander Bulkeley was now in the Executive Department. My surprise occurred when a watch messenger gave me a notice to report to his office. I had no idea why. Bulkeley left me standing at attention in front of his desk while he chewed me up and spit me out! I had committed some infraction of Navy protocol and when he finished with me I felt I was about to be drummed out of the Brigade. I really believe he enjoyed putting the terror into midshipmen.

In a Hollywood movie released at the end of 1945 entitled *They Were Expendable*, the part of Bulkeley was played by Robert Montgomery, while John Wayne played the part of Kelly.

Commander Kelly was in the Marine Engineering Department. He could bring trauma to his classes with his teaching methods. Both he and Bulkeley were reputed to have shortwave radios in their automobiles so they could communicate as they did on the PT boats. I never knew whether or not this was fact, but it sounded logical to me at the time.

I enjoyed both the Marine Engineering and Electrical Engineering Departments in particular. I do recall trying to innovate my way out of a problem in an electrical engineering laboratory one day. We each worked at our own test benches and when we wired up our lab problem for the day we had to request power from the professor. If all was okay, he would authorize a power slip that had to be presented to the power board before they would put power to your worktable. I was having difficulty wiring correctly. Finally I thought I saw a way to circumvent my problem. If I could just bypass one of the safety breakers on my board, I could make it all work. I must have caught the professor at a busy time or else he figured that no one would dream of bypassing one of the two safety breakers. Anyway, he gave me a power slip and I took it to the power board. When they put power to my test panel, it blew one of the main breakers in the Academy electrical power plant. Much of the electric power to the whole Academy was temporarily out. There was a full inquiry as to what happened and I believe my professor had to bear the brunt of the inquiry. Of course it all filtered down to me and the embarrassment seemed like punishment enough. I had also smoked up my test board and other equipment as well. Rather than attempt excuses, I felt I could be best defended by my golden silence.

During Youngster year I was taking a special interest in the Department of Aviation. Our upcoming summer cruise would be a carrier cruise and word was already coming down that it would be a Scandinavian cruise. Since we would be flying off the carriers in dive-bombers and torpedo bombers, it was necessary that we learned how to escape from an aircraft which might be forced down in the water. To demonstrate correct procedure, the Aviation Department rigged a Navy aircraft fuselage on a high track which led to the water at a very steep angle. We would be wearing our flight gear, including parachutes and life jackets, and be strapped into a seat just as though we were flying. Suddenly the fuselage would be released and you would crash into the water. The fuselage would overturn and, because of being submerged, you only had the briefest of time to extricate yourself and get safely away. We thought it was a lot of fun, but when we actually went to sea on the carriers the training became invaluable. There were several crashes that summer, but the only fatality was one pilot flying a fighter plane.

By the time Christmas leave came in 1946, there was some relief in the movement of military personnel. Consequently, I was able to get reservations from Union Station in Washington all the way to Gillette. No hitchhiking was necessary this time and I was thankful for that.

On the return trip following Christmas, I phoned my uncle in Chicago. Since I had a train change and also a station change, my uncle, John Albert Ostlund, arranged to meet me. My father's younger brother, Albert, was a bachelor and I was fond of him. He had red hair and always managed to stay in trim condition. He also enjoyed drinking whiskey. I had a few hours layover before catching a train to Washington and Albert and one of his pals would meet my train and we would go nightclubbing. I can still remember sitting in those crowded, smoky clubs on South Clark Street watching strippers do their dances. I would drink gin and tonic and felt I was really quite big-time. At midnight my train would depart for Washington. During the ensuing years my Uncle Albert began bringing his girlfriend with him. Her name was Edna and I was pleased for them when they finally decided to get married. Even at that relatively late stage in life they set up housekeeping in Des Plains, Illinois, and lived happily for many years.

Since the rifle team was my best athletic endeavor, it was quite a struggle for me to decide not to go out for the varsity team as a Youngster. I was so dedicated to getting good academic reports I did not want to lose the time required for me to participate in varsity rifle. Instead I used my required athletic time in company sports and participated in soccer, lacrosse, softball, and similar events. It was better for me and I had a lot of fun. Handball was a great new sport for me and I appreciated the many courts the Academy had available.

During my plebe year, one weekend I explored Bancroft Hall and discovered an attic in the Rotunda area and a small room with an old upright piano. I had not taken a lesson since I was twelve years old, but I remember being taught by my mother. I began to slip into that little room on Sundays when I was not sailing or busy and began to teach myself to play the piano by ear. For four years I used to do that from time to time and for the rest of my life I have been trying to improve my piano playing.

During the 1946 football season, we went to Baltimore and Philadelphia for football games. This time we took buses. With the end of fuel rationing there was no more need for us to use ferryboats. I always enjoyed the march-ons and regardless of the score the Brigade would sing "Navy Blue and Gold" at the end of the game. I usually went out with friends following the game. Time was such a limiting factor that nothing very memorable ever occurred. At least nothing worth writing about.

When June Week of 1947 came around, we went directly to Norfolk to commence our cruise. Possibly the ships came to us at Annapolis, but I really don't remember. This time I was assigned to the carrier *Kearsarge*. Her sister ship, the *Randolph*, was also in our task force. What a difference a year makes. We were beginning to be treated as future officers and we were the only class on the carriers. It was exciting to think of being launched off that huge flight deck either by catapult or by normal take-off procedures. We were also thrilled about the excellent quality of the food which was served on the *Kearsarge*. Our crew quarters were much nicer than the battleship and we were heading for Europe. How wonderful life could be!

We were advised long before the cruise commenced that if we could identify bona fide relatives in any of the countries we were to visit, we could request leave at that port. I put in for leave when our ship was in Edinburgh and also when our ship reached Goteburg, Sweden. Our first port of call after leaving Norfolk was Edinburgh, Scotland.

Our huge aircraft carrier steamed under the magnificent bridge over the Firth of Fourth, where we anchored. I carried my camera and remember the first picture I snapped ashore. We had disembarked from the launches and began walking toward the city. Two young Scotch lassies wearing kilts were walking toward me and I asked if I could take their picture. They were grinning as they posed for the photograph, which I believe is still in one of my picture albums. Young Scotch boys would walk by us and ask, "Gum, Chum?" This is something they picked up during the war years. World War II only ended two years before our visit to Scotland. In retrospect there were no tourists as we visited Europe over the next couple of years. This never occurred to me until years later when the tourists were everywhere.

My three-day pass to visit my Great Aunt Polly and Great-Great Aunt Jane Steel began the following day. I carried a small bag which contained mostly underwear and socks plus one change of uniform. I went to the train station in Edinburgh and booked passage to Glasgow. I loved the British trains and thoroughly enjoyed the ride from eastern to western Scotland. As I recall, I then booked a bus from Glasgow to Ardrossan where my aunties lived. Recalling the photographs taken earlier by my mother, Ardrossan turned out to be the same lovely Scotch town which my mother had described to me. It was right on the ocean. I was so thrilled as I walked to my Aunt Polly Orr's house. I had seen a picture of it which was taken years ago and nothing had changed. When I knocked on the door this grand rosy-cheeked lady opened it and gave me such a warm welcome. This was the only sister of my deceased grandmother who lived with her own Aunt Jane. Aunt Jane must have been close to a hundred, but her mind was sharp. Of course, first we had to have tea. The teakettle was swung over the coals in the fireplace and soon began boiling. The tea was a traditional ceremony and this lovely tea was served with scones and biscuits. As I recall what they called biscuits, we called cookies in the United States.

The next day Aunt Polly took me to the market with her. She carried her basket and no sacks were used as we do in our present-day supermarkets. We bought our breads from the bakery and our meats from the butcher. Every little store had its own specialty. Best of all was the congeniality of everyone.

Aunt Polly invited her preacher to the house to meet me. She wanted him to take me walking around the area, which he did. There was no rail service in Ardrossan; there were few automobiles and a lot of bicycles, but mostly people just walked. And walk we did. I recall walking all the way to Saltcoats, which must have been about five miles. The views were beautiful. I recall my grandmother had once lived in Saltcoats.

The ruins of an ancient castle were on a hill behind Aunt Polly's house. I enjoyed thinking about all the activities which might have taken place there centuries before. Aunt Polly's husband was a sea captain and Captain Orr is all I can recall now. In later years he was one of the principals at the Ardrossan Ship Works, but those days of ship fitting were long past. That was my only visit to this lovely town and I was never to see my aunties again. How my own mother loved for me to tell her about my visit and, of course, I had many pictures and movies to share with her.

I left Ardrossan early to spend my final night in Edinburgh. I remember checking into a hotel and going to the pub for a beverage. I happened to meet a young lady and her mother and we enjoyed talking with one another. The next day the girl, Sheila, guided me around Edinburgh. The Edinburgh Castle was a magnificent structure high on the hill. We entered the castle and saw many other beautiful sights. I have recollections of sitting on a grassy hillside known as Arthur's Seat, overlooking a residence used by the royal family called Balmoral Castle. My only regret is that Mary and I never traveled there together to experience that unique beauty.

When I returned to the ship, it was only because my leave was over. I was not ready to leave Scotland and would have enjoyed staying another week. I had certainly fallen in love with the country and the people. Although I have been to England several times, I never did get to return to that lovely land called Scotland.

Shipboard life on the carrier was glorious. Perhaps this was because we were no longer doing the grunt work. There was a certain glamour attached to flying off the carrier. We carried four different aircraft. The torpedo bombers had a pilot, a radio gunner, and a torpedo man. The SB2C dive-bombers had a pilot and a radio gunner. Also we had the new Grumman Bearcat fighters as well as the older gull-winged Vought Corsairs. Of course they were strictly single-seaters. All were gasoline-burning, piston driven engines. Jet engines had not yet come into service. Prior to flights, we would take seats in the Pilot Ready Rooms. This was an unusual luxury for us. At these sessions we would be told our mission and exactly what we were to accomplish. After these briefings, we would go directly to the flight lines on deck.

The dive-bombers were my favorite. What a thrill it was to be at altitude in formation and then get the attack order. We would roll back our hatch covers and then peel off. Usually we would be attacking a towed sled, but it would seem as though we were traveling straight down. As we released our bombs and pulled out of the dive, it felt like your body must have weighed a ton as you were pressed into the seat beneath you. One day I decided to take my movie camera with me. In those days the cameras were not battery-powered, you wound them up. As we went into our dive I carefully tried to lean my head out to point the camera and begin filming and I thought the wind was going to tear the camera out of my hands. I believe the G forces actually stopped the camera from rolling and I hardly got any pictures. I did feel lucky that my camera was not torn out of my hands by the force of the wind.

During the summer cruise we lost several planes off both carriers. As we cruised from Scotland to Sweden we lost a Bearcat fighter and the pilot. As I was observing, he came in for a landing and got a wave off from the landing signal officer. When he poured the power to that big gasoline-driven piston engine, the torque seemed to flip him right over and into the sea. It sank within seconds and, unfortunately, the pilot never got out.

The first crash, which occurred with midshipmen aboard, was a TBM torpedo bomber. It was set to be launched from the catapult at the forward end of the ship. The plane was set with full power on the engine and was attached to the catapult by a locking-ring device. In this instance, the locking ring fractured before the catapult fired, so the TBM taxied off the forward end of the flight deck and crashed into the sea just ahead of the carrier. The ship was traveling at about thirty knots, which was necessary in launching planes. Fortunately, the pilot and both midshipmen were recovered safely. We were thankful for our escape training at the Academy.

Of all the general quarters stations I had on the carrier, I liked the twin 20-millimeter machine guns the best. Robot-controlled planes with a wing span of about five feet would sometimes be launched. They were painted bright red and as they flew in to "attack" the carrier, we would open up with our machine guns. Every fifth bullet would be a tracer that would assist with our aim. Our guns were mounted about five feet below the flight deck. Instead of being a part of a team, like the larger gun stations, these 20-millimeter batteries were each a one-man operation. Some fun!

The ship itself was enormous. I don't recall the dimensions, but it seemed awesome. We had two or three huge flight elevators that took the landed aircraft to the hangar deck below, which kept the flight deck clear for landing other aircraft.

When our ship arrived at Goteburg, Sweden, I was prepared for another three-day pass. However, this time both Dick Mergl and Bill Jones put in for passes to accompany me to visit my relatives. No one in my father's family had kept good track of these relatives, but they were sure that the address they gave me was in order. Our bags were packed and we stood in line at the gangway off the hangar deck to disembark. It was then we noticed we had a double gangway. The one going off to the right led to a destroyer and the gangway to the left led to the launches which would take us to the Goteburg docks. As we neared the head of the line, I asked someone where the destroyer was going.

"Copenhagen," I was told. "Some of the ship's company are taking a few days leave there." I turned to Dick and Bill and on impulse said to them, "Let's go to Copenhagen. We can come back to the southern end of Sweden and take the train to visit my relatives just as well as we can from Goteburg."

There was no time to discuss it, so we all turned right and boarded the destroyer.

It was a beautiful morning to cruise to Denmark. The swift destroyer did not take long to make the trip. Steaming into Copenhagen harbor, I will always remember the sculpture of the Mermaid on a Rock in the harbor—we had found heaven on earth in Copenhagen. Cigarettes were like gold and right after the war the black markets did a great business with American cigarettes and you could take a taxi most anywhere in Copenhagen for two cigarettes. We checked into a nice small hotel and went out on the town.

Tivoli Gardens was the drawing nightlife attraction and that is where we spent a lot of our nights. We almost forgot about visiting my relatives in Sweden. However, good sense finally prevailed and we checked out of the hotel by bartering with the hotel owner with some silver dollars I had taken with me. In our low order of finances, we were always looking for the best bargain. We caught a train to the point on the coast that supplied ferry crossings from Denmark to Sweden. That is where we ran into our first major problem. We came into Denmark on a Navy ship and there was no need for passports or other identification. The same or similar Navy destroyer was planning to return the same group to Goteburg they had taken to Copenhagen. Those people only needed to show their leave papers to board the ship. Here we were, running off like tourists without any identification other than a Navy leave paper. It never occurred to us, but trying to leave Denmark and gain admittance to Sweden was another matter. I suppose the look of innocence coupled with a lot of glib talking finally got us through. All the papers we had to go on were the official stamps on our three-day leave papers and that did not include a visit to Denmark. For a little while I began to worry that someone was going to call the Navy or an Ambassador or perhaps put us in jail, but I have a tendency to worry too much.

When we reached Sweden again, we discovered we only had time to get to Goteburg before our passes expired. Immediately we bought train tickets to Goteburg and enjoyed the beautiful countryside scenes. We had three days of wonderful adventures, but I never did get to see my relatives in Sweden. However, there is some limit to what you can accomplish in three days!

Some of our task force ships visited Norway while we were in Sweden. But after departing the Scandinavian countries, we formed up again for sea exercises. The next port of call was on the southern coast of England. My ship was in the group that went to Weymouth while some of the others went to Portsmouth. The City of Weymouth put on a nice reception for us midshipmen. The mayor of the city was the official host and I was impressed by his wearing of the badge of office, a heavy gold-link chain around his neck with a symbol of office on it. Chaperons were out in force and all of the young ladies in Weymouth seemed to have an invitation to the party.

It was a nice affair and so very, very proper. That was the first time I ever danced the hokey-pokey. The band played the tune, "You put your right foot in, you put your right foot out," and so on.

The next day some of us left for London in buses. We spent several days touring the areas surrounding London. I recall being at Stonehenge and many other historic sites. Anxious to get to London, imagine my surprise when I did arrive and accidentally ran into an old pal of mine from Gillette named Warren Taft. Warren had played trumpet in our high school dance band. He was a commissioned naval officer and assigned to duty in London. He took me around a couple of nights and we had a great time. Although the country was under severe rationing and suffering from many shortages, you could still buy anything you really wanted in 1947 London. Warren took me to black market restaurants where the offerings were exquisite, but costly. Fortunately, I was Warren's guest.

At that time London was still busy trying to recover from so much of the damage inflicted by the German Air Force plus the German rockets. There seemed to be no end to the cleanup and rebuilding.

It was a requirement for midshipmen to check the bulletin board in the hotel every morning. Sometimes official duties were called for and listed midshipmen had to be in a certain place at a certain time. My name was on the list one morning and I sighed in dismay. As it turned out, we were part of the official Naval Academy group which was invited to a garden reception honoring the engagement of Princess Elizabeth to Prince Phillip Mountbatten. At the time I was not too impressed, but as time marches on, we take on a different perspective. Princess Elizabeth has now served as Queen of England for many years. The party was tediously formal and, at the time, I was definitely anxious to put this party behind me so I might return to the excitement of Piccadilly Circus.

At the Tower of London, as well as the other usual places, I took many pictures. This past year of 1998, many of our family members gathered to view old movie films which I had taken during my years at the Naval Academy. Imagine my surprise, as well as theirs, when movies of this carrier voyage were shown, as well as pictures of Scotland and England. Hopefully, we will get those old films placed on videotape for all my family members.

I was especially impressed with Windsor Castle. It was about thirty-three years later before I returned there with Mary. We surely enjoyed that opportunity to reminisce!

We never made a summer cruise without putting into the naval base at Guantanamo Bay in Cuba. From there we were back to Norfolk for a different kind of training. This was called Operation Camid II and only the second year in which the Naval Academy did a joint operation with the Military Academy. We did an amphibious assault on some island off the coast of Virginia. Of course with all the amphibious assault vessels we had in those days, it was no problem to find equipment. There could well have been literally hundreds of vessels in the operation, both large and small. We midshipmen even had army combat helmets and uniforms. As I recall, the cadets did more of the duties normally assigned to navy people.

Somewhere, we midshipmen were picked up by the troop ship-type vessels. I only remember one of them was the USS *Noble*. We had been training to go over the side by using what I might call a webbed-rope device so that we could climb down to the waiting landing craft. We proceeded ashore in full-scale attack. From the first wave of landing craft, the attack was followed with tanks, more troops, and flame-throwers. Navy fighter planes strafed the emplacements and underwater demolition teams blew up tank traps. It was full-scale amphibious war going on that day.

Returning to the Naval Academy, we were immediately turned loose for our late summer leave. I was ready and anxious to begin. While I was home in September, my Academy pal, Bill O'Flaherty from Richmond, paid me a visit. His mother and sister, Mayme Frayser, drove with him to visit Yellowstone Park. As strange as it seems, I had never been to Yellowstone Park. They invited me to go along. After visiting the park they headed south and I volunteered to get off at a place named on the Wyoming map as Muddy Gap. I had never been there before, but no stranger to hitchhiking, I knew I could get back to Gillette without any difficulty. I guess I had failed to mention to my friends that Muddy Gap had zero population.

We were driving down the highway in the O'Flaherty Packard when I cautioned Mayme Frayser that we were approaching Muddy Gap, a junction where two highways met. There were no buildings and, at that time, definitely no people lived there. The O'Flahertys were shocked and would not consider leaving me on a bare stretch of highway. While we talked, a car approached. Mayme Frayser got out of her car and actually caused the oncoming car to stop. I still believe the driver thought there was serious distress. Never one to ask questions, I grabbed my bag, waved good-bye to the O'Flahertys, and jumped in the front seat of the car. Imagine my surprise when the driver told me he was not supposed to pick up hitchhikers. As I watched my friend's car drive away, I was afraid he was going to ask me to get out, but he didn't.

We headed for Casper when suddenly his fan belt broke. While examining the broken belt he said, "You see, I knew I should not have picked you up."

I tried to be comforting when I told him that I had heard that if you drive about sixty miles an hour you get enough air through the radiator to keep it from boiling. He allowed that he might as well try it because we really had no choice. We did reach Casper without further incident and I felt he was probably glad to finally be rid of me!

Next I caught a ride from Casper to Midwest, but hanging around a filling station in Midwest was not very promising. There was not much traffic going to Gillette. Finally, an empty cattle truck drove in for fuel and the driver told me he was heading for Gillette. "Got no room in front, but if you want to ride in the stock trailer, you can." I said that I was happy to get the ride and jumped aboard. He had just unloaded a bunch of cattle and the crap and the smell in that trailer was really powerful. I had to stand up all the way to Gillette because you didn't dare sit down. We find the life of the wanderer can be varied and colorful!

Leaving home in late September, I felt returning to the Academy with the privileges of being a second classman were benefits of monumental importance. As a second classman I could now use Gate #2, better known as "second class gate." Wow!

John visited his mother's relatives, Jane Steel and Polly Orr, in Ardrossan, Scotland, 1947.

Aboard the aircraft carrier, USS Kearsarge.
John with the pilot and a SB2C dive bomber, 1947.

9

1947–48
USNA Second Class Year

THE ADVENT OF TWO GOLD DIAGONAL STRIPES ON ONE FOREARM OF MY BLUE service uniforms made me pretty proud. As a second classman, we could now use Second Class Gate. I had been planning for that event for over a year. Through my first classman, C. G. Batt, I had been introduced to a nice lady by the name of Fannie Bright. Mrs. Bright had weekend rooms for girls and she only lived about six doors up the street from Second Class Gate. I had the world by the tail; instead of running back to Bancroft Hall through the Main Gate, I now had a terrific shortcut both ways. After taking my girl to her residence, I now had fifteen minutes more than I did as a Youngster—the distance from Mrs. Bright's house, through Gate #2 to Bancroft Hall had to be the best deal in Annapolis. I could hardly wait to try it out.

Second Class Year also meant getting our class rings. Our class, the Class of '49, had been quite daring in the design of their class crest; daring for the forties, our class crest had two bare-chested mermaids. No other class had ever been so forward or so willing to face the bare facts.

Now was the time for actually selecting our personal class rings. One side of the ring has the class crest, and the other side carries the Naval Academy seal. I had examined the various gold colors and stones which were available and finally chose a blue spinel stone with an old English *O* on the stone. Medium Burmese gold in a size nine and one half was the order. The inside was inscribed with my full name. The jewelers were Bailey, Banks, and Biddle of Philadelphia. It is difficult to express how important that ring became to me because it represented the fulfillment of one of my most important goals.

The Ring Dance was the first occasion you were formally presented with your ring. The tradition was probably as old as the Academy and the ritual might still be the same today. You invited a girl for the weekend and if you had a really special girl then, of course, she would definitely be the one to invite. After all, this occasion was the most important social event of our Naval Academy lives! The night of the Ring Dance, decked out in your formal midshipman attire, your girl wore your ring on a ribbon around her neck. On this important evening we took our ladies to an exclusive dinner at the midshipmen dining room. Tradition required that during the Ring Dance the couple walked through a huge replica of a class ring, paused when they were in the ring, and then the girl removed the ring from her neck. She dipped the ring in a binnacle that supposedly contained water from all of the seven seas, then placed the ring on your finger and the photographer snapped our picture and we continued to dance. For this occasion I invited Ann Worsham, from Richmond, Virginia. I still have our picture in one of my old scrapbooks, and it was a beautiful ceremony—to have that ring on my finger was a very memorable moment in my life.

One of the academic highlights of second class year was in the Aviation Department. We were to receive eight hours of actual flying instruction. The Naval Academy had no runways, but in lieu of that seaplanes were used. We received our instruction in N3N single-engine floatplanes. What a thrill! These were two-wing, fabric-covered, open cockpit planes. They did not have electric starting, but instead, a crewman would crank up the flywheel with increasing speed before engaging the inertia starting, and the pilot would holler "contact" when engaging the engine. If the engine started, then we could proceed. If the engine failed to start, then the hand cranking had to begin again. The plane sat on a sled which had wheels and when the towing tractor pushed the plane down the ramp into the Bay, suddenly we would be riding the waves.

I felt the thrill of a lifetime. I was wearing a helmet with goggles and a flight jacket and was assigned to the front cockpit. I could not communicate with the instructor in the rear cockpit except for nodding my head in a 'yes' or 'no' convention. Communication took place through the tubes that were fastened to my soft leather helmet by my ears. The instructor gave me orders, but I could not ask questions.

The instrumentation was about as basic as could be achieved. As I recall, we had a magnetic compass, a ball to show if we were in level flight, a throttle, a stick, and two rudder pedals. There may have been another instrument or two in the rear cockpit, but I was never in that position. Of course there were no radios or sophisticated devices. The thrill of flying was there and it was joyous!

During these eight hours of flight instruction, I discovered I did not have good depth perception. This happened one day when my instructor told me to make landing approaches over the water. I had no buildings or other objects to relate to. I was leveling off for a landing when my instructor said, "Ostlund, are you about to land?"

When I nodded in the affirmative, he came back with, "You are about one hundred feet off the water!" A further test on some devices, which demonstrated your depth perception ability, bore out the fact that mine was not up to flying standards. This caused me some consternation because I had already decided that naval aviation was to be my career path. Having just spent the previous summer flying off carriers, I could think of no more glorious way to live than being a carrier pilot.

Our flight instructors were all Navy pilots who had just come from carrier assignments. All had previous combat flying. Instructing biplanes had to be quite dull for them. So many times before returning to base, they would take the controls and do a bit of simulated combat flying. These were very heady days for a young midshipman.

For me, my academic subjects were far more interesting than they were the first two years. I especially liked celestial navigation. Foreign language seemed easier and this was probably because I was much more conversant in Spanish. Also we were utilizing our Spanish during the summer cruises.

We were required to learn the amenities associated with formal dinner meetings, including after-dinner speaking. Marine engineering dealt with equipment and theory that I was now familiar with through shipboard life. The pressures of being an underclassman were gone and I knew within a few months I would be one of the privileged first classmen. Life was good!

I was now living in a four-man room. The main room was where John Greene and I resided. We slept in a double-decker bunk bed and we each had a desk and locker. The four-feet wide steel lockers were standard equipment for every midshipman and every bit of clothing you owned was stored neatly inside. Your hanging garments were on the left along with your various shoes on the bottom shelf; the right-hand side of the locker was separated into shelves. The procedure for folding and storing your laundry properly was learned as a plebe. During the years I was a midshipman, we were not allowed to have any civilian clothing at the Academy.

On either side of the main room were smaller identical rooms. Herman W. "Bill" Jones lived in one of these side rooms and Edgerton Ten Eycke "Tenny" Sprague lived in the other. We had a large shower stall, plus a lavatory, and that comprised our quarters as I recall them. Bancroft Hall had five stories, or aboveground decks, as they were known, plus a full basement. Although we changed rooms every year, it seems I rotated from the first deck to the fifth deck with regularity. However, I liked the fifth deck because it was such good exercise to run up and down all those steps so many times each day.

Periodically, each of us would be assigned watch duty, a job which excused you from attending classes that day. Each year the responsibility of your watch duty increased. As a plebe you were more or less a messenger. By the time you were a first classman, you were probably wearing a sword and responsible for the watch staff.

With the war over for two years, transportation was no longer difficult. When the Brigade went to football games, we now took buses. When we went to Philadelphia for the Army-Navy game, we took the train from Baltimore. I spent less time sailing and more time dating than during the first two years. I also spent more time thinking about my naval career—what I would now choose after learning that naval aviation was no longer possible. I was looking forward to first-class cruise. We were going to the Mediterranean for our final cruise as midshipmen and I wanted destroyers. As it turned out, I was assigned to a destroyer and during that summer I was on two different destroyers plus one submarine.

When we shipped out of Norfolk in June of 1948, we went right into the aftermath of an Atlantic hurricane. Previously, I had been on a battleship and a carrier. Now I was on the destroyer that I thought I would love, but the rough weather was almost my undoing. I could not believe how that ship could roll and pitch. One day we were alongside the battleship *Missouri* and I could see my friends eating ice cream. At that moment I would have given most anything to have traded places, but would never admit it.

Under bad weather conditions it is impossible to cook meals on a destroyer. But who wanted to eat anyway? Most of us were sick and vomiting, but in Navy tradition the work must go on. I remember classes in torpedo launching where we hung on for dear life. I longed for the class to be over so I could just go somewhere and privately be sick.

We took turns having our meals in the officers' wardroom. Our skipper, a Navy commander named Barnes, was always jovial. A "storm top", that had insets to supposedly hold the dishes in place, was placed on the table. Commander Barnes liked to tell the story about one storm he was in where a cup of coffee left the table, splashed all over the overhead (ceiling), and never a drop touched the bulkheads (walls). Later that summer during a violent Mediterranean storm, I actually witnessed this described event.

I always remember a midshipman friend of mine, Ping Collins, who was so sick. He slept in the bottom bunk. I felt badly for him. He seemed to be moaning and hoping to die. He laid in his bunk and vomited and just lay in it and moaned. The odor was enough to make me sick. Finally, one day I began silently lecturing myself. It seemed to work and I actually got over being seasick! I believe that was the last time I was sick, although I saw a lot of very bad weather on destroyers during the balance of the time I spent in the Navy.

I liked the destroyer life; especially as a first classman. I was learning to be a destroyer officer. I stood bridge watches with the regular watch officer and practiced a lot of navigation and maneuvering board work.

While we were still traveling in very rough seas, I was on watch in the CIC (Combat Information Center). This center is manned on a twenty-four hour basis at sea. All of the radar and sonar information, plus the tracking equipment and plotting boards were located there. Communication from there extended throughout the ship and also to planes in the air. This particular day I was stationed there along with a petty officer. All movable equipment was lashed down and we were hanging on with every roll of the ship. Then it happened! A typewriter broke loose from its lashings and sailed across the table. We both made a grab for it and missed. Unfortunately, the petty officer lost footing and was carried through the air and out of the hatchway into the passageway, literally hurled, the back of his head striking a steel beam in the passageway. He was unconscious and I immediately called the bridge for medics to CIC. The sailor suffered a fractured skull, but since we did not carry a doctor on board, this was the best judgment of the medics. We had to transfer the sailor to a battleship where he could receive the proper attention in a hospital. In that terrible sea we came alongside and shot a line across to the battleship. Soon we had rigged a canvas carrier to support the unconscious sailor. As I watched the transfer taking place, I thought perhaps it was a blessing the sailor was still unconscious. The sea was so violent and the transfer seemed precarious. Somewhere in my movies I have pictures of that transfer. Safely aboard the *Missouri* and in their hospital, they discovered a fractured skull. Later I heard he survived the incident, although I never saw him again.

After sixteen straight days at sea, our first port of call was Lisbon, Portugal. The weather was perfect and we enjoyed visiting the many ports. Once a few of us pooled our money and rented a taxi for the day. We ended up in Estoril, which even then was known as a resort with much gambling. I recall some of us won a little money which could not be changed into American dollars and we had a great celebration on our last night in Portugal.

I also remember the beaches in Estoril. It was unfitting for men to be on the beach with only swimming trunks. We were required by local custom and regulations to wear our undershirts. In recent years I am told that many of the beaches don't even require a person to wear anything at all. How the times do change!

When the task force sailed through the Straits of Gibraltar, I was certainly impressed to view that prominent and historic rock. This was to be the first of many trips past the Rock of Gibraltar which I would make during my lifetime. When we arrived at Genoa, Italy, a group of us boarded a train for Rome. We had a three-day package leave to visit Rome. I remember the train stopping in Pisa where I looked at the Leaning Tower of Pisa out the train window. At the station we bought food and since we were warned about the water, I bought a bottle of Chianti wine. I thought it tasted terrible, but that was my first introduction to cheap Italian wine. I have since learned to relish the many better ones. What I would have really enjoyed would have been a cold Coca-Cola!

As I was trying, without success, to remember the hotel where we stayed in Rome, my grandson, Patrick Ostlund Jr., asked if he could look at my Naval Academy scrapbook. It had not been opened for at least twenty years. Among other memorabilia he asked about the picture of Pope Pius XII and also the book of matches naming the hotel where we resided—Hotel Quirinale Roma.

Having previously learned the world substitute for money, I had a bag full of tax-free cigarettes. We could buy them aboard ship for six cents per package, but we were only supposed to carry two packages for each day ashore. I easily found the black market and sold my cigarettes for enough Italian lira to last me for the three days.

Throughout Italy in 1948 there was much evidence of the destruction from World War II, but, fortunately, Rome was spared. How I enjoyed walking through the ancient Coliseum. I could picture the gladiators and lions facing one another across the sand. Having always enjoyed history, I loved this wonderful opportunity and as I previously mentioned, there were no crowds of tourists in those days! In fact there were no tourists at all.

We made a tour through the Vatican and I will always remember the wonderful beauty and masterful artistry of the ages. The following morning my name was on a list at the hotel to be a member of an official visiting party the next day. We were the official Navy group to visit the Pope, Pope Pius XII, as I recall. I was not Catholic at the time, but the visit was a humbling experience. I was in awe as we were taken through the private rooms at the Vatican and finally to a room where the Pope was to receive us. When he entered, I was struck by his appearance. I found him to be a handsome man and even though he was in white robes, I could tell that he kept himself in reasonably good shape. He spoke to us in English and then approached us individually. We each knelt and kissed his ring. He handed each of us a medal and blessed us. I believe that in my scrapbooks I still have a picture of us kneeling with the Pope offering a prayer. This was indeed a memorable and moving experience. I later gave my good friend, Father James Power, the medal that I had personally received from the Pope.

Our destroyer went to Casablanca, French Morocco. The task force split up and visited a number of North African ports, but I was particularly glad to go to Casablanca. I remembered the movie done by Humphrey Bogart and Ingrid Bergman that carried the name, *Casablanca*, which is now recognized as a film classic.

Viewing Casablanca for the first time from the destroyer, it appeared to be an oasis in the desert. The green palm trees were set against the white of the buildings under a hot desert sun. Visiting around Casablanca was memorable. I was impressed to see the French Foreign Legion forces for the first time. I recalled the Gary Cooper movie, *Beau Geste*. Some of us took advantage of a bus going to Rabat, the capital. In those days it was an ancient bus. At Rabat I walked up to the walled gates of the Sultan's palace and had one of my buddies take my picture standing with one of the Sultan's guards who carried a rifle with the bayonet attached. I always liked that picture.

We wanted to walk through the Old Medina area, which is the Arab marketplace. We were warned not to do so unless we were walking with several in a group, which we did. I shall never forget the scenes. The narrow crowded streets were only for walking. There was no room for vehicles and none were wanted. We were eyed suspiciously. I tried to barter a knife away from an old Arab, but he wanted no part of me. Finally, I did have an opportunity to barter for a sheathed knife that was inscribed with many Arabic markings. I believe I still have that knife with its sheath among my possessions. I was unimpressed at all the sheep and goat meat hanging for sale in the open air—whole sheep heads toasting over a charcoal fire seemed to be the delicacy of the market. I was glad we made the visit to the Medina. I suppose I could have read about it, but one look was worth a thousand words.

At one time that summer, when we were in Caribbean waters, the heat in the forward compartment where we midshipmen lived was like an oven. Our compartment was immediately under the main deck forward. There is an old Navy saying ascribed to some admiral whose name I can no longer remember. When faced with a problem requiring a solution the fellow would say, "I'll find a way or make one!" That was a motto that I took unto myself and at the time when our living compartment was so hot, I knew there must be a way to improve it. Down in one of the engine rooms, I found what I thought was an extra emergency blower. These were used to blow air in or out of a compartment under emergency conditions. It was portable, but very heavy. I talked Tex Lauderdale into helping me 'borrow' this blower. We had to first get it out of the engine room without being seen. I recall getting a long rope and we actually pulled it topside through a deck hatch. We covered it with a blanket and moved it into our compartment without being discovered. We also acquired many feet of flexible air tubing that was about a foot in diameter. Our plan was to suck air from topside and blow it throughout the sleeping compartment during the evening after the main rays of the sun were ebbing.

As it happened, we first demonstrated our great idea just as the captain and ship's officers were sitting down to their evening meal in the Officers Wardroom. One problem: we could not find a place to plug our blower into electricity. The only way to solve this, in my opinion, was to dismantle a red battle lantern and hook into that source. We did that. I remember calling to Tex, "Turn it on, Tex!" When Tex threw the switch, the blower started revving up. Gaining momentum, the resulting air began to blow all the mattresses off the bunks. About that time it began drawing too much power and a circuit blew. It was a bit reminiscent of the day I blew a breaker in the Academy Power House. Over the ship's speakers came the command, "Attention, the Chief Electrician report to the bridge on the double!"

In my mind I thought, "Here we go again." Of course we were discovered, but I actually believe maybe the captain saw enough humor in the event that we were not severely reprimanded. I might add, we continued to suffer the heat of the tropics in that compartment without benefit of our blower!

From the Mediterranean we returned to Norfolk where we changed destroyers. Later, at Guantanamo Bay in the Caribbean, we performed hunter-killer operations with submarines. My experience on destroyers that summer made me decide to apply for destroyer duty upon graduation. I liked the feeling of less formality usually observed on destroyers. As I recall, such a ship carried less than three hundred men and perhaps seven or eight officers. By that time, I was also convinced I had overcome seasickness.

A brand new experience was forthcoming when we were assigned to submarines for three days and nights. For me, the ultimate highpoint finally arrived when we were carefully depth charged while submerged. This was done so we could experience both the sound and feeling that accompanied the detonation.

We had been hunting for subs from our destroyers and now it was time for us to experience the attack from the point of view of the submerged subs. On the sub we were actually keeping track of the destroyers and it made for an exciting game of cat and mouse.

On the sub my berthing place was alongside a torpedo. Living space aboard these World War II diesel subs was cramped and precious, however the submarine service boasted of the finest food in the Navy. It was true! That is how the Navy kept the sub service so filled with good men. I remember glancing into the skipper's tiny quarters and thinking, "He certainly has little room to enjoy being a Navy skipper."

When the cruise was completed, we had our usual thirty days' leave coming. I had convinced two of my roommates to drive to Wyoming with me. Bill Jones and Tenny Sprague were both from Indiana and this was our first destination. We went to Tenny Sprague's home in Michigan City, Indiana. His father manufactured precision instruments, many of which were used on shipboard. I believe they were named Hayes

Instruments and Tenny's older brother, Phil, was beginning to take over the family business from Tenny's father. We had a wonderful time with the Sprague family. They lived over the hill from Lake Michigan and we spent some very delightful times on that beach. Their beautiful stone house was known as Castle Abri.

We also drove from Michigan City to Gillette because Tenny had become the proud owner of a black Lincoln convertible. Although he was not allowed to drive his car in Annapolis until our June Week, it was wonderful just to own one of these. This Lincoln was kept in the garage of Commander Paul Gill who was married to Tenny's older sister.

While we were in Gillette, we helped my father work cattle and we all enjoyed riding horses. I later took them to Meadowlark Lake in the Big Horn Mountains above Buffalo. We stayed in one of the rustic cabins and I did the cooking on a wood-burning stove. We trolled in the lake and had good luck catching trout. After returning to Gillette we went to the ranch of my good friend, Burt Reno. To give them the full flavor of our western life, we went antelope hunting. Tenny and Bill were impressed with both the Reno ranch and my friend, Burt.

We played a lot of bridge in those days, but when we had the opportunity, we also played a lot of golf. I had played golf at our naval base in Cuba that summer. If you knocked your ball into the rough in Cuba, you hated to explore for it. Tenny and Bill gave me a hard time over the golf course in Gillette. In those days it was only a nine-hole course with oiled sand greens which they had never seen before. There was no planted grass simply because there was no water!

Looking back to those days and those times, I think about how happy and carefree we were. We had completed three years at the Academy. Our new careers were about to begin. As second classmen we had even taken advantage of a new program at the Academy. We had been allocated two weekends. Can you imagine that?

Returning to Annapolis following our leave was a time we looked forward to with much anticipation. The Class of 1949 had less than nine months until graduation!

John with a gate guard at the Sultan's Palace.
Rabat, French Morocco, 1948.

Men aboard a destroyer.
(John in helmet, lower center)

10

1948–49 USNA First Class Year

Returning to Bancroft Hall in September of 1948, one of the urgencies for first classmen was to check the "grease sheet." For the previous three years we were never concerned with any report other than our grade standing. Beginning with first-class cruise, we were now receiving a separate report on our potential leadership qualities. These in turn were mixed with our academic standings and the whole thing was referred to as our "grease" standing. I was pleasantly surprised to note I had received quite high marks from my destroyer training that summer. Since I was never a "star" student, my overall average downplayed the summer scores. I was still made a midshipman officer for the fall term. This meant that while in formations, the midshipmen officers were duly given a position in accordance with their rank. As a "one striper" I no longer had to carry a rifle on parades. Instead, I only wore a belt with a bayonet. I assumed that not having to tote a rifle demonstrated I was really making significant progress. (I smile as I write this!)

During the previous couple of years when flying between Washington and Billings, Montana, I had flown on Northwest Airlines. I often flew with Eddie Briggs, a classmate who lived in Minneapolis. It was not until our fortieth class reunion, while talking with Eddie Briggs, did I discover he retired from the Navy as a vice admiral.

However, on more than one flight I had the same stewardess, named Mickey Corbett. In those days there was only one stewardess on an airplane and she also had to be a registered nurse. Since I had become acquainted with Mickey Corbett, I thought I would invite her to the Academy for a weekend sometime. I really had no steady girlfriend, so I invited Mickey Corbett to June Week that year. Many of my classmates were getting married following graduation, but I had absolutely no interest in marriage. My social life was purely social and I had no ties that could be considered binding.

Looking back, my first class year was probably my best because it was all about to culminate with graduation during June Week. All of the academic departments had more interesting class work because it was of a very professional nature. In seamanship and navigation we were actually commanding the YP's which were known as Yard Patrol boats. They were twin-screw vessels and the maneuvering and docking were very similar to a larger twin screwed ship.

Ordinance and gunnery, electrical engineering, and marine engineering were not at all intimidating. English, history, and government were still my favorite subjects. It seemed that almost every aspect of first class year had such practical applications.

My decision was made for my first choice of duty preference. I had decided to apply for destroyer duty in the Mediterranean. When the preference numbers were drawn, I lucked out with a preference number of ninety. That meant I could have any duty assignment I wanted. As it turned out, I was ordered to the USS *Meredith*, a fairly new destroyer numbered the DD890. She was in the Mediterranean fleet, the Sixth Fleet, and my official written orders were to report aboard whenever I found her. My explicit orders were to board the USS *Grand Canyon*, a destroyer tender bound for the Mediterranean.

As the spring of 1949 approached, I finally decided to buy an officer's cap. When I made the purchase and stored the new cap in my locker, I could not help but take a peek at it from time to time. Sometimes I thought about the fact that some college graduates became naval officers after ninety days of training and were sometimes referred to as "Ninety-Day Wonders." After four years of Naval Academy, I felt certain I had earned the right to wear an officer's cap. In fact, it felt great as I began buying other insignia which would also be needed.

We seemed to undergo a kind of transformation as we prepared for graduation. Several official trips were made to Washington in relatively small groups. These trips were for the purpose of demonstrating the better side of a life, which we were about to enter. We even visited the Army-Navy Town Club and the equally prestigious Army-Navy Country Club. We were offered memberships without the usual initiation fees. Of course, determined to join both clubs, I paid a nonresident membership for many years following my graduation.

Other trips took us to the Naval Gun Factory and the Naval Research Institute. One memorable day, a small group of us went to the Capitol where we were seated in the office of the Vice President of the United States, Albin Barkley. He was a former Senator from Kentucky who was chosen as Harry Truman's running mate. We enjoyed the intimate, casual, and humorous way that the Vice President talked with us. All in all, we were beginning to feel that it was going to be truly fine to live life as newly commissioned naval officers!

The privilege of leaving the Academy grounds on weekends had been afforded us twice during second class year. As first classmen we now had at least four weekends, or perhaps even more. I cannot recall any particular weekends I took, other than going to Richmond. Those trips were always pleasant—the fact that we were allowed to do these things was important in itself.

I recall the time Mrs. O'Flaherty drove me to Richmond for my weekend. It was indeed a pleasure for me to ride with Mrs. Oaf, as we affectionately called her. As we drove along in her beautiful Packard, she related the significant events which occurred during the War between the States. Unlike northerners, Mrs. Oaf never called it the Civil War. I was intrigued to listen as the miles slipped away. At graduation the O'Flaherty family gave me such a wonderful gift—a key to their home. The identification tag, which was chained to the key, carried my name and their address. I was moved by their expression of love. So were the few others who were given the same gift. We felt very special!

As graduation time approached, we began to make our June Week plans. My parents had never been to Annapolis and that was true for many parents. Bill Jones and I rented a house for June Week. This was a common practice. Many residents of Annapolis left town during June Week with the money they made by renting their house to parents. We found a very nice home and made all the arrangements, including a deposit. The house was large enough to provide room for our parents, our dates, and another couple from Indiana who were special friends of the Jones family.

My folks bought a new car for the big trip and my father seemed especially proud to be undertaking this trip to Annapolis. I had sent them maps of Washington, D.C. and had arranged to meet them in D.C. on a particular Saturday afternoon. I said I would be standing in front of the Statler Hotel at a certain time and sure enough, it worked out exactly that way. My father said he did not want to drive another mile, so I gladly took over—as first classmen we were allowed to drive during June Week.

Compared to present days, there were very few traffic problems in Washington, D.C. in 1949. I drove them around so they might view the famous buildings. Unlike my first trip in 1945, all the one-story temporary buildings, which had been hastily thrown together on the Mall, were now gone. During the war there had been no thought concerning looks—it was an emergency situation and a necessity to get it done!

June Week was a grand and memorable time. My parents were impressed with tea at the Superintendent's house, plus all the many parades and other activities. Even President Harry Truman was there. My parents really enjoyed a couple from Indiana, Fred and Ida Hans, who were there as friends of Bill Jones's family. One day my parents went with them to Mount Vernon and both Fred and my father smoked cigars and enjoyed telling stories to each other. I was pleased about their new friendships.

One night after one of the June Week dances, I returned my date, Mickey Corbett, to our June Week home in my father's new Cadillac. Since this house was on the outskirts of town, there was no curb and gutter. In my haste to return to Bancroft on time, I backed off the end of a culvert, and wrinkled the right rear fender of his new car. The next morning I called the Cadillac garage and talked them into repairing the fender on an emergency basis. It took all day to repair and overnight for the paint to dry. I told my mother about what had happened and what I was doing about it, but I saw no need to burden my father with this mishap for he was involved in other activities. Of course Fred Hans also had a car and by then Axel and Fred were beer-drinking buddies.

When graduation day finally arrived, we were more than ready. Our "cruise boxes" were loaded to be shipped to our home addresses. These padlocked cruise boxes were large wooden boxes in which we deposited all our belongings whenever we went on cruise. Each year, when we returned to Bancroft Hall, our cruise boxes would be sitting outside our newly assigned rooms. At graduation they were used for the last time to ship our belongings to our new homes or, in my case, my old one.

The final assembly of our class in Dahlgren Hall was the culmination of four hard years. This also was the final event for our class at the Academy. We received those precious sheepskin diplomas—mine hangs on my wall to this day. The traditional cheers for those graduating was led by the president of the Second Class. This was followed by the president of the Class of '49, Pete Williams, who led the three cheers for those we would leave behind. On the final cheer, all 770 of us threw our midshipmen caps into the air!

The crowds awaited their chances to grab souvenir caps which we had thrown into the air. Going to our rooms for the last time to return with our officers' insignia we would now put on our new commissioned officers' caps. Traditionally, one of your new shoulder boards is placed by your mother and the other shoulder board is placed by your girlfriend. This was accomplished and following proper hugs and kisses I stood ready for my new career!

June 1949 was special: John received his commission as an Ensign, USN. Polly and Axel celebrated their 25th wedding anniversary. Bob graduated from the University of Wyoming.

25th Company just before graduation from the USNA, 1949. John, front row, second from left.
Photo provided by Jack Rupe

John Chapman Ostlund, United States Naval
Academy, Class of 1949.

11

A Short Naval Career

FOLLOWING MY GRADUATION AT ANNAPOLIS, MY MOTHER FLEW TO DENVER where she was met by my brother, Bob, and driven to Laramie to attend his graduation from the University of Wyoming.

My thirty days leave began with my father and I heading west in his new car. We had a very nice trip, as it was one of the few occasions in my life when I spent time with my father without interruption. We stopped in Paxton, Illinois, my dad's hometown, to visit Aunt Rose and Uncle Walter Carlson at their farm. Axel loved telling them about Annapolis and Washington, D.C. The Carlsons sat entranced as he embellished his most recent experiences.

By the time we reached Gillette, I was glad to get off the road and relax. I was anticipating the coming events and my return to the Mediterranean. My orders were to report to the Naval Station at Norfolk and report aboard the destroyer tender *USS Grand Canyon*. The *Grand Canyon* would service fleet destroyers on duty in the Mediterranean and when we came across the destroyer *Meredith*, I was to report aboard for my duty assignment.

The *Grand Canyon* seemed both large and comfortable. There were several new ensigns aboard including my last roommate, John L. Greene, who was also assigned to the *Meredith*. It was a long shot for two roommates to receive assignments to the same destroyer and I was certainly pleased.

We had a most relaxing trip out of Norfolk. Our duties were light and we made the most of the occasion. Our time was spent working out, reading, playing bridge, and examining the ship. We were transporting a few new automobiles which were to be off-loaded in Gibraltar and an art treasure in the form of Michelangelo's statue of *David*. This statue had been reposing in the United States during the war and now we were to off-load it at Naples, Italy, from where it would be returned to reside in Florence permanently.

It was the first time I had ever put into port in Gibraltar. We had sailed past the famous rock several times before, but now I had a close look at the place. I was intrigued by a few sights, especially the Barbary Apes and the interesting rainwater collection system built by the British. Although we did not spend much time in port at

Gibraltar, I always imagined the history of the Rock would be a fascinating historical study. We off-loaded a couple of passenger cars at Gibraltar before returning to sea.

Docking at Naples caused a general sigh of relief after the statue of *David* was turned over to the proper Italian authorities. It was to be at least thirty-four years later before Mary and I would have the opportunity to see the actual statue of *David* in Florence—at which time my thoughts returned to the day we delivered *David* to Naples.

Some of us went ashore in Naples and even took a boat to Capri, a beautiful resort island. The days were pleasant—always my thoughts were how lucky I was. I had no thoughts of getting married and felt I was living the most perfect life imaginable.

When the *Grand Canyon* arrived at Piraeus Pyres, Greece, we found the *USS Meredith*. John Greene and I were anxious to report aboard. Captain H. C. Schwaner, Jr. was the skipper. He called John Greene and me into the wardroom for our introductory meeting and said he needed a gunnery officer and an engineering officer. His present engineering officer and gunnery officer were being detached from the ship when we returned to the United States in the fall. It made little difference to John Greene and me, so I volunteered to become Assistant Gunnery Officer, to be promoted to Gunnery Officer upon returning to the United States.

The *Meredith* carried two twin five-inch gun turrets forward and one aft, five torpedo tubes amidships, and a quantity of twin forty-millimeter antiaircraft guns. In addition, we carried various and assorted depth charges for antisubmarine duty. I was very pleased with my good fortune to have the *Meredith* as my first duty. In 1949 the *Meredith*, the #890, was of recent vintage.

My assigned stateroom was next to a supply officer who was out of the Class of '47. He told me that the *Meredith* had acquired a jeep and whenever they were in port they took the jeep ashore. In other words, the officers used it. He asked if I would like to go into Athens that night. Since my friend, John Greene, had drawn the duty watch his first day, I said I would like to go. Three of us, along with our driver, went to Athens, approximately five miles distance from the port of Piraeus. In those days you actually drove through countryside traveling between the two places—thirty-four years later, when Mary and I drove the same route, it was solid, polluted city all the way from the port.

In 1949 there was a civil war going on in Greece. Officers going ashore were instructed to be back at the boat dock no later than midnight. When our jeep arrived in Athens, everyone bailed out and agreed to meet at the same hotel before eleven-thirty. The other fellows had been in Athens and knew where they were going, but I was strictly on my own. Of course, I was back at the meeting place by eleven and so was the driver, but it was long past eleven-thirty when the last officer showed up. We had five miles to drive and we all knew the roadblocks went up before midnight.

Sure enough, we came to the first roadblock manned by Greek soldiers. They checked our identification and took our names before allowing us to proceed. By the time we reached the boat dock it was past twelve-thirty and there was no boat waiting.

About that time the admiral's barge from the flagship came alongside the dock. At the same time, Greek officials in a car delivered the Sixth Fleet Task Force Commander, Admiral Forrest Sherman, to the barge. The admiral coolly eyed us and inquired, "Do you gentlemen need a ride to your ship?" Of course we did, but it was embarrassing, especially for me.

The next morning was a good deal more embarrassing. I was called to the stateroom of our executive officer. Lt. Commander Thatcher proceeded to ream me royally. He said it was bad enough to display such disregard for the captain's orders, but on top of that, having the fleet admiral deliver me home was just too much. He made me feel as though I had planned and carried out the whole affair by my own initiative. I felt he probably gave me the worst reprimand since I was the newest officer aboard. What a great beginning!

At the time I joined the *Meredith*, the Sixth Fleet was carrying out amphibious landing operations on various Mediterranean islands. Consequently, every ship was loaded to the brim with men and material. The *Meredith* had to carry extra men who were combat marines to be used for assault landings. This situation caused crowding and water shortages, which caused complaining. The sailors felt the marines were at fault for the crowded conditions and the marines had their own complaints, including rationing of fresh water. I did not realize how bad the situation was until we put into Salonica, Greece, one day. We were due for some relaxation after being at sea for a while, however, I drew the duty the first day in port. It was a 24-hour tour of duty and we were anchored in the bay at Salonica. A series of events followed which kept me very busy. This was a surprise because I thought there would be little to do while at anchorage. All the other officers, plus two-thirds of the crew, had gone ashore. The one-third remaining were on the duty watch with me.

About mid-morning the soft breeze gradually changed directions, so subtle, I was hardly aware of it. The petty officer that was on deck watch brought to my attention that the destroyers were swinging on their anchors to head into the new wind direction. The immediate problem was that we were swinging in a direction which seemed opposite to the destroyer anchored to our starboard. It was a nervous situation for me. I could envision my record showing that on my first day as officer of the watch my ship was involved in a collision and, incredibly, doing this while at anchor! I can laugh about it now at this writing—of course nothing like that happened, however, standing my first in-port duty as officer of the watch was again an important learning experience.

Following the evening meal and at dusk, we followed normal routine and had the movies commence for those still on board. From our ship the liberty boats were making trips to the docks every hour on the hour, but only two or three men ever returned to the ship. I began to have some apprehension about what kind of shape these men were going to be in when their liberty expired. Enlisted men were due by eleven, chief petty officers by eleven-thirty, and the officers' liberty would expire at midnight.

By nine o'clock I ran liberty boats every half-hour, but the ten-thirty boat only had about four sailors in it. The eleven o'clock boat brought home the problem. The boat came alongside with drunken sailors and the coxswain told me the docks were full of sailors and marines in the same condition. Calling up my on-duty sailors and marines, they laid these fellows on the deck like cordwood. Our pharmacist mate quickly checked them for injury and I tried to get the deck cleared before the next boatload returned to the ship. It is not unusual for drunkenness to turn into belligerence and that is what happened between the sailors and marines. The movie had still been running on the aft deck when a sailor reported a marine with a knife was after a sailor! Fortunately, he handed the knife over to my duty people and they put each man in his own crew compartment. About this time I hoped officers would arrive, but no one wanted to return to the ship before liberty was over.

This demonstrates what happens when overcrowding and water rationing goes on. These men were desperate to go ashore and wash away their problems with booze. I was glad when the night finally ended and I looked forward to going ashore myself the next day.

At sea again a few sailors who wanted to ask me a favor approached me. They hemmed and hawed, but it came out that they wanted me to also be athletic officer. They told me they were without one ever since someone left a few months prior to my arrival. This particular group liked to play basketball, but their problem was that no one would schedule games for them. I agreed to help. I talked with the skipper and said I really needed to be the first one ashore at each port in order to line up games in that port city.

Our next visit was Istanbul and, sure enough, I was in the first boat ashore. In those days it seemed like there was nothing I felt I could not accomplish. My mind was set to schedule a basketball game in the capitol of Turkey, where I had never been before. Undaunted by the fact I could not speak a word of Turkish, I charged ahead. As the boat approached the dock, fascinated by the mosques and the prayer towers, suddenly I thought, "I wonder if they even know what basketball is in this country?" I caught a taxi and after using English, Spanish, Latin, and sign language, I conveyed the idea to the driver that I wanted to go to a school. He took me to a building which looked as though it could pass for a school. How delighted I was to find a young Turk who not only spoke English, but also had spent a year in the United States and loved to play basketball.

We arranged for a game that afternoon. My *Meredith* boys played well during the first half, but their lack of conditioning caught up with them. The Turks took the second half, and my team could hardly put one foot in front of the other by the end of the game. Most importantly, they were happy! They thought that my arranging a game for them was the absolute greatest event and they truly appreciated it. From then on I knew I would have to accomplish the same thing in every port.

One afternoon John Greene and I were in Istanbul sitting at a patio table at a hotel high on the hill. The view was expansive and magnificent and we sipped a glass of wine as we contemplated our new lifestyle. I thought it could not get any better!

While on bridge watch, one of my most memorable days was while steaming through the Dardanelles Strait. This waterway is about forty miles long and varies from a mile to four miles in width. This strait connects the Aegean Sea to the Sea of Mamara. It was a pleasure to navigate that narrow waterway, especially on a warm summer day. My recollection of history is sometimes faulty, but as I recall, Winston Churchill made his first reputation as a reporter while serving in this Crimea area. This is also near the area where the vaunted "Charge of the Light Brigade" took place! What wonderful history was found in this extraordinary land. While in Istanbul, I also viewed the beautiful Bosphorous which connects the Black Sea to the Sea of Mamara.

To me, life aboard the *Meredith* was more than I could have ever hoped for. At sea I enjoyed the responsibility of standing my bridge watches and I was scheduled to have my full qualification as a bridge-watch officer well under way by the time we returned to the United States in the fall. However, I began to experience a thirst that, at times, seemed to be unquenchable. I became aware that during a four-hour bridge watch I would sometimes easily consume a pitcher of water. Also, there were times when I felt so fatigued and I could not understand this.

The *Meredith* put into the island of Crete one weekend for rest and relaxation. The officers had been challenged to a softball game by the petty officers and I began the game and could hardly wait for the end to come. I was so tired and weak and my thirst was unbearable. I remember returning to our anchored ship. It was a very warm day and someone had organized a swimming party off the ship. I joined the swimmers and dove off the side. We were anchored out as usual and all it required was a shark watch from the deck of the ship. The cool water felt glorious and it did perk me up somewhat.

Since there was only one medical doctor for every destroyer division, I had no access to a doctor aboard the *Meredith*. However, when we departed from Crete, the division doctor came aboard the *Meredith* to reside for a while. He was a young doctor who had gone to medical school under the Navy program and I really liked him. Unfortunately, I can no longer recall his name. One night I talked with him about my symptoms and after I described them he said I had described the symptoms for diabetes mellitus. He did a urine test—I was loaded with sugar. After a pretty complete examination, he was increasingly concerned I was diabetic.

We were already at sea with the fleet preparing for a major amphibious operation. The doctor, fortunately, found that one of the cruisers had a bottle of regular insulin aboard. Our destroyer came alongside while we were under way and we transferred the bottle to the *Meredith*. The doctor gave me small doses of regular insulin and monitored my blood glucose by urine specimen. I immediately felt like my old self again. I thought that was all there would be to it, but life was to become full of new surprises!

As soon as the fleet operations had been concluded, the *Meredith* was dispatched to Trieste. I carried orders from Admiral Sherman to be admitted to the Seventh Station Military Hospital in the free territory of Trieste for treatment and transportation to the United States. I was to be evacuated on the earliest available transportation.

Our ship docked at Trieste and I was feeling low in spirits. Leaving that ship was tough and I really felt that the whole ship was sorry to see me go.

Docking at Trieste left another indelible memory in my mind. The previous ship to dock there was a cruiser that came in too fast. Unable to stop, the cruiser tore out the front one hundred feet of concrete dock. I felt sympathy for the poor docking officer.

Following World War II, in 1949 Trieste was still an "open city" and the Allies were still pondering whether Trieste should be a part of Italy or Yugoslavia. Combat among partisans was still going on north of Trieste. The military hospital where I was taken was an army hospital. What a blow to my ego. Since I only would be there until transportation was available, those Army doctors did not want me to get into any treatment program, so I still took regular insulin before each meal.

After a day or two I learned that a military transport ship was leaving Trieste for New York and I was to be aboard that ship. The transport was named USAT *Pvt. Eldon H. Johnson*. Of all my sea duty in the Navy, that was the easiest assignment I ever had. All of the passengers returning home were Army personnel and their dependents. I was the only Naval officer aboard and the officers and crew were probably Merchant Marines. I did enjoy the trip, although it seemed to take about ten days to make New York. All that time I felt well.

One day I had gone to a utility room to wash out underwear and socks. Automatic washing machines had not yet been invented and the washers were all wringer types. A soldier came up to me and asked if I could show his wife how to use the washer. I began speaking to her, but she looked puzzled. The soldier explained that his wife did not speak English, only Italian. I volunteered to give instructions to the soldier and he could translate to his wife. Imagine my surprise when he told me he could not speak Italian either. That was the way life was following World War II.

During the trip to New York, I came to know the ship's officers well and they used to invite me to the bridge. It was unusual for military transport people to have a naval officer aboard, but we enjoyed visiting with one another.

As we proceeded, I was making plans on what I would do when we reached New York. I determined that I would leave the ship, catch a train for Washington, D.C. and check into Bethesda Naval Hospital. The last night out of New York my friendship with the crew proved my undoing. The radio operator came to me and said he had radioed the Navy in New York and they would have a Navy ambulance at shipside to take me to St. Albans Naval Hospital on Long Island. I choked up. That was the last thing I wanted to do. I knew many people in the Annapolis/Washington area and it seemed like a good idea to go to Bethesda. The next morning, as we docked in New Jersey, there was indeed a Navy ambulance and I was the first person off the ship. I refused to lie down in the ambulance, but had no choice but to be driven to St. Albans Naval Hospital.

Obviously, this hospital had been built in a hurry during the war. It had many separate single-story wooden buildings which served as wards and were connected by a long wooden corridor. Alongside was a new, permanent hospital now under construction, which was to be a multistoried brick building. My address for the next six months was to be SOQ, #108, St. Albans Naval Hospital. For the uninitiated, SOQ stands for Sick Officers Quarters.

At this time the Department of Defense was newly organized. Following World War II, the Department of War, and the Navy Department were separate cabinet posts and the military was in no way unified. The new Department of Defense was supposed to change all that and St. Albans had both Army and Navy doctors serving there. The first Secretary of Defense was James Forrestal. He had previously been Secretary of the Navy. In fact, he signed my first paper which signified my being a midshipman. The new job must have crushed Forrestal for he soon ended his life by leaping out a window at Bethesda Naval Hospital. What a shame to lose such a talented gentleman.

It was a surprise to learn I was assigned to an Army doctor named Captain Karlin. I learned to like him and appreciated his special interest in diabetes. His wife was also a diabetic. The first day we talked he caught me by surprise. He told me if the tests showed I was diabetic and since I was regular Navy, I would be retired.

"Retired! I just started my career and besides, now, since I am taking insulin, I feel great!" I pleaded.

Karlin made it very plain that remaining in the service with insulin-dependent diabetes was absolutely out of the question. He took the opportunity to let me know, if I indeed was diabetic, I could look forward to early arterial disease; loss of one or both feet or legs, blindness, and perhaps kidney failure. I was assured of a shortened life span. The doctor gave it to me straight from the shoulder. He described my future outlook, which seemed pretty bleak at that moment.

I made a lot of friends and acquaintances on Ward 108 and it was not long before I was taking advantage of the free Broadway tickets. The Red Cross made these tickets available and I learned to take the Long Island Railway to Jamaica and then the subway to Manhattan. An Army chief warrant officer showed me how. I forget his full name, but he liked to be called Shugg, which was his last name. We regularly took advantage of the free tickets. I do recall seeing *Death of a Salesman*, with Lee J. Cobb, *Mr. Roberts* starring Henry Fonda, and *South Pacific*, starring Mary Martin and Enzio Pinza. We also took in the New York Giants first pro game of the season at the Polo Grounds.

All this time I believed my stay in New York would be short. It probably would have been if the United States Congress had not decided to pass a new military pay bill. This congressional action caused confusion in the pay status of retired officers. This confusion finally ended by the passing of legislation that allowed officers awaiting medical retirement to be able to choose whether or not they wished to retire under the old law or the new one. That was the reason I had to remain at St. Albans and, consequently, was not officially retired until April 1, 1950, six months after my arrival. And I was never a bed patient!

My routine at St. Albans developed in a casual manner. I arose in the morning, took a shower and shaved, injected my insulin, and then went to the dining room for breakfast, where I read both the *Daily News* and also the *Daily Mirror*. I liked to work the crossword puzzles in both papers each day. Then I went to the front glassed porch and usually found a chess game. I discovered there were a few very serious chess players on #108.

One day a corpsman named Ivory came to me and said, "Mr. Ostlund, Mr. Martone in room number three would sure like to play chess with you."

I begged off with Ivory. I had never met Mr. Martone, except I knew he was an old fellow. However, a couple of days later Mr. Martone, dressed in bathrobe and slippers, came to me as I was getting dressed. He spoke with an accent, which I later discovered was Hungarian.

"Would you like to play a game with me?" he inquired.

"Certainly!" I volunteered. I felt that I might just as well get it over with and be done with it.

My goodness! What a surprise I was in for that morning.

Mr. Martone won so easily I began to feel foolish! I especially felt that way when he turned his back to the chessboard and called his moves to me without ever seeing the board. By then a crowd had gathered around my bed. You see, my bed was where Mr. Martone found me and he just plopped his chessboard on top of my bed. Since it was narrow, he sat on one side of the bed while I sat across from him. He beat me at chess with his back turned!

I discovered some of the onlookers were there to visit Mr. Martone. They were members of the New York Chess Club. I was happy to relinquish my seat to one of them. I had suffered all the chess I could enjoy for one day!

Mr. Martone had one bad habit. He smoked cigarettes constantly. He would place a cigarette into his holder and light it. Then, under mental concentration, he would forget about it. The ashes would grow longer and longer as he held on to his cigarette holder. Finally, the ashes would fall on my bed. By the time the crowd left that day, my bed was a sorry sight—resembling an ash pit.

The next morning Mr. Martone returned. I had no intention of suffering more defeat another day, however, he only wanted to give me a book. He said, "You play very well. Perhaps you would like to improve yourself and you might find this book helpful."

It was then that I discovered Mr. Martone had written the book. He was an Hungarian national champion while still in his early teens and he was a rocket scientist whom we had brought to the United States after the war. He was a civilian working at Sands Point Naval Research Center on Long Island. My respect for Mr. Martone expanded greatly. It also gave me some consolation for the defeats I suffered the previous day.

Later, I witnessed Mr. Martone playing six of the best members of the New York Chess Club at one time. He walked from table to table and made his moves without taking an inordinate amount of time. What a master! I felt relief just knowing that Mr. Martone, as a scientist, was on our side.

My education was broadened a great deal and that included going to the race tracks. There were three important tracks around St. Albans: Belmont, Aqueduct, and Jamaica. When one was closed, another would open on a rotational basis. In retrospect, I was on my way to becoming a real worthless kind of a person. But then, this routine was changed in November of 1949.

During the first week of November, a most wonderful event happened in my life. I came out of the bathroom one morning where I just finished shaving and saw this lovely nurse making my bed. I walked over and introduced myself to Ensign Mary Virginia Ryan. She had just joined the Navy Nurse Corps after graduating the previous year from St. Vincent's Hospital of Nursing in Manhattan. She told me she joined the Navy to see the world, but so far she was only a 45-minute ride from her home in Mount Vernon, New York. Then, for some reason, she was not to be seen on my ward for several days. When I did see her again, I thought I would try to make a date some-time. One afternoon I called her at nurses' quarters and invited her to see a movie in St. Albans. Neither one of us had a car, so we walked down the main street and saw the movie *Crash Dive*. Afterward we had a drink in a local tavern and I walked her back to nurses' quarters.

Since I knew I would be leaving the Navy, I began to think seriously about purchas-ing a car. I had established a checking account with a bank in Scranton, Pennsylvania. This was because, even prior to graduation, they had solicited my business as a Naval Academy graduate. Included in their pitch was the offer to finance a car anytime I desired it. I wrote to them and they readily agreed to do it. I looked at Fords and Chevrolets, but I finally decided on a blue, four-door 1949 Ford that had overdrive plus an eight-tube radio. And since the 1950 models were already out, supposedly they made good deals on the old models. I believe I may have paid seventeen hundred dollars for that car and I was so proud of it. The first thing I did was phone Mary Ryan and invite her on a date. When I called for her at nurses' quarters, she was surprised to see me open the car door of my new auto.

With the advent of my new car, I began to drive in ever-larger circles around St. Albans. I found neat little places to take Mary dancing and our friendship blossomed.

Unfortunately, I also discovered how easy it was to drive to the racetracks. I was becoming quite a horseplayer. I read the *Daily Racing News* in order to supposedly bet more wisely. At least that is how I excused myself. One day I came home from the tracks after learning that the seventh race at Jamaica the next day had a "sure" winner. Now, in order to learn that sort of thing you had to be rubbing elbows with some pretty colorful and sometimes unsavory characters. Probably I should speak more plainly and state that most of these fellows would qualify as real track bums.

However, at that time I also felt some certainty and told a few of my hospital friends about how Golden Boy was a sure winner at Jamaica in the seventh tomorrow. Some of them even gave me money to bet for them. My sweetheart, Mary Ryan, was a skeptic, bless her heart, but since I seemed so confident, Mary and another nurse, Sherry Pierce, each gave me money to buy them a ticket.

Golden Boy did win the seventh race the next day! I was excited as I began heading for the winner's window at Jamaica. Suddenly the tote board that showed Golden Boy winning, paying four to one, went on "hold." A complaint had been registered against Golden Boy. Suddenly the tote board showed a new winner. Golden Boy had been disqualified for fouling another horse or jockey. I don't recall the explicit incident, but I will never forget having to face my backers with the bad news. Mary had been saving her money to buy a new pair of shoes. I believe I probably lost all further interest in going to the tracks. In retrospect, perhaps it was a good thing to happen when it did. In the long run it may have saved me from becoming a derelict at the New York tracks.

My Navy records indicated I had been in the hospital for several months and this qualified me for sick leave. I applied for leave over Christmas and decided to drive to Gillette. I remember very well the long trip out west and also remember worrying about Mary Ryan while I was gone. One of the other patients at the hospital, John

McFeaters, told me reassuringly that he would look after Mary while I was away. I felt a bit uneasy about leaving her to those wolves at St. Albans. John McFeaters sent me a Christmas card at my Gillette address. John was a good friend, but he certainly enjoyed teasing. Or was it really teasing? His card said he was taking Mary out that evening.

After Christmas I decided I needed to get back to New York and I drove in record time. As I remember, I only spent two nights on the road and made New York in one piece with no accidents.

Winter turned into spring and Mary Ryan became a very important lady in my life. Mary had invited me to Mount Vernon to meet her family. They had an apartment at 425 Bedford Avenue and I learned to drive there with no problems. In fact, I could now drive all over New York and did so with regularity.

While I was in New York, I received word from Jane and Otis Hall. Their son Dick and I were pals from kindergarten days. Otis worked for the Burlington Railroad and he and Jane received passes to travel. This was their first trip to New York and they were hoping to see me. I arranged to meet them at Penn Station and drove them all over New York. Traffic was simple compared to conditions in present-day New York. Jane sat in the middle between Otis and me. I became aware that as I sped through the traffic, Jane pressed her feet on the floorboard as though she were stepping on the brakes. At first I laughed about it, but then slowed down so Jane could see the sights better. I enjoyed their visit and I felt the Halls did too.

I liked Mary's family, however, I had the feeling her parents hoped Mary would not get involved with a guy who lived so incredibly far from Mount Vernon. As it turned out, the entire family was to end up in Wyoming and that would happen sooner than later.

At that time between the late forties and early fifties, television was just beginning to come into regular use. Tom Ryan had a TV set in his apartment and the screen was about five inches square (the size television was at first offered). He surely liked to watch his TV and every night there was boxing. I learned early on that TV was going to destroy conversation in the home. Unfortunately, Tom Ryan also used to watch the nightly weather report and more often than not, Big Piney, Wyoming, would get the prize for the coldest spot in the nation! At least that is the way Tom Ryan reported it to me.

As well as John McFeaters, another classmate also was at St. Albans Hospital; Jack Benoit who had married Rosemarie following graduation. As it turned out, Jack Benoit and I both received our official notification that we were now Ensigns USN retired as of April 1, 1950.

A week after my retirement, when I departed St. Albans officially, it was very tough to leave Mary. Our last date together was full of assurances that we would stay in close touch with each other. We also talked about Mary coming to Wyoming to visit in the fall. Nevertheless, the next day I pulled out and headed my blue Ford south to Richmond. I was going to visit the O'Flaherty family for a day or two before heading west. I called Mary often because my heart was with her.

While writing this day, April 17, 1992, I asked Mary if she would try to find an old Navy file for me. I was revising this very chapter. Among other papers she discovered the Christmas card that John McFeaters sent to me at Christmas of 1949. Almost forty-three years later, Mary finally read it! She laughed as she said, "So that's how you knew that Mac took me out over the Christmas holidays!"

The USS Meredith, DD 890.

Nurse Mary Virginia Ryan.

Ensign Mary V. Ryan and Ensign John C. Ostlund at an Annapolis dock, 1950.

12

Early Business Years

As I departed from New York, I tried to concentrate on looking ahead and not lamenting my Navy career, which I was leaving behind. I wanted very badly to get to work and earn money. I had seriously considered remaining in New York and going to work for Merrill Lynch, however, I also knew that living in New York was never going to suit me. Other than feeling badly about leaving Mary, I had good feelings as I saw the city in my rearview mirror.

After seven months of injecting my own insulin, I was beginning to get used to the routine. It was a constant concern to try to regulate my food and beverage intake to match my insulin. In 1949 we did not have throwaway syringes. Syringes were made of glass with heavy gauge steel needles; sturdy needles that could be sharpened on a whetstone. I purchased Bakelite cases so I could keep the syringe in alcohol at all times, otherwise, they had to be boiled for sterilization. Insulin also had to be kept refrigerated. Urine testing had to be done with test tubes, chemicals, and an alcohol burner. The whole procedure was not only awkward and time-consuming, but the information received was of small value—this was the way it was—the only way then known.

My brother, Bob, and I had been talking about going into business together. The most recent occasion was during our last Christmas holiday. We both were confident that Wyoming had plenty of potential to offer. Originally, in 1950 we talked about going into highway construction. During the war years hardly any new highways were built and so much catching up needed to be done. In order to build highways, a person needed capital for equipment. As with most people, this was our immediate shortfall.

In the beginning we were going to join my father in the plumbing, heating, and farm equipment business. My father had already expressed a desire to take it easy if my brother and I would come into the business. Formally, we organized a partnership known as Axel W. Ostlund & Sons. We also agreed to the amount to be paid to my father for our interests.

With almost no new farm equipment made during the war years, there was a demand for farm machinery. Wheat farmers had become well-off during the war and the price of wheat was still very favorable. There were many more farmers in Wyoming in those days than there were to be thirty years later. As I returned to Gillette, I was undaunted by how much I had to learn. Instead, I was excited about the challenge and anxious to get after it.

Our plumbing shop was located on the east side of Gillette Avenue between Third and Fourth Streets. The location is now occupied by the First National Bank building. The fifty-foot lot on the corner of Fourth Street and Gillette Avenue was the remains of a garage that had burned down in 1939. It had never been rebuilt and although there were no sidewalls or roof, the old floor was still somewhat useable. The basement underneath the floor was full of junk. I mention this location because that is where we kept our machinery. We did not even rent the space, but since it was there and no one seemed to care, we used it.

Our store was to the north and consisted of two of the oldest buildings in Gillette. Each framed building was situated on a twenty-five-foot lot and was uninsulated and heated by coal stoves. When we started out, tools, supplies, and storage were kept in old sheds that had accumulated over the years and our pickups, parked outside in the elements, endured the cold of winter, which was a trial.

My father had been doing plumbing business in this small shop for almost thirty years and nothing had changed. Although we rented these two buildings from an older rancher, an astute businessman named W. R. Wright, my father did own the property across the alley from the shop at the corner of Kendrick Avenue and Fourth Street. That old building was the original courthouse for Campbell County. Later it became a schoolhouse and was used as a school until 1937. In fact, both my brother and I attended first and second grades in that building. My father acquired the property in 1937 after a new grade school was built and we used the old building as a warehouse. It had no heat or electricity, but we did not need those luxuries.

Hans Gregersen worked in the John Deere business and Pat Heinbaugh worked as a plumber. My brother, Bob, had been working since his graduation from the University of Wyoming in June of 1949. My father worked from time to time, but his interest was in his small ranch—formerly Lawrence J. Rick's ranch, which was about eight miles northwest of town. Following the death of our father in 1982, through an exchange this ranch became my brother's and was sold to the Dalys.

As I look back on this arrangement, I can't help but recall how naïve we were. Although we all had good hands-on working experience, none of us had any understanding of business accounting. My father had always operated on a cash basis and if he had some money, everything was fine. This lack of practical accounting knowledge was to plague us during our first years of growing our business.

There was no shortage of ambition or dedication to the work ethic. We started work by at least six o'clock in the morning and never closed until six at night. In those days everyone worked a six-day week and Sunday was the only respite in the work week. Since farm machinery would break down on holidays as well as weekdays, we were never unavailable to our customers needing repairs.

At first we had no truck for hauling farm equipment, but we hired someone to deliver when the situation called for it. Farm equipment was brought in by truck or railcar. Of course, first it had to be assembled. For example, I had never seen a side-delivery rake work in my life, only the old horse-drawn sulky rakes. But side-delivery rakes were the new way of making hay and were necessary when you used a hay baler. I remember starting about daylight to assemble a steel-wheeled side-delivery rake. Soon I could do it in just a few hours. The delivered price of such a rake was $294. All John Deere tractors were two-cylinder in those days, as they always had been. It was not until the late 1950s that John Deere began making tractors with more than two cylinders. They did not have electric starting, lights, or hydraulics. You hand-cranked them to start by spinning a flywheel with your hands. Rubber tires were the big thing and we even converted a few of the old steel-wheel tractors to rubber.

Customers came to us for pipe and fittings. We also were the Maytag dealers and in those days we only had three models of wringer washers to sell. Our Maytag representative, who called on us from Colorado Springs, was a young fellow named Chuck Winslow. Now, forty years later, we still know him. Chuck and his wife, Celeste, live in Phoenix, Arizona, and Chuck is a very successful businessman.

My brother took care of the plumbing side of the business. Probably by default, I carried forward with our customers' need for sheet metal, which included making roof jacks and stovepipes, installing gutters and downspouts, and warm-air heating. All of the furnaces we installed were coal-fired. Coal was available from the Wyodak mine and if you took your own vehicle you could load it yourself for just two dollars a ton. The sales tax was one percent or maybe two percent.

Another very important part of our business was selling windmills. My father had always sold Aermotor windmills that he bought directly from the factory in Chicago. Windmills were practically impossible to get during the war and most every rural customer needed windmills for stock water. Growing up I had occasionally helped my father install windmills, but now I was determined to take that over. One day three of us loaded up an eight-foot diameter wheel windmill along with a twenty-seven-foot-high steel tower. A fellow, whose last name was Austin, dug the postholes and my father showed me how to assemble the mill and tower. When the assembly was completed and the anchor postholes dug, the windmill was ready to raise up in the air. Without detailing how this was done, I was now convinced I could handle the windmill business, and I did. By the time I was through with the windmill business, I had assembled every size made including the smallest, a six-foot wheel, to the largest, a twenty-foot diameter wheel which required at least a forty-foot tower. In northeast Wyoming there are many windmills still standing that I erected.

Besides selling the windmill and tower, we also sold the pipe, rods, and cylinders to get the water into the tanks and, of course, the stock tanks. Usually we sold steel tanks, but redwood tanks were considered a better investment.

That year the Wyoming Highway Department granted a contract to build a new shop building in Newcastle, about seventy miles from Gillette. A Gillette general contractor named Max Luton got the job and gave the plumbing and heating contract to us. My brother, Bob, spent most of his time at this job. As time went on, we were successful in getting a new school job in Hulett and also in Moorcroft. Bob worked the jobs in Newcastle and Moorcroft, so we urged Axel to manage the job in Hulett. The benefit of Hulett was that it was such a nice small and quiet town, which suited our father very well. As previously mentioned, none of us had any training in business accounting and, unfortunately, I remember my father saying that all we needed to do was set up a separate checking account for each job and whatever was left in the bank when the job was finished would be our profit. That seemed simple enough, but oh, if only it were so!

After finishing our first year, we had to make out a partnership income tax return. I took our records, such as they were, to a local accountant. When I learned the results I was shocked. We not only had not made any profit, but in fact we had lost money! I remember questioning the accountant, "You mean to say that we have worked like hell all year and not only did not make any money, but donated some of what we had for the privilege?"

"That is about right," he said.

"I swear we'll never let that happen again," was my response.

I actually did not know what to do about it, but my immediate answer was to learn accounting. There were no CPAs in town at that time. There was only one public accounting firm to my recollection: Cassidy and Snearly. Current trade magazines carried advertising about various schools and business opportunities. I enrolled in the LaSalle School of Accounting which offered correspondence training. I was excited when my books arrived and I dove into the course the first night. I soon learned that after working a ten-to twelve-hour day it was easy to lose your appetite for correspondence training at night. I did persevere and learned accounting. I have never regretted that action and, in fact, I owe whatever degree of success I have achieved to my accounting training.

With my newly acquired understanding of accounting, we began immediate action. I became dedicated to proper, departmentalized, balanced, monthly records. My first attempts seemed rather ambitious, but we organized into five departments: New and Used Machinery, Merchandise and Repairs, Plumbing and Heating, Sheet Metal and Air-Conditioning, and Appliances. This served our needs for many, many years. My mother liked to work in the shop and enjoyed keeping records, so the job of posting the books was hers.

As time went on, I wanted to mechanize the posting and finally bought an NCR posting machine. After a while we upgraded this with a newer and more modern machine. Today, in 1990, I think how incredible it would have been to have one of today's personal computers in our business. It would have truly been a miracle. We were just born too soon for that. The constant problem in our hand-posted system was balancing. Every column of figures was hand-posted and it was so easy to transpose a number or two. It kept my mother busy and, fortunately, the volume kept climbing.

One day in 1951 something occurred that was to have far-reaching implications for us. One of the three doctors in town named Dr. J. C. McHenry, who was a good doctor and had been in Gillette for many years, had become interested in flying. After the war several people wanted to learn to fly. Dr. McHenry, Larry Butler, and Norris Taylor bought about two hundred acres of land east of Gillette. At that time this land was as flat as a billiard table and the dry creek bed that wound through the property was actually drainage for the City of Gillette. Years before, the creek ran with open sewage from the city, but by this time the sewage was contained in an underground sewer pipe.

McHenry and Butler, along with Norris Taylor, had built a private airport on the location. There were three hangars of various sizes plus a storage building. Water came from a very shallow well. The water was poor quality and the best that could be said was that it was wet. Electricity came from the city system. The three runways were gravel-covered. In addition there was a bountiful hay crop on this land.

The day Dr. McHenry came into the plumbing shop he talked about several inconsequential things before stating his real purpose. He was not satisfied with the arrangement that he had with Larry Butler and he wanted to sell this private airport. He came to me because he figured we needed the room for our implement business. And how true this was. The old corner with the burned-down garage was just not adequate for us. We had no room to do overhaul business and business was good. I asked McHenry how much he wanted and he told me twenty thousand dollars. In some respects that sounded like an impossible amount, but I told him that we would be back in touch soon.

My father and my brother and I talked over the prospect of acquiring this large property and decided to take it. Bob and I each felt we could get GI Loans. That sounded good, although we really should have first checked with the bank. Instead, we went to Thomas Morgan, Attorney, and asked him to draw the papers. The papers were drawn and Tom Morgan was to examine the abstract to render title opinion and then we were to pay.

It was at that point that I went to the Stockmen's Bank to arrange for the money. In 1951 I was quite naïve. I talked with Jess Spielman who was the main man at the bank. He asked me about the deal and when I told him we needed twenty thousand dollars to buy the property, he said, "Young man, don't try to borrow yourself into prosperity!"

I later thought he probably said that to all new borrowers. He would not give me an answer, but instead told me to appear before the Board of Directors the following morning. What an experience that was! As I can best recall, some of the directors were J. A. Allison, Hubert Dickey, Elwood Anderson, and W. R. Wright. Their small bank building was located midway between Second and Third Streets on the west side of Gillette Avenue. They were the only bank in town and although it was a small building, it was large enough to handle the business needs of the time. To say that there was no privacy would be a serious understatement. The small officers' area had absolutely no privacy at all. People going to the tellers' cages could curiously lean on the marble railing and listen to the bank officers talking with their customers. I was told to be there before the bank opened to the public and was admitted and told to sit and wait. The directors joked and visited until the bank opened for business. About that time someone remembered me and called on me to make my request. I had no balance sheet, no income statements, nor did I have any projections. I just had faith that through hard work we could repay the loan. I soon learned the bank did not loan on faith, nor did they consider that we had enough collateral for such a loan. Our great idea of a GI Loan was only met with silence. However, they did have a way to approve the request. They seemed to know that my mother had inherited certain stocks from her father and they were willing to take those shares as additional security. My mother agreed to do it and we bought the land. That six percent mortgage remained on the land for several years and we learned early that borrowed money was seldom easy to repay.

We did move our farm equipment to the 'airport' as we continued to call it. The largest hangar became our shop building and since we had over half a mile of highway frontage, we had excellent display for our equipment.

At the time of this writing (1990), I will describe the location of that airport in today's terms. The Butler-Spaith Road bounded the property on the west and the State Highway 14-16 bounded the property on the north. The University of Wyoming Agricultural Experiment Station was on the east. Today that is the site of the Cam-plex facilities. Today the East Interchange for Interstate 90 is located in the middle of that former airport land.

Soon after returning to Gillette in 1950, I was invited by Bill Ryan, a local furniture dealer, to attend a meeting of the Gillette Rotary Club. They had only organized the previous month of March. After attending the evening meeting held in the back room of the Goings Café, I was invited to join. John Ilsley and I became the first members to join after the club was chartered. Dr. McHenry was president, Bill Edelman was vice president, and Archie Lindsey was secretary. One of the first goals of Dr. McHenry was to raise enough money to buy a piano, for he felt we should sing at the meetings. When the piano arrived, I played for the club while they sang, and to my recollection we usually only sang "America."

Mary Ryan came to visit in the fall of 1950 and flew into Billings. I drove to meet her and bring her home to Gillette. It was so wonderful to have her there. My parents gave their bedroom to Mary and they slept in a bedroom upstairs for the several days she was there. I took Mary to my father's ranch where we carried a picnic lunch. We rode horses and had what I thought was a very romantic picnic in a secluded location on the ranch. I am sure Mary felt the same way about it. We went to Devil's Tower one day where we walked around and marveled at the scenes.

Since I had to deliver a tractor to Broadus, Montana, I invited Mary to go with me. We had just purchased a red Ford two-ton truck for deliveries and I was quite proud to offer Mary a ride in it. I'm sure that it was a very different experience for Mary.

While Mary was here, probably the most different thing we experienced was antelope hunting. The Rotary Club had just sponsored an 'Antelope Roundup' in an effort to induce more out-of-state hunters to come to town. It was quite a success. A prize was offered for the biggest antelope and I felt I knew where there was one that would qualify for being the largest. We didn't win, but we did have a lot of fun. I hoped Mary found it to be an exciting experience. I so wanted her to like the West.

Before Mary made her visit that fall, I had only been back to New York one time. This happened on the spur-of-the-moment, but I certainly took advantage of the opportunity. Maytag had just come out with their first automatic washer, however, dealers could not receive one until they sent a repairman to be trained at the Maytag facility in Colorado Springs. I became the Maytag automatic washer repairman.

I drove from Gillette to Colorado Springs in my blue Ford sedan. There were no four-lane highways in those days and driving through Denver at noon on the way to Colorado Springs was unforgettable. Just as my blue Ford inched to the middle of the intersection of Colfax and Broadway, the motor quit. This was my first experience with high-altitude vapor lock, but what an embarrassment it was. The cop at the intersection yelled at me to get the car out of there and, of course, nothing would have pleased me more. Finally, someone told me to blow into the gas tank, and that did the trick.

Following the completion of automatic washer school, I had determined to drive all night and catch a plane out of Omaha, Nebraska. I figured I could spend the weekend in New York and then fly back to Omaha to get my car. My Ford could then take me to Missouri to see a Mrs. Bridwell about land I wanted my father to buy to enlarge his ranch.

When you are young there is nothing that you can't do. I drove all night and arrived in Omaha with about an hour to spare before the plane left. I flew into LaGuardia in New York and checked into the Algonquin Hotel. It was wonderful to see Mary again and I knew that I really wanted to marry this lady. But in June of 1950, the Korean War began and Mary could not get out of the Navy. Wasn't that a switch! Usually it was the man who was in the service, but I was now out and Mary was unable to separate from the military.

When I returned to Omaha I had another surprise. My car battery was dead. Having previously driven all night and arriving in Omaha after daybreak, I had forgotten to turn my lights off. For that reason I was a bit delayed in heading for Missouri.

There was a section of land joining my father's place that I thought we should have. It had been homesteaded by the Bridwells and was now being leased by Jimmy McKenzie. I found Mrs. Bridwell, but she had no interest in selling the land. The trip on to Missouri was for naught, but the trip to New York will stay in my memories forever.

It was about that time when we really needed to expand our farm equipment business. I suggested we do some cold canvassing and loaded my blue Ford sedan with catalogs and literature and took off for new country. Working the area out of Moorcroft led me into the Devil's Tower country.

One spring day, I was following a dirt trail through the pine country not really knowing where I was going. I knew that I would arrive at a farmer's house eventually. When I found a place it was a rather weird experience. A man lived there in a dugout along with a bunch of goats. I had not seen so many goats except at "Barefoot" Nelson's place. Barefoot Nelson never wore shoes, even in the wintertime; his feet were so callused that I swear he could walk on cactus. However, Barefoot lived close to Rozet.

At this place the man's name was Young. He had not seen a visitor for months, so was glad to see me. He told me about his wife running off many years before with his brother and how he had lived out here in the hills ever since. He farmed with horses, but admitted that he always wanted a tractor. I sold him a John Deere MT tractor with a small plow. Before I got back to the highway I got stuck a couple of times, but that was the way things were in those days. Making a sale and finding a new customer was what it was all about!

One day I pulled into another place back in those pine-covered hills. The farmer, John Aurand, loved to talk and really liked people to call on him. He had two sons, but they never got to say a word. John was a timber-cutter and sawmill operator. He wanted every piece of equipment in the book, but he had no way of paying for it. I asked if he could cut some heavy stuff, like six by six posts and three-inch thick plank.

"Why, you're talking to the best sawman in Wyoming when you're talking to me!" he retorted. "I can cut you all the posts and planks you want!"

I agreed to sell him a John Deere MT tractor and other equipment if he would deliver some heavy timbers and planking to Gillette for the down payment. We needed the posts and planking to make a loading dock at the "airport." It took John a long time to get it together, but he finally showed up with my load of posts and planking. It was always a problem collecting payments from John, but eventually he got the equipment paid out, and the loading dock became indispensable in our operations.

In 1951 we took on the General Electric line of major appliances. A guy named Bruce Francisco convinced us that we could accommodate the line. We also carried General Electric small appliances plus a whole line of kitchen cabinets and since the cabinets were made of metal, we decided they should be a part of the sheet metal department. This was said with a smile!

The first kitchen job I did was for my parents. My mother had always dreamed of remodeling her kitchen, so I drew up the plans. I was proud of the way it turned out and so were my parents. That was the first big kitchen job and many more were to follow. We did the layouts, furnished the appliances, cabinets, countertops, and the plumbing. Any carpenter work or painting was farmed out so we were always the prime and responsible contractor.

In November of 1950 I drove to New York to see Mary. I had purchased tickets to the Army-Navy game in Philadelphia and was looking forward to showing Mary off to any of my classmates who were attending the game. Following the football game, we drove to Richmond, Virginia, to visit the O'Flaherty family. I wanted them to meet Mary, also. It was during this trip that I showed Mary the diamond engagement ring I had purchased from L & C Mayer and Company in New York. Instead of giving her that ring, I had already decided I could afford to buy one with a slightly larger stone. Mary was happy with this one, but I persisted. At Christmas I sent Mary's ring to her and hoped it would arrive on time. Then I called her on Christmas Eve. When Mary answered the phone I hesitated to say all the things I really wanted to say because I had the uncomfortable feeling that my parents were listening. That kind of cools your expressions. I hope Mary was not disappointed in my proposal, but I know that I was!

In the spring of 1951, I was elected secretary of the Gillette Rotary Club. Bill Edelman, the incoming president and I, the incoming secretary, were expected to attend the District Rotary Conference in Colorado Springs. This would take place at the famous Broadmoor Hotel. Immediately, I invited Mary to come to Colorado Springs and join me. We planned far enough in advance for her to arrange for leave, so it came about. When Bill Edelman made the reservations, the Rotary people called and asked about John Ostlund and Mary Ryan having separate accommodations. Bill Edelman explained that Mary was my fiancée and we were planning to get married. Immediately the Colorado Springs Club, the host club, began to get ideas. They thought it would be terrific if we got married during the conference. They were offering the bridal suite at the Broadmoor, plus they planned to get *Life* magazine to do a spread on the wedding. Of course I thought that would be great. When I put the plan to Mary, she made me understand that her wedding should take place at home with her family and friends present. Although we turned down the Rotary wedding invitation, we did have a great few days at Colorado Springs.

The day we left we went to Denver and stayed at the Cosmopolitan Hotel. Bill and Coramay Edelman took us to dinner that night and then we all went to the Ice Capades Show. I had never been to such a spectacular show on ice and with my future wife at my side I was in heaven.

The summer of 1951 consisted of long hours with much work. It was great, but I was so darn lonesome for Mary. She wrote to me almost every day and going to the post office was the high point of my day. Unfortunately, my letter writing was never as good as my intentions and Mary would go for many days without a letter. I know that I must have disappointed her and I have always felt badly to have caused her any distress.

By this time, following a year of naval service, Mary had been sent to serve at the Naval Hospital at Annapolis, a hospital that served all naval personnel in that area. At one time she even had Admiral Chester Nimitz's wife as her patient. Mary told me Mrs. Nimitz was a most gracious lady, even though she was suffering from a broken collarbone.

Finally, about November of 1951, Mary received permission to leave her active-duty status as a Lieutenant J.G., United States Naval Reserve. I made arrangements to go to New York so that Mary and I could make our wedding plans.

As a bachelor in Gillette I really had little social life. I was a good friend of the Catholic priest, Father James Power, and we played a lot of chess together. After Rotary Club on Tuesday evenings I was invited to play poker with a few of the Rotarians, including Dutch Dahlman, Kelly Swenson, Dr. Bob Wade, LeRoy Mankin, Charlie Broadhurst, John Ilsley, Bill Ryan, and Neil McLain. I never really enjoyed playing poker, but did it as a diversion. For that reason I was never a good poker player. However, bridge, pitch, and cribbage were games I did enjoy and played reasonably well.

Dr. McHenry took a young doctor into his practice who was also single. His name was John Saycich and we played golf together on Sunday on the nine-hole sand greens at the municipal airport. We both played at about the same level and we had a lot of fun trying to improve our games.

When November finally arrived, I could hardly wait to go to New York. I stayed at Tom and Peg Ryan's apartment on a sofa bed in the living room and I was delighted to be invited to stay there. The wedding date was set for Saturday, January 13, 1952, and Mary's sister, Barbara, was to be her maid of honor. My brother, Bob, was to be best man. The wedding was to take place at Sacred Heart Catholic Church in Mount Vernon.

One day, Tom Ryan asked if I would like to take a trip with him. He said he felt badly that he could not take any time off from the Mount Vernon Police where he worked as a detective. He said that he and his partner had to go to Ossining, New York, to pick up a prisoner being released from Sing Sing Prison. I told him I would love to do that. The day we went to Sing Sing we first stopped at the police station where Tom gave me a detective shield for identification.

The day was cold and rainy. I would describe it as being much like you would see in a typical movie of a prison scene. When we arrived at the prison, we parked the car and were allowed to walk through a series of locked steel doors. At one room we were told we would have to leave our weapons until we checked out. The two regular detectives gave up their guns, handcuffs, and blackjacks. I looked a bit sheepish and offered that since I was just a beginner, I carried no weapons.

We finally entered the warden's office. Wanting to make a bit of conversation while we were waiting for the prisoner I asked, "How many prisoners do you have in here now, Warden?"

"After you take Jones out of here I'll be down to 2,019," he said crisply.

Actually I cannot recall the exact number. Jones was a black man who had been doing time for a liquor store robbery. The Mount Vernon police were waiting for his parole so they could charge him with another liquor store robbery. I felt that Jones did not have much to look forward to and the last I ever saw of Jones was watching him get locked up in the Mount Vernon jail.

Returning to Wyoming, I decided to trade in my '49 blue Ford sedan for a new 1952 Ford Victoria. This was about the first of the two-door hardtop designs that were to be offered. It was a two-tone green color and I thought it had to be the best-looking car on the road. I decided to keep it as a surprise for Mary for our wedding the following month. I also ordered a necklace of real pearls to give Mary as my wedding gift. Living in Gillette in those days, I seldom spent any money—consequently I had money saved up for our wedding and honeymoon to follow.

While Mary and her family were busy making plans in New York, I was busy in Wyoming doing the same thing. My brother, Bob, was to be my best man and we talked with our friend, Tom Gill, of Cheyenne, about driving to New York with us. Tom agreed to serve as an usher at our wedding. My father did not go, but volunteered to stay at the shop while Bob and I were gone. My mother, along with her sister, Lucille, and my cousin, Elizabeth Culver, were to make the trip on the train. Bob's wife of three months, RoseMary, also went on the train, while Bob, Tom Gill, and I drove my new car to New York. I had made reservations at the Hotel Roosevelt in Manhattan for all of us.

The first leg of our journey was to Cheyenne to pick up Tom Gill. We spent the night at Tom's mother's house and after a hearty breakfast the next morning, we took to the highways. Imagine my surprise when a Nebraska Highway Patrol stopped me later that morning and I was not speeding! He reported that Mrs. Gill had called the patrol to tell me that I had left my insulin in the bedroom where I slept the previous night. Oh, my! Rather than retrace our journey, I stopped at Grand Island and bought a new supply. We took turns driving, but I recall being the one at the wheel in Pennsylvania, driving on the famous Turnpike going at least seventy. A state patrol car came alongside and pulled me over for speeding. He claimed I was doing seventy-five. He not only wrote a ticket, but also made me follow him off the Turnpike to appear before a justice of the peace. I noted that while following him to an exit, we exceeded seventy-five miles per hour several times. There was no use arguing; I just had to pay. At that time the Pennsylvania Turnpike was the only four-lane highway between Gillette and New York.

We reached New York without any mishaps and we arrived a few days before the wedding day. Tom and Bob had plans to see New York while I had plans to see Mary. I drove carefully to Mount Vernon each day so that on the following Saturday I could make the trip without any problem. I would head west and take the Hudson River Parkway to Mount Vernon, a trip that took about forty-five minutes. I used to worry about getting a flat tire on the big day, but nothing like that ever happened.

Each night I returned to the hotel rather late and the streets were fairly deserted. With no parking space, I just parked on the street across from the hotel so that I could see my car from the hotel window. The signs clearly stated that there was to be no parking after seven in the morning. I hoped the cop would just figure that the Wyoming license plate meant he had a real country kid with this car. The very last day, as I was leaving to drive to the wedding, the cop met me as I was getting into my car.

"I've been wanting to catch you every day when I'm out here directing traffic around your car. Can't you read these signs?" he added sternly. "Now don't let this happen again or I'll have you in traffic court."

Naturally I apologized because I had seen his problem one morning when I looked out the hotel window from high above. But this last morning I told him I was off to get married and he would probably never see me again. I believe he smiled when he waved me away.

I will always remember what a beautiful bride Mary was as she walked down the aisle with her father. I was so proud and so happy to take her hand and become her husband. We had a double-ring ceremony and to this day (now past forty years) I still wear my ring daily. Inside of the ring Mary had it inscribed and the gold band was made to fit around my Naval Academy class ring.

The photographer took great pictures, which are still in our wedding album. Mary's father had hired a limousine to take us from the church to the Hartley Hotel for the reception. Tom Ryan spared no expense in putting on a wonderful reception, which included a sit-down dinner. This was followed by dancing, cake cutting, and toasting. I kept thinking that we should be getting away, but her father insisted that I not hurry. I realized they were thinking that it would be a long, long time before they would see Mary again. Finally, they let Mary go to the room and change into her traveling clothes. The Mount Vernon Police had assisted us in hiding my car to keep it from being decorated and this was successful. We said our many, many good-byes and headed out.

Except for telling Mary, I did not tell anyone where we were going, but I had chosen the Walt Whitman Hotel in Jamaica for our wedding night. It was not much of a hotel, but I had requested their best suite and there was to be cold champagne waiting. It had been a very long and emotional day for both of us, but with Mary moving so far from home it had to be especially emotional for her. She was very brave and only occasionally shed a wee tear for those she left behind.

We had planned to drive down the east coast to Florida and we did. The second night we stayed in a motel in Delaware and I remember how everything was a totally new adventure. We had a wonderful time on our honeymoon. In Charleston, South Carolina, we stopped and visited my former roommate, Tenny Sprague, who was still in the Navy at that time. When Tenny did retire as a commander a few years later, he decided to remain in South Carolina where he lives at this writing.

While traveling through the South, I began to develop a real affinity toward grits. I would have bacon and eggs for breakfast and instead of putting on hash brown pota- toes, they would serve grits. Now, at this stage of my life, Mary often cooks grits for me on a Sunday morning. Bless her heart!

Soon after passing Jacksonville, Florida, we turned west and drove through Pensacola. That day we were crossing a river when I noticed the sign on the bridge: SUWANNEE RIVER. I stopped on the other side and felt we should explore this river. We assumed this was the river Stephen Foster had made famous with his song. We learned that we could take horse-drawn carriage rides up and down this scenic river and a horse named Maude drew our carriage. The leisurely pace of the carriage moving along the river under the huge trees dripping with Spanish moss was most memorable. What a grand way to spend time together on our wonderful days of honeymooning. I would love to do it all over again.

We stayed at a new motel in Biloxi, Mississippi, that we were to recall a few years later. Perhaps in 1959, a hurricane came ashore in Biloxi and *Life* magazine pictures showed the aftermath that included the rubble of the Sun and Sand Motel where we spent one January night in 1952. Years later, in 1977, we returned to Biloxi. I was a state senator and serving on a national committee studying the future of satellite pictures and imaging. We found no Sun and Sand Motel, but we did find some very wonderful seafood places.

Since our wedding trip had no strict plan or schedule, we talked about possibly going to New Orleans, but decided instead to head north. Mary wanted to begin getting settled in Wyoming—our first step in that direction was Omaha.

My Uncle Scotchie Roberts had given us introductions to furniture and carpet wholesale houses in Omaha where he had accounts. We were to select our furniture to be shipped home to Gillette. I had already lined up a small one-bedroom apartment which was part of a duplex on Kendrick Avenue. Presently this is the location of the Guarantee Savings and Loan facility.

While we were in Omaha I called upon the U.S. Supply Company, a plumbing wholesale house where we did business. The president of the company, Mr. Dilly and his wife, lived at the Blackstone Hotel and invited us to dinner. We enjoyed a wonderful meal in a very elegant dining room that night.

We had perfect weather during our trip. Considering it was the latter part of January, it was phenomenal. There was no snow as we pushed our way west into Wyoming. When we arrived in Douglas, we stopped at the LaBonte Hotel for a lunch break. Mary had never been to Douglas and I felt that I should explain that there were no facilities available for the next 114 miles. I brought the matter up by suggesting, "You will probably want to visit the ladies' room before we start on to Gillette." For years after this happened, Mary would laugh as she shared that event, "We had only been married for two weeks and John was already telling me when to go to the bathroom!"

At the time of this writing there is quite a settlement at Reno Junction, including the town of Wright, but in 1952, there were no facilities other than an outhouse at Bill, Wyoming.

Mary and I lived in an upstairs bedroom at the home of my parents until our furniture arrived. We had hardly returned before receiving an invitation to a bridge party on a Saturday night. Mary had been trying to learn to play in New York because she was aware that playing bridge was the chief social activity in Gillette. But this early invitation scared her and I sensed a bit of panic as she thought about the approaching event. Of course, it all turned out well, but we did laugh about it. She can still recall trumping her partner's ace more than once, but it was all in fun.

The most humorous event happened while playing bridge at LeRoy and Ora Mankin's house. Mary was wearing a pair of eyeglasses which may have seen better days. She sneezed rather suddenly and when that happened both her lenses fell on the table in front of her—an act that almost broke up the game. Best of all, Mary could laugh about those kinds of stories as well as anyone.

The usual program for a bridge party was to arrive, visit, and draw numbers for your table and partner assignment. There was little or no alcohol. About midnight, or after playing three tables, we would break for a late snack and coffee. After refreshments, sometimes a pitch game developed among a few of the fellows, but normally everyone would say good night.

In those days, there was no television or radio station and going to a dance was the biggest social affair. Sometimes we would stop in at the Lobby Bar and Lounge for a drink and dance. Other than that, the Fiesta Theatre was the only movie house in town.

Toward the end of 1952, Mary and I bought our first house. Dr. Werntz, a dentist, had died and his widow, Harriet Werntz, decided to sell their home at 400 Rockpile Boulevard. She wanted twenty thousand for the property and also agreed to carry the balance at five percent interest. I felt we could handle it; we were expecting our first baby to arrive the following March. Our one-bedroom apartment was not going to suffice. We closed the deal and our lawyer, Earl Dunlap, drafted the paperwork.

We were very happy to move into the house on the first of October in 1952. The carpet was worn, but the house had three bedrooms and a full basement. It was built on a 75-foot frontage lot and the yard was nice. The house was heated by a coal-fired furnace, as were most homes in Gillette.

Earlier that summer, Mary's folks came to Gillette to visit and slept in the basement of our apartment on a dubious kind of bed. To make things easier and, hopefully better, I had taken the coal-burning water heater out and installed a General Electric water heater. However, a basement is still a basement and the coal-burning furnace still had a dusty coal bin that also took up part of the area. Buying the new house seemed like the most wonderful thing for us and yet I continually thought about the burden of getting it paid out. However, we did have confidence.

The previous year, in 1951, Campbell County voted a bond issue to build the badly needed Campbell County Memorial Hospital. The contract went to a Sheridan builder named Herman Bondi. We were successful in getting the subcontract for the mechanical work. This was our biggest job to date. We knew for certain we had to get capable help and expand our meager workforce.

Dean Marrington agreed to move to Gillette from Rapid City where he had an excellent reputation as a plumber and welder. Since the new hospital was utilizing radiant heat with more than a mile of black pipe to be buried under the concrete floor, we really needed someone with his capabilities. Additionally, we needed a sheet-metal man and Wayne Walters agreed to come to Gillette also. At this writing these two men are still in Gillette and I have a high regard for both men and their families. The job went well except that Herman Bondi went broke and the bonding company had to finish it. Our work was well accepted and we were paid for it.

Also during 1951, a business opportunity presented itself that we took advantage of. There were three propane dealers in Gillette, as propane was being installed more and more on many farms and ranches in the area. One of the companies was owned by George Gibson of Lusk, along with Ira Lamb of Torrington, plus a Gillette partner who also ran the business. We learned through the accountants, Cassidy and Snearly, that Gibson and Lamb wanted out. We knew our old friend, Jerry Jasper, could run a gas company, so we decided to make an offer on the company. Ostlunds were to have a third, Cassidy and Snearly were to have a third, and Jerry Jasper was to have a third. We negotiated the deal in the offices of Cassidy and Snearly who occupied space upstairs in the old Ace Hotel. This old wooden structure, since burned down, was situated at the present site of the Eagles Lodge building. We met one evening and hammered out a deal. I sat down at the typewriter and put the deal in writing with a place for all to sign. All parties were present except the Gillette partner of Gibson and Lamb. They just said, "Get it ready, we'll see that he signs." They called their man on the phone and when he arrived they told him, "Sign that paper!" And he did.

We again entered into a deal without the money to pay for it. My brother and I needed six thousand dollars to pay for our one-third. Bob and I decided that I should drive to Newcastle and talk with our Uncle George Culver. Uncle George had evidently made a lot of money in the Newcastle oil boom and was now president of his newly organized Plains Pipeline Company. With some trepidation I entered his office and told my story. Without showing negative signs of any kind, George took out his checkbook and wrote me a check for six thousand dollars and also wrote out a note for me to sign for the same amount. He said, "I'm putting in six percent interest because that is what I am paying to borrow money." It never occurred to me that George was borrowing money—in my naïveté that was another economic lesson I was learning. I appreciated his confidence, plus the fact that he stepped up to help when requested.

Years later I recalled the kindness of Uncle George and consequently did the same for a nephew of ours.

We began our business by setting up a corporation known as the Gillette Gas Company. Jasper was president and I was secretary. My first education in keeping corporate records began at this time. We rented space at the corner of the Douglas Highway and Highway 14-16, a corner now occupied by an Exxon service station. Cattails were growing in the back lot where the Sands Restaurant was later built. (Note: Since 1988 when this story was first written, there has been a significant change. In 1990 the Exxon Station and the Sands Restaurant were demolished and a new Hardees restaurant is now occupying the same ground.)

The old building that we used for an office was about the size of a small trailer, but we had plenty of room for our storage tanks. In order to swing the deal we had to sell off extra equipment, like a large tractor with a huge trailer for hauling propane that we leased back to Gibson and Lamb as part of the deal. Gibson and Lamb each had their own successful propane operations and shook their heads when they figured that they were leasing their own truck and trailer for our benefit.

Jerry Jasper did a great job running Gillette Gas Company. Later on, Cassidy and Snearly dismantled their partnership and needed to sell their interest. My brother and I bought out their third. That left Jasper with a third and my brother and I with a third each. In 1955 we approached our biggest competitor, Ted Wassenberg. We finally put a deal together to buy him out, but the financing was intricate.

If it had not been for the fact that the Stockmen's Bank brought in a new executive vice president named Howard Esmay, we would never have been able to accomplish it. I went to Howard with all the facts, including our business plan, our financing plan, and our projections on repaying the loan. At the time of closing the Wassenberg buyout, we had to simultaneously sell a good deal of excess equipment. Jasper took orders for the extra equipment and farmed it into dealers in Montana, South Dakota, Wyoming and other places.

Howard Esmay agreed to finance us and we made the deal. It all transpired like clockwork. Now we owned our own land and building and had a huge bottle business, plus several delivery trucks for supplying our bulk customer tanks. We paid off the bank at the rate of over one thousand dollars per month, which for the fifties was a lot of money. We always felt that word of this payoff leaked out of the bank and within a couple of years the Farmers' Co-op decided to go into the propane business.

By 1956 business was really good and we noticed in the trade publications that a company called Petrolane was buying more and more local outlets coming east from California. They had just bought out several local outlets in Montana. Instead of fighting them, we decided to join them. I put together what I considered to be an impressive history of our Gillette Gas Company along with our financial statements showing the huge volume of gas we were moving. We sent this off to the Petrolane President, Rudy Munzer, at their headquarters in California. We received a letter evidencing their interest that said one of their vice presidents, Harold Goerke, would call on us. This began a long series of negotiations. Petrolane had no operations in Wyoming, but they obviously wanted some and our company was of sufficient size to warrant their acquiring it. They determined that Gillette would lend itself to being piped for a gas-air installation. The terms of the deal were finally worked out and a closing date in May of 1957 was set.

Just before closing, the Farmers' Co-op announced that they were starting up their own propane business. Petrolane figured that the Co-op would drastically take a lot of our customers and the deal almost fell through. Finally, we added a price-adjuster agreement that stipulated that if our gallonage over the next twelve months fell short of our estimates, we had to return part of the purchase price. If it exceeded our estimates then they would pay us additional. We worried about this for the next twelve months and we worried more when the winter seemed unusually mild. As it turned out, our gallonage figures hit the median and neither side had to pay any excess. Petrolane purchased everything except the land and buildings. However, they agreed to a long-term lease on the property, which turned out to be very beneficial to us.

At this time I was concerned about how much federal income tax we would have to pay. I made a trip to Casper and visited the offices of Rabb, Roush, and Gamon where I worked with a CPA named Donald Tempest. I was to enjoy that association until his untimely death in an auto accident in 1969. Don Tempest saved us a lot of taxes by liquidating the corporation at the time of sale.

Never before in our lifetimes had we ever received this amount of money and it felt good. By today's standards it would not represent a lot, but to us, in 1957, it was a small fortune. Howard Esmay even bought some government bonds for us that paid three percent interest until maturity.

My brother and I wanted to utilize our money toward building a motel on part of our "airport" site. We hired a couple of Casper architects named Bence and Stein to do the design. About the time the design was moving forward, we were notified by the Highway Department not to begin any construction. They advised us they were laying out a route for Interstate 90 and it might go right through our property. With that thought our plans were placed on hold.

John working at the plumbing shop with Bob and employee.

Ostlund's plumbing shop, under the John Deere sign, was on Gillette's main street in 1950.

John up in a windmill.

John on his way to the bank.

John Deere Days at the airport property.

Mary visiting Wyoming, 1950.

John and Mary's wedding at Sacred Heart Church in Mt. Vernon, New York, January 13, 1952.

John and Mary's first home, 400 Rockpile Boulevard, Gillette, Wyoming, 1952.

Mary and her parents, Tom and Peg Ryan, visiting Yellowstone.

13

Motel and Restaurant Years

WITH OUR MOTEL PLANS ON HOLD, WE WAITED PATIENTLY FOR THE HIGHWAY Department to finish their survey. Business people in Gillette wanted the Interstate Highway to come up the south side of the railroad tracks as it presently did. This meant removing a large portion of the trees at the University of Wyoming Experimental Farm. They felt that the interchange in sight of the city was the most important aspect.

However, about that time federal coal leases were being picked up by Kerr McGee Coal and others. Wyodak Resources were probably shocked to discover that they were not the only ones interested in coal leases in this area. Wyodak had been renewing these leases for many years without any competition. The coal people wanted the Interstate to go north of town and that began a long period of controversy. By the time 1959 arrived and nothing had been concluded, we decided to look for a new site for the motel and restaurant.

The property at the corner of Douglas Highway and Highway 14-16, the original Gillette Gas Company location, seemed ideal for our purposes. This property belonged to Humble Oil Company, which later became known as Exxon. I learned that the decision makers were located in Billings, so I called and made an appointment with them. I prepared to offer them twelve thousand dollars for the partial block of land. They had no idea about the property and called for someone to bring the Gillette file. As they examined the information, they said that their only plans were to set bulk storage tanks at the rear of the property. I mentioned that we had other property which would be better suited for storage tanks and that this site would lend itself well for a much-needed restaurant in Gillette.

It took several weeks for them to prepare their papers which had to receive final approval from Houston, Texas. Just about the time I thought we had it, they received another bid from another party. Thurman Decker from Newcastle, decided this location would be good for a new Deckers Super Market in Gillette. All of a sudden Humble Oil thought they had a real good thing going. In the end we did acquire the property, but not to my liking. Humble chose to reserve the very corner for a service station and we had to take an L-shaped piece for our restaurant. I felt that we had to go ahead or we were going to be left in the dust by others. I believe we paid about twenty thousand dollars for the L-shape instead of twelve thousand dollars for the whole piece. Humble also received a fifteen-year lease from Ostlunds for a bulk plant site for which they paid fifteen dollars per month. This site was selected at the airport property in what we thought would be a site undesirable for anything else.

D. J. "Peanuts" Dalby was mayor in those days and one of the first things I did was to approach the city council with a request for a liquor license. After examining the preliminary plans I carried to the city council meeting, they conditionally agreed to give us a city license once the facility was actually in place. Across Miller Avenue was a small twenty-four hour café. This building faced north toward Highway 14-16. It would logically work for our motel addition, so we put a deal together to buy this half-block with the intention of having it available to one day build a motel there.

The first need was to get a fine restaurant in operation. The whole deal was going to exceed our ability to finance, so we looked for partners. We invited two ranchers to join us. James R. Daly and Quentin Marquiss both became shareholders and directors along with my brother and me. We set up two corporations: one to own the land and the new building, called the Northern Development Company and the other would be the operating corporation called Western Sands, Inc.

By that time the Wyoming Highway Department had determined to acquire the center of our 'airport' property to build their interchange for Interstate 90. We had gone to a lot of effort to establish the value of the property they were acquiring and the deal was made. My brother and I decided to use the funds paid by the Highway Department to finance our share of the restaurant facilities. We determined to put aside any development at the airport until later, when things were more definite there. My CPA friend, Don Tempest, again proved his worth in saving taxes on the money we received from the Highway Department. He termed the sale of the airport land and the subsequent purchase of the Humble site an "involuntary land conversion" and the remaining land at the airport had a somewhat reduced basis.

To save both time and money, we determined to utilize a steel building for the restaurant. Plan after plan was prepared attempting various layouts for the completed facility. I had been studying by reading many books available at that time on such subjects as parking lots, driveways, traffic flows, kitchen layouts, and dining room flexibility. We needed such flexibility in order to meet the needs of the community and had to be able to hold relatively large banquets (about two hundred seats). We also needed to take care of small parties while leaving a public dining room available for drop-in trade. We finally chose Pella wood-folding doors. We contracted with Bob Smithisler of the Sheridan Iron Works for a steel building that was seventy-five feet by one hundred feet. Reiman and Wuerth of Cheyenne got the contract for the footings and basement which they installed while the building was on order. Charley Johnson of Sheridan received the contract to do the finish work on the building after it had been erected by Smithiesler. Somehow it all went well.

Meanwhile, I was in Denver working with Dag Arnold, of Carsons, Inc., a restaurant supply house who was trying to properly outfit us. During a session with Carsons, I became acquainted with an interior designer named Claus Heppner. This was early in 1960 and I knew that our new facility had to have great public drawing power—it had to be different from the usual florescent lights and chrome furniture which was the norm for that particular era. Claus Heppner was working in a furniture store which belonged to Cape Coe and they took on my project with the understanding that we had to have something classy while operating on a low budget. Claus really did a fine job for the few dollars we allowed him.

Again, I worked with Howard Esmay of the Stockmen's Bank for financing. By that time we were establishing a good credit record with that bank. With little restaurant experience, I decided to meet with the Gulleys in Newcastle. They were a family operation and had a reputation for delivering a good product and running a good establishment. Don Gulley and his wife, Dorothy, showed a lot of interest in coming to Gillette. By that time Newcastle was beginning to slow down from their oil boom and it looked as though Gillette might possibly have new potential. A deal was struck with Don and Dorothy and they moved to Gillette. They had a large family, which would grow to thirteen children before they finished. They found a house to rent on Miller Avenue and they were set to begin with a new business.

We were hoping to be ready to open before the 1960 fall hunting season, but as things worked out, we opened the day after the hunting season ended. That was not what is called great timing!

Of course, there were many things we were forced to do without, but the most troublesome was the lack of paving on the parking lot. It was to prove a disaster before that was finally blacktopped. At the beginning we knew we had a drainage problem on the property and as I mentioned in another chapter, the property along Third Street was actually growing cattails.

We needed a lot of fill dirt and that was not easy to come by in the quantity we had to have. South on Miller Avenue the street finally ended about where the old Burlington ditch flowed through town, a ditch that was no longer in use, but still existed in places. I went to the city and offered to remove a good portion where it crossed some city land, if we could have the dirt. Alva Wilson took the contract to fill our new lot with dirt which he hauled down Miller Avenue from the old ditch. (The present County Recreation Center is now located in the area that the old ditch formerly occupied.) There were no paved streets in the east end of Gillette, so there was no worry about hauling big loads over the paving—there just was no paving. It was not until 1964 that Miller Avenue and the Sands parking lot finally got paved.

I met with Don Gulley almost daily. Our first menus were taking shape and the concerns over pricing were a matter of the utmost importance. I knew that our food costs had to be lower than our competition, but I also knew that we had to observe limitations on pricing. For example, coffee was selling for a nickel per cup all over town and that included a refill. We felt that we should get a dime for coffee, but our fears were that we would immediately be called the place of outrageous prices. We left coffee at a nickel. Our first breakfast menu priced two eggs, bacon, hash browns, toast, and coffee all for one dollar. Our competition was selling the same product for ninety cents, but we felt we could attract the patrons to our new place.

A few years later, when I had a food and beverage manager named Howard Clark, we actually raised the price of coffee to ten cents. One of our regular customers, a colorful guy named George Keeline, was a retired rancher and just naturally talked with a great deal of profanity. Howard was new on the job and he sat down at the counter in the coffee shop right next to George Keeline. George looked over at Howard and opened with, "I'd sure like to meet the son-of-a-bitch who raised the price of coffee!"

Howard looked at George, stuck out his right hand and said, "My name is Howard Clark and I'm the son-of-a-bitch who put coffee to a dime!" Howard was off to a good start.

My father asked me what we planned to charge for a shot of whiskey. I told him a shot would cost forty cents. He shook his head sadly and told me he had never paid more than thirty—we just would not get the business. I told him we didn't plan to get it all and we did not want the bar trade that some of the others catered to. I felt that especially during tourist season the travelers were more interested in a good place than cheap drinks. My father just knew that we were probably doomed to fail.

In the design of the restaurant we tried to think of all the negative aspects we had encountered in other facilities. One of these was the smoke-filled stuffy atmosphere you encountered when a place was crowded. Since air-conditioning was my field, we designed a heating and air-conditioning system that was divided into five separate zones. The bar and liquor store, the lounge and banquet room, the dining room, the coffee shop, and the kitchen made up the separate areas. We used the new Rheem refrigeration type air-conditioning condensers that were mounted on the roof of the building. To save precious dollars, I used the entire basement and crawl space as a return-air plenum chamber. The real key to the success of the system was the installation of new electronic air cleaners with each unit, which proved to be exceptionally good at removing smoke from the air. In fact, when these units were backwashed for cleaning, the drain water would run brown from the tars and nicotine. The public acceptance was excellent and regardless of how big a crowd we had, the air was usually always comfortable.

We had no money for carpeting and the only room with carpet was a small section of the cocktail lounge. Claus designed the tile floors with compatible colors and layouts. We soon learned that without paving and with customers tracking in mud or dust, keeping these floors polished was a heavy burden.

The last week in October of 1960 we were about finished. Claus and Cape Coe had flown Cape's single-engine Cessna airplane up from Denver for the final touches. That week we had a heavy wet snow and they slogged through muddy streets to the Triangle Motel where they were staying. Their only diversion was playing pool at night in one of the local pool halls.

One thing was for certain, the Sands Restaurant had no equal in the entire area. I have to admit there were many glances that seemed to bespeak disbelief at first. This was especially true on entering the coffee shop. There on the end of a planter Claus had mounted a statue which was about four-feet tall—like a woman in long robes carrying a sheep hook. I never did understand the connotation and the real truth was that it was probably something Claus wanted to get rid of. It did cause comment, but that was okay with me.

On the back wall of the bar were four long framed pictures that contained artificial flowers. One was labeled fall and then of course, winter, spring, and summer. For all the oil trade and traffic that came into the Sands bar, they seemed out of place. However, I kept reminding myself of my admonition to Claus, "Make it something different, very special, with modest cost!" He certainly did.

A facility this large also needed a good sound system that could page people for phone messages. I tracked down a fellow named Berdon Smith in Sheridan who designed and installed our system. It was great in that we could play taped music and radio, page, use a microphone in certain areas, and override the mike with paging if we so desired. Of course, the more features we had, the more complicated the system was to operate. The operating controls were at the hostess station at the front entrance. I can still remember wincing at banquets when the after-dinner speaker was interrupted by a telephone page. Finally, I had Berdon install another switch that was a "no page" switch when the public address was in operation in another area.

Through that winter we had many bookings for private parties. Usually they were held on Sunday afternoon with several couples hosting together. Although liquor-dispensing places had to be closed after midnight on Saturdays, hosts ordered their drink requirements before Sunday and dispensing took place at a bar which was not set in the regular dispensing area. So drinks were served, dancing was enjoyed, and usually a buffet dinner followed. This was something new in Gillette and it became very popular. However, for all of this, I was not impressed with our ability or inability to turn profits. In later years I was amazed at my own naïveté. I had so much to learn about portion control and food costs in general. In the eleven years I spent in restaurant operations, I did learn that the three rules of profit were control, control, and control—but that enlightenment and education was still yet to be acquired.

Meanwhile, we set to work on the motel plans. Henry Therkildsen of Casper, our architect, designed a two-story motel that fit the half-block of property which we already owned. There were three buildings: two contained motel units consisting of fifty-six rooms, the third was the registration facility, offices, and an upstairs meeting room. The design was unique and we felt that we had the best layout for the property. Of course there was a nice outdoor swimming pool area, which would be the first motel pool in Gillette. My brother and I drove to Casper to talk with the people at the First National Bank about financing the motel. We met with Executive Vice President Norvil Currance. After that, we met with Bob Miracle, a longtime friend of ours at the Wyoming National Bank. At that time Bob was in the Trust Department and a fellow named Rex Rafferty was executive vice president. Bob Miracle wanted us to let Wyoming National have a look at the motel deal and we did. As it turned out, Wyoming National did make the loan, so our financing was completed.

Reiman and Wuerth of Cheyenne got the contract on the motel and, of course, Ostlunds did the plumbing, heating, and air-conditioning. We were hoping that by the time the motel was completed that the street would be paved also, but the proposed improvement district was voted down. We ended up pouring concrete paving in the motel yard. The big obstacle was still that dirt and gravel street between the motel and restaurant. Without curb and gutter, that street could become a regular bog hole and it did. The following year in 1964, the improvement district was finally voted in and we did receive the long overdue paving.

Attempting to find a good manager for the new Sands Motor Lodge, I interviewed a number of applicants. The fellow we hired was named Jim. (I choose not to use his last name in case it might lead to some embarrassment for someone.) He was then manager of the Fiesta Theatre and his reputation was good and my mother mentioned that he was a good member of the Episcopal Church, which she attended. Jim was young, eager, and enthusiastic. I made a deal with Jim and he approached his new job with vigor. It was not for a few months that I began to question his ability as motel manager.

Always trying to have the best system for accounting purposes, we had purchased an NCR register system designed for motels. We ran a three-shift desk operation and Estelle Cutler, the night clerk, came on before midnight and performed what was known as the night audit. Week after week, we never had a night audit that ever balanced. Estelle Cutler would shake her head and tell me that she didn't know and Jim seemed of little help in trying to assist her in balancing the night audit. I studied the system carefully and began to go to the motel at midnight to work with Estelle at the night audit. Strange entries began to surface. It finally became evident that Jim was covering certain entries and even a few checks written from our motel operating account were questionable. When I discovered that we had paid for the diamond engagement ring that Jim gave his fiancée, I called him in and presented the factual evidence. Without hesitation Jim left immediately and I have never heard about him since that time.

Aubrey Thornton had been running the Western Motel and we had known Aubrey and his wife for many years. I called on them and offered the Sands Motel job. They took it.

It was during this time that serious competition began to form. To people on the outside, it seemed that we had a bonanza going and, of course, that made others want to do the same. A group got together that included Stan Wenkus. Stan's father-in-law had left Stan and his wife some very nice property and it was most suitable for a motel and restaurant site. The group included Frank Parks, a successful rancher, and Sonny Moore, another rancher. The promoters came up with a conception of a facility like ours, only their place was to be known as Park Manor. This was flattering to Frank Parks.

I phoned Frank Parks and asked him to visit with me one day. When he came to town I told him what I considered to be the realities of the business and how I seriously questioned the ability of Gillette to support a duplication of the same thing. He listened politely and then responded with the thought, "Well, it sure ought to beat bank interest on my money!" As it turned out, it not only didn't beat bank interest, it actually cost Frank his ranch in order to pay off their debtors.

They went ahead with Park Manor and were successful in receiving a county liquor license. The Park Manor was located on the site presently occupied by the Ramada Inn in Gillette. At that time, in 1964, they had purchased a big Quonset building which had been put there for a dry goods store and a grocery store. This Quonset steel building was remodeled into a bar, lounge, dining room, and coffee shop. I was worried. I knew that we were not making enough profits and to share this business could be disastrous. This also happened during a time when I was concerned about our entire operation. I felt that even our own plumbing, heating, appliance, and farm equipment business was lacking proper organization and controls. My brother, Bob, agreed with me. We needed to bring in outside consultants and we chose a company named the George S. May Company. We asked them to look at Ostlunds, Inc., the Sands Motor Lodge, and the Sands Restaurant. They spent a good deal of time examining all aspects of the business, but it was their final conclusions that changed the course of my life.

They urged for control systems to be put into place in everything. Their concerns over the lack of good management at the motel and restaurant were suggested to be resolved by positioning me as the overall manager, removing Aubrey Thornton, and reducing Don Gulley to food manager. Dorothy Gulley was picked to head the hostess and cashier people.

My brother and I took this very seriously. We felt that either Wayne Walters or John Hoveskelund, both top-notch men, could run the sheet metal department at Ostlunds, and we had a person who was capable of running the appliance department. We had hired a new man named Lance to head the farm machinery end of the business, so I convinced myself, and my brother agreed, that I should move to the motel and restaurant. I talked it over with my family and then determined to do it.

A lot of planning went into my decision. I did not want to take the time that would allow rumors to surface and cause employees to wonder what was happening. I left word at the restaurant for all employees to remain after closing on Saturday night, as we stopped serving liquor at midnight. Those employees who were off duty came in at midnight anyway. I had worked out my plans and brought an organizational chart with me. I explained to the employees that I was taking over as actual manager of the combined operations of both the restaurant and motel and hereafter all employees would be working within one of five departments: food department with Don Gulley as department head, liquor department with Mary's father, Tom Ryan, as department head, maintenance with Tom Davis as department head, housekeeping with Edna Davis as department head, and accounting department, which also included the desk clerks (I can't recall that department head at this time, but it was probably me). I stressed the importance of thinking of the entire operation as a single unit. I said we would work with each department head to develop a manual of policy, benefits, and procedures so that each employee would understand our operations completely. Of course, I asked for cooperation and understanding. There seemed to be some shock, but no one objected and no one quit—jobs were not that plentiful.

The following Saturday night was quite a letdown. Park Manor had brought in "live" music and they were drawing huge crowds, especially on Saturday nights. I called

Sheridan and hired Don Diers, a photographer who also had a Saturday night dance band. I was planning a big Saturday night at the Sands. I opened up the whole dining room, banquet room, and lounge and put in a raised platform for the orchestra. We put tablecloths on each table along with a lighted candle. The atmosphere was beautiful. I thought, "Isn't this magnificent for Gillette or anywhere else for that matter?"

It was like being all dressed up with nowhere to go. Only one table of four people came. Park Manor was jammed as usual and driving by there really upset me. I told myself that this would be the last time we got put down in such a way.

Returning to my restaurant office, I found a fairly recent circular from a booking agent in Hollywood named Johnny Robinson. He had a twenty-four-hour telephone, so I called him. Over the ensuing years we developed a good friendship, but during that first conversation I was very apprehensive. I told him my problem and asked about entertainment that could draw a real crowd. Of course he had just the thing for me. Donny James and the James Gang would be the answer and he could deliver them by next Saturday. I thought the price was too high, but at that time I was in no position to argue.

This meant quite a change in program because hiring Donny James meant that we would have entertainment every night except Sunday. I figured that in order to make this pay off, we had to have additional revenue as well as more customers. Rather than go to a cover charge, I decided to put an additional twenty-five cent charge on every bar drink served after the music started. I advertised on the only radio station we had, KIML. For greater media impact, I even booked them to do a live broadcast from the Sands, featuring the James Gang on opening night.

When Saturday night came I was still a little disappointed in the size of the dining crowd, but I suppose we were about half-filled. Once the James Gang began playing and the music was going out over KIML land, more and more people began to show. Before long every seat was filled and people were standing in line waiting to be seated. The James Gang made a terrific hit and from that night on the Sands Restaurant became the place to be!

We had to hire extra people and the reservations came in every night. There was hardly a complaint about the extra twenty-five-cent drink charge and that really made profits for us. I had counters on the cash registers in the bar and I had these read before the music commenced each night. That way I could better track the bar volume attributable to the music. My nighttime bartenders worked feverishly to keep up until closing and we had to hire more bartenders.

It was during this time that I was constantly putting new controls into effect. During May of 1964, I had attended a conference in Breckenridge, Colorado, for restaurant operators. The conference was put on by the Denver University School of Hotel and Restaurant Management. Ralph Wilson was the head of the school and we became good friends as the years passed.

I learned a lot about portion controls, which I decided to perfect in our own operation. I also began to understand the hundreds of ways that you could lose your profits in a liquor operation. Although some of my systems were probably tedious, we were making great profits. In fact, by 1966 we had paid off the Stockmen's Bank on their mortgage they held against the Sands Restaurant. We had been making monthly payments, but I even surprised my partners and myself by our ability to accelerate the entire loan.

Meanwhile, the competition from Park Manor dwindled. It became evident that they were not going to be able to begin a motel as previously announced and I even began to hear rumors of financial problems affecting the Park Manor. I realized they were running an operation without controls and even though they were doing business, they had no profits. One day in 1965 I called Frank Parks and asked it he would stop by for a visit when he was in town. I didn't know how this would fly, but I offered to buy the Park Manor. He showed a lot of interest until I mentioned the price—my low dollar offer left him cold. "Well," I thought, "nothing ventured, nothing gained."

It was not until the summer of 1966 when he called me back one day and asked, "Would you still be interested in giving that price for Park Manor?" He said he needed to know right away. I really had forgotten about trying to make the deal and now wondered what I would do with it if we could acquire it. Park Manor had been undergoing different management during this time, but one fact remained evident to me—their lack of good controls was killing them. If they only had good food and liquor controls, they would probably have made it. However, that holds true for every food and beverage operation ever started anywhere! No controls, no profits!

At the time we were considering buying Park Manor, a couple of other ideas were also brewing. In 1965 the Wyoming legislature had reapportioned itself. For the first time, both Campbell and Johnson Counties were to make up a single senatorial district with only one senator. With my long and fairly active interest in Republican politics, I was contemplating running for that Senate seat. Dick Greene, who had been in the Wyoming Senate from Johnson County for so many years, had already said he was not going to seek reelection. Johnson County knew that Campbell County could now outvote them, so they were interested in getting a Republican candidate whom they felt would be acceptable to them. I had made overtures in Johnson County and the political leaders seemed to agree with my candidacy. Filing time would come in July of 1966.

Meanwhile, Don Gulley had talked with me about leaving the Sands to start a drive-in business. I had interviewed food and beverage manager prospects at the University of Denver. I chose a new graduate named Ken Hall who came to work and the Gulleys left to build Big Don's Drive-In. Ken was going to work out okay, so at that time in my life I felt I had enough control of the business so that I could run for the Senate. But now, if we bought Park Manor, I knew that I should forgo the political race. We went ahead and made the deal to buy Park Manor and even though the price was quite modest, I still didn't know exactly how to utilize the facility.

Park Manor had become strictly a dinner place. The coffee shop equipment had either been sold for cash or repossessed and the operation was being handled by Gregg and Louise Williams. Gregg was a good cook, but he was losing ground due to lack of food and bar controls. I talked with Gregg and Louise because the word was already out that Frank Parks was selling to the Sands. Talking to Gregg and Louise was not easy because they seemed to hold me responsible for their state of affairs. I guess there was some truth in that.

Arrangements were made to take possession of Park Manor on a Sunday. I soon learned that the last Saturday night was quite a blowout for the Park Manor employees. But on Sunday I moved in with my people and everyone knew the job that had to be done. We inventoried the liquor and tagged each bottle. This was the perpetual inventory system I had developed at the Sands. My food people inventoried the kitchen and, in accordance with our purchase agreement, we paid additional for the inventories. I offered each employee at Park Manor a job with our organization, which was conditional upon their willingness to accept our manuals of procedure and strict control systems. I told them that Gregg and Louise would work under Ken Hall, the food department manager, and the bartenders would work under Tom Ryan as head of the liquor department. Maintenance would be under Tom Davis and everything and everybody would be fitted into our organization and welcomed there. We also had unusual fringe benefits to offer these potential new employees—we paid all of an employee's medical insurance and all of our employees received paid vacation benefits. We were among the very first in the Wyoming Hotel industry to innovate this. However, I had to wonder if many of these employees, especially bartenders, were not making more on the side than these fringe benefits could possibly offer. After all, Park Manor had done a lot of business and someone had to be making some money.

Gregg and Louise Williams were the first to go and I understood. They had been used to running things their way and probably resented our takeover. In addition, they had lost their mobile home in a small tornado that literally picked up their mobile home and dropped it over the fence. At that time their mobile home was on Park Manor property. Later they sued to collect Workmen's Compensation for Louise because she was in the trailer at the time, but the state of Wyoming would not allow it. When we went to court where the Williamses sued both the Sands and the State of Wyoming, Gregg and Louise lost the case.

Before actually acquiring Park Manor, Ken Hall and I had been studying what we could do to change it. We decided that since they had always competed with the Sands, then we would take it out of competition. To give the place a new atmosphere and a new menu, we changed the name to the "Gay Nineties." We would feature good draft beer, which was unavailable in town, plus offer terrific sandwiches and pizza. Of course, we would still offer steak and seafood. Although we still ran entertainment at the Sands, we thought we would gradually offer nightly entertainment only at the "Gay Nineties".

We closed Park Manor for about one week. We put red-checkered tablecloths on every table, bought a good pizza oven and installed draft beer taps. We also installed a large and appropriate GAY 90'S outdoor sign to draw attention. It was a success from the day we opened. We were tapping a new market by offering items otherwise unavailable to our normal trade area.

Before opening the "Gay Nineties" I also installed the same new bar system that we had put into the Sands. Each bar station had seven electronic dispensers and the liquor product flowed from the larger half-gallon size containers. We used the most popular drinks: gin, vodka, bar bourbon, bar scotch, as well as Cutty Sark, Walkers

Deluxe, and Canadian Club. We set our dispensers to issue an exact one-ounce portion, which additionally benefited our operation because the counters kept track of each time the dispenser was used. Over eighty percent of our output was dispensed in that very exact manner, at the lowest possible cost.

Additionally, we used the carbonated-dispensing handles which contained the soda, Coke, SevenUp, and others; products we made in our own system from the big containers of syrup which were remote from the bar. At the Sands, we also had dispensers in the coffee shop and dining room so that our soft drink costs were as low and convenient as possible. With all of the records and daily statistics that we accumulated, I charted important and useful management control numbers. One of these was my calculated wholesale cost per drinks served. Any variation in this monthly cost was an immediate tip off that someone was getting to us. More than one bartender was surprised when we discovered his own little system for making extra money. I don't mean to denigrate bartenders, but human nature being what it is, if you have loose controls you are actually inviting someone to participate in your profits.

About this time I began adding a second entertainment agent from Wichita Falls, Texas, named Sam Gibbs, who was really a gentleman. I remember how badly I felt for Sam when he got the news that his only son, who had become a Marine, had been killed in Vietnam. What a tragedy! Sam used to visit me in Gillette because he liked to see how his groups were working and performing. I liked this approach to business and Sam had good groups.

Some of the groups I worked with really developed a great local following. One of the most popular trios was Audie and the Forget-Me-Nots, three gals who played guitars, banjo, and drums and sang up a storm. When I booked them in for two weeks, I could do so knowing they would always play to a full house. Another great popular group was "Taller O'Shea," a Canadian quartet. Even after I sold the business, Taller O'Shea came to Gillette to visit me one time. Changing entertainment every couple of weeks for several years allowed me to know many great groups.

One entertainment experience I shall never forget occurred prior to my buying Park Manor. Business was in a real slump, which coincided with the oil business being down also. I felt that we needed to generate new enthusiasm and I was searching for new ideas. Talking with Johnny Robinson in Hollywood, he told me about places that were using dance contests as drawing cards. He said he could send a good-looking dancer to work with one of my bands and she would demonstrate the latest dances such as the Watusi, the shrug, jerk, and many others. I thought that we should at least try it and after scheduling this dancer to come we began advertising the new feature.

This gal arrived on the bus one day and we registered her into the Sands Motor Lodge. She showed me her costumes, which she planned to wear and wanted my approval. With exaggeration, I offered that most of them would fit into my shirt pocket. I made it clear to her that, although we started our music at eight o'clock, we did not consider ourselves a cabaret until ten. By that time dining was over and no one under twenty-one was allowed into the dining room. Until ten o'clock, I admonished her to wear a proper gown while singing with the band.

She opened on a Friday night, which was usual, but on this particular Friday night, with a hometown basketball game, the Sands was crowded with people going to or coming from the game. We were so jammed that I was even working the cash register at the hostess station. The band was playing in the dining room and the girl was singing. Then I heard the band begin playing a rock number and this was followed by a lot of clapping and cheering. I stepped over to peer into the dining room and there the dancer had dropped her gown and proceeded to demonstrate dance steps in her brief costume. Since we still had families present, I was chagrined, but determined not to make more of a scene at the moment. They were due to break in less than five minutes. At break time I scolded her for failing to follow my explicit instructions. She told me how sorry she was for misunderstanding and promised she would not make that mistake again.

All went well until close to midnight. A lot of people were watching the dancing and we had awarded small prizes to couples we chose as winners. Around midnight she performed a solo dance, when all of a sudden she dropped what little clothing she was wearing. Here I discovered I had a stripper on my hands. The cheering was wild. I thought I had an outbreak of pandemonium. I was burning. Later she told me that a lot of people had been asking her to do this and she only wanted to improve my business. I told her to either follow orders or take the next bus out of town! She agreed in a way that was becoming her anticipated response.

The next day the phone rang constantly. People called for reservations wanting to know if the stripper was still on for tonight. I asked my hostesses to inform the callers that although there was no stripper or no stripping, we would take their reservation for dinner or dancing or both. Good music was what we had, but no stripper! We sold out anyway.

It was a Saturday night and at that time we still had to close at midnight. People came to me during the evening and asked if I was going to allow the stripper to perform. Even the sheriff and his wife had a dinner reservation—people who only seldom dined out were there that night. I gave an emphatic "No", to all questions about whether she was going to strip. About eleven forty-five that evening I felt we had gotten through another Saturday night when the cheering started again. My dancer had been wearing plenty of clothes, but during a dance she reached back and dropped her clothes and of course she had nothing else on. I went straight to the phone, called Johnny Robinson for the second time, and told him she would be on the bus to California the next day.

Well, the next day she would not open her motel room. The whole day went by and she would not come to the phone or unlock her door. I began to worry and with a policeman, I opened her door with an emergency key. She seemed to be breathing, but also seemed to be out cold. I felt she was faking. I called Dr. Jerry Hannum and he arrived shortly. He thought we should admit her to the hospital and he phoned for an ambulance. No sooner than she was checked to the hospital, she slipped out and disappeared. Park Manor heard that I had fired her, so they tried to hire her, but at the moment no one could find her. By telephoning Johnnie Robinson I learned later that she had called him and he demanded she board a bus for California immediately. When I was certain she was out of town I was greatly relieved.

The whole incident left me embarrassed. Many of my customers congratulated me for really opening up the entertainment in Gillette, but I surprised them when I said it was not only unintentional, but I would endeavor to never again have that happen at the Sands. My reputation as a good operator and as a good husband and family man were definitely on the line and I knew that only time could heal the bruises. In retrospect, I also wonder if part of my embarrassment was due to the fact that, for the first time, I had momentarily lost control of my own operations.

Keeping control of operations in those days required a lot of planning. We had established a simple code of conduct for our patrons to not only understand, but also to strictly follow. Our bar patrons understood, by example, that if anyone started a fight in or on our premises, I would file disorderly conduct and breach of the peace charges against them. I never made an exception. I even barred some customers from ever using our facilities. One man used to call me on special occasions, like his wife's birthday, and plead to be allowed to have dinner in our dining room. I used to say, "Sorry, Charlie, but you sorely violated our rules. Never again!"

During the sixties, with the population of Gillette beginning to expand with oil exploration, we could have chosen to soft-pedal disorderly customers and if we had decided to operate this way, we would never have regained control. As it was, I was put to the test on many occasions. It is a wonder I didn't get my block knocked off, but I never did. In fact, I truly believe that a lot of the so-called tough guys developed a respect for the fair way everyone was treated in accordance with our established rules. We would not even allow men to wear hats in our dining room.

In 1966 we had the opportunity to buy a one hundred-foot lot adjacent to Third Street and facing Miller Avenue. I had also been trying to buy the front footage facing the Douglas Highway between Third and Fourth Streets. These lands were across the street, south from the Sands Restaurant. I wanted very badly to add more rooms to the Sands Motor Lodge. We just didn't have enough rooms and the additional overhead caused by adding more rooms would be minimal. By this time our stockholder and director, Quentin Marquiss, had been killed in an unfortunate plane crash at the Buffalo Ranch. His wife, Opal "Toots" Marquiss, took his place and was an excellent board member. The board agreed with my suggestion for additional units, so Henry Thirkildsen again drew plans for a twenty-unit annex. These rooms were planned to answer the need for a room for no more than two people. I put all queen-sized beds in this annex and built the beds solid to the floor. The carpet we saved by not having to put carpet under the bed was utilized to cover the luggage rack built onto the wall. There was no freestanding furniture other than the chairs and a single game table. Access to these rooms were from an inside corridor instead of directly from the outside and these rooms became popular with our steady customers.

When we first opened the Sands Motor Lodge in 1963, the most commonly asked question was, "What will be your commercial rate?"

We pondered that one for quite a while. The highest commercial rate at that time was six dollars and the lowest was about two dollars. I felt that we had to receive at least eight dollars to make things work. When you considered giving that rate the year-round, even at the expense of turning away tourist business, you knew you needed to make it high enough. We had many who said they just could not spend eight dollars. This was especially true with State employees. As it turned out, we did charge eight dollars and that held for a few years before we raised another fifty cents.

One of the biggest problems in facilities such as ours could have been the maintenance. About the time we began building the motel, we had problems keeping good maintenance people at the restaurant. While working on plumbing and heating contracts at the Moorcroft school system, my brother observed that their maintenance was exceptional. They had a fellow named Tom Davis who had worked for the school for a long time and his wife, Edna, also worked with him. I talked with Tom and Edna about coming to Gillette and offered Edna the job as head housekeeper at the new motel, with Tom heading the maintenance department for both the motel and restaurant. They finally agreed to make the change and it was most fortunate for us to acquire such capable and dedicated people. They had one son and one daughter when they moved to Gillette in 1963 and were still living there when we sold the business in 1971. Tom Davis loved to raise English bulldogs and he had some dandies.

In the plumbing and machinery business most transactions were handled by check, therefore I never realized how much cash went through a restaurant and lounge facility because it was mostly cash. Banks were closed on Saturday, Sunday, and holidays, so it took a great deal of planning to always have sufficient cash. In addition, there was a security problem. During the first year of the Sands Restaurant operation, Don Gulley said he needed a safe. Jim Daly said his father had a big safe that was not being used, so we moved it to the restaurant. There was no good place for it and it finally resided in the kitchen. It was huge and stood almost six-feet high; it certainly seemed secure, but soon proved to be no problem for professional safecrackers. Early one Monday morning when the first cook arrived for work, he found the safe peeled and everything missing. The next safe we purchased was a two-door, two-compartment safe, with the top portion supposedly both torchproof as well as burglarproof. A few years later when our next break-in occurred, they successfully opened the bottom, but the top proved to be impervious. So I later bought three additional safes like the unopened one.

However, after running entertainment our daily cash intake was huge and we had to have certain amounts of cash available for opening the next day—the restaurant opened at six in the morning, the bar and liquor store opened at eight. I arranged a program with the Stockmen's Bank wherein we could drop our cash bags in their night depository every night. But upon closing, there were seven separate bags of cash each day for both the Gay Nineties and the motel. I hated to drive to the bank at two-thirty in the morning with all that cash, so to avoid danger, I arranged for the police department to escort us. At closing time each evening we called the police. Not until they arrived would we carry the cash bags to the car and then pick up the other money bags at the various locations. We performed this ritual every night without fail.

The following business day, the bank opened our bags, deposited our cash, and made new bags with the proper amounts of wrapped coins and bills. This was a tremendous service and the fact that the Stockmen's Bank did this was not only unique, but very much appreciated by us. My thanks always will go to Kenneth Naramore, the president of the Stockmen's Bank, for this great service. On those weekends with a Monday holiday following, it took a whole suitcase full of cash bags from the bank to each proper safe and it is a wonder we were not held up just returning those bags in daylight to their proper place.

It was our good fortune to have the twenty-room Sands Motor Lodge annex built in 1967. In the fall of that year Jeff Hawks, one of my favorite oil men, was drilling a wildcat well about ten miles west of Gillette. In the muddy formation that well came in with such pressure that they experienced a blowout. Oil and gas blew up through the drilling rig and attempts were made to control it. Unfortunately, a spark caused the well to catch fire, resulting in an immediate meltdown of the rig. Jeff Hawks called Red Adair in Texas to come and get the well under control. That well fire caused more excitement than anything that had ever occurred in Gillette.

I received a call from Universal Studios in Hollywood asking for room reservations for picture crews. They were just getting to work on a movie with John Wayne called *Hellfighters* and they needed authentic footage of an uncontrolled well fire. Not only did Universal move in, but so did Red Adair along with his men named Boots and Coots. They cut quite a swath in their fire red coveralls. Universal Pictures not only needed rooms, but they also needed lunches sent out with them each day. Business had never been so good—our motel was filled and, I would venture to say, that except for Christmas there were few days for the next couple of years when we had any vacancies.

The Jeff Hawks well fire was finally extinguished and that was the beginning of the Kitty Field. The Recluse Fields came in next and that was followed by the Bell Creek fields just north of the Wyoming-Montana line.

During this time our facilities were the principal place for most everyone to head-quarter and also the Gay Nineties gave us an extra advantage. In 1968 I proposed that we build a second motel at the Gay Nineties location. We had acquired plenty of prop-erty when we bought Park Manor and there was a need now. This time we hired a Denver architect named Richard DeGette. He developed plans for an eighty-unit fa-cility we named the Thunder Basin Inn and also aligned it with Best Western. Once again the builders of this facility were Reiman/Wuerth, with mechanical contracting done by the Ostlunds.

This time I wanted an in-house laundry. I fully realized the advantages that could accrue with our own laundry facility. Imagine doing all the linens for both restaurants as well as both motels! Thanks to Edna Davis, this worked very well for us and added a good deal to our bottom line.

We had already acquired the highway frontage along the Douglas Highway between Third and Fourth Streets and I wanted to improve the appearance of the area as people approached the Sands Restaurant from the south. Although the property was a full-block in length, it was only about thirty-five-feet deep between the highway and the alley. I thought it would work well for a couple of small office buildings with ample parking for each building. We built the first office building at 302 Douglas Highway in 1968 with Kirk Coulter as the contractor. I arranged the north side of the building to house the Sands Corporation offices and leased the south half of the building to Sinclair Oil Company. It worked out so well we built the second one at 304 Douglas Highway the following year. Reiman Wuerth constructed that one while they were working on the Thunder Basin Inn. Jerry Dines of Casper was the architect. Bob Hays and Sam Ratcliff rented the south half of the second building, while McCullough Gas rented the north half. At the time of this writing (1990), McCullough is still at the same location under the name MGIC.

In 1968 when we moved the Sands Corporation offices to their new quarters; we really felt as though we had come of age. We also purchased the best NCR accounting machine available at that time. It was huge and of course we thought it was the most remarkable and sophisticated machine ever built. When you entered a ledger card, the machine picked up the balances off the magnetic stripe on the card. When doing payroll, the machine gathered all the information except for hours, computed the check and then printed it. Today's computers would put it to shame, but in 1968 it was the latest equipment available.

It was during this time that I felt our organization could benefit by having our own in-house CPA. With the approval of my board of directors, I hired Jerry Record who brought new professionalism to our organization.

When I first left Ostlunds, Inc. to take over the Sands operations in 1964, I had no business vehicle. I had always driven a pickup while at Ostlunds. I bought what I thought I could afford. I paid one hundred dollars for an old blue Ford station wagon. I took a bit of ribbing during the time I drove that car. One day a guy said to me, "You really ought to drive a better car, especially a man in your position." I told him the one benefit of driving that car was that it was paid for!

As conditions improved, I finally decided it was time to drive a new car. I bought my first Cadillac from Cliff Davis. My brother and I had agreed that Ostlund Investments should be buying and depreciating our vehicles. For the next fourteen years we traded every year. Bob's favorite vehicle was a Lincoln Mark Series.

In 1961, about the time the local oil business first began to develop, we started getting inquiries about the availability of land at our airport. The first serious request we received was from an oil-field supply company called Mountain Iron & Supply who needed a yard which they felt should be about two hundred-feet wide and four hundred-feet in length. We measured a plot and fenced it for them and also built a wooden frame single-story building for their store. They also wanted a couple of mobile home hookups for their personnel. Bob Drieling and Jim LaOrange were the first employees who came to work for Mountain Iron—the beginning of a long relationship with that company that lasted for about twenty years when they were finally forced into bankruptcy. Over a period of time, we developed a good deal of rental property there which was to provide good income. Of course, with the advent of the Interstate 90 interchange, several oil companies talked with us about acquiring a location. At that time, my brother and I dealt with Texaco about interstate service stations and we ended up building, owning, and leasing a total of five different locations to Texaco in Buffalo, Gillette,

Sturgis, and Rapid City, South Dakota, as well as acquiring a site in Douglas, which we were to later sell.

Perhaps in another chapter I might relate the period of time that led to our decision to sell the Sands Corporation. As I write these lines, I tend to forget or perhaps neglect to write many of the humorous situations that happened in the motel and restaurant business. I hope we can find the opportunity to recall some of those incidents. I would not want my grandchildren to think I never had any fun!

The Sands restaurant dining room. *Wyoming Division of Cultural Resources*

Sands Motor Lodge.

Park Manor. *Wyoming Division of Cultural Resources*

Gillette's new night spot, the Gay 90s.

Family picture—Front row, left to right: Patrick, Karin, John, Mary with Scott, and Jane. Back row, left to right: Tom, Peg, John, Jr., and Nancy, 1964.

14

Political Pauses

YEARS AGO, WHEN VISITING MY GRANDFATHER'S HOUSE IN NEWCASTLE, Wyoming, I remember admiring his picture as a member of the 16th Wyoming legislature in 1921. This was when I was probably six years old. I was not even certain about what the legislature was, but I knew it must be a very important position. I was always proud of Grandfather Matthew Chapman Roberts.

I also have recollections of my own parents going off to political rallies in Campbell County in the early 1930s. My dad had served as chairman of the Campbell County Republican organization for a few years in the late 1920s. In the early 1930s he was running for State Representative. He tried twice to win that post, but he was never successful. From that background, I seemed to have inherited some interest in the political process.

A classmate of mine was Jack Nicholas. We were not only good friends, but our mothers were also close friends. Jack's father was Thomas A. Nicholas, an attorney. I was impressed when Jack's father ran for governor on the Republican ticket in 1938. Unfortunately, his opponent, Nels Smith, won the primary and then went on to become governor. However, I do remember admiring his dad for that effort.

Jack and his wife, Alice, now reside in Lander where Jack was at one time a District Judge. His interests are varied and include ranching. We get to visit with them from time to time in Cheyenne.

When I returned from the Navy in 1950, I already had plenty to think about, and politics was not on my agenda. Then one day an attorney friend of ours, John Ilsley, stopped by to chat. His conversation led around to the coming meeting of the Campbell County Republican Central Committee. John told me there was a lot of dissension among Campbell County Republicans and he thought it would take a new person to get Campbell County Republicans working together again. Since I had only recently returned to Gillette from the Navy, Ilsley reasoned that I should run for chairman at the county Republican election to be held the following week. Of course Ilsley felt I would probably be acceptable to both factions.

Without giving it much thought, I agreed to be nominated for the office and could probably even say that I won, but it was only because no one else wanted the job.

In those days some of the Republican stalwarts included John and Helen Ilsley, Bill and Hazel Norman, Eric and Thelma Ohman, George and Mary Heald, Harris and Josephine Swartz, U. S. "Staley" Archibald, William Taylor, Charlie Miller, Alice Spielman, Jess and Patty Jessen, and Lynn Tarver, to mention just a few who easily come to mind.

We always met in the courtroom of the old courthouse, an old building that sat on the corner of Gillette Avenue and Fifth Street. In earlier days it was known as the Daly residence, but it had been converted to a courthouse. A brick and concrete addition on the rear of the wooden building provided for the necessary jail. The courtroom was on the second story just above the jailhouse. Now, at this writing, 1990, the present court-house not only covers the original site, but Fifth Street was also closed to accommodate the newest courthouse. My parents lived across the alley from the old courthouse at the corner of Fifth Street and Warren Avenue.

Of course, I approached the chairmanship with vigor and enthusiasm. Our Executive Committee met to give guidance more frequently than the regular meetings of the Central Committee, which did not meet very often.

The first big job came in 1952 at the state convention. That year the convention was being held in Casper and the Henning Hotel was the headquarters. In those days the Henning was on one corner, the old Gladstone Hotel on the opposite corner, and the Townsend Hotel across the street from the Gladstone. Those three big hotels were where everyone met everyone else.

Our county convention had named the county delegates to the state convention and as county chairman, I headed the delegation. I remember old Bill Taylor came to me asking that I back him as a Wyoming delegate to the National Convention. He said he had never had that privilege and at his age he felt this might be his last opportunity. It was then that I learned that Campbell, Johnson, and Sheridan Counties alternated that delegate selection every four years, and this was the year for Johnson County to name the delegate. Bill Taylor was very disappointed, and although he could have had an alternate appointment, he turned that down. The Republican National Convention nominated Dwight Eisenhower to become President in 1952. The Eisenhower years were good ones. The period from 1952 through 1960 was productive— no inflation and relatively small amounts of world tension. The United States had all of the military power and the rest of the world was trying to recover from the devastation of World War II.

I held the job of county chairman for about eight or ten years. When I turned down another term, Dr. Frank Hadley, an optometrist, was elected. I then became the Republican state committeeman, a job I held for about another eight or ten years. During that time I enjoyed meeting many other stalwart Wyoming Republicans through the state conventions and other political meetings.

My first acquaintance with a person who was actually holding office was Frank A. Barrett. As a congressman in 1944, Frank appointed me to the Naval Academy. Later he became governor and then United States Senator from Wyoming. He was always the advocate for the western states to receive a higher amount of the federal mineral royalties. It was through his efforts that the Alaska Statehood Charter allows that state to receive ninety percent of their own royalties. If Frank Barrett could have remained a U.S. Senator, he would have worked to accomplish the same thing for the rest of our western states. His sons, Frank Jr. and James, plus his daughter, Marialyce Tobin, made their own fine contributions to this State of Wyoming.

Another most impressive political person was Stanley K. Hathaway, who was elected governor in 1966 at what I would term a critical time for Wyoming. Few people seemed to be aware that we were on the verge of enormous mineral development. In 1967 the revenues of the State were pitifully low and the State General Fund was very lean. Hathaway proposed a mineral severance tax of one percent, which failed in the House. However in 1969, he not only again proposed the same tax, but this time, through his persuasion, it was indeed successful.

Following that legislation, the permanent mineral trust fund was established in 1974 by constitutional amendment, an amendment that Wyoming people should have been grateful for. But without the foresight and ability of Stan Hathaway, it is difficult to guess if that would ever have happened. That accomplishment alone should place Stan Hathaway in a most prominent position in Wyoming history!

Books could be written of other strong Republican men and women who deserve having their accomplishments added to our historical libraries and happily this has occurred to several. However, I do choose to mention some who come to mind and I dare to do this even though I fear committing the serious sin of omission.

Some of these include names such as Jim and Carolyn Griffith, Ed and Eleanor Witzenburger, Harry and Inga Thorsen, Stan and Bobby Hathaway, John and Jane Wold, Milward and Lorna Simpson, Estelle Stacey Carrier, Keith and Thyra Thomson, Cliff and Martha Hansen, Harry and Toni Roberts, Harold and Peggy Helbaum, Bob and Barbara Gossman, Jeral and Marjorie Rainwater, Tom and Marta Strook, Dick and Estes Jones, Stan and Harriet Smith, Malcolm Wallop, Alan and Ann Simpson, Dick and Lynn Cheney, and Warren and Kathy Morton, to randomly mention a few.

After selling the Sands Corporation in 1971, I wanted to run for the State Senate. Neal Stafford had been the single senator from the Campbell-Johnson District since the 1966 election and was running again. With two positions now open, not only did I file for one of the two seats, but also R. A. "Dick" Mader filed as well. It was a tight primary race. Since I was not well-known in Johnson County, I chose to do a lot of campaigning there. I met a lot of great people in Buffalo who agreed to help me. Probably my best supporter and friend turned out to be the Catholic priest named Father James Ruddy. His support brought me a lot of votes in that area. George Knepper, Bob and Jane Ferrill, Leon and Lee Keith, Jim and Mary Hicks, Bob and Marie McBride, Simon and Dolly Iberlin, and Emerson Scott were just a few of my great Johnson County friends who helped me win the campaign.

In Buffalo I campaigned door-to-door. My wife, Mary, and our daughter, Peg, helped me. I appeared at public gatherings in both counties and learned that campaigning was hard, tedious work.

Neal Stafford and I won with Dick Mader coming in third. With such strong Republican registration in both counties, we did not feel that the general election held any problems for us and it did not. I was happy to know that when the forty-second legislature convened in January of 1973, I would be taking my seat in the Senate. That would be just fifty-two years after my grandfather, M. C. Roberts, had served his legislative term.

Now let me take you, the reader, back to the legislative session of 1967, when I had been working the legislature as a lobbyist. Late in 1966, after Stan Hathaway was elected governor for the first time, I received a call from my dear friend, Harry P. Smith. Harry and his wife Mildred owned the Hitching Post facilities in Cheyenne. Since we both were in the same business and served together on the Colorado-Wyoming Hotel and Restaurant Board of Directors, we were really good friends. We also respected each other for running good operations. This particular day Harry was on the phone.

"John," Harry opened, "I think we ought to get together and try to get the legislature to open the bars on Sunday!"

"Harry, why don't you ask me to jump over the moon? That might be easier," I responded.

"I hear the new governor will be trying to raise more taxes off beer and liquor and instead of doing that he ought to let us sell more product, especially to the tourists," Harry added in his usual sensible and reasonable manner.

"Harry, you have always been willing to help me when I asked you. Although I don't know how to begin on this effort, I will be glad to help," I added.

Harry had been giving this matter a lot of thought and I was not surprised when he suggested that the first thing we do was meet with the new governor. Harry figured that if we were successful we would not want the governor to then veto the bill. Harry set up a meeting in Cheyenne with the new Governor Stan Hathaway and I drove to Cheyenne for the meeting.

In the meantime, I began working on a strategy to convince both the legislature and myself that this could be beneficial for both the State of Wyoming and the economy. Harry's thought about selling beer and liquor to tourists made a lot of sense to me. In those days in Wyoming, all retail liquor establishments had to close at midnight on Saturday night and not reopen until Monday. However, the private clubs were exempt from this law. Clubs such as the Legion, the VFW, the Elks, the Eagles, and the Moose were allowed to remain open until 2:00 A.M. every night including Sunday. It seemed reasonable and, hopefully, convincing that only the tourists were denied the opportunity to purchase beer and liquor on Sunday.

Operating on that premise, but not knowing where it might lead, I posted a large map of the State of Wyoming. From the Wyoming Liquor Commission I received the data on how many licenses were in each county and also the total dollar amount of liquor purchases made from the State in each county. From other sources I then obtained the data on how many motel and hotel units were in each county. That information began to present a totally new and untold story about the liquor business in Wyoming.

There was a direct relationship between the amount of liquor purchased from the

Commission and the number of motel units in each county and not necessarily proportional to the actual resident population. The conclusions to be drawn were that Wyoming citizens were being well served by their liquor outlets, but the majority of the Wyoming liquor business was directly related to tourism. And rather than up the taxes on Wyoming citizens who consumed alcohol, we should give the tourists a chance to buy on Sunday; the same opportunity that the locals were already receiving in their private clubs. To me, this was factual and should not be ignored.

Stan Hathaway later told me he was really puzzled when he learned that Harry Smith and I had made an appointment. He could not imagine what we wanted. When we proposed to Stan that he hold off on increasing taxes on liquor and give us a chance to open the bars on Sunday, he was surprised. At that time, he probably had little confidence we could do it, but he did agree that if the bill was passed, he certainly would not veto it.

Since most all of the legislators stayed at the Hitching Post, it was easy for Harry Smith to organize a small luncheon to be held in one of the meeting rooms for a few House members. I recall that the Speaker of the House, Ward Meyers, Ed Sensabaugh and Newell Sargent were three of the six or eight fellows he collected that day. Since they were always in a hurry, I told them that I would make my presentation while they were eating. I put up my map of Wyoming and showed them how the sales of liquor were directly proportional to the number of motel units in each county. I explained to them that for Wyoming to benefit from the tourist industry, we should allow limited sales on Sunday. By limited, we were only suggesting opening from ten in the morning until ten at night.

The group listened intently and to my gratification they were impressed. I was surprised when Ward Meyers suggested that I give the same presentation to the entire House of Representatives. Someone then reminded them that only House members could speak from the floor while the House was in session. Ward Meyers said, "I think the House of Representatives should hear this presentation and I will adjourn the House early on Thursday and then ask that everyone remain in their seats to hear from a Wyoming businessman." And he did!

On the appointed day I was a bit nervous about what was going to transpire. Ward Meyers gave me a nice introduction with a statement that he felt the Wyoming legislature should hear what I, a businessman, had to say. I remember Campbell County Representative Cliff Davis looked surprised as I went to the podium to use the loudspeaker. I also recall Representative Nels Smith pausing in the balcony to listen. I gave them the story and they listened with obvious interest. Harry and I had not endeavored to get the liquor dealers behind us, but we had informed their lobby, headed by Al Risha, about what was going to happen that afternoon. There were crowds in the gallery. This new and evidently refreshing story received attention and a few House members volunteered to sponsor a bill.

The bill was introduced in the House and from that time on there was constant lobbying to get it through. Being a neophyte in legislative process, I thought my job was completed when the bill finally passed the House on third and final reading. Imagine my surprise when I found that the same long procedure had to take place again in the Senate. I had already spent a great deal of time away from my family and our business. But it passed the Senate and became law in 1967.

During the legislative session of 1969, to my surprise, Governor Stan Hathaway called me and asked me if I would take an appointment to the Board of Trustees at the University of Wyoming. I well remember his words. "There are always a lot of people wanting to be appointed and I get all kinds of suggestions on who to appoint, but I want you to take this appointment because I want a businessman who knows how to get things done."

I told Stan that I was honored to be asked, but I also reminded him that I had never sought such an appointment. He told me that he knew all that, but he still asked me to take it and, of course, I did.

Besides me, Stan made three other appointments to the University Board that year. Al Pence, an attorney from Laramie, Bob McBride, a banker from Buffalo and Win Hickey, a former First Lady of Wyoming. Win's husband was Joe J. Hickey, a Federal Judge, and a former governor and United States Senator as well. I made great and lasting friendships while serving on that board. At this writing (now editing in 1992), many former board member friends are now deceased, including Al Pence of Laramie, Eph Johnson of Rawlins, Gordon Brodrick of Powell, and Paul Hines of Lander.

Bill Carlson was University President and my good friend, Elliot Hays, was Vice President for Finance. Besides the four new members mentioned above, Jerry Hollon from Lusk, Dave True from Casper, Joe Sullivan from Douglas, Bill Jones from Wheatland, Gordon Broderick from Powell, Eph Johnson from Rawlins, Cris Bunning, who replaced Eph Johnson, Patrick Quealy from Kemmerer, and Paul Hines from Lander made up the balance of the Board. Of course, Harry Roberts as Superintendent of Public Instruction and Stan Hathaway as Governor were ex officio members. I used to spend several days each month in Laramie and I thought I surely must have memorized the highway between Gillette and the University.

The period of 1969 through 1972, my term of service, was one of campus unrest due to the ongoing Vietnam War. Although Wyoming had few incidents, there were some. The infamous "Black Fourteen" and the "Flag Pole" incidents were two that easily come to mind.

The so-called Black Fourteen incident happened during my tenure. Lloyd Eaton was a successful and popular Wyoming football coach. Several days before Wyoming was scheduled to play BYU in Laramie, the incident took place. Some of the Wyoming team members, who happened to be black, decided to wear black armbands during the game as a protest against BYU religious practices which they found offensive.

Lloyd Eaton made it plain to the team members that he would not tolerate such protests and no player on the Wyoming Cowboy team would wear anything other than his regular football uniform during the game. When the blacks protested, he finally removed them from the football team and the game was played without them.

Only recently I had an opportunity to ask former Attorney General Jim Barrett about the details of the court case. This was instigated by the lawyers for the Black

Fourteen and it was scheduled before Federal Judge Ewing Kerr, who was trying to resolve the matter so the fourteen could play in the game. Professional scouts were going to be present and all the players who hoped to be picked for an NFL team certainly wanted to show their skills.

However, the lead attorney for the Black Fourteen, a fellow imported from Michigan, would not allow his clients to meet individually with Judge Kerr and Coach Eaton and he also did not inform any of the Fourteen of that fact. That was the bad deal the fourteen players ended up with and it could have been so easily resolved!

The incident received immediate national attention and strong protests were raised, both pro and con, at the University and in the media. We, as a board, supported Lloyd Eaton. However, the incident proved to be more than Lloyd Eaton wanted to take, later he resigned his position as football coach and Wyoming began a downhill slide in football that lasted for a few years.

These were the Vietnam years of protest and nothing was too sacred to prevent ridicule from somewhere during that unfortunate era.

During my tenure as a trustee, the most prominent new construction to be added was the Fine Arts Center. Also, the first expansion to the football stadium took place, including the press box and a new pharmacy building was also constructed. However, expanding the University facilities is an ongoing and never-ending project as it should be.

In 1970 the University Board decided to tour the University of Wyoming Experimental Farms. There were several located within the state. Many felt that the Trustees needed to update their own selves about the relevance of the research being conducted at these sites. The Trustees also had to be able to talk with legislators who may be inquiring as to whether or not the State of Wyoming was receiving benefits to match the expenditures.

Gillette had a large farm just east of the city. I arranged for the Board to meet in Gillette and stay overnight during their tour. I was anxious to show off our good hospitality at the new Thunder Basin Inn. Additionally, we had overhauled the old coffee shop area at the Gay Nineties into an elegant new room called the Wine Room. It was the finest small dining room in Wyoming at that time. I write this with a smile—I hope the reader certainly understands my personal bias by now.

The Board of Trustees had a great time at our facilities. Enjoying the festivities of the Gay Nineties, we all remained far too late that night for our own good. But then, it was indeed fun!

When I was elected to the State Senate in 1972, I chose to resign my Trustee position at the University. I had served four years of a six-year appointment. The two positions were incompatible and I did not ask for an opinion from the Attorney General; I knew it would be bad form. Governor Hathaway appointed Dr. Vernon Thorpe from Newcastle to fill my unexpired term.

Stan Hathaway easily won a second term as governor in the 1970 elections. Sadly, during that time Joe J. Hickey died and my good friend, Win Hickey, was widowed. Mary and I had become such good friends with both Joe and Win, as well as with their two sons, John and Paul. She and her fine family remain wonderful friends to this day.

In 1973, the President of the Senate was Dick Tobin from Casper. Dick was a remarkable gentleman and a true friend of mine. He probably had more friends than anyone in Wyoming, for that matter. Dick asked me to serve on the Judiciary Committee as well as on Mines, Minerals, and Industrial Development, my real choice. Just after the session began, the United States Supreme Court declared our statutes banning abortion remembered as the Roe versus Wade decision to be unconstitutional. Many in Wyoming wanted the legislature to pass new abortion laws which would meet the criteria that the federal court had established. Dick Tobin had a bill drawn and asked me to carry that legislation in the Senate. Although the arguments were heated and emotional, the new laws were passed defining the three trimesters of the pregnancy. At that time the federal court would only permit abortions during the first trimester, as I remember it.

From that work in the Senate that year, Bishop Hubert Newell unexpectedly expressed his appreciation and gave me a beautiful statue of the Madonna which I have always treasured. Bishop Newell always remained a close and very dear friend until his death. He also was admired and respected by everyone whoever had the opportunity to meet him.

During the summer of 1973, I received a surprise phone call from Dick Tobin. "John, I want you to go to Chicago with me!"

In his own humorous style, he finally told me about a meeting of the National Conference of State Governments in Chicago and he thought we should go. I will add here for those who did not know Dick Tobin, that he suffered from spinal problems which left him unable to bend. He used crutches, but he could not even bend to put on shoes or socks. He was magnificent in his efforts to overcome his handicap, but there were still limits. I was glad when he asked me to go with him.

We had a great time together. We worked hard all week and then Dick surprised me on Friday with two baseball tickets which he received from Jack Rosenthal for a Chicago Cubs game. We went to Wrigley Field and I cannot remember who their opposition was that day. During the seventh-inning stretch we went to the hot dog stand and imagine the coincidence of running into Ed Herschler. Of course we did enjoy our beer and hot dogs which always taste better at a ball game!

We attended an evening reception given by Mayor Richard J. Daly and other Chicago officials. One of the highlights of the week was watching the incredible Austrian Lipizzaner white stallions perform. Years later, Mary and I were to watch the Lipizzaners work out at their home in Vienna.

Something else happened at one of our work sessions that I was also to remember. Representative Gerald Ford, who was Republican minority floor leader of the House of Representatives, came and spoke at one of our workshops. I had an opportunity to visit with him after the workshop. A few years later Mary and I were to be guests of then President Ford at the White House. We certainly never know what surprises the future might hold for us.

Also in 1973, Governor Hathaway asked me to represent the State of Wyoming with the Industry Task Force which met about every six weeks in anticipation of opening the Powder River Basin for coal. I gained a good deal of insight into the problems as perceived by industry and their approach to solutions. In turn, they were receptive to my own suggestions as well.

In December of 1973, Dick Tobin had to undergo bypass surgery. He immediately resigned from the Senate since he would be unable to attend the budget session which was due to begin in January. We all felt badly about Dick, but fortunately his surgery was successful. It was not until 1986, that Dick Tobin passed away. He left a huge host of wonderful friends who were blessed to know him. Mary and I remain fortunate to have both Dick's widow, Marialyce, and also his sister, Peg Tobin, as our very good friends.

At the General Election in 1972, a Constitutional Amendment was approved allowing the legislature to meet on even numbered years as a budget session, limited to a twenty-day session. The very first of these budget sessions occurred in 1974 and during that session the legislature appointed a Select Committee to study Industrial Development Impact. Both Neal Stafford and I were on that committee since the Powder River Basin would bear the brunt of the anticipated impact. If I remember correctly, we only proposed and passed one piece of legislation during the 1974 session. That was the optional one percent sales tax which a county could levy upon themselves for two years at a time. As I recall, it was Teton County who declared the real need for this. We probably also passed the creation of the Joint Powers Board Act.

Before the end of the budget session, Neal Stafford resigned as chairman to head up Dick Jones's campaign for governor, so the Legislative Management Council appointed me as chairman.

Two other fine senators were on the committee, Dr. Pete Madsen from Sheridan and Dick Sedar from Casper. From the House side I had Walt Oslund from Newcastle, Orin Geesey from Kemmerer, and Jack Jones from Rock Springs. All were dedicated to the task. The legislature had approved a significant appropriation for us to use, if necessary, and we went right to work. I wanted a full-time person to work for the committee, so I asked Bob Pettigrew of Casper if he would take the job. I had worked with Bob when he headed the Wyoming Industrial Development Corporation and also knew he did outstanding work. Bob Pettigrew, one of the most capable individuals in Wyoming, had just left WIDC and fortunately he accepted our job offer.

When I reported this to the LSO (Legislative Service Office) they seemed to take some offense to my action and later I was asked to meet with the Legislative Management Council. They wanted to know why I did not choose to use the LSO people. I told them that the LSO would have more than enough to do with all the work I had in mind. The basis of finding solutions to impact problems required the full-time approach of an experienced businessman with uncommonly good judgment. I told the council Robert Pettigrew was the perfect man for the job and there was never another expression of concern.

Our Select Committee set up a rigorous schedule for meetings throughout the State. We wanted input from people everywhere and we received it. It was invaluable. Our goal was to put a sound legislative program together which could be presented to the 1975 session of the legislature. We would have a new governor, but at that time I had no idea it would be Ed Herschler. The Republicans fielded Malcom Wallop, Dick Jones, Roy Peck, Bud Brimmer, and at one time Frank Barrett Jr. Dick Jones barely beat out Malcom Wallop in the primary and then went on to lose to Ed Herschler in the general election by a significant margin.

The work of the committee was completed on time and the legislative recommendations were printed and bound in what my editor friend, Jim Flinchum, described as the most comprehensive legislative program he had ever seen presented before that body. The cornerstone of the proposals was the bill to establish the Wyoming Community Development Authority. Originally, this would authorize the sale of tax-free revenue bonds and use the proceeds to provide mortgage money for not only housing, but also municipal needs as well. Another bill gave the cities and counties a larger share of the State Sales Tax distribution. Another bill gave the cities and counties, for the first time, a share of the State Use Tax. Another bill removed the sales and use tax exemption that many had previously enjoyed. For the first time the railroads, the interstate pipelines, and interstate truckers were no longer exempt. We knew that the counties and cities had to be able to handle impact better; previously they lacked the funds to do so.

Another major bill was the Coal Tax for Impact Assistance. This levied a new and progressive tax which would ultimately be at two percent of the value of the extracted coal. The tax was to remain until 120 million dollars had been raised, but was amended by me a year or two later to bring at least another forty million dollars into that fund.

In 1975 Ed Herschler was inaugurated as governor and the Democrats and Republicans tied in the Senate—fifteen to fifteen. The organizational makeup of the Senate had to be done through compromise. The Republicans offered the Democrats the position of President of the Senate. They accepted this offer and made Wes Meyers president. The Republicans then wanted the majority of the committee leadership positions, which we received. In order to put our Select Committee's program before the legislature, I wanted to be chairman of the Mines, Minerals, and Industrial Development Committee. I also knew that with only two years of service I lacked the seniority to get it and now sharing the leadership with the Democrats, it would be almost impossible. But you don't often get things without asking. I asked and through the courtesy of Senator Pete Madsen, I received!

As chairman of the Mines, Minerals and Industrial Development Committee, I introduced our program through our Senate standing committee; that is with the exception of the Coal Tax for Impact Assistance, which had to originate in the House of Representatives as a tax bill. We were successful in passing our entire package without serious amendments. Day after day debates went on. I looked forward to it since we seemed to be winning; not only because it was an excellent and necessary program, but also because of Senators Pete Madsen and Dick Sedar urging the Senate for passage.

In the House, Walt Oslund was floor manager for all the impact legislation. I was certainly proud of every member of the committee and the dedication and perseverance which every member demonstrated throughout. The successful legislative solutions brought by our Select Committee were far-reaching in their effectiveness. I will add that the industry supported our legislative package, even though it meant higher taxes for them.

Meanwhile, government policies were again about to determine the economics of the Powder River Basin. Amax Coal Company was preparing to open their new mine at the Clabaugh Ranch. Bob James moved to Gillette to become mine manager. I smiled when he told me, "When a coal miner looks up and sees that eighty-foot wall of coal, he thinks he has died and gone to heaven." This was the first of many new mines to open in later years.

However, about 1974, in a suit between the Sierra Club and Secretary of Interior Rogers Morton, the Sierra Club got a federal injunction against the Interior that prevented them from approving any additional mining permits. The Sierra Club maintained the uncertain notion that the soils in this region were unsuitable for reclamation.

During the 1973 legislative session, the Wyoming legislature, adopting proposals of Governor Stan Hathaway, created the Department of Environmental Quality. We were proud of the way Wyoming was preparing for the new Coal Age that was coming.

With the passage of the legislative package during the 1975 session, I returned to Gillette and went back to business. To my surprise, one day I received a phone call from the office of the Secretary of Interior. They inquired if I could find it possible to come to Washington to offer testimony at a meeting chaired by Secretary of the Interior, Rogers Morton, and Frank Zarb, then designated Energy Czar.

I inquired as to who else would be testifying and was told it would be limited to about five or six people. Mary and I made the trip and it was my first and only time to offer testimony to the federal government. By letter we were requested to meet at the State Department building. Once identified, we were escorted to a meeting room and I was surprised—it appeared to be what I would term small and unpretentious.

Soon the few others who had been invited began to identify themselves. Governor Edwards of Louisiana, the mayor of Portland, who was also the president of the National Mayors' organization, the Speaker of the California Assembly, Jesse Unruh and another who I can no longer remember.

We were then led into a huge room, which I recall was like an amphitheater, covered with purple carpeting. At the center of the room was an appropriate table with two or three seats on each side. This is where I sat. At the head of the table were seats for Rogers Morton and Frank Zarb. Television cameras were present along with necessary lighting. Thus the program began.

Of course Secretary Morton opened the meeting, followed by Energy Czar Frank Zarb, who also commented and thanked us before we testified.

To my surprise most of the other gentlemen testifying were asking for government money in order to resolve their supposed energy problems. Possibly I have forgotten much of the testimony by now, but I doubt it. Of course, I remember my own testimony. Essentially it came down to these facts:

1. Wyoming does not need federal money in resolving this energy crisis.

2. Wyoming does not need or want federal legislation dealing with reclamation of open-pit mined lands. We already have them and I bring a copy of our laws as evidence of our good preparations.

3. Wyoming has prepared itself for dealing with industrial impact by enacting legislation to mitigate the pressures which could result from new mining, new oil development, or new electric power plants. For your reference I submit a copy of those enrolled acts.

4. However, there is one thing that Wyoming does need and invite from the federal government and that is your cooperation!

Following that conference a couple of the other fellows approached me saying, "We never heard of anyone coming here and not asking for money!"

The Sierra Club and others were pushing on the United States Congress to write mined land reclamation laws for all fifty states. During my testimony, I told Morton and Zarb why this federal intervention and duplication would only lead to confusion and excessive administrative costs. Twice Congress voted it in and twice President Ford vetoed the bills.

When Jimmy Carter became President in 1977, he signed the Federal Mined Land Reclamation Law and we have been saddled with it ever since. During the 1960s, Campbell County had gone through a very rough time in trying to get their thirteen school districts organized into a single countywide district. Three county commissioners with the courage to lawfully do it simply by meeting as the Boundary Board, finally accomplished this. My memory tells me those three were Eric Ohman, Lynn Tarver, and Bill Fitch. They did a wonderful thing for all the children of Campbell County.

Our own children had attended tough classroom conditions. During the oil boom of the sixties in Campbell County, every available space was taken or converted to a classroom by a school system that had insufficient tax base to support their immediate needs. From the viewpoint of the rest of the state, exclusive of counties that had mineral development, their attitude was one of "let's all share the mineral wealth". Legislation to amend the State Constitution was passed in 1974, but failed to get the required vote of the people.

In the Senate, I was always outspoken about this proposed constitutional change. I used to say that this proposed legislation was a solution to a problem that had not yet been properly identified. Of course, my opponents found it easy to paint me with a brush that said, "he only wants to keep the wealth in Campbell County". I used to remark that I had lived in one of the poorest school districts in Wyoming and also one of the richest and never changed my address. I felt that I knew the problems attendant to impact situations which the balance of the State, with the exception of Sweetwater County, had never had to contend or address.

However, instead of being on the defensive year after year, I determined to take the offense. Working with J. 0. Reed, the Superintendent of the Campbell County School District and also with Bill Fulkerson, a school board member and treasurer of the Board, we drafted what we thought was the legislation that really needed to be put in place. After properly filing the bill, I took it to the Senate Education Committee and they were enthusiastic. Over in the House, Jack Sidi, chairman of the House Education Committee, brought out the old and tired twelve-mill levy Constitutional Amendment once more. This amendment would again try to increase the statewide tax support for school foundation funds from six mills to twelve mills.

My bill would have given relief to a problem that had never before been addressed. While the school foundation program put a monetary floor under each classroom unit for operations, it could never do anything to provide the necessary funds to build or equalize the building of a classroom. This is a problem especially faced by any area undergoing industrial impact because the immediate needs for classrooms cannot be met by the existing tax base. My bill essentially proposed a school foundation for capital facilities and the support was great. The bill easily passed the Senate and, even with the foot dragging of the House Education Committee Chairman, the bill passed the legislature. For a few years I was very proud to have that legislation referred to as the "Ostlund Bill."

The Wyoming School Boards Association gave me a nice award which hangs in my office to this day. Of all my legislative accomplishments, this one stands out in my mind because it did so much good for all the kids in Wyoming.

Now, for the reader to pause and review a little Wyoming history: for the first two years of my legislative career I served under Governor Stan Hathaway. I first became aware of Stan when he became secretary/treasurer of the State Republican Central Committee. Harry Thorsen was chairman. When Stan decided to run for Governor in 1966, there were just two Republicans running in the primary campaign. Wyoming was indeed fortunate to have two such capable gentlemen running as Stan Hathaway from Torrington and Joe Burke from Casper. Early in the campaign, Stan came to Gillette and stayed at the Sands Motor Lodge. I believe he was not only impressed with the facilities, but also the way we were running the operations. At the same time, I was impressed with Stan. This was the beginning of a long friendship that we still maintain. Of course Stan not only won in 1966, but also easily won his second term as Governor in 1970 and he did a terrific job of running the State.

During the 1974 General Election campaign between Dick Jones and Ed Herschler, I began to look ahead at how the State would fare under new leadership. As it turned out, to my surprise, Ed Herschler beat Dick Jones and Wyoming again had a Democrat as Governor. Following the election of Herschler, I provided him with a rather detailed summary of all of our material relating to the impact legislation.

Soon after the 1975 session commenced, I began to get a bit impatient with Ed Herschler. I just had not adjusted to his casual style of being Governor. I felt there was too much work that needed to be done and I was anxious to go forward. It was this impatience that led to my resigning as State Senator following the 1978 Budget Session and attempting to unseat Ed. When the votes were tallied following the 1978 general election, Ed had 2,370 more votes than I did. That was not many, but after all, he only needed one more vote than I received. I used to labor over where I could have caused 1,200 voters to change their ballots; a totally futile exercise.

I enjoyed working in the legislature and accomplishing worthwhile legislation. Of course, each person might argue about what is or is not worthwhile, but that is the ongoing debate in public service.

After my 1973 trip to Chicago with Dick Tobin where we took part in the National Council of State Governments meeting, I continued to be interested in that kind of endeavor. Wyoming also belonged to the National Conference of State Legislatures. The first organization dealt with state governments on all levels. This included not only the legislature, but also the Attorney General, other state officials, and various state departments. During my six years in the Senate, I became quite involved with these organizations. Some would say that those of us who participated just liked to travel and there may be some truth in that. However, I found that serving on various committees within these organizations brought forth some good responses to common problems. All in all, I believe these states more than get their investment back if their legislators go to the meetings to work.

My involvement led me to Anchorage one time. Mary and I had never been to Alaska and we scheduled a side trip following the conclusion of the meeting. I shall interrupt here to say that Mary's expenses were paid by me and not the State. We were planning to take a flight to spectacular Glacier Bay. The day our meeting ended we received bad news, a phone call from Gillette. Our son, Scott, had broken his knee in a bicycle accident. We immediately returned to Gillette. Scott eventually had two operations on his knee and, thanks to good surgery and good physical therapy, he regained full use of his knee.

During the last three years I served in the Legislature, I was elected to the Executive Committee of the National Conference of State Legislatures. I did enjoy that group and the work we accomplished. Those meetings took us to Hilton Head Island, Annapolis, Biloxi, Mississippi, Detroit, and many other places. Whether or not the legislative money is well spent always depends upon the dedication of each member involved.

While serving on this Executive Committee, I had the opportunity to visit mainland China in 1977. However, the trip to China, as well as my run for Governor, shall be taken up in other chapters.

University of Wyoming Board of Trustees. Back row: Robert Schrader, Chris Bunning, Albert Pence, Patrick Quealy, Joseph Sullivan, Jerry Hollon, ASUW President Cal Rerucha, and John Ostlund. Front row: Paul Hines, Robert McBride, Winifred Hickey, Governor Stan Hathaway, H.A. "Dave" True, and UW President William Carlson, 1971.

John C. Ostlund, presiding over the Wyoming Senate, 1977.

15

Picking a President

The Bicentennial Year of 1976 marked the Independence of the United States. It was also a presidential election year, as well as my reelection for my second term as State Senator from the Johnson-Campbell Senatorial District.

Chronologically, the county conventions were in March and the state conventions in Cheyenne were in May. I had set my sights on going to the Republican National Convention in Kansas City as a delegate. Since by rotation, it was Campbell County's turn to name the delegate and our county convention had elected me to fill that position.

The unprecedented resignation of Richard Nixon as President of the United States a couple of years earlier was still the hottest political subject. Gerald Ford was the sitting President. By virtue of his being appointed Vice President following the resignation of Spiro Agnew, Ford now filled the vacancy left by Nixon's resignation. I had become personally acquainted with Gerald Ford in 1973, but that contact had never matured.

Spiro Agnew had been elected Vice President on the Nixon ticket in 1972, but the pressure of his own wrong doing while Governor of Maryland finally forced his resignation from office. That is when Nixon appointed Gerald Ford, who was then serving as minority leader of the House of Representatives. Ford had earned the respect of his colleagues and his appointment as Vice President was well received. However, the shock to this nation over the resignation of Nixon was only preceded by the disclosures of the Select Congressional Committee looking into the Watergate scandal. Gerald Ford was holding the office of President of the United States although he had never been elected by a vote of the people.

Meanwhile, on the national political scene, Ronald Reagan was coming on strong. Reagan had come into the national political limelight in 1964 when he delivered a spellbinding keynote address at that Republican National Convention. He was a master at using the electronic media and at this time he still has no equal as a political figure in front of the camera. In 1976 there was a big move to nominate Ronald Reagan for the office of President. In some ways it seemed to me that Gerald Ford, as President, should have earned the right to carry the banner, but my concerns went beyond that.

Having completed my first term as State Senator, I was becoming increasingly aware of the huge role the federal government was playing in Wyoming. They seemed to be pushing their way into what I thought should be Wyoming decisions. The state legislature had worked hard in conjunction with the Hathaway Administration to put the Department of Environmental Quality into effect. That legislation was passed in 1973, and although it established sub departments of Water, Air, and Land, my role was working on the Mined Land Reclamation part of that legislation. By 1974 the federal government was trying to do the same thing with mined land reclamation, and they were insisting upon setting up a new federal bureaucracy to accomplish what Congress wanted. To me, it was just another example of federal encroachment on state's rights. I believe that the environmental lobby was responsible for this vigorous federal effort. By this time the environmental lobby people had learned that if they concentrated their efforts on Washington they could spend less effort in the various state legislatures. Already the Congress had twice passed this federal legislation, but Gerald Ford vetoed the bill both times. I was convinced that each state could better determine their own needs than Congress. This has been proven time and time again, and Congress only accomplishes one thing for certain—spend more money.

At the Campbell County Republican Convention I was approved as the official delegate selected by our county process. I was also named to the Nominating Committee at the State Convention. This convention was held in Cheyenne that year. That was the same time that Malcolm Wallop decided to run for United States Senator, trying to beat the incumbent Democrat, Gale McGee. Of course, you are already aware that Malcomb did win his race quite decisively.

However, ardent Ronald Reagan supporters determined in advance of the convention to send only committed Reagan delegates to the National Convention in Kansas City that year. During the first meeting of the State Republican Nominating Committee, I absolutely refused to make that commitment and told them the reason. I said that Wyoming has little opportunity to communicate with the President of the United States, and we had many issues to raise with the next President. I said that if we went committed, then neither candidate had to bother talking with us. Our only opportunity was in a tight race for the nomination, with each candidate trying to get our support. I wanted to know where both Ford and Reagan stood with regard to mined land reclamation, energy development, water development, federal lands policy, and other concerns that were important to Wyoming and the West. Mary Garmon of Sundance took the same stand. No one tried to railroad our United States Senator Cliff Hansen because it was felt that he had to support the President, Gerald Ford.

Dick Jones of Cody was the leader in this effort to commit to Reagan. He had resigned from the Senate in 1974 to run for Governor. Dick had won the primary race, but lost to Ed Herschler in the General Election. Now, in 1976, he was going to be state chairman of the Reagan for President Committee. He had enlisted a lot of help to send only committed delegates to Kansas City. Mary Garmon and I were not nominated by the committee that day. The following day the committee report had to be presented to the convention. My position was that Dick Jones nor anyone else was going to dictate to

Campbell County whom they were going to send to the National Convention. Dick talked with me that evening, but I was adamant. I never knew until over nine years later how Dick Jones finally gave in. All I knew, at the time, was that both my name and Mary Garmon's were presented to the convention and we were both officially named as delegates.

Unknown to me at that time was the beginning of a rift between Dick Jones and me that was to probably decide the outcome of my race for Governor in 1978. To my surprise, one day in the fall of 1985, Dick called me at the ranch to say he wanted to be friends again. Following our telephone conversation, Dick drove to Remount for a personal visit. I told him that I had never understood why he became so upset following my vote in Kansas City. I said I was unwavering in my position to remain uncommitted until the convention and I did. When I made up my mind to vote with Gerald Ford, Dick never got over it.

"What ever gave you to understand I was going for Reagan?" I asked.

"The night before the election at the State Convention in Cheyenne, I talked with your County Chairman, Sam Ratcliff. Sam told me that he was pretty sure that you would vote for Reagan when the vote came," Dick stated.

I told Dick, "I never had a conversation with Sam Ratcliff about how I would vote and, obviously, Sam was trying to make peace and prevent a floor fight. You mean you have carried that misunderstanding around for the past nine years?"

"Yes, and I am sure that it cost you the Governor's seat in 1978," Dick stated somberly.

"It is certainly too late to change what has already transpired, but I am glad to solve that mystery that has plagued me since 1976," I told him. "But why you didn't ask me about it will probably always remain a mystery."

During June and July of 1976, I received the opportunity to talk with both Reagan and Ford. Mary Garmon and I were both recognized as uncommitted delegates and, by all counts, every vote was important to break a possible deadlock in nominating a presidential candidate. The news accounts of that time clearly showed why I was uncommitted and I said that my decision would be based upon which candidate I felt could and would do the best for Wyoming as well as the nation. I asked myself privately, more than once, if I was not allowing myself to take an ego trip. Twice, the President called me at my office and once I had a call from Ronald Reagan. I made a trip to Casper to meet with Ronald and Nancy Reagan along with the other delegates. I had asked for a private meeting and received it. I wanted to talk about the issues which were important to Wyoming. Although Ronald Reagan was very personable and comfortable to talk with, I felt that his understanding of these matters was a bit shallow. I also had to consider that Gerald Ford had spent many years in the Congress and it was natural that he had a better understanding of these issues than Ronald Reagan.

President Ford was also using pressure to win votes from Mary Garmon and me. We both received invitations to a White House state dinner in honor of Prime Minister Malcolm Fraser of Australia. I talked with my wife and we decided it might be the only opportunity we would ever have to do this. We gave a very prompt and positive response. I found out that Mary Garmon and her husband, Neal, had also accepted.

Mary and I went off to Washington in high spirits. We stayed at the Madison Hotel because of its close proximity to the White House. The dinner was held on Thursday night, July 27, 1976, and it was very memorable. Mary wore a beautiful aqua gown and we decided that we looked quite appropriate for this special occasion.

A taxi took us to the designated entrance where we showed our invitations. As soon as we stepped out of the cab, we were asked questions by reporters. I recall Ann Compton, White House Correspondent for ABC, asking me if I had decided to support President Ford. Of course, I gave the usual undecided response. A photographer snapped our picture as we were entering the White House. Imagine our surprise when we discovered our picture on the front page of the *Washington Post* Society Section the next day! However, under our picture were the wrong names. The caption stated "Uncommitted delegate Allen Young and Mrs. Young and Senator and Mrs. Strom Thurman arrive for the dinner last night." Wyoming Congressman Teno Roncalio and State Auditor Jim Griffith both sent us clippings from that paper along with humorous notes about the misidentifications. Anyway, it was a good picture!

We entered the White House at ground level and shortly thereafter we were escorted to a stairway where people were advancing upstairs leisurely. Wyoming Senator Cliff Hansen and Martha were directly in front of us and Paul Harvey, the broadcaster, was immediately behind us. When we reached the top of the stairs, Mary was escorted by a Marine officer and I followed behind. Someone announced "Senator and Mrs. John Ostlund" to the people waiting to meet the dignitaries. As we went through the receiving line, we first encountered Chief of Protocol, Shirley Temple Black, who presented us to the President and Betty Ford. Then we met Malcolm Fraser and his wife. After that we were directed to a very large room where cocktails were served.

At that time, White House Chief of Staff Dick Cheney and his wife, Lynn, of Casper made us feel very welcome. During the course of the evening Dick introduced us to Mr. and Mrs. Frank O'Conner of New York. I told Mrs. O'Conner I was more honored in meeting her than the President. Mrs. O'Conner is better known as Ayn Rand, author of *The Fountainhead* and *Atlas Shrugged* to name two of her most prominent books. A recent biography called *The Passions of Ayn Rand* states that she felt honored to be invited to that particular White House dinner because her presence had been requested by Prime Minister Fraser.

Following the cocktails, we went outside to the Rose Garden and entered a huge air-conditioned tent which had been erected. Previously, this had been used for a state dinner for Queen Elizabeth. It was beautifully done. With the carpet on the floor you didn't feel that you were really outside. We sat at round tables of eight. The head table was elevated and seated Secretary of State Henry Kissinger and his wife, Nancy. Mary and I had been presented with our seating assignments. Mary was delighted to sit with Gregory Peck!

Mary and I were at separate tables, as were all couples. Paul Harvey was at my table and we reminisced about his visit to Gillette in 1964. At that time the Chamber of Commerce had Paul Harvey speak at the high school gym to a capacity crowd. Governor Cliff Hansen was there and I was pleased to act as master of ceremonies. We had a dinner for Paul Harvey at the Sands preceding the speaking engagement and he stayed at our new Sands Motor Lodge.

Now, at the White House dinner, the lady sitting at my left was the wife of Chief of Naval Operations, Admiral James Holloway. I told her that her husband's father was Superintendent of the Naval Academy when I graduated. I also told her that when her husband was a pilot flying off the carrier *Kearsarge*, I flew with him in an SB2C dive-bomber. She said, "Oh, Jimmy will be so glad to see you again! Let's get together right after the dinner."

Without voicing my skepticism, I thought about the CNO being happy to meet a former second-class midshipman who flew with him in 1947, but we did get together. Immediately following the dinner we returned inside for cordials and cigars. I also had a brief conversation with Admiral James Holloway, the CNO.

Mary and I felt that the evening was ending, but to our surprise there was much more to come. We took seats in a music room where we were entertained by Sherril Milne, the opera star. And if that were not enough, following the music interlude, there was ballroom dancing. We danced alongside couples who included Rod Steiger, Gregory Peck, Jimmy Conners, and on and on. We will always be glad we went. It was past midnight when Mary and I took a leisurely stroll through the White House. We came to the front entrance when we decided to call it an evening. As we stood there looking out from that famous entrance seen in countless pictures, we felt inspired.

The reader needs to understand the setting. We were alone. It was the magic of midnight. The warm summer evening carried the fragrance of flowers. The lighting of the White House grounds was enchanting. It was such a memorable sight. We leisurely strolled out the front door and down the walk. Several times we stopped and looked back at the magnificent White House. As we neared the gate we thought about returning to the ballroom, but decided it could not end any nicer than the present moment. We walked past the guard and bid him a very pleasant, "Good evening!" As we strolled back to our hotel, it was the end of a rather fairy-tale day!

The Republican National Convention convened in Kansas City early in August. Wyoming was fortunate to have Estelle Stacey Carrier as national secretary of the GOP. The Wyoming delegation stayed at a Marriott Hotel on the outskirts of Kansas City, but the accommodations were very good. Regular bus service took us directly to the arena and returned to the hotel at convenient times. The weather was hot and humid, but that was expected. Estelle Stacey Carrier, from Douglas, had an important position on the podium. In fact, Estelle called for each vote from the states in her official capacity as secretary. I believe that is the reason Wyoming had such a prominent place practically in front of the podium.

All of the media service people, especially the TV crews, worked the delegations on the floor. About the second day, I was asked by Dan Rather of CBS to do an interview. We were on camera with a national audience when he commented about my being an uncommitted delegate and asked when I was going to decide. I told him that the decision had been made and I also told him how fortunate I felt the Republican Party was to have two such qualified candidates. He commented that I should announce my decision on national TV! I told him I was going to support President Ford for the nomination. I found out later that President Ford was watching CBS at the time I made that announcement and later that day he had Senator Cliff Hansen bring me to his hotel suite to thank me.

My Aunt Rosie in Paxton, Illinois, was also watching TV at that moment and she excitedly recognized me. When the convention came to the final close and a prayer was being offered, I stood amid all the other delegates on the floor with bowed head. For some reason, the TV cameras zoomed in on me as I stood praying and many friends from around the country commented about seeing me. Those were my few big moments in the sun!

As history already records, Ford beat Reagan in the nomination battle and then picked Bob Dole of Kansas as his Vice Presidential nominee. History also shows that a little known guy named Jimmy Carter from Georgia beat the Ford ticket and we had a Democrat in the White House for the next four years. Ronald Reagan got his shot again in 1980 and this time won two successive terms in the White House. Of course, he never invited Mary and me, but that's politics!

Following the selection of Ford for President, Dick Jones was hot-under-the-collar. He felt he had been betrayed by the delegation and, evidently, there were some delegates who had pledged themselves to Reagan at Jones' insistence and who later voted for Ford. I was not one of those and why he was upset with me was covered earlier in this chapter. The failure of the Ford faction and the Reagan faction to unify caused the Republicans to lose the election that year. The same thing was to happen to me in 1978 when I ran for Governor. I won the primary over Gus Fleischli, but the failure to unify after the primary cost me the General Election by about 2,370 votes.

In retrospect, it was fun to attend a National Convention where there was a real contest. This year, 1988, the nominees were chosen before the convention even began. Instead of a selection process, it was more like a coronation. I am happy that I was able to be a delegate at a National GOP Convention. My grandfather Roberts was a delegate to the Republican Convention when the GOP selected Wendell Willke to run against Franklin Roosevelt in 1940. I feel certain we both enjoyed it!

President Gerald Ford, State Senator John C. Ostlund, and U.S. Senator Clifford Hansen during the 1976 Republican National Convention in Kansas City.

16

Tour of Mainland China

To my best recollection, the Chinese Nationalists were driven out of mainland China by the Communists in 1949. At that time, led by Chiang Kai-Shek, the Nationalists set up their government in Formosa, now called Taiwan. From 1949 until the visit of President Nixon to China in 1973, the People's Republic of China remained closed to the United States and its citizens. It was a surprise announcement by President Richard Nixon that he was making an official visit to mainland China. The trip had been prepared by Secretary of State Henry Kissinger.

Following the visit in 1973, there was still limited travel in China and by a very few U.S. citizens. In 1976 the National Conference of State Legislatures received a formal invitation from the People's Republic of China to send twenty state legislators on an official visit to Peking and other cities. Since I was serving on the Executive Committee of the National Conference, I was anxious to go. But I also remembered that I was running for reelection to the State Senate that year and reluctantly chose not to go. As it turned out, about twenty people made the trip in 1976. They brought back some very interesting stories about this ancient country which had been virtually closed to the free world for over twenty-five years.

However in 1977, the NCSL received a second invitation and I was among the first to volunteer. The trip was to commence from San Francisco about the tenth of September and we were scheduled to return to Honolulu on the twenty-fifth of September. Talking with members of the 1976 delegation, I learned some good pointers. They cautioned about not taking too much baggage. Take only one suit, or of greater value, one blue blazer with gray trousers. People in China mostly wear gray Mao jackets and pants. We were also cautioned to take plenty of 35mm color film because it could not be purchased in China. I believe I ended up taking about forty rolls of thirty-six-exposure Kodak film and I was glad I did. I also took comfortable clothes that did not require dry cleaning and good walking shoes.

One day in California, I bought what I thought would be a perfect set of luggage for the China trip. I knew that I would need lots of luggage space to bring home many gifts that I hoped to acquire in China. In a luggage store I saw matched, soft-sided luggage. One of the regular-sized bags could fit completely inside one of the larger bags. I felt that I could travel with one bag and come home with two. It really worked out that way, however, an incident at the San Francisco Airport left me momentarily disgruntled. After deplaning and watching the endless belt for my luggage, I spied my new dark blue soft-sided bag coming toward me. It was distinctive in that it carried small stripes of bright color around the middle of the bag. When I leaned over to grab it off the belt, I noticed that part of the handle was completely torn away from the bag. I immediately thought that on my very first trip I would lose my ability to carry my suitcase. Then I noticed another one just like it coming on the moving belt. I was greatly relieved to find that my bag was okay, but that someone else had a bag just like mine.

I checked into the Hilton Hotel at the airport which was our designated meeting place. That evening and again the next morning our group met with China experts from Stanford University. It was then that I began to realize just how difficult it was for people from the United States to get into China. When I returned from my trip and was interviewed by the Central Intelligence Agency, I began to appreciate even more how significant our opportunity was at that time.

The names of our group of twenty people had to be submitted to the Chinese about four months before our trip was to commence. If our passports had carried a visa stamp to Taiwan, we had to apply for a new passport. Mine did not. I had to carry International Medical Certificates showing I had received two cholera shots plus a smallpox vaccination. The smallpox vaccine was hard to come by since smallpox had been eradicated in this country years ago. During this four-month period, there were three members of our delegation who had to withdraw. Because of the time constraints, we could not substitute new names, so a total of seventeen people actually made the trip. Dr. Karl Kurtz was coordinator from the NCSL, and Speaker of the Tennessee Legislature, Tom Jensen, was our group chairman. A list of the delegation follows:

Representative Tom Jensen, Leader, Tennessee
Senator Walter Baker, Kentucky
Assemblyman Willie H. Brown, Jr., California
Mr. Timothy R. Campbell, Illinois
Speaker Billy Wayne Clayton, Texas
Senator George Firestone, Florida
Representative Robert E. Hosack, Idaho
Representative Hannah D. Atkins, Oklahoma
Dr. Karl Kurtz, NCSL, Colorado
Mr. John N. Lattimer, Illinois
Senator Albert B. Lewis, New York
Senator James A. McDermott, Washington
Speaker Ned McWherter, Tennessee
Senator John C. Ostlund, Wyoming
Mr. Arthur J. Palmer, Nevada

Senator E. D. Potts, Oregon
Speaker George B. Roberts, New Hampshire
Delegate Steven Sklar, Maryland
Senator Bernard C. Smith, New York
Delegate Robert Washington, Virginia
Mr. Al Abrams, New York

Before leaving on this exciting trip, I asked my daughter, Karin, to pick out a proper camera. She chose a 35mm Pentax with two additional lens; one a wide-angle lens; and the other a telephoto lens. Karin gave me a crash course on the utilization of my equipment and she certainly did a great job—I brought home some wonderful pictures.

I received many requests to show my slides to different schools and civic groups and I enjoyed the opportunity. Sometimes when I could not keep a school lecture date, Mary would substitute for me. She could do my China presentation even better than I could.

On the day of our departure from San Francisco, we were driven to the international departure concourse to board Japan Air Lines. I did not want any hassle when returning so I made a point of going to the customs office to validate my camera and equipment plus my watch. I did not want to be accused of buying this new equipment out of the country and be charged duty for it.

I had never flown on Japan Air Lines and I was pleased we were flying a Boeing 747 jumbo jet. We flew nonstop to Tokyo and crossed the international date line where we skipped one day. The service was superb! The hostesses wore traditional Japanese kimonos and the food was excellent. Since we had plenty of time and no place to go, during the trip I practiced using chopsticks. I knew these would be my utensils for the next two weeks and I became quite proficient with them. During the flight, I happened to meet an Eastman Kodak representative. We conversed about the film I was carrying. My film had an ASA speed of 200, which was the fastest at that time. He told me the company was going to be making an ASA 400 later on, but if I was in a situation where there was not sufficient light, I could set my camera on ASA 400 and give special instructions when the film was processed. I was glad to learn that and later on in China I made good use of that information.

Arriving in Tokyo marked the completion of my longest air flight, but also in Tokyo I was about to witness the largest congestion of people I had ever experienced in an airport. These huge jet aircraft were disgorging people at an enormous rate and locating baggage, plus going through customs and passport control, was a big job. I was anxious to see Tokyo. Having ended a long war with Japan just thirty-one years before had caused me to want to view this very different culture.

We were driven to the New Otani Hotel. Driving through the city was exciting and I was impressed by all the various sights of the city and the people. The New Otani Hotel was very nice. When I was shown to my room I was struck by the size of the bed. It was small and, by western standards, would not have been considered comfortable. The real shock came when we had dinner. Of course the food was wonderful, but the prices were sky-high. At that time we received about 240 yen for a dollar. Now in 1992, we only receive 123 yen for a dollar. That makes prices in Japan twice as much as we paid in 1977. I would not want to visit Japan with present-day exchange rates.

One of the highlights of our Tokyo visit was going to the Japanese Diet. Although the Diet was adjourned, we were received by the Diet leaders and several of the senior staff people. I recall being impressed with the chambers and, most of all, with the beautiful wood so skillfully used in the furnishings. We enjoyed talking about their relations with China and what we might expect during our visit.

Another highlight of Tokyo was our visit to the U.S. Embassy. I thought the architecture of the Embassy to be rather strangely unimpressive. We did meet with Ambassador Mike Mansfield, from Montana, who was formerly the majority floor leader of the U.S. Senate. President Jimmy Carter had designated Mike Mansfield to serve as Ambassador to Japan. It seemed as though it would be a very comfortable posting.

We toured some of the interesting places in Tokyo, including the Emperor's palace and grounds. We could not go into the palace, but to view it was impressive. I recall my surprise when visiting an ancient temple. There was a platoon of young uniformed Japanese fellows doing a military drill. At one point they all shouted, "Banzai!" I thought that had all disappeared following World War II. It gave me a rather uncomfortable feeling to view this drill. Before leaving Tokyo a few of us used the subway system and although nobody could speak Japanese, we did return to our hotel without incident. The subway system was very clean and well maintained.

Having had a Seiko watch, I decided to buy myself a new one while in Japan. I did that and, of course, was impressed with all the newer features of this watch. In China some of the Chinese used to like to examine it also. Sitting in the main lobby of the New Otoni Hotel, I recall enjoying the international variety of the passing parade. First of all, the view out the main windows was an extensive Japanese garden complete with waterfall. One night in one of the restaurants, I ordered the famous Kobe beef that the Japanese farmer raises on beer and grain until it is slaughtered. It was extraordinary, but the price was outrageous.

On the day we were to leave Tokyo for Peking, we went to the airport to catch the weekly flight of Japan Air Lines, which flew directly to Peking. As the plane broke out above the overcast, I recall seeing Mount Fuji, which was the only terrain high enough above the surrounding clouds. It made a beautiful picture. Our route was not a straight line because we were not allowed to fly over North Korea, so we altered our direct route to bypass North Korea before crossing the mainland Chinese border. As we lowered to land at Peking, I was quite excited. I was impressed by how green the landscape appeared and as we flew lower it was evident that most of the land was being tilled for agriculture.

As we taxied toward the terminal building, it was obvious that there was no other air traffic. I saw what looked like Russian Mig fighter planes on the ground nearby. The JAL plane stopped a considerable distance from the terminal and we all exited the plane. The ominous quiet and complete lack of any kind of noise was almost scary. There we were at the airport of the capital of China and you could not hear the sound of another aircraft or any vehicle sounds at all. As we walked toward the terminal building, I noticed about a hundred Chinese men standing on the balcony overlooking the airport staring at us. There was not a sound, except for our own footsteps on the pavement.

As we passed through the admitting door, there were no greetings and no smiles from the Chinese. Immediately our papers were examined. It was discovered that two of our party, Willie Brown of California and a Senator for New York, did not have the required smallpox vaccinations. Since they had been forewarned, the Chinese removed their jackets and rolled up their shirt sleeves. Meanwhile, Willie and Al protested loudly that their doctors said they should be excused, but the Chinese did not offer a word of explanation, apology, or give any indication they could even understand English. They just held and vaccinated them on the spot. The rest of us were quite amused by the incident and showed no sympathy.

Since we were an official visiting party, I discovered we were to be provided with official transportation during our entire visit. Four-door sedans waited for us outside the terminal building. My recollections of the terminal building was the huge statue of Chairman Mao, plus all the red banners on the walls. Later I found these all over China. Although I suspected the drivers understood English, there was never a word spoken by the driver to us. Whenever one of our official translators was in the same car, they would, on occasion, converse with the driver in Chinese. Driving to our hotel from the airport, I was amazed at all the shacks we passed along the way. I was told that the bad earthquake of the previous year had made it necessary to throw up a huge number of shelters for the refugees. There were thousands of these makeshift, cracker box-type buildings.

I don't now recall the name of the hotel where we stayed, but it was large as well as old. We were probably within half a block of the main Tiananmen Square in the heart of Peking. I was told that Senator Walter Baker and I would be sharing a room together. It was easy to tell that our hotel facility was prerevolutionary and that the plumbers, electricians, and other technical types were not available to service our hotel in this Communist regime. I found the same thing in Shanghai, where we were to visit later. I missed having a shower, but soon learned to shower with a spray in the bathtub.

Outside our hotel window, we saw hundreds more of the cardboardlike, refugee-looking shacks. The corrugated tin roofing sheets were weighted down with stones because they had no roofing nails. The Chinese families occupying these shacks cooked their meals on an outdoor fire. Sanitary facilities were not evident, but I could imagine.

When our group took their meal, we were the only people in this huge room which had no carpet and a bare wooden floor. The sparse walls had only the usual pictures of Mao and sometimes Lenin. The food was interesting, to say the least. We never suffered a shortage of food and in an attempt to avoid the water, we usually drank the quarts of beer which were placed on the table. There was no menu selection and no alcoholic beverages were ever offered or requested.

China was suffering from a shortage of protein and it was well-known that there were no cats or dogs left in all of China. The basic food offering was rice and with this we mixed a variety of different cooked vegetables. When fish, duck, or chicken was served, they offered everything, including the head, feet, and entrails, mixed with rice and vegetables. You soon learned to ignore what you were eating. The only food item I had problems with were the slippery, black sea leeches. I learned to pass over them unless the leeches were the only protein available. At breakfast, we learned they were going to offer us an American breakfast, so we had toast and eggs. They also had a "sour milk" that I found out was yogurt and I liked this very much. Karl stated he wanted an authentic Chinese breakfast, so they gave him one—a huge bowl of gruel made out of soybeans—quite tasteless, but I suppose a very necessary foundation for the millions of Chinese who labored so long each day.

Immediately after breakfast the first morning, Walt Baker and I walked to the huge Tiananmen Square. I wish I knew dimensions for reference, but it looked as though you could stand a few million people there without difficulty. The picture of Mao must have been thirty-feet tall and the fact that Chairman Mao had recently died created a new happening. Mao's body was on display in a glass box within a special building built for his resting place and the Chinese were lined up in front of each door waiting to walk by his coffin; lines were probably a half-mile-long. Later that day our group was taken to the head of the line so that we could view Chairman Mao's body. The Chinese people made no protest, but I could only imagine the reaction to this maneuver if it had been pulled in an American city.

Since it was September and just a trifle cool, I was aware that the smoke from various chimneys was hanging low to the ground. I was also to learn the low-grade coal that they burned caused a huge problem of air pollution in Peking.

Without a doubt, the most impressive thing about the streets of Peking were the millions of bicycles. There were no private vehicles on the streets, only military trucks and the government vehicles like the ones in which we were escorted from place to place. Other than the jammed public buses, people rode bicycles. The other very impressive view was the tremendous quantity of beautiful paper flowers that adorned the pictures and statues of Chairman Mao. They were really incredible and I was unaware that they were made from paper until it rained one day and the flowers "wilted."

Near the center of the city is a huge walled enclosure which was the former residence of the emperor. This is known as the "Forbidden City." Its existence goes back for well over a thousand years and the Communist government kept it open so the citizens could view the decadent way the government of China used to live. It was both magnificent and impressive—like everything I saw in China, I took lots of pictures.

Often our schedule for the day was full of surprises. The first night in Peking we were told suddenly that we would have an official dinner at the Peking Restaurant. We were dining in the room which was used for the official dinner for President Nixon. When our cars took us there it was already dark. We climbed a stairway to the second floor of this restaurant, which was supposedly famous for serving, of all things, Peking duck. It was impressive by its drabness. As we took seats in an unusual assortment of old upholstered easy chairs, we were served tea. The mayor of Peking and an assortment of other Chinese officials were present along with our interpreters. In the adjacent dining room, we were seated at round tables of about eight persons per table. I sat next to one of our interpreters, as I usually tried to do.

The dinner was quite formal and commenced with the waiters presenting and displaying several whole plucked ducks. We viewed them and gave appropriate nods of approval. We were served an eight-course dinner—all made with duck. I did not realize this at first and it was not until after the appetizer that I asked Mrs. Wang, the translator, what we had eaten. It was like a puff pastry that was really quite good. She explained that the webfoot of the duck was skinned to form the container for the stuffing that we had just eaten. And that was the way with each course. We ate every piece of that duck except the "Quack", including all of the entrails. But my biggest surprise was yet to come.

A plate was placed in front of me and I noted that only two people at my table had this offering. I asked Mrs. Wang about it. She said, "You have been honored by receiving the head of the duck!" I wanted to explain this was an honor I could readily do without, but the Chinese at my table were beaming at me, so I picked it up like finger food and did my best to act out my enjoyment.

Following the dinner, small liquor glasses were placed in front of each of us and a clear liquid called Mai Tai was poured. I referred to the drink as white lightning, but many toasts were offered. I noted that some of the Chinese drained their glasses at every toast, but I quickly learned this drink was for sipping, not for belting. The toasts, as well as the several speeches, took a great deal of time because of all the translations. It also became quite clear the ban on alcohol was strictly for the masses and not for the leadership. Of course they dodged behind the truth used by most all communists, that offering toasts was an international tradition. I suspect they learned this from the Russians.

Another night in Peking we went to an opera. The opera house was jammed full and again the building and the interiors were without imagination. The opera was a purely communist propaganda piece and demonstrated how bad the nationalists were. It showed how the peasants suffered under the old nationalist regime and how the Communists ultimately prevailed and won out in the end. One peasant girl was the heroine of the opera and the crowds cheered when she became victorious at the ending. Mrs. Wang explained it all to me as the opera progressed.

One morning at breakfast we were told that, by special consideration, we were going to be shown the Peking underground defense system. We were told that in case of a nuclear attack, most of the millions of residents could take refuge underground. So I thought that really had to be something because Peking was a huge city and how could they have a city underground large enough to hold everyone? Afterward I felt this was truly a propaganda effort meant to impress us because I could not buy it.

Our cars took us to a crowded and busy street in Peking where we unloaded. We were led into a clothing store where the tables were piled deep with Mao jackets and pants. Everyone in the store stood aside and they opened a trapdoor on the floor behind one of the counters.

We descended into an underground passage where we walked for some length. The translators were instructed to inform us that this underground system covered most of

Peking. I had many questions that never received satisfactory answers and, to me, the whole affair was a giant hoax. I thought it probably gave jobs to a lot of Chinese who really needed them, but the lack of ventilation, storerooms, food and medical supplies, and adequate generators caused the whole thing to look suspect to me.

The trip to the Great Wall was traditional and remains so to this day. On the way to the Wall we paused at the Ming Tombs excavations. These huge underground tombs reminded me of the kind of efforts that went into building the pyramids in Egypt, or the Great Wall of China. When an emperor wanted to leave the world in high fashion, he had all the resources in China available to him. Incredible work and effort was expended in giving these emperors their final resting place. As an example, we viewed one huge underground room containing an army of carved soldiers who were meant to accompany their emperor and protect him in the afterworld.

Although the Ming Tombs were impressive, in most respects they paled in their efforts compared to the Great Wall of China. I recall the astronauts commenting how the Great Wall could be seen from space orbit. As I stood on the Wall looking out on Outer Mongolia, I could almost imagine the hoards attempting to breach this huge defensive structure. It was easy to recall the many times I had looked at pictures of the Great Wall and finally I was there. I enjoyed taking pictures and walking from tower to tower.

Our most important meeting in China took place in the Great Hall of the People. This huge structure is also impressively furnished. When we went to the Hall, the Chinese officials joined us for a photograph. I believe the present chairman of the Communist Party, a fellow named Dung, was with us in that photo shoot. Our reception took place in a huge, high ceiling room that had rich carpet and a good deal of artwork. Like all Chinese affairs, tea was served. Speeches were made and translated and then we were allowed to ask questions. It was during this session when my dictaphone ran out of tape and began squealing. I taped most of our conferences and it did not take long to learn to stop taping when only Chinese was spoken. That saved a good deal of tape.

Immediately following our meeting at the Great Hall, we were whisked away to the American consul's home for a debriefing. No other American officials were allowed to be present at our meeting and this necessitated the use of this roundabout approach to the dissemination of information.

I was ready and anxious to leave Peking. When the time came, we returned to the airport and boarded a Russian-built jet airplane to fly to Shanghai.

Shanghai was a complete change from Peking. The most obvious reason: Shanghai is a southern seaport as well as an industrial city. The harbor area of Shanghai was always busy and a great deal of the traffic was due to the Chinese junks which were interesting to observe. Our hotel in Shanghai was an old traditional hotel which lacked the needed maintenance. I was given a large bedroom which also had a good deal of old-style upholstered furniture probably dating back to the thirties. The carpet was of the same vintage. The large tiled bathroom had a big showerhead and I was anxious to make use of it. When I turned on the shower, the water leaked from many joints everywhere. I felt there were probably few plumbers or electricians left in Communist China.

The first morning in Shanghai, it was a brilliant morning and I was anxious to get out on the streets to shoot pictures. I walked to the sea wall. Unlike Peking, where everyone wore gray Mao outfits, I saw mostly white shirts and many were short-sleeved. Shanghai was a much warmer climate than Peking, especially late in September. As I took a picture from the sea wall, I noticed I needed to replace the roll of film. I had become an expert and could do this quickly. When I finished that small chore, I looked up in surprise. There were about a hundred Chinese surrounding me trying to get a glimpse of what I was doing. I smiled and waved at them and I believe I could understand their curiosity. After all, they had seldom ever had the opportunity to view an American.

We were driven to a hospital the first morning in Shanghai and that was fascinating. I had never seen major surgery performed before. I was about to witness the removal of a brain tumor from a patient who had acupuncture instead of a general anesthetic. I took pictures all during the surgery and, situated directly above the top of the operating table, my many pictures are terrific. Meeting with the surgeons following the operation, they told us the patient would recover much faster than if he had received a general anesthetic. I shall never forget seeing them remove a four-inch square piece of that man's skull, remove the tumor and then replace the skull and sew it up.

One day we went to visit an agricultural commune. While there we were invited to visit one of the worker's homes. The family members were obviously very proud of their facilities, but I thought it rather incredible that so many people could live together under one roof. On reflection, there was hardly any privacy in China. And when you think of their billion population, the problem becomes more obvious. When young Chinese wanted to get married, they must not only seek family approval, but also approval of the government. They must set up housekeeping with one of the families because there are just not enough shelters to go around. Some of the apartments which we visited in the city had several families sharing one kitchen and one bathroom. In the rural areas there were no bathrooms. I believe the human wastes were sometimes used as fertilizer.

My favorite time in China was our visit to Kweilin. During World War II I believe this was the base for the Flying Tigers. We flew from Shanghai in a twin-engine turbo prop airplane and I could not believe so many people could fit in such a small plane. The pint-size seats were packed so close together, I felt like my knees were riding under my chin. I also remember it was a warm day and how terribly hot the inside of that plane was before we finally got into the air.

Landing at Kweilin brought us to some of the most unique natural surroundings in the world. The mountains around Kweilin look as though they were painted in a picture. They are called karsts and although I bought some artwork depicting these scenes, they just don't look real.

Kweilin, a smaller community, is in western China. I had the opportunity to walk through the streets and snap pictures of local artisans at work. We visited the local industry, a silk factory, where we watched their old equipment take the raw silk from the cocoons and turn it into silk threads that eventually became bolts of silk cloth. I wanted to buy some and after long negotiations, they finally offered us the opportunity. However, I don't believe anyone in our family ever made use of the silk I brought home—the quality was not outstanding.

One day we boarded a passenger barge pulled by a powered boat and went down the Li Chiang River. This river eventually empties out in the South China Sea. I had the opportunity to take pictures and view a lifestyle which probably had not changed for centuries. The countryside was so beautiful and peaceful, however, it was jarring to see the Chinese bringing barges upstream. They lacked power equipment, so men waded at the edge of the river pulling on long ropes tied to the barge. Imagine spending your life at that seemingly endless drudgery.

Another great day was spent visiting a local school in Kweilin. Although the schoolhouse was certainly ancient, the kids were really impressive. Many of the kids took part in a talent display that included dancing and singing. Even at the elementary level, there were political overtones in the presentation. All school productions that we witnessed demonstrated the disdain held for the notorious "Gang of Four." One of the so-called "Gang of Four" was the widow of revered Chairman Mao, but they had all been convicted of attempting to subvert the political goals of Communist China. At appropriate times during the performance, the kids showed their contempt for caricatures of the "Gang of Four".

During the conference with the school administrators, I asked why no children wore glasses. I assumed that they probably could not afford them, or perhaps there was no appropriate way of testing them. The administrators called in a couple of students and asked them to demonstrate their eye exercises. We were told the daily use of these exercises strengthened the eyes and the wearing of glasses in China was a rare condition. Because of my own eye problems relating to my diabetic condition, I was particularly interested. In fact I practiced these Chinese eye exercises for several years after returning from China.

While writing this in 1989, twelve years since visiting China, I can't help but recall the philosophy of the government then and now. In 1977 the Chinese recognized they were certainly deficient in industrial production and technology. Their attitude was, "we will do it ourselves without foreign investment taking control of China again." Since that time I have observed that China is becoming more liberal in allowing both foreign investment and also a bit more individual freedom. I would hope this can continue for the benefit of a billion or more Chinese.

Our final visit in China was at the city of Kwangchowan, formerly Canton. We invited our Chinese translators and guides to dinner the final night. We enjoyed the occasion and even witnessed some good smiles and a few laughs out of our normally somber Chinese guides. The following day, we boarded a train which was to take us to the border at Hong Kong. We had been in China for almost two weeks and I was looking forward to Hong Kong. The train ride was a few hours and I took many pictures of interesting scenes along the way. Thousands of people worked the agricultural fields and although they used water buffalo a good deal, I never saw a tractor in use in China.

I was really unprepared for the cultural shock upon leaving the People's Republic of China. I had become used to the absence of billboards and outdoor advertising. Also there was never any litter in China. I suppose this comes from the fact that nothing in China could be wasted and also people kept the streets swept. When the train arrived at the bridge that crossed the river separating China from Hong Kong, we had to get off the train. Our luggage was also unloaded and put on carts and we walked across the bridge, then boarded another train and proceeded to Hong Kong. Once across the bridge vendors were hawking Coca-Cola, postcards, ice cream, and countless other items we had never seen in China. Also, the dirt and litter was apparent immediately. Hong Kong was a monument to entrepreneurial free enterprise. We checked into the Hyatt Regency Hotel and I felt like a king in my palace.

After a world-class dinner, I walked out into a blaze of neon lights and honking traffic, neither of which were found on the mainland. The second night we were guests of the United States Ambassador at his home atop a high hill overlooking Hong Kong. All of the Embassy personnel were invited to join us for cocktails and snacks. Looking out over the water surrounding Hong Kong at the million lights, both moving and stationary, was a welcome sight after the austerity of China.

We toured Hong Kong by bus and I would support anyone's intentions to visit that area. Through the efforts of Willie Brown, we enjoyed an unexpected highlight in Hong Kong. At this writing Willie is currently Speaker of the California Assembly, but at that time he was also a private practicing lawyer. He had connections with the British in Hong Kong and arranged for our group to be invited by the management of the Hong Kong banking system. We were invited to have lunch aboard their yacht, but the weather developed with uncertainty. Consequently, we had lunch in their private chambers. It was superbly elegant. The rooms were what I would call "old world charm". We were served cocktails, and then seated at round tables with about six persons to a table. I sat with the Britisher whose name was signed on the Hong Kong currency and he autographed the bill over his inked signature. I don't know whatever happened to that bill, but I am sure it is around somewhere.

The day we departed Hong Kong we flew back to Tokyo. We stayed at the airport and waited for a Japan Air flight to Honolulu. On the way to the Hawaiian Islands, I began to wish Mary was going to meet me so we could relax and enjoy a vacation. However, my original plans were to meet Mary in Denver. After landing in Honolulu, I spent an hour or two just going through customs. The customs agent was obviously not pleased that I had returned from mainland Communist China and he gave me a hard time about it. There was no doubt that I was returning home with many gifts, but I was always glad that I took advantage of the opportunity.

I flew Western Airlines from Honolulu to San Diego and my daughter, Nancy, met me at the airport. I was already exhausted from the flying hours from Hong Kong and I certainly dreaded getting aboard another flight to go to Denver. Anxious to see Mary, that was all the incentive I needed to hurry along. It must have been well past midnight by the time Mary and I moved my baggage into the Brown Palace Hotel.

The next morning I slept late and then had breakfast served in the room. I took my favorite recuperative treatment at the Brown Palace by making an appointment with the barbershop. I told them I wanted one of everything they offered: a shampoo, a haircut, a shave, a massage, a manicure, and finally a shoe shine. There is nothing like that to make you feel like a new man.

After returning home I was invited to many places to talk about China and show my pictures. But the strangest of all calls was the one from the Central Intelligence Agency. The fellow wanted to come to Gillette and visit with me about my trip and what I saw. I suggested that he come on a weekend when I would have more time. We made jokes at our house about the spy coming to dinner. I picked him up at the airport and he wore what we think of as the traditional trenchcoat and soft hat. He was interested in my pictures and also what was talked about at our conferences. I told him I could make it very easy for him because I had everything on dictaphone tape. He wanted to take them to Denver with him and I finally agreed to let him borrow them. They were returned to me after a few weeks. I really can't believe I had anything to offer the CIA that enlightened them on mainland China, but it was the conclusion to a very wonderful experience.

U.S. delegation with Chinese officials in the Great Hall of the People in Beijing, 1977. John is in the second row, third from right.

John at the Great Wall of China, 1977.

17

We Loved those Vacations!

ON JANUARY 13, 1952, MARY AND I WERE MARRIED AND THE HONEYMOON
that followed was the last real vacation we were to have for many years.
There were business trips, of course, but not what we could call real vacations.

In June of 1953, after Peg was about nine weeks old, Mary took her to visit Mary's
parents in New York. Although they were actually gone for a month, it seemed liked
years. Then in March of 1955, Mary and I took both Peg and John Jr. to New York for
another visit to the Grandparents Ryan. Peg celebrated her second birthday in New
York while John had his first. Thereafter, with Tom Ryan retiring from the police force,
there was hardly any reason to return to New York. Mary's parents had moved to
Florida, as most all New York police dream of doing.

It seemed as though I spent all my time working. Of course we did open our business on Main Street at 7 A.M. and never closed before 6 P.M. The only day we remained
closed was Sunday, so there was really little time for other activities. For several years
we did try to go to the mountains for a weekend. Once or twice we went to Forshay
Acres above Buffalo and then a few times we went over the Powder River pass to
Meadowlark Lake. In those places we rented a cabin, a rough shelter with beds but no
plumbing, and where the woodstove served as a heater as well as for cooking. There
was a shower house with toilet facilities for many cabins. We thought it was great fun, at
least I felt it was. If anyone had to take a pee at night, they used an empty coffee can. In
retrospect I have to continually admire the patience and great planning ability of Mary,
who really bore the brunt of packing and organizing for everyone.

One cold day early in 1963, I spoke with Mary about the two of us taking a vacation.
I told Mary about talking with our friend, Howard Esmay, who told me about the great
hotels and entertainment in Las Vegas and I thought we ought to go there. We had
been married for eleven years and Mary was then pregnant with Scott. We talked with
Norma Tanner about moving into our house to take care of the family and she agreed.
So off we went!

We drove to Casper to board a Western Airlines flight and it registered twenty-
eight degrees below zero when we boarded the plane. When we landed at Las Vegas it

was a lovely seventy-two degrees and it felt like heaven. We had made reservations at the Sahara Hotel and everything was lovely and elegant. Mary loved to sun at the swimming pool each day and I went to the Country Club where I took golf instruction. Every night we attended a different dinner show and enjoyed fabulous entertainment. In those days everyone attending the large hotel's entertainment spectaculars always dressed for dinner; the clothes you wore were usually your very best.

At that time I did not realize I would be returning to Las Vegas every year for the next eight years. This was because the Best Western Motel Convention was held in Las Vegas annually.

During our first trip in 1963, we were to meet another couple who have remained our good friends to this very day. We were at the Tropicana Hotel dinner show where Eleanor Powell was featured. We were fairly close to the stage and everyone was sitting quite close to one another. The couple sitting next to us did not open a conversation until the show was over. Then we introduced ourselves and began visiting on the way out with Joe and Vivian Blaise from New York. Joe was a Secret Service Agent who was assigned to the Presidential detail at the White House. Vivian worked for AT&T and through all these years we have remained close.

With each passing year, we began to talk about taking a real family vacation. Late in 1967, we spoke about going to Disneyland in California. This seemed to be everyone's idea of the perfect place to go and Mary and I both agreed. We soon discovered that part of the great fun of a family vacation is the planning and subsequent anticipation of the trip.

Scott would be five years old by the end of May in 1968 and Peg would be fifteen. We conceived the idea of implementing the "buddy system" to keep track of everyone. At the start of each day any two youngsters could agree and announce who their buddy would be for the day. Buddies had to stay together and keep track of each other. If they had an argument or tiff of some kind, they still had to hang with the other until a new formal arrangement could be announced and accepted by the parents. Mother would pack clothes with two children to a single suitcase. We were fortunate to have the same number of both boys and girls.

Reservations were made at the Disneyland Hotel. I learned that flying into Los Angeles International Airport was a goodly distance from Anaheim and studied the available transportation. A great idea developed! You could take a scheduled helicopter from Los Angeles airport to Disneyland and wasn't that going to be neat? It was, until just a few weeks before our scheduled departure when one of those passenger helicopters crashed. Many persons were killed and questions were asked at our dinner table after that news was announced. It was with great confidence that I summed up my position on this difficult question.

"Think of it this way," I said gravely. "This only happens once in many millions of miles traveled and now that this has occurred, we can be sure it won't happen again for a long, long time."

I noted thoughtful expressions passing among the family members and fortunately, a few nods of understanding began to be exhibited. The reader can imagine my chagrin when a second passenger helicopter crashed shortly after we returned from our vacation!

On the exciting day when school was over, the bags were packed, the station wagon loaded, and we commenced our great adventure. Ten people in a nine-passenger station wagon can always find reason to become a little testy, but we frowned on discouraging words this day. We sang the song of the open road! Our first stop was at the Natrona County line when one or two had to vomit from car sickness, but what the heck, soon we would be airborne!

We offloaded our bags and parked the car at the Natrona County Airport. Marching up to the Western Airlines counter, I displayed our ten ticket envelopes in front of the lady, and she looked up and exclaimed, "Oh Mr. Ostlund, this must be a tour group!"

"You sure called that one right," I responded.

As I recall we had to change planes in either Denver or Salt Lake City, but in the end we not only arrived in Los Angeles with all ten of us, but we also had every piece of luggage as well. But now came the time to show true grit. It was the appointed hour to take what might be described as the fateful helicopter ride to Anaheim. As the passengers were called to board the craft, few smiled. The craft was a large and ungainly looking creature with two giant sets of blades overhead. After taking seats I was discouraged to find the windows were dirty. I had told the family we would get such good views of Los Angeles and Disneyland from the air. It probably took thirty minutes to make the flight, but however long it was, we were all glad to get off safely. Disneyland electric carts picked us up and took us to the hotel in grand style. Now this was transportation we could understand and appreciate. We had great accommodations on the ground floor with a garden outside our front door. It was the first time our kids had seen palm trees. Everything seemed new, exciting, and very wonderful.

It did not take long for the kids to get acclimated to hotel living. They became quite popular with the service personnel in the dining room and they were soon ordering at will and signing off on tickets. What a way to live!

Scott celebrated his fifth birthday while we were there. The hotel furnished the birthday cake and it was a great party.

We purchased coupon books for admission to Disneyland including rides. Each child had saved religiously so they would have extra money for this big event. We were all excited as we took the monorail from the hotel to the park. As we walked up the main street, the Matterhorn was the most prominent feature and I could hardly wait to take that ride up and down the mountain. Scott seemed a little reluctant to ride on it, especially when he heard riders screaming. Confidently, I assured him that both of us would ride together. Somehow, at least in my own mind, I felt riding with Scott would reassure him. Now, looking back, I did take a lot for granted. We all did make the ride, but I did not realize how frightened Scott was at the time. Afterward, I felt badly that I had not considered his true feelings. I am certain that I did that with each of our children at least once in their life, but we can't ever do it over again.

We decided to go through "It's a Small, Small World" event. At this event, tragedy struck for Nancy. We all loved the boat ride through the small world, but as we were leaving the pavilion, Nancy discovered her wallet was missing. We went back to ask if it had been turned in, but Nancy's new wallet and all her money was gone forever. I felt so badly for her. I believe she had at least twenty dollars she had saved so carefully. We all did our best to cheer her up, but I know it was dismaying to Nancy on her first day at Disneyland. The money was replaceable, but the hurt feelings over the embarrassing loss were not.

We did enjoy a marvelous time at Disneyland, but three days were all we had allocated. I did not want to return home immediately, so we had preplanned to fly on to San Diego. We had made reservations at the Hilton Inn on Mission Bay for a couple of days and then we would return to Gillette. So another fateful ride in the big helicopter awaited us and we were all relieved to eventually land in San Diego.

We rented a station wagon and we were right at home in that vehicle. We thoroughly enjoyed our time; the pressure seemed to be off now that Disneyland was no longer outside our front door. We seemed to relax more. We found Sea World to be an outstanding attraction for all of us and I thought the San Diego Zoo was one of the best ever.

At the Hilton Inn on Mission Bay the kids loved to swim in the pool. This was probably because the pool was equipped with both a low diving board and also a very high board. The boys began coaxing Nancy to cannonball off the high board. Finally Nancy agreed to do it. She properly clutched her knees as she went off the board and thus hugged up, hit the water with a terrific blast. Nancy still remembers how she thought the hit on the water tore the skin off her backside!

Each of us has our own great memories of that wonderful time. One of the best things about that trip was that I lost any apprehension about taking ten people on a vacation. We did prove it could be done and done well. After returning home we had a few critiques on the trip. We thought the only thing wrong was that we missed having some good home-cooked meals. Before long we were talking about the possibility of taking another trip the following year. We decided if we could find a big house near the ocean to rent, one with a good cook and also someone to do the laundry and housecleaning, why that would be next to perfect!

We began looking in travel magazines for vacation rental properties. From time to time during the year, I made telephone contacts about rentals and really became interested in foreign rentals. By foreign, our interest was Mexico. I found a place in California which had a good reputation for meeting the needs of their clients and began working with them. I set out a list of conditions which I felt could not be fulfilled, but I was proven wrong. My conditions were: We wanted a rental in Mexico that we could fly to; the house must have five bedrooms, with at least one of them air-conditioned; we must be within walking distance of the beach; we must have a cook and a laundress; and we must be within reasonable distance of a Catholic church. The great rental folks came up with three different locations. We narrowed it down to two after looking at pictures and descriptions of each place. One was in Acapulco and the other was in Puerto Vallarta. Acapulco won out because this house showed a swimming pool on the patio. We made a deposit on the house for half a month.

Our decision was made at least six months before we were to leave. We were going in May of 1969, right after school was out. We spent all that time planning. The house came with a staff of five service people, none of whom spoke English. I was delighted about that because it would give me a wonderful opportunity to review the Spanish I had learned and used in the Navy. Peg was taking first year Spanish in high school that year and we began practicing Spanish words and phrases at the table.

We all needed certified birth certificates and we had to get Mary's from Yonkers, New York. Again there was real dedication to the saving of money, plus a great incentive to make extra funds for spending in Mexico. Again, armed with ten airline tickets, we presented ourselves in Casper to begin our new adventure. I believe we flew Frontier to Dallas where we then caught an American Airline flight direct to Acapulco.

It was about seven in the evening when we arrived at the airport in Acapulco. Departing the plane I recall going down the stairway with Peg and trying to lighten things up with a little humor. I whispered to Peg, "Did you ever see so many Mexicans in your life?" I don't recall her returning the smile, but everyone was perhaps a bit apprehensive about charging off into the unknown.

Fortunately, we again received all of our baggage and I called our rental house to let them know we had arrived. They gave me instructions to give to the taxi driver on how to get to Casa Los Techitos on Boulevard Aleman. Take a right after passing the Hotel Presidente. Of course, like every time we needed a taxi, I had to get two so that the ten of us could be properly accommodated. At the airport we were about fifteen miles from the city, but the two cabs remained together. The cab drivers had difficulty locating the house and after arriving I understood the problem. The street which turned right off the boulevard was a dirt street which went up hill. After winding around, you came to a stone wall and there was no house in sight. The gardener had been stationed at the entrance to the stone stairway at the wall to watch for the taxis. He finally waved down the cabs as we passed by. The houseboy, Beto, was also on hand and they verified that, indeed, we had arrived at Casa Los Techitos. We climbed up a long stairway which went through a veritable forest of plantings. There were a few acres in this estate. At the top of the stairs we walked onto a lovely patio that was illuminated with small lamps. Tomasa, the cook, and the laundress, Maria, and the housekeeper, whose name I can't remember, were also there to greet us. Since one of the bedrooms was air conditioned, they correctly surmised who was going to sleep in that room. Pat and Scott stayed together, John and Tom had their own guest house, Peg and Nancy were roommates, as were Karin and Jane. Of course, it was warm and humid and very strange for all of us to be in this new environment. Everyone finally got located and settled in for the night.

Following breakfast the first morning, Tomasa talked with us about what we liked to eat. She was asking this so she could not only do her grocery shopping, but also to do her best to satisfy our wishes. In those days I had not yet developed the good sense to not imbibe in hard liquor, so I volunteered that I liked martinis before dinner. By afternoon Beto had purchased about a gallon of gin along with some dry vermouth. For a while, every time I stepped on the patio he would want to put a martini in my hand.

Of course we were anxious to go swimming, so we walked to the street, crossed the boulevard, and swam in Acapulco Bay. I could easily discern the boys were disappointed by so little surf. They wanted large waves, so I inquired about a beach directly facing the ocean.

The staff recommended Revolcadero, but they added that it would be a long drive. Undaunted by that, I called for dos taxis and told them, "Playa Revolcadero." We also learned later that tourists were advised not to use Revolcadero, but we loved it and went almost every day. It never occurred to me we were the only gringos there.

The surf was tremendous and everyone enjoyed it. Even six-year-old Scott took to the heavy waves and seven-year-old Jane was always fearless in the water.

On Sundays we would go to Mass by phoning for the usual dos taxis. All of us seemed to enjoy hearing Mass spoken in Spanish—the language we now heard on a daily basis.

During the planning of our trip, we looked at pictures of the Mexican divers doing their high dives from the cliffs of the Quebrada into the ocean waters between two narrow rocky walls. At the Quebrada a patio near the cliff top afforded an excellent view of these skilled divers doing their dangerous performance. We were anxious to get there and we certainly were not disappointed in what we saw and we returned there a second time while we were in Acapulco.

One of my lifelong desires was to go deep-sea fishing. Remembering watching movies of people hooking sail fish or marlin, some of the kids and I thought what a wonderful experience that would be. Now we were in the real deep-sea fishing country and I was determined to go fishing. I checked on the best charter references and booked a boat.

Since the entire family would overload the craft, we decided I should take the four older children. Trying to quietly slip away early the next morning, Peg, John, Tom, Nancy, and I walked to the Hilton Hotel for a hearty breakfast. While we were eating, I noticed Tom was looking rather pale and peaked. I paid the check and we were walking across the marble floor when Tom had to vomit. The nearest container was a large urn with sand in it for cigarette disposal, so Tom left his newly acquired breakfast right there on the clean sand. We quickly evacuated the hotel lobby, but I can imagine the distress of the poor devil that had to clean that one. Unfortunately, Tom was coming down with the Mexican disease that frequently catches up with tourists. Before we returned to Wyoming, most of the family, more or less, came down with the same distress. Anyway, we took poor Tom on board the fishing vessel with us, but I know what a miserable day he must have experienced. The skipper packed a great lunch, including cold pop and beer, but Tom couldn't handle a thing. The boat did have some bunks in it, so Tom did get to lie down during the day.

Meanwhile, the fishing was great. A sailfish hit our bait first thing out and Peg got in the chair with the harness set. While reeling in the other line, a second sailfish struck, so John Jr. harnessed up to the second one. We had already decided we would keep one sailfish for mounting and release any others. With two hooked, Peg got her fish to the boat first and what a fish it was. I believe it was about eight-feet-long and so beautiful. John brought his alongside and the skipper released it. I am certain that the second fish was just as large, but we were happy to release it. Shortly thereafter, we hooked another fish and the skipper was sure it was a marlin. I got to bring this one in. That marlin was a bit over nine-feet-long. We have pictures of both these fish. Unknown to me, the kids had the nose bill sawed off this marlin and they had it mounted for me. We also had the sailfish mounted and it was hung on the basement wall of our home in Gillette for many years.

Everyone enjoyed going downtown shopping. It was a new experience for the family to shop where you bartered over the price. I believe some of our boys traded their tennis shoes on some kind of a swap with some Mexican boys. The kids would tease Peg because some of the Mexican boys were offering her the best deals if she would just throw in a kiss for them.

Deciding to get with the program, I went shopping for a pair of sandals. They certainly seemed to be the most appropriate footwear for that climate. I approached Beto one day and told him I wanted to go shopping with him. I explained my need for new sandals and he surely knew where to go. He took me to a place where they must have had twenty thousand pair of sandals if they had any at all. I found a pair which were just right, but Beto would not give the price. I knew that he had to maintain his pride and I was patiently allowing him to trade. I was about to give up when he finally made a deal for about eighty-five cents for the pair. I also wanted to buy Mary something made from Mexican silver, so I told Beto we better keep on shopping. We did find some nice gifts. If I could have only retained Beto full-time, I would have been well served.

Beto was nineteen years old and like many Mexicans, he came from a poor family. Now Beto was working for this family in Acapulco and saving his money. One day I talked with Beto about looking after the kids for one evening. I told him I wanted to take Mary to a nightclub for dinner and dancing and Beto said, "Sure!" Beto told me he would love to entertain the kids. The next day the kids told me Beto gave them karate demonstrations. He was breaking boards with his bare hands and could even break bricks. I asked Beto about this and he told me he learned karate from a book. In fact he showed me the book. Anyone would be very impressed with the dedication and abilities of this young man.

The swimming pool on the patio always looked cool and inviting. Early one morning I found out who maintained it. Alberto, the gardener, looked after the pool, among other duties. I also learned that the water for the pool had to be carried up from a faucet at the foot of the eighty-nine stone steps. Alberto carried a five-gallon pail in each hand and trudged up those eighty-nine steps to pour the new water into the pool. Just observing this drudgery caused me to feel badly whenever I splashed any water out of this lovely pool.

Two other roommates came down with the bug, Peg and Nancy. They were so sickly, I took them to the doctor. In my best Spanish we described their symptoms and the doctor prescribed medicine for them. Karin and Jane and then John Jr. all suffered for a day. Everyone seemed to agree that Scott was the last to catch it and he had the misfortune of carrying the malady all the way back home.

One day Tomasa told me she was worried because the kids were not eating. Mary thought they really would like hamburgers and chocolate malts. So Tomasa set out to try to do just that. She did well and even found the ingredients to make the milk shakes. Of course they were not like you could buy at home, but we asked the kids to please drink them and grin. With everyone saying "gracias," Tomasa felt rewarded for her efforts. She even found catsup for the burgers.

One morning Alberto saw me on the patio early and he promised me a great reward. He put a machete in his belt and began climbing to the top of a tall coconut tree. When he reached the top, he cut off several coconuts and dropped them to the ground. Then he climbed down, as nimble as a monkey, and expertly attacked the coconuts. Working with the machete, he made a flat bottom for the coconuts to sit upright and then neatly cleaved the top off of them. He picked some fresh limes out of another tree and squeezed them into the coconuts. He took straws off the bar and politely offered us this very excellent drink of coconut milk. He was very proud of his efforts. He wanted to do something nice for us because we had given him Polaroid pictures we had taken of his little daughter, Merlinda. This was his way of saying thank you.

Our family got their first views of real poverty on that trip to Mexico. From the beautiful facilities of Casa Los Techitos, you stepped onto a dirt street. The short walk down to the boulevard showed poor families living under conditions of absolute poverty. I believe the experience for all of us was truly a learning one. Mary and I both wanted to broaden our children's outlook and we felt that travel was probably one of the best educational opportunities.

In retrospect, I believe we can all tell of various stories concerning forms of bugs and lizards we encountered. Mary also recalls the mystery of the missing clothes. Each time any of us changed our clothes, they would disappear. Mary asked me to look into it. I talked with Maria, the laundress. Maria said that she was supposed to wash our clothes, so she picked up everything as a matter of course. However, without a clothes dryer and with the excessive humidity, it would take about two days for clothes to dry. Trying not to hurt Maria's feelings, I explained that she was only to wash clothes which Mary had set out for that purpose. All was well again.

Each of us carried a special souvenir home with us. I don't recall all of them, but Nancy was set on buying an ornate Mexican sombrero, which she still has. Pat bought a wooden hand-carved bull head complete with horns. He actually gave it to his Grandfather Axel and Grandpa hung it on his front porch for several years. I hope Pat still has it now.

The last night before we were to leave for Wyoming was festive and a bit sad. Our staff had never before had a family stay at the house, only adult couples. Our kids found their way into the hearts of our staff even though they could not really communicate by spoken language. They did wonderfully well by communicating with smiles, enthusiasm, and thoughtfulness. Following dinner that evening, I invited all the staff to join us on the patio. We had purchased small gifts for each of them and we had also discretely placed monetary gratuities in their packages. I delivered a speech in Spanish and we passed out the gifts. We felt a bit emotional before it was over because we had really gotten to know everyone. Beto really touched me. He wanted to extend a gift to reciprocate our gesture. He had very few possessions and little money, so he presented me with his Spanish karate book. I really hated to accept it, but I knew that if I did not, his pride would be hurt. I thanked him and although I never studied it, the book remained on my bookshelf for a long, long time.

The next morning we called our dos taxis and everyone cheered us off as we departed for the airport. We had truly enjoyed a very wonderful and special vacation.

As almost a footnote, I would add the following comment. About eleven years later, in 1980, Mary and I were to return to Acapulco. We had boarded the Cunard liner, Queen Elizabeth II, in New York. After transiting the Panama Canal we anchored in Acapulco Bay. When we took the boat to go ashore, we decided to get a taxi and find Casa Los Techitos again. I directed the cab to the best of my memory. As we approached the El Presidente Hotel and as I looked for the intersection to go to the hacienda, I could not get my bearings. Too much had changed. Finally, we put it all together. It was a bit sad to see that over the site of our vacation home, a large high-rise condo had been constructed. All was gone and so were the beautiful friendships we had made there. But then, that is the story of life.

Next we went to our favorite beach, Revolcadero. At that site now stood the newest hotel called the Princess. Of course it was lovely and the crowds of people indicated how their accommodations were, undoubtedly, fully booked. All in all, we did enjoy the return visit.

OTHER VACATIONS

As our family progressed through different levels of school, it became more evident that taking vacations as a group of ten was going to become more difficult. This was only because of the various interests which were developing in all the kids, plus the different times when college and secondary schools ended. We resolved this by taking the four oldest at different times from the four youngest. Each group still had two boys and two girls. I recall in 1975, we had been talking of renting a house in Hawaii. However, Mary's father, Tom Ryan, was very sick with lung cancer and we canceled our plans. Unfortunately, Tom Ryan passed away in Gillette later that summer.

We did take the four youngest to Denver. Pat was most interested in buying a used car and we also wanted to go to Elitch Gardens, the amusement center. The six of us drove to Denver in order to take a short vacation for two or three days. Pat did look at most of the used cars in the city, but ended up buying an El Camino from Spedding Chevrolet. That year we stayed at our favorite, the Brown Palace Hotel. Since it was August, everyone got to do their get-ready-for-school-shopping. We also took in most of the rides at Elitch Gardens. Again, Scott and I rode together on the big roller coaster. Karin, Jane, Pat, along with Mary, Scott and I were all screaming on that wild ride. I think I had as much fun as anyone.

About 1970 I had undergone shoulder surgery at the Scripps Hospital in La Jolla, California. About a year later I returned to have my other shoulder freed of the adhesions which were crippling my use of the arm. So around 1973 and, probably again in 1974, Mary and I took the four oldest on a Las Vegas and California vacation. We were determined to stay in the new MGM Hotel. We took a suite of three rooms for the six of us. There was a good deal of excitement about going to Las Vegas and I could also sense a little bit of apprehension from Nancy, who was in high school at that time. She was concerned about whether or not she could attend the dinner shows and late shows for which Las Vegas was so famous.

As we drove our rented car up to that huge new hotel, I voiced my usual admonition to my family. "Always drive into a hotel like you own it." I never wanted them to make a timid approach where lack of self-assurance never paid off. The service people unloaded our baggage while we marched into the hotel to register. Big eyes were looking at that vast casino which seemed to spread as far as a football field. The rich carpet kept the sounds subdued, but the constant clicking of chips and dice, plus the casino crowds, made the whole atmosphere seem unreal. We all agreed our accommodations were very elegant.

That night we booked reservations for both a dinner show and a late show. Since Nancy still seemed apprehensive about being allowed to be at the main show, her mother offered to let Nancy wear her short mink coat in order to give Nancy more of a "sophisticated" appearance. In reality it was probably to offer Nancy more self-assurance. It worked, but there was a moment of humorous embarrassment for Nancy. We were at the Flamingo Hotel show where Connie Stevens was starring, seated at the first table adjacent to the stage and Nancy had hung her mink jacket on the back of the chair where she was positioned at stage center. A warm-up comedian was telling rapid fire jokes when he reached down and plucked Nancy's jacket off the back of the chair! Holding it high up, he explained to the audience that this garment was known as a Jewish windbreaker! Nancy was momentarily more than embarrassed, probably because she never dreamed of suddenly becoming the most noticed person in the room!

Another evening we had dinner at the Tropicana, which always featured the Follies Bergere. When the magnificent show and the parade of beautiful showgirls, including the bare-breasted, began, Mary noticed a son gaping and called across the table, "Tom, close your mouth!"

The next day we left John and Tom in Las Vegas while Peg, Nancy, Mary, and I flew to San Diego. I drove a rented car to La Jolla to visit my orthopedic surgeon, Robert Cummings. Following that visit we walked to the Valencia Hotel. Behind the hotel is a park that fronts on the sea wall. It has always been a favorite place of mine and that day we walked along the sea front and out on one of the breakwaters where we snapped some pictures. That trip may have contributed to Nancy's desire to live in San Diego, where she has happily resided since 1977.

Meanwhile back in Las Vegas, it had been a big day for John and Tom. They played golf at the Dunes Hotel course and then attempted to beat the casino at the MGM. John was within a few days of becoming twenty-one years old. When carded, his identification showed he lacked a few days of being twenty-one; he was asked to leave the casino. John told me that on the way out he felt a quarter still remaining in his pocket, so he slipped it into a slot machine. That caused the security guard to take him off the floor and into the security office. The guard told John he used to be on the police force in Gillette and that he knew his father and grandfather. With that, he admonished him to stop gambling and turned him loose. John was somewhat indignant since his younger brother, Tom, was never requested to show his identification and had free run of the casino.

About the following year we took Pat, Karin, Jane, and Scott back to San Diego. As we left Gillette in our station wagon, we felt we were traveling with a lighter load. After all, leaving the four oldest behind caused the four youngest to feel a bit more important.

Driving to Casper, a most unforgettable event occurred. I was driving our Mercury wagon. Because of a dispute involving Patrick, I had Patrick sit in front between Mary and me. A flock of small birds flew up from the roadway and one hit the car. Instead of hitting the windshield, or fender, or grillwork, this bird hit the hood ornament on our Mercury wagon. In fact, he became impaled upon the small spike, which was a part of this ornament. While the poor bird remained impaled on the ornament, all his guts splattered smack on the windshield directly in front of Pat's face!

Patrick cried out, "Oh my God!! I'm going to be sick!" Each time Patrick opened his eyes he could only see guts splattered in front of him. Meanwhile, the bird stayed right out there on the hood ornament, dead of course. I was amazed the bird remained at the speed of seventy miles per hour blasting him.

I asked Pat if he would wipe off the windshield if I stopped. His reply was, "No way! I couldn't do it without throwing up!"

I believe the bird finally blew off, but we parked the car with the windshield still dirty. After all, we were on vacation. We could tidy up when we returned to Casper! As a matter of interest, when we did return, we pulled into a gas station, filled our tank, and had the windows washed. No problem.

At San Diego we stayed at the PSA Hotel Islandia. This was a very nice accommodation with a large boat dock. We rented a sailboat and had great fun on the water. Of course, I would only take the kids out one at a time. We also bought tickets to a baseball game where the Cincinnati Reds played the San Diego Padres. Catcher Johnny Bench was the star performer. Of course we had to go back to Sea World and the San Diego Zoo.

From time to time Mary and I began to slip away on our own little trips. The first time was to Jamaica in 1974, following a legislative session. We landed at Kingston airport and then bussed to the northern Jamaica coast to Ocho Rios. We stayed at the Playboy Hotel for about a week and even went deep-sea fishing one day with another couple named Brown from Cheyenne; and although three of us got seasick, Mary never did. We caught dolphin, which I had never seen or tasted before, but it was quite delicious. I also learned that a dolphin was certainly a different fish from a porpoise.

One day Mary and I enjoyed taking a tour of a banana plantation and we found that to be something new and different. Then in 1976, we finally realized a promise I had been making to Mary for the previous twenty-five years. I had been telling her that I wanted us to take an ocean voyage sometime, but sometime seemed a long while coming. We booked passage on the Royal Viking Liner Star. A good friend of ours in Sheridan, named Charles Adams, was good friends with the president of Royal Viking and through his request we were assigned to sit at the captain's table for the whole voyage. We flew to San Francisco where we stayed at the very elegant Stanford Court across from the Fairmont. We did some last minute shopping, including buying a small foot locker. I went to my favorite men's store in San Francisco, called Bullock and Jones, where I not only added to my seagoing wardrobe, but also bought a new dinner jacket. I thought it a bit loud as it was plaid, but they assured me this was very stylish for my purpose—a jacket I had for several years and enjoyed wearing.

Sailing out of Frisco was a wonderful sight, especially as we steamed under the Golden Gate Bridge. We stopped overnight in Los Angeles where we took on more passengers.

After stopping at Mazatlan our next Mexican port was Puerto Vallarta. Mary and I walked about the city and we became fascinated with the parachute rides. This was done along the beachfront and after being harnessed into the chute, a speedboat towed you around the bay while you were silently aloft. I thoughtfully decided I must do this and it was a wonderful experience. I flew right over our ship. After a gentle landing I suggested that Mary try it. I also wanted to get my movie camera and take another ride, which I also did. And Mary flew also. We both enjoyed it.

Life aboard ship was wonderful. The food was superb and the people were charming. We made such good friends, especially with Russ and Thyra Fellows from Rancho Santa Fe in California. He grew lemons. We still exchange Christmas cards at the time of this writing.

We went through the Panama Canal from west to east and it was a very educational and interesting day. I had been to the Canal in 1946 while I was in the Navy, but this trip was like being on a royal yacht. Leaving Panama we stopped at Cartagena, Columbia, a city with a violent history since the opening of the Spanish Main. We enjoyed touring the ancient city with the old fortresses and prisons, but on the whole, if you think you have seen poverty in Mexico, Columbia has the most pitiful. We visited Willemstad, Curacao, in the Dutch Antilles. We were to make a second trip there a few years later and that delightful Dutch community is considered a shopper's paradise. We stopped at Table Bay in Jamaica and then went on to Fort Lauderdale, Florida, where our trip ended.

Renting a car, we drove to Miami Beach where we checked into the Carillon Hotel. That night we went to the rooftop of the Doral Hotel and enjoyed dinner and dancing until late. We had been taking dance instructions aboard ship, so we felt as though we really performed well in front of the big orchestra at the Doral Rooftop. Actually, you only think about such things when you are the only couple out there dancing!

We checked on the construction of the Omni Hotel in Miami because we had a financial interest in that project then under construction. We swam and relaxed before flying on to Washington, D.C. With our sea voyage now behind us, we dispatched the foot locker containing extra clothes which were no longer needed.

Our son, John, was with the "UP with People" group that year and they were performing at the Capital Centre. He stayed with my cousin, Bill Parker.

Mary and I stayed at the new Plaza Hotel, which was very elegant. We invited Senator Cliff and Martha Hansen to join us for dinner and then went on to the show. It was a very successful evening. I always remember watching the performance that night.

The Arena was huge. At one point our son, John, sang a solo and the TV camera did a close-up on him. The huge screens carried his image and tears came to my eyes as I listened to him sing a song about his dad.

The next day we picked up John and his friend, Pat Gamache, in our rental car. We drove to Annapolis where I proudly showed them the Naval Academy. We really had a very fine day. John's group closed their performance in Washington, so John flew home with us the following day.

I well remember dropping John Jr. and Mary off at the American Airlines terminal and then I was going to drop our rental car off at Avis. Unfortunately, with some construction confusion I missed the detour to go to the Avis lot and suddenly I found myself on the freeway heading for Memorial Bridge. I was desperate, but there were no exits. If I crossed the Potomac River I would have a heck of a time trying to figure out how to get back and I had little time before the plane was to depart. I did the only thing possible to save my flight; I did a U-turn across the grass median strip. If a cop saw me I would be arrested, but if I didn't get caught, it was the only way to make my flight. Well, I did not get stopped and pulled into Avis where I flashed five bucks at the yard employee and said, "Drive me to American." He did. Mary and John were relieved to see me approaching. And upon finally reaching Gillette, it was so wonderful to have all ten of us reunited once again.

Following the unsuccessful election campaign of 1978, Mary and I sorely needed a vacation. Ruth Ann Norris, who then worked for Air Lansee Travel, suggested we go to Palm Springs and she booked us into a delightful place called Ingleside Hotel. It was formerly a mission and each room was custom built with no two accommodations the same. The morning we were scheduled to depart, a terrible winter storm hit Gillette and we had to move our reservations ahead one week.

Neither Mary nor I had ever been to Palm Springs. We really enjoyed it and with our rental car we traveled the area extensively. Nancy and Jim drove from San Diego to visit us. Before they arrived the hotel management wanted a conference with us. I could not imagine what was going to happen and I was certainly curious. The manager explained that a man who was a frequent guest at the hotel had just gotten married and he wanted to bring his new bride to Palm Springs to stay in "their usual accommodation", which Mary and I were occupying. To add to the manager's consternation, there were no vacancies left at the hotel either. Delicately, the manager invited our indulgence long enough so that she could show us their condominiums adjacent to the hotel, which were owned by the hotel. We took a look and loved what we saw. It was a beautiful situation; large landscaped grounds surrounded the building and a lovely swimming pool was in the middle of the lawn. Our refrigerator was to be stocked, including a supply of champagne and hotel room service was to be given to us any time we phoned. They made it an attractive offer. It was perfect for us with Jim and Nancy coming, although, in front of the manager, I agreed rather reluctantly to make the move.

While in Palm Springs I took advantage of the bathhouses for which Palm Springs is famous. Following the bath in the mineral water, I had a rubdown that really made you feel great. I could take that life all winter, but that was our first and only time in

Palm Springs.

The second sea voyage that Mary and I took began in 1979. We flew to Venice where we boarded a small Greek liner named the *Stella Maris*. We spent a couple of days in Venice and that was just enough time to whet your appetite for more. It was a fine trip, visiting the Greek Islands. We even spent one day ashore at Ephesus, Turkey, which was the most remarkable and memorable ancient ruins I have ever visited. We can certainly recommend that visit to anyone. Our trip ended in Athens about two weeks later.

Thirty years had passed. I had not been in Athens since 1949. Now the buildup of industry from the seaport all the way into Athens made it seem like one continuous city. The air pollution was terrible and I understood that many of the ancient marble buildings and statues were eroding from the air pollution. It was marvelous to return to the Acropolis with Mary. We enjoyed viewing the ancient structures built so many centuries before us.

The casual informality aboard the Stella Maris made for a most enjoyable trip. A couple of years later we cruised on the QE2, which was rigid in its formality—quite a contrast.

In October of 1980, we cruised the Western Mediterranean aboard another Greek ship named the Daphne. We began and ended our cruise in Genoa, Italy, and visited Cannes, Nice, Barcelona, Palma de Mallorca, Tunis, Palermo, Naples, and Livorno. Again, the food and facilities were great. We had flown Pan American from Dallas. Wanting to unpack and get organized first thing, I began the task. Imagine my surprise and embarrassment when I put my first large bag on the bed, unlocked the familiar padlock, unzipped the soft-sided luggage lid, and opened it—the bag contained nothing but women's wearing apparel! Remembering how careful I had been to claim my luggage in Dallas, I realized the awful truth. I had grabbed the wrong bag for one that was identical to my own. Here I had carried someone else's luggage to Italy. I informed the ship and they immediately took the bag to place on a departing flight to the United States. Meanwhile, I called my office in Gillette and left a message on my answering machine for my secretary. "Please call Braniff Airlines in Dallas, claim my luggage and ask that it be sent to Gillette to await my homecoming."

That incident made me realize just how well I could get along with half the things I usually took with me. I did feel sorry for the woman raising cane with Braniff Airlines in Dallas about her missing luggage. Little did she realize some guy had hijacked it off to Italy!

BEHIND THE IRON CURTAIN!

Through the travel service named INTRAV, Mary and I scheduled a month-long trip which was to take us behind the Iron Curtain. We had never selected a land tour before, for we had found it so convenient to go by ship. We had such good luck with INTRAV and particularly liked them because their policy stated that no INTRAV customer would ever carry luggage. That warms the heart of a seasoned traveler.

We flew to Berlin in the fall of 1981. We had never previously been in that city. The ominous Berlin wall was something to behold. From the West Berlin side of the wall we climbed up on a platform in order to view over the top of the wall into East Berlin. The wall was not keeping people out of East Berlin, but rather it was there to keep the East Berliners at home. We stayed in Berlin for several days before heading east by bus. There were twenty-seven people in our group— a nice collection of folks who were most congenial to be with.

The day we first went into East Berlin was a cultural shock. East Berlin seemed almost vacated when observed through a bus window. In contrast, West Berlin was a beehive of activity. Unfortunately in future years, those people who never had the opportunity to view both the west side and the east side of the wall will find it difficult to imagine or believe how capitalism and communism could be so totally different! May communism never again prevail!

When we left our fine hotel in West Berlin to go into Poland, we were to live with this severe social order for many days. Crossing into East Berlin was traumatic every time. Russian or East German border guards would cautiously inspect each bus. They would even slide low-wheeled mirrored carts beneath the bus to check for possible occupants who might be clinging underneath. What a way to live!

The most prominent sights throughout eastern Europe were the Russian war memorials exhibited everywhere. According to Russian history, Russia won World War II all by themselves.

Our tour guide spoke many languages, which was important as we crossed the different borders. Sometimes border crossings could take as long as two or three hours. Usually, it was necessary to provide bribes of vodka, chocolate, dollars, or other things to get expeditious treatment.

Life in Poland was terrible! In fact, a month after we departed Poland martial law was declared. People were subjugated. Throughout Poland people were seen standing in lines everywhere awaiting food stores to be restocked. We visited and stayed over in several Polish cities: Krackow, Warsaw, Poznan, Zakopane, Czestochowa, and Wieliczka, which was at the base of the Polish Alps and was the last city we were to be in before leaving Poland for Hungary.

Zakopane was at a higher altitude. We reached it in October and it was quite chilly. Unfortunately, the Polish coal miners had been slowing or halting production for lack of pay. Coal supplies were limited and the hotel was only providing hot water and small amounts of heat on a strict regimen. I would have given many dollars for a suit of long underwear.

After checking into the hotel there and examining our cold room, I set out to try and find some place with heat. Discovering the hotel supposedly had a sauna on the premises and the fact that most people went there to get warm, I hurried back to the room and told Mary there was a sauna in the basement. Mary declined to go with me, but I went anyway. First of all, I was surprised not to see more people using it. I was directed to a locker in which to place my street clothes. The attendant was a male, so I assumed I was in the proper men's locker room.

To my surprise, there was only one other man in the large sauna room. There were three or four layers of benches rising up from the floor level. I took the first bench I came to, placed my towel on the bench to sit on and relaxed as the heat soaked into my cold body. The door to the sauna opened to admit some other devotees and I observed them picking a place to sit. Then to my utter surprise, two naked women walked in and took places beside me. Now I don't speak Polish, but I probably could not have protested anyway. Obviously, they knew what they were doing and I assumed I was the only person in there who was surprised. Well, in Rome, do as the Romans do!

My next surprise came when one or two at a time left the sauna to jump into that massive tub of icy water which was outside, then, back they came for more heat. I chose not to follow that routine.

When I returned to the room, I certainly had many new things to talk about with Mary. Since we were in Poland for a week, we tried to call the family in Gillette. There was always an excuse from the government for not being able to do that. I don't believe they wanted telephone calls going out of Poland at all. We had no luck until we reached Hungary.

This trip could extend the length of this chapter extensively. I shall attempt to abbreviate!

The most troublesome and traumatic day we spent in Poland was visiting the death camp at Auschwitz. Much of this camp has been preserved as a reminder of the horrible Nazi program to eliminate the Jews. Touring Auschwitz left me sick at heart. The gruesome piles of human hair, clothes, luggage, shoes, and other mementos of people gassed and burned to ashes were an unforgettable reminder of man's inhumanity to men!

We crossed Czechoslovakia without staying on our way to Hungary. We stayed in a very nice hotel in Budapest. In fact, we could direct dial Gillette and talk with our kids. Hungary was far and away the best and most progressive of the communist controlled countries we visited and we enjoyed going to a nightclub where both the food and entertainment were great. The new wine crop was ready and we celebrated the "hoorigan" as the new wine was called. Delightful!

We left Budapest by boat up the Danube to Vienna. I loved that trip and enjoyed the scenery. Vienna quickly became our very favorite place to visit. Being back in a democratic country was wonderful. We stayed at the Intercontinental Hotel, a terrific accommodation. One of the benefits of arriving in Vienna was to see a doctor. I picked up a virus in Poland which had been troubling me for many days. When I went to the doctor and described my symptoms he said, "You must have been to Poland!"

When I acknowledged that I had spent over a week there he replied, "I just treated the President of Columbia University for the same ailment yesterday." He gave me some pills which quickly overcame the troublesome virus. I was so appreciative.

Mary and I took a carriage ride around Vienna one day, which we enjoyed. One of the highlights was seeing the Lipizzaner stallions perform. We watched them practice at their own fine building. I had seen the stallions perform in Chicago during the summer of 1973 and seeing them again was indeed a treat.

Next we traveled by bus to Prague, Czechoslovakia, a letdown compared to Hungary. However, we came to see and enjoy and we certainly did that. Leaving Prague for

Germany we passed through Lidice. I vividly recalled Hitler ordering this town to be destroyed. One of his SS generals was shot and to make the residents an example, he had the men dig a ditch. All males in the town were lined up, shot, and buried where they fell into the ditch. The females were trucked off to be used in other ways. The town was completely razed and buried. There was to be no sign or indication that people ever resided there. Now a memorial has been erected where the former town of Lidice once stood and it has a sombering effect, as is fitting. Additionally, it is another grim reminder of the horrors perpetrated by the Nazi party under Adolph Hitler. May the people of the world never forget this.

SOUTH AFRICA

Early in 1983, Mary and I were to take our last major vacation trip. We both had expressed an interest in visiting South Africa. Again we arranged with the INTRAV folks who had served us so well.

We flew from New York on South Africa Airlines in a Boeing 747. After eight hours in flight we looked forward to the stop to be made at Cape Verde Island. Since this was a fueling stop, we had to leave the aircraft, but we were anxious to do this anyway. However, Cape Verde was indeed disappointing. Only one other plane was there at the same time and it was a Russian jet. Inside the terminal we viewed an unpleasant place and the rest rooms were neglected. Other than having the pleasure of stretching our legs for about twenty minutes, we were glad to leave that place behind.

Another eight hours of flight brought us to Johannesburg, South Africa, where we were treated to fine hotel accommodations, good food, and some of the most outstanding wines I had ever tasted. It was news to me to learn that vineyards had been established there for more than three hundred years.

Within a couple of days, a few of us flew off to visit a lovely private game preserve called Mala Mala. Although we were living in what you might call thatched roof units, they had air-conditioning as well as all the modern conveniences you would expect in any fine city. The difference was that we could sit on our front porch and observe wild animals nearby, such as baboons, chimps, and others. An interesting place was what I termed the outdoor "dining room." The food was excellent, but it was all cooked without modern appliances at the center of this encampment. To prevent intruders from entering the circular area within which we dined, it was enclosed by a high wooden fence made of native materials. Of course the food and service was exquisite!

Mary and I were driven out to view wild animals by a guide who drove a Land Rover vehicle. We took many beautiful slides which, of course, never seem to be shown anymore.

Attempting to give the reader only a bare flavor, we went on to Durbin, on the Indian Ocean side of Africa. While there, we made a bus trip north to the Zulu country. On the way we passed mile after mile of sugar cane—I never dreamed there was so much cane growing anywhere. Years before I had seen it growing in Cuba, but this was impressive by the sheer magnitude of the endless fields. The Zulu encampment was very interesting and the Zulus performed ritual dances for us.

Returning to Durbin we later went to Cape Town, which is made impressive by the fabled Table Mountain rising to the east of the city.

For me, the most impressive visit was traveling to the very tip of the Cape of Good Hope. Standing on a high granite point, which was as far as a person could safely go, and looking across that black granite to the very tip of the continent, was a memorable picture I carry in my mind. More than 2,500 ships each day round that point where the Indian Ocean meets the South Atlantic—as they have for many centuries.

Finally a lovely overnight ride on the famous Blue train carried us back to Johannesburg and from there we returned to New York.

Perhaps this very abbreviated account will encourage those who have not yet visited South Africa to do so some day. My accounts barely scratched the surface of the many beautiful and fascinating places to go and see.

Through the pages of this chapter I have attempted to recall the fun and good times enjoyed by our family doing things together. Hopefully, it will refresh the memories of everyone, and thus bring forth more now forgotten stories of those wonderful days.

Meadowlark Lake. Left to right: Nancy, Tom, John Jr., and Peg, 1959.

The Fishermen: Tom, John Jr., and Patrick, 1965.

Disneyland. Left to right: Nancy, Jane, Goofy, Pat, Pluto, Scott, and Tom, 1968.

Successful deep-sea fishing in Acapulco. Left to right: Tom, Nancy, Peg, and John Jr., 1969.

John and Mary on the beach in Jamaica, 1974.

First Cruise, 1976.

18

Chelation, a Lifesaver!

As a twenty-two year old naval officer, the military diagnosed me as being diabetic. As well as that shocker, I was also forewarned that my death would probably be earlier than normal and either kidney failure or arteriosclerosis would probably be the cause. Additionally, I was told that most diabetics could expect to experience amputations of a foot or a leg, if they lived long enough. I failed to inquire if they had any good news. By the way, this was happening to me in the fall of 1949.

However, by the time I was forty-five, I still felt in fairly good health and fully ready to take up new challenges. Having sold the Sands Corporation in October of 1971, I was ready to run for the State Senate, a decision which had been delayed. (That political race is taken up in a separate chapter.) This chapter is devoted to a medical treatment that, in my opinion, certainly saved, enhanced, and extended my life. To introduce this therapy, I should offer the reader a bit of personal medical history.

During my years at the Naval Academy, I had begun smoking cigarettes. By 1972 that bad habit had been going on for twenty-six years. During the primary campaign for the State Senate, I began to realize I was sometimes smoking almost three packages each day. I determined that when the primary was over I would quit smoking. Of course it is much easier to say than to do. I felt I should not delay because I doubted that I could quit smoking while I was beginning my term as a State Senator. Quit I did! Considering the very best decision in my life was marrying my wife, Mary, the decision to quit smoking also has to rank close to the top of my "best decisions" list.

In 1972 it was not yet proven that smoking was injurious to your health, but of course, we now know that it aggravates arteriosclerosis, as well as countless other health problems. By smoking I was only encouraging the process to hasten. Unfortunately, I had also forgotten the value of exercise and when I quit I gained weight. This should have been a temporary condition, but I seemed to be oblivious to the problem. At that time it never even occurred to me to exercise to prevent the weight gain. I should also admit that I probably only visited a doctor every year or two for the first twenty-three years of being diabetic. Now, too late, I confess that was a pathetic practice.

By the time I took the oath of office and commenced serving in the 1973 Wyoming Senate, I weighed about 182 pounds. This was far above the 168 I had been carrying and far above the 150 I presently weigh. To make matters worse, I was still not exercising. Unknown to me, my cardiovascular system was and had been deteriorating rapidly, diabetic retinopathy had already begun to work its devastation on my eyes. All this was soon to come to the forefront of my life in a big way!

During the Senate session one day in January, I was about to enter debate on a bill when I became aware that my heart was beating rapidly. I also felt as though I was running out of oxygen. Instead of rising to speak, I just sat there. In due course the Senate adjourned and I remained seated trying to cope with what seemed to be a lack of oxygen.

Finally I stood up and slowly walked over to the "Doctor for the Day" and I told him about how I felt. I don't remember that doctor, but he was not from Cheyenne. He felt that I should check into the hospital and he asked if I thought I could drive myself. I thought I could. On the way to DePaul Hospital I recall thinking how strange it was to have my heart beating so rapidly, but I made the trip without incident.

At DePaul Hospital I was put in intensive care where my heart was monitored. It was concluded that instead of a heart attack, I probably suffered heart failure. I was advised to go to General Rose Hospital in Denver. Dr. Frank Barrett, my friend from Cheyenne, drove me to Denver. At General Rose Hospital I was examined by a Doctor Craddock, a cardiologist who told me they wanted to do an angiogram the next morning. He explained that they would open an artery at my elbow and then run a probe to my heart. He also described how dye would be injected into my system from time to time to take pictures to determine if and where I had blockages in my circulatory system. The procedure was done the next morning. It was not long before Dr. Craddock viewed the video with both Mary and me. Serious blockages in the arteries from my heart were shown—the cause of my problems. I was placed on prescriptions of anturane, digoxin, and nitroglycerin. I was a candidate for bypass surgery, although that operation was not a common practice in 1973 as it is today.

Returning to Cheyenne, I took up my duties in the legislature. I could not walk up stairs, so I used the elevator instead. I walked slowly and was constantly fighting for breath. In the meantime, I lost some weight and I have never allowed myself to get heavy again. Following the legislative session, it still seemed as though I could not regain my strength to do much of anything. However, we had arranged for an appointment at the Mayo Clinic in Rochester, Minnesota, where I wanted a second opinion.

Meanwhile my friend, Jerry Jasper, called. Jerry and I were good friends from years ago when we were part of the group who started the Gillette Gas Company. Jerry and Dorothy Jasper had a daughter, Pat Addison Borden, who was the head administrator of a hospital near Euliss, Texas. Euliss is between Dallas and Fort Worth. Jerry told me that Pat felt that a process known as chelation therapy had been quite successful with certain patients. Jerry urged me to call Pat and finally, after much foot-dragging, I did.

Pat Borden told me that a Doctor Steven Cordas had been giving chelation therapy to patients with circulation problems and that the results had been quite impressive. Chelation was given to patients intravenously and it took three hours for a treatment. Pat advised me to come to Texas and talk with Dr. Cordas. I was already scheduled to go through the Mayo Clinic, so I thought about first going to Texas.

When I attempted to explain to Mary what my understanding of the process was, she grew skeptical. Mary is a registered nurse and the idea of allowing an osteopath to give me intravenous treatments, which few people seemed to know about, made her both suspicious and apprehensive. Her concerns seemed fully justified.

At that time I did not have a regular doctor in Gillette. Dr. Charles Lowe in Casper was the medical doctor whom I visited annually. I recall talking with Dr. Lowe about chelation and he knew nothing about it. He told me that one of his classmates was in charge of a large veterans' hospital in Dallas and he would be glad to ask him to look into it. After a short time, I received a call from Dr. Lowe who said his friend had talked with Dr. Cordas in Euliss and concluded that Cordas was a very capable and earnest doctor. He could not conclude that chelation was good or bad, but he seemed to be impressed with what he understood from Cordas.

Since I was not really improving and I was apprehensive about any kind of heart surgery, I decided to fly to Dallas and talk with Dr. Cordas. I flew Braniff and then rented a car and stayed in the Six Flags Over Texas Inn, which is actually in Arlington, Texas. I had never been there before. I studied my map and took off on Monday morning to find Dr. Cordas.

The small office occupied by Dr. Cordas in Euliss was unimpressive. He was the only doctor in his practice, but the place was crowded. When I first met Dr. Cordas, for some reason, I was reminded of the story of Ichabod Crane. Steven Cordas was very tall and lean. His reputation was built on his ability to treat allergies. He patiently explained the history behind chelation.

The word chelation comes from the Greek or Latin meaning "to grab onto". It was found that chelation was very effective for treating people with lead poisoning. The EDTA substance, more properly known as ethylene diamine tetracetic acid, when injected into the bloodstream, grabs onto the lead in the blood and is disposed of through urine. When chelating it's important to check the kidneys. Of course, chelation is not so selective that it takes only the lead out of the blood. It also removes other minerals and when chelating it's necessary to take additional minerals and vitamins.

While treating people for lead poisoning, it was also discovered that those patients who suffered from high blood pressure and circulatory problems would also find relief after chelating. It was then determined that the plaque coating the interior walls of blood vessels and arteries could be diminished with chelation.

I was skeptical, mostly because I thought, "If this works, why doesn't the rest of the world know about it? Why should I have to learn about this in a small doctor's office in Euliss, Texas? There must be a catch to this." I told Dr. Cordas I was scheduled to go to the Mayo Clinic soon and I would make my decision after visiting at Mayos.

Mary went with me to the Mayo Clinic. I recall taking James Michener's new book, *Centennial*, and was glad, because there is so much waiting when going through the clinic. As a diabetic patient, my lead doctors were diabetic specialists and when introduced to a new doctor I usually began by asking the question, "Do you know anything about chelation?"

The response was always negative and the question was usually turned back to me, "What is chelation?"

My brief explanation usually left them shaking their heads as though chelation must be some kind of scam. One doctor even ventured that, "they do a lot of strange things down in Texas!" Consequently, it was a surprise to me when I first spoke to the cardiologist at Mayo's. I asked the same question regarding chelation and his response was, "Why yes, in fact we are doing research in chelation at this time."

"Well, how does it look?" I asked.

"Oh, it looks very promising," the cardiologist replied.

"Could I come here and get chelated?" I asked.

"Oh my, no," the doctor said. "We are only doing it to animals. It may well be years before we might do it to a human."

That response made the decision for me. I decided right then to go back to Texas and start chelation. The only thing that Mayo could offer me was more pills, with perhaps a surgical alternative. Mayo had already affirmed that my circulation in my feet was so poor that no pulse could be found, which accounted for why my feet were cold and numb. I had not had any feeling in my feet for a long time; my arteriosclerosis was more advanced than anyone had previously told me. I had a lot to gain and very little to lose by trying chelation. Without the chelation I might soon lose one or both of my feet!

Once again I headed for Texas. I did not realize then that I would be making many trips to Texas over the next six or seven years. I checked into Pat Borden's hospital because Dr. Cordas wanted to give my first few chelations while confined in a hospital.

Since I had trouble getting my breath under any slight exertion, this was undoubtedly a good idea. At my first chelation I learned that my veins were difficult to find, let alone insert a needle into. After a "blowout" or perhaps two, I took my first treatment and found the chelation mixture burned if the substance began to infiltrate. To help my kidneys, they insisted I drink lots of water and when chelating I also took a lot of various mineral pills and vitamins to replace those being depleted by chelation.

Following the first few chelations, I felt no different. I was hoping and expecting to feel better, instead, there only was increased difficulty in starting my IVs. After seven treatments, Dr. Cordas told me that I could leave the hospital and come to his office as an outpatient to receive the balance of the twenty treatments he prescribed. However, after my tenth treatment and the problem of my veins not taking the IVs, Steven Cordas suggested I go home for a while and give my veins a chance to build up. I returned to Gillette for a couple of weeks and then returned to Texas.

In retrospect, I now believe my inactivity and lack of exercise undoubtedly were contributing factors leading to my problem of flaccid veins. I finished the twenty treatments and, although now I don't recall how I felt, there is one incident that I shall never forget. I was told that even after concluding the IVs the body would keep on chelating for a period of time. More and more I discovered for myself the truth of this, which is the reason you keep taking minerals and vitamins for some time following chelation. About a month after returning home, I awoke early one morning sleeping under a sheet and blanket and felt a strange sensation. I wiggled my toes and for the first time in several years I could actually feel my toes rubbing against the sheets. Glory be! Years later my diabetes doctor, Dr. Paul Sheridan in Denver, told me he felt if I had not gotten chelated, I probably would have lost both my feet to amputation. On occasion I have heard my doctor tell other medical doctors in his office about what a great pulse I have in my feet—especially after I have just finished more chelation.

Shortly after I began regaining circulation in my feet, I would wake up at night with terrible cramps in the calves of my leg. At first I thought this must be chelation, but I misunderstood the signals. I was actually getting careless about taking my minerals and Dr. Cordas told me that the lack of calcium was the reason for the "Charlie horses" in my legs.

A few years later, again I became lax about taking my pills every day following chelation. This time there was a different signal. I awoke from sleep one night and felt my heart skipping a beat every once in a while. When I reported that incident, Dr. Cordas immediately asked if I had stopped taking my pills because heart skipping a beat was from a shortage of magnesium. Now, when chelating, I remember to take my minerals and vitamins without fail.

When I first began chelation, Dr. Cordas was charging about twenty dollars each treatment. Now, some twenty-five years later, I am chelating in Denver for about eighty-five dollars pcr trcatment. By now, I suppose I must have taken more than three hundred fifty treatments and my only problem occurred when I would put off getting a monthly booster chelation. Sometimes I used to experience slight numbness returning to my toes—a strong reminder to get chelated. My former high blood pressure now consistently stays about 120/70, but if I delay getting chelated, I can usually count on my blood pressure to rise.

During 1987 when I was going to Guide Dog School, I put off getting chelated. By early 1988 I developed a severe earache, which I had not had since I was a child. Dr. Bill Gibbons told me I had an ulcer in my ear and that my eardrum had a white coating on it. Responding to my question, he acknowledged that my circulation was evidently poor in that eardrum and he felt that I was going to develop a hole in the eardrum. I did. But I told Dr. Gibbons that I would work on my circulation to get my eardrum healthy again.

I went to Denver each week for one or two chelations until I had taken at least six or more. When I returned to Dr. Gibbon's office he peered into my ear with his microscope. He seemed surprised that the hole had healed itself and the eardrum tissue looked healthy again. He asked what I had been doing and I told him about riding my bicycle every day. I did not talk about the chelation then, but told him later for I had found most medical doctors don't believe in chelation. Dr. Gibbons told me his partner, Dr. Smith, had an uncle who chelated with good results, so he was not a stranger to chelation therapy.

The combination of chelation and exercise is great. I don't believe that exercise alone can open clogged veins, but once chelation has opened them, exercise plus proper nutrition can keep them that way. With my long diabetic history and ongoing vascular disease, I continue to take monthly maintenance chelations and plan to do so until my final days. It is really no different from taking a shot of insulin three times each day. Already during my life, I have taken well over 50,000 injections of insulin—a simple matter of keeping fit by the best available technology!

For a guy who could not walk upstairs in 1973, I made a great comeback. By 1974 I was walking and jogging and by 1975 I was playing racquetball every day unless I was out of town. I loved that hard physical exercise and was in great shape. My veins in my arms became large and strong, the fat disappeared from my body and I felt terrific. I still maintain my weight at around 150 pounds and best of all, I do feel great!

As I contemplated running for Governor in 1978, I knew I must get a clean bill of health before commencing the race. My examining doctors were impressed with the way I breezed through the stress EKG. I performed great on the lung machine where you blow into a device. There was no resemblance to the guy who had heart failure five years before in 1973.

In all my years of chelating, I have made a lot of friends and witnessed a lot of wonderful results from chelation therapy. Only after chelation treatments were offered in Denver did I stop going to Texas. In 1980 I began with Dr. John Bumpus, D.O., who handled my chelation in Denver for several years until he retired. Then I chelated with Dr. Edward Anderson. After his retirement, I was a patient of Dr. William Doell, also of Denver, who has since moved to California. Next I began chelating with Dr. George Juetersonke, D.O. of Colorado Springs. Somehow it seemed comforting when I learned that Dr. Juetersonke had interned in the office of Dr. Steven Cordas in Texas. Then I began traveling to Gillette where the good Doctor Rebecca Painter was offering chelation therapy to those who requested it.

During this period I have met several hundred other patients receiving chelation therapy. Some of these people, before discovering chelation, had already undergone their second bypass surgery and were looking at chelation as an alternative to another surgery. I have seen remarkable examples of people who have either already lost one foot or leg and were about to lose another, but instead of a second surgery, they tried chelation and successfully saved their limbs.

At the time of this revision, it is now 1999. Although I have been fully aware of chelation therapy for twenty-six years, I am increasingly convinced that the opposition to chelation therapy has to be coming from the drug makers—the pharmaceuticals— the old simple theory of following the money trail. Since the patents on EDTA have long ago expired, there is no big money in making EDTA anymore, compared to the huge pipeline of new drug products constantly flowing from the global drug industry. Anyone who is an investor in equities is fully aware of these facts.

Probably most doctors learn about drugs from relying on the representatives of the drug makers. Drug companies rely on profits and push whatever makes money. Their subtle pitch against the use of chelation has been effective. They have long ago convinced the medical insurers to not allow for payments of chelation therapy and, of course, that includes Medicare. However, people have been increasingly aware of the benefits of chelation and more and more usage comes about each year. The irksome part is how the people unable to afford the treatments are left to the amputators. In all my years of chelation, I still have not spent as much as the cost of a single bypass surgery. Yet Medicare, Medicaid, and private insurers do pay for the increasing costs of both amputations and bypass surgery.

Books have been written on both sides of the chelation issue. Drugmakers state there is no scientific evidence to show chelation therapy works—a statement that is meant to be the last word on the subject. The problem is that no scientific evidence will ever be recognized by those opposing the use of chelation. Yet in the final analysis, more and more doctors are discovering the benefits of chelation just by observing the good results shown on some of their patients who do chelation therapy. Several times I have sat next to a medical doctor or even the wife of a medical doctor who is receiving chelation.

This chapter is not meant to convince or make believers out of people who have doctors voicing disapproval of the therapy. It is only meant to show how I chose to be a pioneer using the therapy. I shall never regret my decision and will go to my grave knowing full well what a lifesaver chelation therapy has been for me!

19

Recollections

As I begin this chapter (1992), the calendar shows twenty-one years have elapsed since I left the motel and restaurant business. During that time many amusing incidents have become lost from my memory, however, there remain a few interesting stories which I shall attempt to pass along.

When the United States determined to send men into outer space, the government chose seven men to become the very first astronauts. These were John Glenn, Alan Sheppard, Deke Slayton, Scott Carpenter, Virgil Grissom, Wally Schirra, and Gordon Cooper.

A former resident of Cheyenne, Bob Ditman was working for NASA in public relations. I knew Bob from having taken our Cheyenne friends on several antelope hunts in the early 1950s. It was quite a surprise when Bob Ditman called me at the Sands Motor Lodge late in September of 1964. He asked if he could bring Scott Carpenter and Deke Slayton to hunt antelope. He wanted me to make all the arrangements, including licenses.

"Of course I will!" and added, "I'll even try to get the State to offer the two astronauts complimentary licenses."

Bob told me there would be about eight in the party and Deke Slayton was bringing his father with him. There would be others in the NASA program accompanying the astronauts.

I called on my longtime rancher friend, I. A. Pickrel, to help. I wanted to divide the eight into two hunting parties and "Pick" was happy to take four of them. Scott Carpenter was in the group who went to Pickrel's and Deke Slayton was in the group I took to my Dad's ranch. Deke Slayton's father celebrated his birthday the day he bagged his antelope. The hunting was totally successful and everyone had a glorious time. Their antelope were processed at the local locker plant and shipped to them frozen.

We enjoyed a celebration dinner at the Sands Restaurant before they departed. The Sands Corporation Board of Directors was present, as well as the Pickrels plus a few other guests who helped make the trip so enjoyable for the astronauts.

Our guests presented me with a wonderful momento of the occasion—a full-color framed picture of the first Gemini Titan rocket liftoff on April 8, 1964. This launch, from Cape Canaveral, was the first of twelve in the series. It was signed by all members of the hunting party and it still hangs on my office wall and I have much pride in that personalized photo.

Several years after that antelope hunt, I accidentally ran into Scott Carpenter in Denver. While shopping at a store, I noticed the fellow standing next to me. Imagine my surprise when I saw Scott Carpenter. He was in Denver to address the Naval Reserve banquet celebrating Navy Day. We had a good visit.

In the motel business you learn to expect odd behavior from odd people. A few weeks following the opening of the Sands Motor Lodge, I discovered a most unusual event one night. This was the time when I was endeavoring to teach Estelle Cutler the peculiarities of the night audit. I arrived at the motel about eleven forty-five that evening.

The clerk going off duty casually mentioned that one of the guests had handed her a wallet to keep overnight for him. I asked, "How much money is in there?"

"I don't have any idea!" the clerk responded. "He just tossed it on the counter and left, asking us to put it in our safe."

"Didn't he ask for a receipt?" I queried. "I can't believe a guy would just toss his money off to a stranger this way!"

Receiving a negative response to this question, I had witnesses watch me count the contents of the wallet. More than eight thousand dollars in one hundred dollar bills were piled on the desk! In other words, the wallet was loaded with about eighty bills!

Immediately I called the man in his room. "We cannot accept this wallet from you for overnight safekeeping," I told him. "You can either retrieve it now, or else we will place it in the night deposit at the bank. You can pick it up at the bank when they open in the morning at nine."

I imagined being held up during the night by an accomplice of this fellow, then sued for the loss of his money plus damages. It took awhile to convince the fellow, but he reluctantly allowed us to place his wallet in a bag that went into the night deposit at the Stockmen's Bank. We did not even have a safe at the motel in those early days. I was relieved to be rid of the cash and following his retrieval the next morning, we never heard another word about it.

Many lessons were learned the hard way. It never occurred to me that some people liked to cook in their motel room. A band played at the Sands Restaurant for a two-week gig and Edna Davis told me the maids were having a terrible time getting into their room—the occupants never wanted to be disturbed. Edna thought they must have been cooking in the room. Were they ever! When those four people moved out we had a major renovation happening before we could ever rent the room again. With an electric skillet they had fried bacon on the vanity and the bacon grease had seeped behind the wall mirrors and permeated the drapes and carpet. We paid dearly for that lesson!

The lobby at the Sands Motor Lodge was relatively small, but nicely done. It had windows facing north and also facing Highway 14-16. It was used rarely, but on occasion, people would meet there. The lobby contained a pay phone as well as a house phone on the wall. I discovered to my surprise that a young rancher liked to use that pay phone. Odd, I thought. He came in several times a week and talked quietly into this public phone. We paid him no attention, but it still seemed odd to me. A few months following this behavior, I learned that this rancher was leaving his wife. On top of that, he was running off with another local man's wife! It then became evident that the motel lobby pay phone had been the clandestine meeting place for those lovers talking on the telephone. My! My!

Several times during the eleven years spent in the motel and restaurant business, we had special one-night entertainment bonanzas. One of the first of these occasions featured the Jimmy Dorsey orchestra. This great "big band" became famous during the years of World War II.

We felt it was a risk to book them, but we received special pricing for taking them on a one-nighter during the middle of the week. As it turned out, in entertainment starved Gillette, we had a sellout! Our only problem was our limited seating capacity. It worked so well that we booked other big names, although rather infrequently. We did not choose to wear a good thing out by doing it too often and at that time, we were not yet running nightly entertainment.

We contracted the fabulous "Inkspots" who had been around for a long time. Everyone who loved their music tried to make a dinner reservation at the Sands Restaurant that night. About that time Denver had a homegrown entertainment group known as "The Taylors". Later on they even had their own supper club called by the same name. They were an exceptionally fine and multitalented group of five people. We booked them at least twice during my years at the Sands and they were a sellout each time.

For all the times we enjoyed booking advance reservations, the time I least enjoyed was New Year's Eve! Reservations come in early and several days before the event we would be completely full at both the Sands and the Gay Nineties. We squeezed tables in until we hardly had a dance floor worthy of the name.

Large parties were not uncommon. More people grouped together for New Year's than any other event. I suppose the reason I disliked New Year's Eve parties was the fact that more people would drink too much that night than any other night. And of course, at midnight, everyone had to kiss everyone else. It became my habit to disappear into the kitchen office at midnight rather than become the target for so many women heavily under the influence. It became a habit to phone Mary just before midnight on New Year's Eve—wishing I were home with her.

Never wanting our premises to appear worn-out, we were constantly making plans to upgrade. During the early spring of 1967, I planned a major renovation of the Sands Restaurant coffee shop and kitchen area. I had been in Denver studying the operations of many of the most successful restaurant operators there. With the assistance of Ralph Wilson of Denver University, we carefully planned our renovations.

We designed our menu and then modified our facilities to best fit our menu plan. I was excited about getting the remodeling under way. We determined to close early on Saturday night and planned to reopen the following Tuesday. All equipment and furniture changes were on hand. Unfortunately, the weather failed to cooperate. A late April snowstorm began on Saturday night. I had gone home while carpenters were demolishing certain structures and roughing in others. When I looked out the window on Sunday morning, I was amazed at the snow depth. Immediately I went to the restaurant.

As the day wore on, it became evident that we were in for a serious major snowfall. Traffic was crawling and diminishing. Travelers were stopping at the restaurant for a bite to eat, only to learn we were closed for remodeling. By late afternoon, I knew it was impossible for me to try to get home.

About that time we had a complete power failure. Evidently the power lines that supplied Gillette from Wyodak suffered a breakdown. There were no lights and the only water available was what gravity flowed from the tank on the hilltop. I asked one of the workmen to saw the padlock off the walk in refrigerator as we needed access to food. Fortunately, our stoves were gas-fired and we could cook. And I did the cooking!

That night I gave all hands a motel room. I slept little that night, worrying about the possibility of frozen pipes. It never got cold enough for that, thank goodness. The next morning I made pancakes. I was amazed at how many stranded people came by for something to eat. It was the only time in my restaurant career that I actually cooked food. Power was not restored until later on Monday.

I kept in touch with Mary by phone. At home they had been burning wood in the upstairs and basement fireplaces. They not only burned all the wood, but then burned the wooden structure that the wood was stored in. Fortunately, the snow stopped on Monday and we began to dig out. As with most spring storms, when the storm was over, the sun came out, but I feel certain that there are a lot of strangers in the country today who recall spending a night trapped by a snowstorm in Gillette. I hope they carry good memories of some guy giving away pancakes at the Sands Restaurant.

The casual reader of this episode may wonder why I gave the breakfasts away. The reason was quite practical. We had no electricity to keep the cash registers working. On top of that, we also had no money to make change—it had all been placed in the night deposits on Saturday night.

The twenty-four-hour schedule of running two restaurants and two motels began to get to me. I realized that I did not wish to spend the balance of my life doing this activity. And besides, everything was running as smoothly as the proverbial Swiss watch. I contemplated, when anything is running this good, perhaps it is time to sell out. After all, it was not likely that things could get better and it could always get worse! However, the basic reason was that I did not intend to want this operation to last for my lifetime.

In 1970 I read that Ramada Inns were buying existing properties. At that time they would rather buy a good going operation than build new. One day I phoned the Ramada Inn corporate headquarters in Phoenix. Our total volume of business got their attention and they requested I send detailed financials for their perusal. I did.

That began a lengthy period of serious negotiations which almost led to our selling to Ramada. Our monthly financials were detailed and accurate and we were complimented on our presentations. I was invited to Phoenix to meet with their top corporate officers, which might well have been my first visit to Phoenix. Unfortunately, it was during the month of August and I recall the shock of stepping outside the air terminal and getting smacked with 105 degrees of heat. I had reserved a rental car, which turned out to be a black one. When that car sat in the parking lot at Ramada headquarters for several hours, I would defy anyone to unlock it and sit on the seat. My gosh, Phoenix in August will never be for me!

Negotiations went well and we had about agreed on most of the points that would lead to their acquiring our entire Sands Corporation. Then, all of a sudden, a wrench seemed to get into the transmission!

Frankly, I was perplexed at the sudden change of attitude at Ramada; we had just agreed on a takeover date. I learned later what happened to squelch our deal. At that time the largest Ramada in Wyoming was in Casper, owned by Ralph Schauss. I was told in confidence by someone at Ramada in Phoenix that Ralph Schauss urged them not to acquire the Gillette property. Ralph told them we were just a flash in the pan and the oil boom would soon end, spelling the end of the Gillette business. Ramada evidently thought enough of Schauss to terminate our talks.

Ironically, while writing this book, the economy of the Gillette area is still strong, especially from the coal business. Casper was the place that took an economic nose dive. Later, I heard that Ralph Schauss declared bankruptcy, although I don't know the facts—sometimes prophecies can backfire on people.

I was not really disappointed in losing the Ramada sale, although I had devoted considerable time to it. However, all our affairs were in excellent order and all I needed was a customer. Lo and behold! A customer walked into my office. A group of six businesspeople from Rapid City, South Dakota, came. They wanted our motel and restaurant business. Imagine how convenient that turned out to be; we knew exactly what we wanted and we could demonstrate that the value was there for them. We did not take long to negotiate the deal. They were ready, willing, and able and we were agreeable. A deal was struck!

Although I cannot recall the names of all the buyers, some of them were: Clair Weisler, Eugene Van Vleck, Ron Jensen, and Ron Banks. Clair and Eugene planned to move to Gillette to run the operations. Eugene Van Vleck later married Donna Wolf, who had worked faithfully for me for several years. Later Eugene and Donna ended up running everything.

The buyers financing would not stretch to handle the purchase of the two office buildings we had constructed at 302 and 304 Douglas Highway. Also we kept a portion of land on the west side of the Gay Nineties. We had planned on utilizing this piece of ground for a convention site. In less than a year after we sold, the buyers came back and purchased the land west of the Nineties; however, the office buildings were retained by us, the four stockholders under the partnership name of the Jax Company. The name JAX originated from our attorney, Bill Brown, formed by the *J* from Jim or John, and *AX* from Axel. A few years later Ostlund Investments bought the interest of Toots Marquiss. By 1991 we had sold both buildings and eliminated the partnership.

The closing of the Sands Corporation deal was held in Casper. Bill Brown headed the fine law firm of Brown, Drew, Apostolos, Massey, and Sullivan and was an outstanding attorney with a reputation to match. I had the highest regard for Bill. Present at the closing included my brother, Bob and his wife, RoseMary, James R. Daly and Elizabeth, Toots Marquiss, and my wife, Mary. The buyers were there without wives. Bill Brown was meticulous with his paperwork, as always, and ran that closing like the professional he was. I had to admire him for his candor and forthrightness. When the closing was over, we all had checks plus payments due to each of us on a monthly basis. Within a few short years the buyers refinanced and we were paid off completely.

The transition to the new owners seemed to go well. Inside of me there was some pain for I had built this company carefully and painstakingly. It was not easy to see my company organizational chart slowly destroyed. The buyers seemed to believe that department heads only cost extra money which should be put to better use feeding the bottom line profits.

We had inaugurated a waitress system which gave each waitress an opportunity to advance in grades. Basic waitresses were paid the beginning hourly wage. With good performance reports from supervisors and department heads, a waitress could be pro-moted to Blue Star category, which gave a pay raise. Her name badge also carried the blue star insignia.

To earn Gold Star status, a waitress must enroll and complete the California Wine Institute course on the proper knowledge and service of wines. After completing the course, the waitress must pass the final examination by demonstrating her newly acquired knowledge to me. Gold Star waitresses actually had a gold star on their name badge. It was status and they were indeed proud of that distinction.

In addition, all employees had their medical insurance fully paid by the Sands Cor-poration. At that time this was unique in the industry. All employees were also eligible for paid vacation; the length of the vacation depended upon their years of service. I was a stickler about making them take vacations. Many of them preferred to keep working and get paid extra for the vacation time. Absolutely not! At employee meetings I would talk with them about how important I felt it was to get away. "A vacation gives you the opportunity to leave this place for a couple of weeks and come back, hopefully, refreshed and eager to take up again!"

I may not have convinced everyone, but they understood my policy. Our policies were written and every employee was shown the policy manual and advised to read it. They could even be tested on it. Each employee had a personnel file. A copy of our personnel review papers were in the policy manual. Periodically, those files would be updated. The supervisor was required to go over each personnel review with the employee and each review was scored by the supervisor.

The next step, the employee met with me. I had also reviewed the paperwork and every supervisor and department head had to justify their scoring, whether it was a high score or perhaps even a low score. I always felt the employees appreciated the time and effort that went into maintaining their records. The biggest benefit to all this was a dramatic reduction in employee turnover—employee turnover can be a horren-dous hidden cost.

The new owners were renting office space from us at 302 Douglas Highway. Within a year they had relocated to the new available conference room at the Thunder Basin Inn. I was pleased about that move. I hated being so close to my former operation. Employees were finding time to tell me how much they missed me, which of course was nice to hear, but no two bosses work alike. They now owned the Sands Corporation and their own policies and methods were in practice, as they should have been.

What was I doing? I was beginning to do all the things I had been planning. It was opening a whole new chapter in my life and it was great!

One of the best benefits was to be able to retire at night like a normal person—getting a good night's sleep was a luxury. The pressure of a constant twenty-four-hour operation of two motels, two restaurants, and two bars and cocktail lounges had been gently lifted off my shoulders.

It was the fall of 1971 and I had witnessed the increased coal development in the Powder River Basin. I also had my sights on running for the Wyoming Senate in 1972. Amax Coal Company had recently acquired a federal coal lease fifteen miles south of Gillette. Leslie Claybaugh, the surface owner, had been a good customer of Ostlunds for many years. Amax negotiated to buy the Claybaugh ranch at a very significant price. Claybaugh sold it and acquired a much larger ranch in another area. What I wanted to know was just where was the best coal?

I contacted the Bureau of Land Management. From them I learned that their most up-to-date coal information was held at the BLM office in Billings, Montana. I drove to Billings and called on the BLM office. In retrospect it was really amazing. I discovered the Coast and Geodetic Survey had made a map platting the outcrops of coal, most of which were in Campbell County. This survey work was done clear back during the 1930s. I asked the BLM, "May I buy a copy of this map?"

"That's the only copy we have," responded the official.

"Could you make me a copy?" I asked hopefully.

"We don't have a copier that can make a copy of something that big," came the unexpected answer.

"Would you allow me to take this map somewhere that can handle that size?" I pursued.

"That would be all right, but be sure to return it. Like I said, it's the only one we have."

Within the hour I made at least a half-dozen copies and returned the original to BLM with my thanks. Now I could follow the outcrop of the fabulous Smith-Roland coal beds all the way from north of Gillette, through Wyodak, on south into Converse County. On top of that, the map showed coal outcrops both east and west of the Smith-Roland beds. The map also showed all of the federal leases already granted.

For many weeks prior to going to Billings I had been having conversations with George Keeline. I had known George all my life and now, in his retirement, he liked to drop by my office for a visit. Sometimes those visits would get downright tedious, but I always learned something from George. George Keeline prided himself for making the Keeline ranch into a really super-sized and profitable operation. He never gave his own father, Harry W. Keeline, any credit, but his own hero was his Uncle Oscar Keeline.

According to George, Uncle Oscar had more brains than anyone else. He claimed Oscar taught him everything he knew.

Keeline land stretched for miles. They were in Weston, Crook, and Campbell Counties. At one time their ranch exceeded 150,000 acres. To make the marketing of cattle easier, they bought land all the way into a rail site at Moorcroft, Wyoming. They never left Keeline land to put their cattle into railroad cars headed for eastern markets.

George's only sister, CoraMay, married Bill Edelman, and lived in Gillette. George's only brother, Joe, was more interested in turning the ranch over to his two sons and then living a life of retirement. George and his wife, Elaine, the former Elaine Sutherland, had only one daughter who also lived in town. When George finally decided to retire, he sold his interest in the ranch to Harry and Jody Keeline, his nephews. Jody and Harry could not get along as well as was necessary to be good partners. Their father, Joe, died and left his second wife, Peg, a widow. Finally Jody, Harry, and Peg agreed to split the ranch into three parcels—each one would own their own parcel outright and there would be no more partnerships.

That is the way the ranch stood in 1971. George Keeline, on his visits to my office, began talking with me about why I should buy that entire ranch and put it back together. I used to listen to him patiently, but without much enthusiasm, until the day I found the Geodetic survey of the coalfields.

The Roland-Smith coal beds' outcrop ran north and south right across Jody Keeline's ranch. All the present federal coal leases were also noted on my map, yet there were no leases on the Keeline ranch. North of Keeline's was an Atlantic Richfield lease and south of Keeline's, on the Jacobs' ranch, was a lease to Kerr McGee.

What did all that really mean? It only signified that large corporations indeed had an interest in this low-sulfur coal and were positioning themselves for the development. It certainly did not spell instant wealth for anyone; it only provided a possible extra option in the event we were to purchase the ranch.

George literally spent hours telling me how we should run this ranch. I believe George enjoyed giving me the insight he spent years learning. For example, he said, "Don't waste money buying hay for those damned cows. It might be all right to buy a little ear corn. When you ride a horse through those winter pastures and you find a cow looking weak, get up close and look her in the eyes. If she looks glassy-eyed, she is probably ready to die. If she is not glassy-eyed, then you can give her an ear of corn to keep her alive. But don't throw money away buying a lot of feed for those cows. Sure, you'll lose some, but you will be money ahead in the spring."

From time to time, I began visiting with Jody Keeline. Jody had been married several times. The last time he married a very attractive German girl, Marianne, who used to work for me at the Sands Restaurant. Marianne gave Jody his only son. One of his previous wives, Paula, had been the sister of my youthful pal, Burt Reno, and had given Jody perhaps five daughters during their years together.

Jody was ready to sell out and we began to negotiate a deal. It went together relatively easily, because Jody had already decided upon a price.

I talked things over with Equitable Life about putting a mortgage on this Keeline ranch. Equitable agreed and my brother and I bought it. We formed a corporation called Black Thunder Ranch, inasmuch as the creek by the same name went very close to the home place. Following that purchase, I attempted to negotiate with Peg and with Harry Keeline on their ranches. In retrospect, I am glad they never made a deal with us. We only would have had a much larger mortgage to carry.

As well as running his own cattle on the ranch, Jody had also been running about five hundred head of Linkletter cows. Art and Jack Linkletter had limited partnership cattle programs all over the west. For running their cows and using their Charolais bulls, the rancher received fifty percent of the calf crop. The rancher was saved the capital investment of the cows and bulls and for this reason we continued with the Linkletter program.

Our new corporation needed a ranch manager. We hired Kerry Clark and his wife, Glo, the daughter of Toots Marquiss. They were young and newly married.

That fall we also bought a few hundred bred heifers. Most of them were due to calve the following February. That proved to be a fortunate time to calf that winter, for we enjoyed a mild February. However, the big surprise came during late April. We had a massive spring storm move through that was a disaster.

Many sheep owners, in the path of the storm, lost a majority of their flocks. Kerry was caught with unprotected cows and calves and our calf-loss was very high. Cows and calves had drifted with the storm. Upon reaching a fence they began to pile up and smother. We did not determine the full extent of the losses for weeks, not until the drifts melted could we count the piles of calves. What a hell of a way to begin serious ranching!

Our land ran seventeen miles north and south, with various widths east and west. Black Thunder Creek ran just to the south of the ranch buildings. While flying over the entire ranch with Jody Keeline, I had the chance to see all the acreage—what a variety of lands, plains, hill country, timber, and hundreds of miles of fences. One interesting and unique aspect was seen from the air south of Black Thunder Creek; evidence of a one-time Indian village with perhaps thirty tepee rings could be seen. I recalled riding a horse over that area years ago.

Indians placed a circle of rocks around their tepees to keep the wind from blowing underneath the sides. Many times arrowheads could be found in these areas. One day Dick Stull was walking with Mary and me as we examined the tepee rings and Dick discovered a broken arrowhead. I could imagine the reasons the Indians located there; it was high ground overlooking Black Thunder Creek with water, grass, and good observation of game or potential problems that might be advancing on them. In other words, they had a great defensive location.

Meanwhile, following our purchase of the ranch, the Congress addressed another serious problem relating to the mining of coal. The federal government owned most all the coal worthy of being mined, however, the government had deeded most of the surface and about half of the oil and gas minerals to the homesteaders. How could the coal, owned by the Feds, be mined while the surface was held privately?

To soften this problem, the Congress stated that federal coal could only be mined from under surface lands also held by the mining company. The Feds felt that the mining companies could certainly afford to pay a proper price to the surface owners. Let the market determine the price. That was a pretty good idea. Following that declaration of policy, coal companies began buying surface rights in the Powder River Basin. Among the leaders was American Electric Power who bought under the name of a subsidiary, Franklin Real Estate.

One day a fellow named Jack Rause came into my office. He was buying ranch property for Franklin Real Estate and told me he was interested in buying our Black Thunder Ranch. Unlike a lot of people, I never buy anything planning to own it for the rest of my life because in my sense, life is too short anyway!

Before negotiating with the fellow, I talked with my brother about the possible advantages of selling to Franklin. Instead of talking the sale of real estate, I thought there were advantages to just selling Franklin one hundred percent of the stock in Black Thunder Ranch, Inc. We could take a capital gain from the sale of shares. Franklin could dissolve the corporation and pay off Equitable. Ostlunds, in turn, could lease back the ranch, for perhaps ten years, and pay the taxes on the ranch in lieu of lease payments. As it turned out, we actually did make this kind of deal, only we ended up leasing back the ranch for two consecutive ten-year periods instead and rather than operate the ranch, we, in turn, subleased it.

Our first sublease was to Ceres, Inc., headquartered in New York. Their area representative was Buzz Coakley, who lived at Sterling, Colorado. Dick Stull and his wife actually lived on the ranch while working for Ceres. That lease was maintained for several years until Ceres decided to quit the business. Buzz Coakley and Dick Stull determined to carry on as partners. They bought Ceres's feedlot in Sterling, Colorado, and made a new lease for Black Thunder Ranch with Ostlunds.

Stull and Coakley called themselves S & C Ranch Company. They were aggressive; not only did they lease our ranch, but also the adjacent ranch belonging to Peg Keeline, who had about fifty thousand acres. These two fine gentlemen would buy thousands of yearling steers in the spring and run them until fall. The steers would be transferred to the feedlots in Sterling for finishing and then sold into the market.

This lasted until we hit two really dry years in a row. I believe it was 1986 or perhaps 1987 when the drought was so bad that range fire burned off thousands of acres of grass. S & C decided to call it quits.

Since childhood and school days I had known Guy "Bud" Edwards, who neighbored next to the Keeline Ranch. Bud had inquired about the possibility of leasing that ranch from Ostlunds. Now that it was available, I called Bud and we soon signed a new lease. At this writing (1992), we are selling and assigning the final years of our Franklin lease to Guy Edwards and his family. It also brings to an end the ranching years of the Ostlund Investments partnership of my brother and me.

Actually, with Mary and I living at Remount and with our Ostlund Investments holding fewer properties, my brother and I decided to end the Ostlund Investment partnership as well. This began back in the late 1950s. It served its purpose and we believed it was time to close that chapter.

Recently an incident occurred in Laramie while Mary and I were attending a dinner party. The occasion was to honor former trustees, or as Mary says "old" trustees! We thoroughly enjoyed the evening, especially renewing so many old friendships. Several trustees I served with were there, including Jerry and Donabelle Hollon, Bill and Jean Jones, Bob and Marie McBride, Esther Broderick, widow of Gordon Broderick, and Mary Lou Pence, widow of Al Pence.

The following day I saw Jerry Hollon again in Cheyenne. He was laughing as he said to me, "The next time we trustees get together you have to tell the rest of that bunch the story about the time you lost your pickup at Remount Ranch. That was the funniest story I can remember!"

It occurred to me that perhaps I should tell that story in this chapter. I hope you find it worthy of repeating.

I would guess this happened about 1975 or 1976. I was in my office at 304 Douglas Highway in Gillette; in fact, I was preparing to make the move to the Hitching Post in Cheyenne for the forty days of the coming legislative session. There was a lot of snow on the ground, but I knew we had received a huge amount at Remount Ranch. My secretary informed me that Dennis from the ranch was on the phone.

"Hello, Dennis," I began. "How are you making out with all the snow down there?"

"Not too bad," Dennis reported. "The only thing is, we don't have any water!"

Dennis, a fairly new resident at Remount, came from West Virginia and this was his first experience with a Wyoming winter.

I said, "There is probably a fuse blown on the water pump. But you still have gas and electricity, don't you? Why don't you just reach out the front door and scoop up a bucket full of snow? You have plenty of time, just melt it on the stove. You will have plenty of water to get by."

"Well, Mr. Ostlund, Madonna would like to take a bath!" Madonna was the wife of Dennis.

"I think you better stay put until the roads are cleared. You will be a lot better off just waiting there at the ranch. Meanwhile, find that fuse that is blown on the pump. Then you can both take baths if you want to," I suggested.

"Well, Madonna didn't want to wait, so we tried to get out in the pickup," Dennis advised.

"I imagine that was a wasted effort, was it not?" I asked.

"Yes sir," Dennis answered. "The road under the Union Pacific was blown completely closed with snow. Then Madonna and I thought we might get through on east where the Interstate highway goes over the railroad."

"But Dennis," I protested, "you would have to drive over the railroad tracks to get out that way!"

"Yes, sir, that's right, Mr. Ostlund. I figured if we took a run at it we could go right over the tracks and then get onto the Interstate highway. But I didn't get enough of a run at it and we got high-centered on the railroad!" Dennis allowed.

Knowing that the Union Pacific runs a freight on that track about every twenty minutes, first I asked, "Did anyone get hurt?"

"No sir, Mr. Ostlund," Dennis answered lamely. "You see I told Madonna to jump out and run down the track to flag down the train!" Dennis paused waiting for my next question.

"Well, what the hell happened next?" I probably shouted!

"Mr. Ostlund, that train didn't pay any attention to Madonna! They just blew on by her!"

"And the train hit the pickup?" I asked incredulously!

"Yes sir," Dennis responded, relieved to finally get to this point. "And the train didn't even get stopped for more than a mile!"

"And what happened to the pickup?" I asked already expecting the answer.

"Well, the train carried it with them all wrapped up on the front of the locomotive!" Dennis told me weakly. In a meek attempt to possibly make me feel better, he added, "But the box for the pickup didn't go with the truck! It just popped off when the train hit it and it is lying out in the field someplace. It probably isn't even hurt!"

"Where is the pickup now?" I asked gently.

"The railroad ordered me to get it off the right-of-way! So I called a wrecker to come and take it away! That is, after the railroad repair folks got it pried off and out from under the locomotive!"

Mentally beginning to compute the ongoing costs that never seemed to end, I raised my voice to ask, "You mean we had to pay for a damn wrecker to come out there and haul that junk off the railroad property?" I already knew the answer. "I don't suppose it hurt the locomotive, did it?"

"Not too much, sir" Dennis whispered. "They did have to do a little welding before they could move the train though!"

Hesitant to ask further about these rising costs, I asked, "Where are you now, at the ranch?"

"No, sir," Dennis answered. "We rode into Cheyenne with the wrecker so as we could take a bath!"

That was too much! After all that, they still had to do the task they had originally assigned themselves for the day . . . the all-important bath!

The next day I left for Cheyenne for the upcoming legislative session. I checked into the Hitching Post and set up my law books at my desk in the Senate. One of the first people I ran into at the Capitol was Ed Sensabaugh, the Union Pacific lobbyist.

"Say!" said Ed. "I understand one of our locomotives got acquainted with one of your pickups close to Remount!"

"I suppose you will be sending me a big bill for that affair?" I joked halfheartedly.

"You think we would send a bill to a Senator?" Ed laughed. "Oh, my no!"

Nevertheless, a few months after the legislative session was ended, I did receive a bill from the Union Pacific for welding and repairing their engine. I paid without comment.

Meanwhile I did locate the remains of our three-quarter ton, four-wheel drive Chevrolet pickup in the junkyard of Tyrell Chevrolet. I could not recognize it—it looked like a crumpled ball of metal that almost defied anyone to believe it could have been a pickup at one time. Should I add that Dennis and Madonna ended their ranching career at that time?

After losing the gubernatorial campaign of 1978, I began to read the *Wall Street Journal* more thoroughly. During the campaign I seldom had the opportunity to read any business news at all. Now, with inflation increasing, I became interested in precious metals. However, I needed to become educated about the metals market.

After studying metals, I then took advantage of some so-called money conferences in Los Angeles. They were indeed illuminating and meetings were held at the beautiful Century Plaza Hotel. It was a pleasure to experience that lifestyle for a few days. One year I enrolled in a three-day study course on Austrian Economics. I was glad to get this bit of education I had previously lacked. It certainly broadened my outlook on the political and economic happenings of the day.

The realities of inflation were being learned for the first time by most Americans. Interest rates on federally guaranteed certificates of deposit were reaching the incredible rate of sixteen percent! Commercial banks and Savings and Loans were learning hard lessons. The S&L people were making long-term loans with short-term money. For example, they were forced to meet competition in order to keep deposit money. They had made long-term home loans at perhaps eight percent and found themselves paying short-term interest rates on certificates of deposit in excess of fifteen percent. Deep trouble was looming for many of these institutions.

People borrowing short-term commercial loans from banks found themselves looking at paying twenty-one percent interest on their loan. People began to believe the economy was going crazy and they were correct! There were also those who felt we were seeing the demise of the bond market! This was the situation which caused President Jimmy Carter to be a one-term president. Ronald Reagan easily deposed Carter in the 1980 election.

Meanwhile, at 304 Douglas Highway, I was taking care of Ostlund Investments business. Having dropped out of business for the campaign, there was a lot of catching up to do.

My dear mother, Polly Ostlund, died in November of 1980 at the age of seventy-eight. My father, Axel W. Ostlund, died in May of 1982. Our son, Scott, and I were traveling between Zurich, Switzerland, and Vienna, Austria, when my father died. And, unfortunately, Scott and I decided to leave the train in Salzburg, Austria, and proceed to Vienna the following day; consequently, we were unable to be reached by Mary to inform us of that sad news.

We got the message when we checked into the Hilton Hotel in Vienna. Mary and my brother made many of the arrangements for Axel's funeral and everything was well in hand when Scott and I reached Gillette. We flew from Vienna to Paris and while in Paris we took a quick and brief visit around that lovely city. Since it was Scott's nineteenth birthday we took advantage of the three-and-a-half-hour trip from Paris to New York by flying the French Concorde. Scott was thrilled!

Because of excellent preplanning, settling the estate of our parents was relatively easy. We had arranged for each of our parents to execute Revocable Living Trusts. (Mary's mother had also done the same.) And by the way, both Mary and I have followed suit. What a great thing to do for your heirs.

My eye problems were more distressing as time went on. I was making frequent flights to Denver and getting a lot of laser work on my remaining good eye. I felt time was growing short on my available vision, which spurred me into a decision that I have never regretted. Mary and I determined to move from Gillette to Remount Ranch. All I needed to do was to make a deal with my brother on the division of partnership property. That was not done easily, but it was accomplished. In that way Mary and I owned Remount Ranch outright.

Mary and I spent many happy hours trying to determine the extent of the remodeling we chose to accomplish before moving. We involved our longtime designer friend, Claus Heppner & Associates in Denver. On his staff was an architect named Robert Larsen who proved to be a terrific guy to work with and we have always been pleased with the way he remodeled our home at Remount Ranch—but it took time.

The planning and drawings took most of 1982 and the contract for the work was set in June of 1983 and the work was scheduled to be completed by December of 1983. As we learn to expect when living in Wyoming, the snow fell the day after Thanksgiving and it just kept on coming. In order to keep the roads open for workers traveling to the ranch, it was necessary to plow the roads daily. As often happens, after about three weeks the snow stopped and nice weather prevailed again. The snowdrifts had caused work delays, but also change orders seemed to be the rule not the exception.

We did not move until March 9, 1984. But move we did! Looking back, we firmly believe it was the best move we ever made.

While writing this in September of 1992, I am about to celebrate my sixty-fifth birthday. I have been blind for slightly less than eight years. Nevertheless, living these years at Remount have been a most exceptional time. However, with all things considered, we are now probably getting ready to contemplate the close of this chapter; to sell the Remount and move into Cheyenne. When that happens, we feel the next chapter of our lives will also be full of wonder and joy as all the previous ones have been!

The Family at Remount Ranch, 1985. Back row: Tom, Jim, Ginger, John Jr., Karin, Scott, Pat, L'Nette, and Gregg. Front row: Mary with Jason and Jordan, Nancy with Chad, John with Goldie, Mary with P.J., Peg with Michael John, and Jane (expecting Andrew).

20

Blind in Paradise!

It is likely that most everyone, at sometime in their life, dreams of finding a perfect, unique, and peaceful place to get away from everything. In 1969 I was contemplating how desirable it would be if we could find such a retreat. Our businesses were succeeding and the stresses and strains that accompany success were making a getaway more and more desirable. I imagined a place with trees and trout streams, since the immediate areas around Gillette were lacking in both of these amenities.

About that time Ned Murray, a Cheyenne realtor, had a listing on the Remount Ranch. Remount was located halfway between Cheyenne and Laramie off Interstate #80. My brother learned about the listing while visiting with Ned one day.

Each month I was in Laramie while serving on the Board of Trustees at the University of Wyoming. In June of 1970 I called Ned Murray and arranged for a tour of Remount Ranch. While driving from Cheyenne to the ranch, Ned gave me the background. The ranch was once owned by Mary O'Hara, who wrote the books *My Friend Flicka, Thunderhead, Green Grass of Wyoming, Wyoming Summer*, and others. But mostly he talked about how the ranch had become a guest ranch under the next owners, John and Carol Knox. Ned told of all the high profile people who had been guests at Remount, including many movie stars and top entertainers.

Ned did not begin by driving me straight to the ranch house, instead, he wisely drove me to the top of a high hill which he called the "Saddleback." The view was impressive. The day was clear and I looked south on the Colorado Rockies, west to the Snowy Range, north to Vedauwoo, and east to Cheyenne. I later learned that the elevation atop the Saddleback was close to eight thousand feet.

Ned pointed out the landmarks and property lines of the ranch from this wonderful vantage point. At my feet were tiny wildflowers in a variety of sizes and colors. I had hardly ever noticed such a colorful array before in Wyoming. I saw antelope grazing in the pasture close by. Of course, I was anxious to see more!

We came off the Saddleback and entered a road heading north from the County

Road. It was marked, Remount Pines. Ned explained that there was perhaps forty acres that had been platted into subdivision by John Knox. We were approaching a nice looking A-frame house built upon huge granite rocks. Ned described that this house and about four acres belonged to a Chicago stockbroker named Frank Schank. In Remount Pines there was another cabin that belonged to George Oxley. A third lot of three acres had been sold to Norman Cable, but he had never built on it.

We drove through the trees and Ned was about to take a road off to the left. At that moment I saw a doe standing at the side of the road watching us. The scene was so beautiful; the blue sky, the green grass mixed with wildflowers, the ponderosa pine forest, plus the deer made for a perfect picture.

However, another surprise awaited me over the next hill. A dam had been built backing up water flowing in from Guss Creek. This little lake had both brook trout and rainbow. The overflow from the lake flowed on to Lone Tree Creek. Lone Tree flowed year-round across the entire ranch and brook trout abounded in those cold clear waters. In fact, I later learned that Remount has two of the earliest Territorial Water Permits dating back to 1875 and 1876 with irrigation rights on the Lone Tree water.

Leaving the lake, we drove along the hay meadows to the back of the corrals and across a lovely stone bridge over Lone Tree Creek. Again we saw the hay meadows from a different vantage point. Ned took me north to the Union Pacific tracks, which marked the north boundary of the ranch. We then ventured east into a half-section that has been leased from the State of Wyoming for all of this century. There is also a good deal of timber on this part of the ranch. Another old landmark turned out to be a deep shaft, dug by hand, that was the site of a gold claim discovered in the late 1800s. This gold mine shaft is referenced in Mary O'Hara's book, *My Friend Flicka*. The Abstract of Title on Remount refers to this claim as the Alexia Lode. I think it is doubtful that much gold, if any, was ever removed. The very existence of white quartz in the area causes one to think there might be gold, though.

In his opinion, Ned seemed to be saving the best for last. We drove into the yard and I saw this beautiful lawn completely surrounding a large swimming pool. There was a cement shuffleboard alongside the patio area around the pool. Four guest cabins completed the scene that spelled gracious living at its best. But Ned did not stop until we reached the main house. The house was made from granite stonework and seemed inviting.

Inside, it was ruggedly beautiful. Parts of the house dated back to the late 1800s. Ned introduced me to Gertie Trautwein, wife of the banker Arnie Trautwein. We sat in the barroom and enjoyed a cold drink. Gertie explained that their youngest son had just graduated from high school and she wanted to move to town. It seemed that Arnie had reluctantly agreed and that led to my being there.

Returning to Cheyenne, I thought about how the Remount offered everything I had ever dreamed about as a "Shangri-La." Ned and Barbara had invited me for dinner and we dined at Ned's Peppermint Farm, a very lovely and unique development that Ned and Barbara put together on acreage north of Cheyenne.

I called Mary from Murray's and tried my best to describe the Remount to her. I told her I had just seen the most ideal property I could have imagined. Mary was impressed and I said that we should go ahead and make an offer on the ranch.

I talked with my brother because we were going to buy the ranch through our partnership, Ostlund Investments. I wanted to make an offer through Ned Murray that would include Arnie Trautwein taking our shares that we owned in the Stockmen's Bank in Gillette. Arnie loves banks and shares of the Stockmen's were not easy to come by in those days. My brother agreed, so I signed the offer that Ned presented to Arnie Trautwein. Arnie accepted!

We were to have possession in thirty days. There was no furniture or equipment included in the sale. Arnie did leave an old horse named "Horse" and a small pony named "Misty." Also, there was a very nice two-wheel pony cart and harness that remained. This was to provide a lot of fun for the smaller kids in days to come.

The billiard room contained an old ten-foot Brunswick snooker table. It remained because it was practically impossible to take out of the house. Other than that, I realized we had a major job ahead of us in assembling all the furniture and household items we needed to make the place livable.

Being in the motel and restaurant business, I set out to have everything ready by Labor Day. I gave Claus Heppner, our interior designer, a budget for furniture and resolved to acquire everything else through our own outlets. I really enjoyed doing it. About this time Gertie Trautwein told us about a special set of china that they had purchased that carried the Remount brand. She wondered if we would like to buy it. Mentioning this to my mother, Polly Ostlund, she wanted to buy the dishes as her gift to us, so that is how we acquired the dishes with the Remount brand.

When Labor Day arrived, all was completed. Not only was my family here, but also my brother's family. In addition were our parents, Axel and Polly, Mary's parents, Tom and Peg Ryan, and RoseMary's parents, Louie and Alice Shilt from Laramie. It was a wonderful housewarming event!

Since the Remount also contained a two-story house suitable for a ranch manager, we hired a longtime acquaintance named Gilbert Vigil. Gilbert worked full-time for the Burlington Railroad as a section hand. On weekends he worked for Ostlunds. Most of the time he worked at the plumbing shop, but he always mowed Grandpa Axel's lawn in the summer and shoveled his snow in the winter. Gilbert agreed to take his retirement from the railroad and he and his wife, Margaret, became our first resident caretakers.

To make long-range planning easier, we alternated every other week on the calendar so that each family would know in advance whose week it was. This worked rather well and trades could always be arranged. In fact, this arrangement was used for the twelve years it was held by the partnership.

By 1982 I was having more serious eye problems. It was necessary that I make frequent trips to Denver to consult with my eye specialist and my left eye was already blind. I had never forgotten how much Mary loved Remount Ranch. Mary used to ask why we could not just move and live there. For the six years I was in the State Senate, it was impossible to move to a new senatorial district without resigning my Senate seat.

But now I began to take a different view. If I was going to be blind, and it was only a matter of time, then I would rather spend my last days of vision in that beautiful setting called Remount.

Negotiations with my brother began and finally we reached the conclusion which left Mary and me as the sole owners of Remount Ranch. I carefully analyzed our accounts to give us the peace of mind that we could handle it financially through the coming years. Once the deeds were signed, Mary and I began seriously to plan major remodeling at Remount. Although we generally had ideas about what we wanted to accomplish, we needed to have an architect with whom we could place our confidence. We found such a fellow. His name was Robert Larsen and at that time he was on the staff of Claus Heppner and Associates in Denver. Bob Larsen had respect for the historical and seemed to know just how to blend the new with the old. On top of that, he was a pleasure to work with. Since completing our job, Bob Larsen is now self-employed as an independent architect and I understand he is keeping very busy in the Denver area.

Mary and I had attempted to set a dollar limit on the remodeling, but as usual, we ended up investing twice that amount. Of course we also anticipated an early sale on our Gillette home, but actually, we rented it to a very nice couple, Craig and Debbie Mader, for perhaps a year before selling it.

From my point of view, I was especially interested in rewiring everything at the ranch. Much of the old electrical was installed before the benefit of codes and much of the wiring was probably rigged by ranch hands or apprentices. The same was true of the plumbing. Bob Larsen retained Martin and Jones Engineers from Cheyenne to design the mechanical and electrical systems— money well spent.

From a space standpoint, I wanted a large office with plenty of windows looking out at the magnificent scenery. Mary wished for a guest bedroom on the ground floor, for she was thinking ahead about grandchildren spending time with us.

We both thought a relaxing spa would be wonderful. I was anxious for Mary to have a hobby room, because I was hopeful that she would begin serious painting. All of these wishes turned to reality with Bob Larsen. When the bids were submitted, a young contractor named Bill Edwards of Cheyenne turned in the low bid. Bill Edwards happened to be Ned Murray's son-in-law, having married Beth Murray. In retrospect we were fortunate to have Bill Edwards. He did such good work and always had our best interests at heart. Since that 1983 contract, Bill has done additional projects for us almost every year since living at Remount. We think a great deal of Bill Edwards and his family.

While the construction contract was underway, Mary and I used cabin four as our temporary residence. We came often to examine the progress. December of 1983 was rough due to severe winter. The snows turned heavy immediately following Thanksgiving. The cost of keeping the road open was burdensome and I seriously thought about closing down the project until spring. Fortunately, January saw the winter moderating a bit and we continued along. By February we decided to make our permanent move early in March. We did just that and arrived at Remount on March 6, 1984. Our bedroom, kitchen, breakfast room, and the new wing were practically completed. Unfinished yet, were the billiard room, dining room, sitting room, living room, and upstairs bedrooms.

When we first looked at the living room at this stage of construction, it seemed a total disaster. Our ranchman at that time was Danny Cosner and he used the living room as a catchall for everything that had to be stored someplace. Mary thought our living room would make a perfect stage setting for the Broadway show, *Cats*, a show we saw in New York where the setting was the city garbage dump. Mary's comment was certainly appropriate!

People who have been through major remodeling understand that the unexpected becomes the expected. That was true every week with our project. We decided to put electric baseboard heat in the upstairs bedrooms. We had already approved electric floor heat in the dining room and billiard room. Our architect was ingenious in finding effective ways to insulate our home without destroying the historical appearance of it. That effective insulation coupled with our accessing natural gas from the interstate gas line were ideas that will pay off forever. Every cold winter night, I am thankful for all of these good innovations.

Prior to March 6, our moving day, Danny Cosner told me he was desperate to find additional storage space. To alleviate that problem, we rented a large old trailer that is customarily pulled on the highway. I believe it was eighty-feet long. When we moved and two truckloads of our own furniture arrived with us, I was thankful for the long trailer. In fact, we used that storage until the end of June that year. It took that long to sort out what we were keeping and what we were turning to the auction house in Cheyenne.

The spring of 1984 found me in special ecstasy. I moved into my new ranch office where I am writing this manuscript. I furnished my office entirely from the furniture I moved from my former office at 304 Douglas Highway in Gillette. With my lateral two-drawer filing cabinets, storage cabinets, IBM computer, desk, and accessories, I was perfectly and comfortably at home. I had only to glance up and out the windows to see the beautiful, ever-changing scenes before me. Every season presents the beauty of nature in a wonderfully different way.

My architect was clever in placing the office floor about three feet below grade. That puts the bottom of my large windows just above ground level. My windows face north, east, and south. It is not unusual to look up and see deer grazing on the green grass.

At Remount I made an idle dream come true. In one corner of my office, I assembled my graphite fly rod, a rod that Mary won in a drawing at the Buffalo Bill Museum in Cody. Now I assembled it with the thought that I would never have to take it apart again. As a matter-of-fact, it is still there as it was the last time I used it. In my office closet I hung my fishing vest. Over a period of time I had carefully assembled all the gear and collection of wet and dry flies that an ardent fly fisherman feels he must have. About three o'clock one afternoon, I pushed back from my desk and said, "Now it is time to take some joy and go fishing!"

I donned my vest and, carrying my fly rod, walked down to Lone Tree Creek. Many years ago an old dam was built on Lone Tree that once was used to divert irrigation water. The sound of the waterfall pulls you like a magnet. I tied a Royal Coachman on the end of a tapered leader and made a couple of casts. Bingo! a beautiful and colorful brook trout took it. A few minutes later I had a second one. I was only planning to have two for supper; already I had accomplished what I set out to do.

However, catching the fish is the least of it. I used to receive a lot of kidding for taking so long to prepare. Folks that are not into fly fishing just don't seem to realize that the long and careful preparation is part of the wonderful therapy that fly fishing brings. At Remount I have often stopped fishing and quietly sat concealed on the bank to observe beavers working on their dams and lodges. I have watched coyotes and foxes, as well as deer and antelope, come to drink. Nothing can catch your interest like a mother duck teaching her young to find food. I have laid on my back to watch the graceful soaring of eagles and turkey vultures high in the clean blue sky. That, to me, is what fishing is really about! And to have all this within minutes of my office was truly an idle dream finally realized.

Like a good omen, the vision in my right eye began to clear after we moved to Remount. Before that I could no longer read or write by hand. As a proponent of a good walking exercise program, I walked a few miles every day after breakfast. Our golden retriever, Goldie, was ready and anxious each morning, rain or shine.

Goldie and I literally walked every acre of this beautiful ranch. I marveled at the new sights and scenes we discovered each day. For example, I developed a great respect for the tenacity of the ponderosa pine. If you let your imagination run loose, you can picture the way ponderosa overcomes tremendous hardships and survives because of its awesome will to live! We have several pines growing out of solid granite rock. South of the residence, I discovered a growing ponderosa that had been victim to a nearby falling tree. Evidently the crashing tree had bent the young ponderosa to the ground. This would have occurred when the tree was too young and elastic to break off under the impact. Rather than give up and die, this tree continued growing horizontal to the ground for perhaps ten feet. Then, in search of sun and sky, it turned upward and is still growing tall and straight. Can anyone fail to be impressed by this amazing feat of nature?

In another chapter, I mention the University of Wyoming geologist, Robert Houston, who studied this area for many, many summers. He told me that this is the site of a volcano that was once surrounded by an ocean. Later, the constantly moving continent pushed the ocean westward. In response to my question of, "How long ago did this happen?"

He casually offered, "About 1.8 billion years ago!"

The written geology of this entire Sherman Hill area would be fascinating. However, only armed with this very basic information, your eyes can discover amazing things.

On our ranch there is a hillside of once molten granite on the north side of Lone Tree Creek where Guss Creek joins it. There is another hillside of once molten granite on the north bank of Guss Creek where that stream first enters our property. What sights these cold stones have observed over the thousands of centuries!

I can't help but be awed by standing beside some of the gigantic granite rocks which tower over me. There is one group of granite stones that seem to have strayed from the rest, and stand alone on the south side of the county road not far from where the Remount pines road goes northward. I loved to walk among this group of stones. They remind me a bit of Stonehenge in England. Just using your imagination, "What a great hiding place they would make if a posse were pursuing you!"

One of the legends told to me about Remount was that a posse did capture some fellows who had robbed a chest of gold from a stagecoach. Supposedly, by the time they were captured on Remount, they had already buried the gold somewhere. The posse ordered them to show the gold or be hanged. Evidently they refused to talk and one by one their horses were whipped from underneath them. Of course, their necks were already tied by a lariat to the limb of a cottonwood or ponderosa. Supposedly, too late to save him, the last outlaw screamed out, "There's three pine in a line and the gold is buried . . ." Unfortunately, his neck snapped before another word could be heard. So the buried gold is still at Remount, of course!

It was on Christmas Eve morning of 1984 when Goldie and I took our usual morning hike. We were about a mile north of the ranch house when my right eye began to bleed internally. It was so severe that I began to wonder how I was going to be able to return home. Removing my belt, I made a leash for Goldie and she patiently walked me home. That was the day I totally lost my eyesight.

For the previous dozen years we had enjoyed the comfort and luxury of the swimming pool every summer. We did not even crank it up during the remodeling year of 1983. By 1984 we had so much to get completed that we again turned thumbs-down on starting up the pool. 1985 was yet another year of a swimming pool which was looking even more decrepit. Finally, in 1986 we determined to abolish the "old swimming hole" and Bill Edwards did the job for us. We have never regretted that decision. Now that entire area is solid green lawn and the constant work of maintaining a swimming pool is long behind us.

After disposing of the swimming pool early in 1986, we wanted to install an attractive fence around the yard. I had always envisioned a good-looking pole fence. Mary gave me phone numbers from the yellow pages and we actually visited a couple of suppliers on site. I felt the fence posts and poles carefully. I was told that they were pressure-treated and retained a pleasant light green color. Although I could no longer visualize such things, Mary gave her necessary approval. We hired Alco Fence to replace most of the fence around the yard and people tell me it has an attractive appearance.

Learning to walk with a white cane, I would attempt to follow the road from the back patio around to the front entrance, approximately two-tenths of a mile. Sometimes, when obviously lost, I would reach far out with my cane hoping to tap the pole fence. If I could hear that sound, I could better judge where I was.

One day I ventured out the front entrance after announcing my intentions to Mary and our son Scott. I was determined to reach the back patio once more. About halfway around I began to hear sounds coming from far behind me that sounded like a growling bear. The farther I walked, the more convinced I was that, indeed, a bear was on the north side of our house. Fortunately, I reached the fence around the patio and by then the loud growls and grunts were alarming. I was worried that Mary or Scott might come looking for me and run into this obviously angry animal!

As I entered the kitchen door, I called out to Mary. She was relieved to hear my voice and said that Scott had gone searching for me. There was indeed an angry animal just outside the window of the guest bedroom, but not a bear. It was a large and seemingly very angry bull that had gotten access to our yard. Normally, this bull was with the cows in the hay meadow. The bull, in his frustration, had charged a blue spruce tree and had knocked it over so that the top was pushed to the ground. The loud noises coming out of that bull were the sounds that convinced me a bear was in our yard. Of course, one look is worth all the noises I had heard, however, I could not or even would not argue with sighted people.

The bull belonged to Dick Ferguson. We leased our extra grass to Dick in the summer time. We phoned Dick and he and his son, Ed, came right over. After a long chase the bull ended up back with his cows and all was well at Remount once again.

In 1987, acquiring my first guide dog, Jamie, was the best thing that ever happened to me after blindness came. I was so anxious for Jamie to be able to take me various places on the ranch. After we were accustomed to the immediate surroundings, I announced to Mary one day that Jamie and I were going exploring. So that she would not worry, I told her we would be walking along Lone Tree Creek going toward the County Road entrance. We did just that and I was loving the familiar sound of the rushing water. As my mind wandered back to the many times I had walked this way when I was sighted, I forgot a few things I should have remembered. I had been urging Jamie to take me closer and closer to the water. Jamie is careful not to allow tree branches or even willow bushes to brush me, but during various attempts to feel the water, I lost track of where I thought I was. The sound of the water kept getting farther away from us, yet I could not feel the road under my feet. I cursed myself for not checking the direction the breeze was blowing when I first left the road, while Jamie was acting like he never had so much fun before. Remember, Jamie and I had only been together about two-and-a-half months at this time. I said to Jamie rather sharply, "Find home!"

I felt that would cause Jamie to march straight home. But after more up hill and down hill, I began to think that Jamie figured we were out for a lark and he wasn't ready to go home.

Finally Jamie stopped. I heard him sniffing. I put my hand out in front of me and felt the side of a fence, or was it a building? I knew it was wood, because a splinter dug into my finger. The wall rose higher than my head. I pondered what could this be? Aha! I must be at the old cow shed that is built from old railroad ties! As I was determining just how to proceed, I heard a vehicle approaching. It was Mary! Impishly, I heard her ask, "Want a ride, mister?"

"Thank you, Ma'am, would you mind taking a black dog, also?" Mary said she would be delighted, so Jamie and I rode home.

Months later, our daughter Nancy from San Diego, sent me a Braille compass. That has turned out to be the most precious tool I have. I never go walking without it. Even in the city I utilize my compass frequently. Especially on cloudy days when you can't feel the direction the sun is coming from, it is easy to get confused on directions. The compass saves my day every time!

Stories about my adventures with Jamie are recorded in another chapter, but that remarkable dog has allowed me to still enjoy this beautiful paradise. I hear the many sounds, smell the fragrance of nature, love the descriptions I hear from Mary, and keep my outstanding memories always present in my mind. Even blind, paradise is wonderful!

Remount Ranch.

21

Jamie, My Guide Dog, Part 1

DURING THE PERIOD OF FIRST BEING BLIND IN 1985 THROUGH 1986, I BECAME proficient as well as dependent upon the white cane used by blind people. While at the blind camp on Casper Mountain in July of 1986, I took twenty hours of mobility training. I even learned to walk around downtown Casper. It was usually frustrating and, at best, I was having to ask a lot of people for directions.

In Cheyenne I had set a goal that every Thursday I would walk to the Hathaway Building. Following my Thursday morning bank board meeting, I would leave the bank at Seventeenth and Capitol Avenue and walk up Capitol to what would have been Twenty-third Street. On the west side of the street was the main entrance to the Hathaway Building. I would then visit my old friend, Dick Hall, who was in charge of Vital Records and Mary would pick me up later.

Oftentimes I would go astray. My friends would try to help, but I would get provoked at myself for not getting it right.

Then my friend, Warren Oakes, talked to me about getting a guide dog. I really had no interest. Later that summer he was a guest at Remount during a University of Wyoming Foundation dinner. He handed me an envelope which he admonished me to read. It was the paperwork to apply for a guide dog. It remained on my desk for a few weeks and my secretary, Debbie Ferguson, kept suggesting that she read it to me.

"All right," I said, "let's get that out of the way."

It was then when I learned that at the Guide Dog Foundation they also trained you to take country walks. That got my attention and set me to thinking about being able to walk about the ranch again. I immediately phoned the Foundation to inquire about these country walks and said, "Please tell me more about these country walks. I live on a Wyoming ranch and could a dog be trained to walk me to places on my ranch?"

"I know of no reason why that could not be accomplished," came back the polite answer from Emily Biegle.

The paperwork was started and when I first mailed off my application it was with some high hopes that I might be successful. More paperwork followed. I had to have a paper from my eye doctor, Bill Jackson, confirming that I was blind. My diabetes doctor, Paul Sheridan, had to certify my good health. Rachel Miller, of the State Office of the Visual Handicapped, had to recommend me and certify my completion of twenty hours of mobility training, which means getting around with the white cane. I also requested Warren Oakes, Fred Baggs, and Stan Hathaway to write letters of recommendation for me, which they did.

Instead of applying for the January class, I asked to be considered for the March class. I would return home in spring weather instead of wintertime in February. Finally in December, I called the Foundation to inquire about whether or not I might be accepted. I was told the final decision would be made at the January meeting of the Foundation Board of Trustees. Then in January, I received the call from Emily Biegel that I had been chosen for the March class. When I expressed my joy she asked, "Was there ever any doubt in your mind?" She added with a laugh that they did not know whether to just enroll me into the class or perhaps they might canonize me. She was referring to my many fine letters of recommendation. I was so grateful to my many friends and wrote each of them to express my appreciation.

Mary made plans to fly to New York with me, where she would visit many of her friends while I was in school. The instructions from the school made it clear that I would be living in a dormitory with a roommate and Mary would have to reside in a local motel. We booked our reservations through the local AAA office and we traveled United Airlines to LaGuardia. The school is in Smithtown, New York, on Long Island, about a forty-minute ride from the airport.

We made a lot of plans and Mary sent two boxes of clothes to the school before I ever left. I made many arrangements with my secretary in order to be gone four weeks. I was really dismayed to learn that I could not have a telephone in my room. In fact, there was only one pay phone in the dormitory. Later, I found out that this pay phone was not even push-button. I had never worked a dial phone since becoming blind. When I used this phone at school, I just began asking the operator to place the call for me and used my credit card. The operator would usually tell me that I could direct dial the call, but I learned to tell them I was handicapped. Once, an operator asked me what my handicap was and I told her I had no fingers. When I left the school, I suggested they replace the dial phone with a push-button model.

I really liked the school and the people. I was met at the airport by one of the instructors, Bob Weiss, who already had one of the other students in the car. His name was Van-Allen Walstein, about my age, but a bachelor. He roomed next door to me and during the next four weeks I got to know him very well. He had been mugged on a subway and beaten with an iron bar. This left him hospitalized and also blind. However, he still had to ride the subway to get to work and he was really looking forward to receiving a guide dog.

I was assigned to a room at the end of the hall and my roommate was named Dick Bolger. Dick's wife and daughter were helping him unpack. Mary got me squared away. There was one dresser with four drawers and I had two of these and half of a closet. It was a very satisfactory accommodation and we even had our own bathroom with a shower.

This was a new adventure in living which I had not experienced since leaving the Navy in 1950. Later, looking back on it, I really enjoyed it. This was my second opportunity to spend time with other blind people. My first being at the Wyoming Lions' Club Blind Camp on Casper Mountain.

The first day at school I was asked to put away my white cane. I was surprised about this, as I had become so dependent upon the cane to get around. I literally had to feel my way along the walls and furniture, which resulted in a lot of broken fingernails. But, like everything at schools, you found there was always a good reason for these requests.

We were given a tour of the building, which contained a large living room with an adjacent dining room. The men's dorm winged off in one direction from the living room and the women's dorm winged off in the opposite direction. There was a large basement room that contained a washer and dryer; also, the grooming of the dogs took place there.

There were only seven in our class at the beginning. All were from New York except for me. There were four men and Dick, my roommate, was there for the third time. There were three women, but during the four weeks two more women were added. Alan's roommate was washed out of the school after ten days, so when we graduated, there were three men and four women who made it through graduation.

The great thing about the school, and particularly the course, was that they kept us busy morning, noon, and night. That way we did not have time on our hands to think about a lot of other things. Of course, we were anxious to get our dogs and that did not occur until Tuesday, the second day. Prior to that occasion, we had been interviewed by the various trainers and even walked with them so that they could get a better idea of what we considered a comfortable pace. Finally on Tuesday morning, we assembled and were told the names of our dogs. I was told that my dog was a male black Labrador named Jamie and the dogs would come from the kennel about ten o'clock, bathed and readied.

Each student was placed in a room and the dogs were delivered to our room one by one. We were told we would be left together with our dog for about forty-five minutes to get acquainted. It was quite a suspenseful event. When the door opened, in came the trainer with this big dog on a leash that he just handed to me. He then closed the door behind him. Jamie was really not too interested in me, although he appeared to like the petting and conversation, but seemed more interested in getting out of the room and back with the people he knew best. But from that day forward, we have never been apart.

Usually, I was up by about five-thirty in the morning. The official wake-up call came at six A.M. After showering and dressing we fed and watered the dogs and then at seven we had "break." This was to "break" the dogs; that meant we took the dogs to the same specified place for their toilet time. We did this four times a day. The first was at seven in the morning, then at noon, again after feeding at four-thirty, and the last chance was at nine at night. Even to this day Jamie follows the same schedule.

We met in the living room following breakfast for the morning agenda. Then we loaded in two vans. We would go to various and diverse areas to learn to walk with our dog under different conditions. We would return to the school for lunch, unless we were in the city and then we would eat lunch at some church basement or other arrangement. We walked all afternoon and by the time supper was ready, we all had a great appetite.

Following supper, we had another training session. This might cover grooming the dog or other learning sessions which were always beneficial to us and our dogs. Following the last session, we sometimes played Trivial Pursuit, played the piano, or just turned in and went to bed. It was a great and healthy regimen to follow and the exercise was wonderful.

In retrospect, I am amazed at how well a group of blind people can live together. It was such a comfortable feeling and I believe the situation was made comfortable because no one treated us special. Many people, out of the goodness of their hearts and their own compassion for the handicapped, go so far out of their way to be helpful. To a blind person it can almost be uncomfortable in that kind of situation. But at the Guide Dog School, this was never the case. You were hardly ever treated differently from a sighted person.

There was constant joking among the students. The funniest stories were usually about blind people. At the dining room I sat next to a young man named Marcus. One day someone asked if he had heard about the blind skunk who fell in love with a fart! Marcus chuckled over that for days.

Marcus was over six-feet tall and about twenty-three years old. He had suffered a stroke which not only partially paralyzed his left side, but also left him blind. The State of New York had recommended him for a guide dog. The school had especially trained one to work on the right hand side. Unfortunately, after about ten days at the school it became evident that Marcus was not going to be able to work the dog well enough and he was dropped from the program. We all felt badly for Marcus because, by that time, he had won a place in our hearts. It also meant his dog, Desi, had to be dropped from guide dog work. Since he had been trained to work from the right, he could not be retrained.

I will always remember one of the training incidents which involved Marcus and Desi. Marcus was a very soft-spoken black man and we were in a training session which involved training our dogs to respond to voice commands. It was time for Marcus to go through the voice commands with his dog, Desi. The trainer urged us to use a commanding voice—a harder and sharper voice than the voice you used for praising the dog. However, it was very difficult for Marcus to speak in what might be considered a strong and authoritative voice. We were putting our dogs through come, sit, down, up, and so on. Marcus told Desi to sit, but evidently the dog just stood there wagging his tail. The trainer said, "When you tell that dog to sit, don't sound like you are inviting him to a tea party. Let me hear you really get tough."

Marcus drew in his breath, but in the next sentence his voice did not sound any more commanding than it did the first time.

"Really get mad, Marcus. Act like you are talking to a street gang!" the trainer admonished.

In his same soft-spoken monotone Marcus said, "Sit, Desi, you black mudder fucker!" That just about broke up the training session.

Jamie was born at the Guide Dog Foundation kennels on May 17, 1985. After four weeks he was fed baby food cereal as well as his mother's milk. When he was weaned from his mother, at eight weeks, he was assigned to a "puppy walker" family so that he was raised in a home environment. John and Chris Leidner of Stonybrook, New York, had Jamie until he was one year old. They taught him the basic obedience commands and they really loved this dog. I know it must have been very difficult for them to return Jamie to the kennel and if it had not been that they received a new eight-week-old puppy, it would have been even more difficult.

One evening the Leidner family invited me to dinner at their home. They are delightful people and they can be very proud of their two teenage sons. I enjoyed hearing stories of Jamie's first year. I hope one day they will visit us at Remount Ranch and see Jamie working with me.

I also learned Jamie received his name from the Jamesport, New York Lions Club. Through their contribution of three thousand dollars to the Guide Dog Foundation, they were effectively sponsoring a guide dog and also they got to name him. So Jamie received his name from Jamesport. The president of the club and his wife came to visit Jamie and me one Sunday before graduation. They presented me with their club pin, which features a black Labrador guide dog. We had our picture taken together and we each spoke a few words to the assembled public. It was very nice and I have written to the Jamesport Lions Club a couple of times to tell them about Jamie and our progress together.

Mary stayed in New York over a week and with her rental car she visited a number of her former school chums. On Saturday and Sunday nights I was allowed to go out to dinner with Mary. Those were wonderful treats; we found delightful places to have dinner and I missed those occasions after Mary returned to Wyoming.

As we approached graduation, I longed to have a dinner out again and perhaps a glass of wine. I asked one of the trainers if I could take she and her husband to dinner and she thought that would be great. But after talking with the head trainer, John Biegel, she reported that John felt it would cause disharmony if they took me out. So I then suggested we invite the entire class and this was agreed on, provided it was a Dutch treat. After lunch that day I announced that anyone wanting to go out to dinner on Saturday night should call out their name. The whole class responded, so we all went. The group included three trainers, one husband of one of the female trainers, and seven blind students. We had a great time and it was a lot of fun. On that occasion we could not take our dogs, so they were left leashed to our beds until we returned from our party. I laughed to think of how it would have been trying to get seven dogs under our crowded table anyway.

On Saturday afternoon volunteers came to offer rides to go shopping or on other errands. Visitors would also be welcome on Saturday and Sunday afternoons and there were always a lot of people around on weekends. All of the other students were from New York and their families came. Dottie Cassell, a student, was getting her third dog.

Her husband was also blind and he too had a guide dog. When he came to visit it was a lot of fun because the two of them were great entertainers. They sang, played the piano, and told jokes. I surely admired them for the way they handled their lives.

Volunteer workers from the community were available to help students and I asked for a volunteer to take me to Mass on Sunday. Saint Patrick's Church was not far from the school in Smithtown and I enjoyed going there. It was a huge church with a congregation to match. The volunteer lady was so helpful and I hope she enjoyed the outings on Sunday as much as I did.

Before graduation John Biegel told me he would like to take Jamie and me for a walk in the country park area. He felt this would be helpful when I took Jamie to the ranch. We spent a Saturday and Sunday afternoon doing that and it certainly was helpful to me. I knew that I would feel more confident when I returned with Jamie to the ranch. I always enjoyed the time I spent with John Biegel because he was truly a great trainer and teacher who worked with me each day although he was in charge of the whole training program. But the two days we spent in the large park were his days off and I appreciated his efforts and his interest.

When graduation finally came, there was a rush of packing and going home preparations. My return flight on United was already verified and I was one of the first to leave. Meg Hunt, one of the trainers, drove me to LaGuardia Airport. She checked my bag for me and took me to the departure lounge. From then on, Jamie and I were to face the real world for the first time on our own. I checked in at the desk and Jamie found me a seat in the waiting area. I was certain the loading gate was to my back. Shortly, they called the flight and I told Jamie to "find the door out." It was then I learned Jamie does not like to stand in line. He would not have stopped for the ticket taker if she had not called out to me. We boarded the airplane and I put Jamie under my seat. I had a bulkhead window seat and I felt that if Jamie did not get under the seat there could not be enough room for the passenger who would occupy the adjoining seat. I was pleasantly surprised to learn they left the seat next to me vacant. Although Jamie and I have flown together many times since then, we have flown about ninety percent of the time on United. I certainly commend United for the way they take care of us on their flights.

Jamie and I both survived the long flight to Denver and Mary was there to meet us when we landed. How great it was to be home again!

Jamie and I were continuing to learn about each other. My life with Jamie was just beginning. This fine dog was to open new opportunities for me to regain my confidence and independence.

John and Jamie.

22

Jamie, My Guide Dog, Part II

IN EDITING THE PREVIOUS CHAPTER ENTITLED JAMIE, IT MADE ME WANT TO update. First of all, in the previous chapter, I talked mostly about the process of getting Jamie and very little about my dog himself. Now, after being together for over sixty-two months, I believe I can add some comments which will enable the reader to better appreciate what a great partner this fellow really is!

It might be difficult for a reader to understand how it is to live every full day without being separated at least some of the time from your dog. Not that I want to be; quite the contrary. We are a team in the fullest extent of the word.

As I write these pages, Jamie is snoozing at my feet. His favorite place in this ranch office is under the desk where I write. He is not on the leash; he is entirely free to wander about the house or out in his exercise yard as he pleases. He just chooses to be with me and it makes me feel good to know that.

If someone were to knock on our front door, Jamie would bolt like a most ferocious animal and raise cane. He continues to warn the 'intruder' until, holding Jamie tightly at leash, I extend my hand and shake hands with the caller. At that instant Jamie reaches his nose toward the hand of the caller and takes a good sniff. At this point, he is suddenly satisfied and stops barking. He is terribly protective, but I do not complain. In fact, both Mary and I enjoy this extra and comforting bonus. As crime increases, I can't think of a better protector than this fine fellow.

Jamie is well known in the Cheyenne community. His first formal acceptance came in 1987. He was nominated and elected as an honorary member of the Cheyenne Young Men's Literary Club. The short list of honorary members includes former Governors Hansen and Hathaway and the present Governor Mike Sullivan. Since members are listed alphabetically, Jamie Ostlund appears between Hathaway and Sullivan. At the recent black tie-dinner Jamie was on the committee charged with all the arrangements. Jamie was listed as official taster and also was given a front row center position in the membership photograph commemorating the ninetieth anniversary of the Cheyenne Literary Club.

In addition, the Cheyenne Rotary Club feels that Jamie is an honorary member, even though I don't believe they ever took formal action. Jamie and I did a program for Cheyenne Rotary after returning from New York in 1987. Rotary members still talk about that wonderful program. His acceptance was demonstrated when Rotary President Milt Bittinger presented Jamie with his own Rotary badge with his name imprinted —there is no doubt that Jamie is a hit wherever we go.

In 1989 and 1990 we had been going to La Jolla, California, for a few months of escaping the winter. Every member at the La Jolla Rotary admires this beautiful and intelligent partner of mine.

Three times each day are really special for my dog. Early every morning and late each afternoon, Jamie eats! How that fellow loves to eat! I truly believe Labradors must have an insatiable appetite. Nothing gives him more pleasure. But I have only mentioned a twice-a-day occurrence and I mentioned there were three special times per day.

The third occasion follows my own breakfast each morning. I carefully unfold a paper napkin and cover my placemat with it. I feel Jamie is eyeing me from his position on the throw rug by the backdoor. When I push back my chair and turn it ninety degrees, I take the few steps needed to reach the pantry door. From Jamie's own box I withdraw a plastic bag containing his brush and comb. Jamie bounds forward to meet me and we begin a grooming period which follows a program we have worked out together.

First, I slip his chain choke collar off his head and lay it on the paper napkin. At that time Jamie carefully places both his front feet on the seat of my chair and stands there with tail wagging. I massage his coat vigorously, always stroking his hair in the opposite direction. I especially scratch his neck thoroughly and Jamie almost purrs. I do this for a very practical reason. My dog rarely ever scratches his neck anymore for I have learned that by loosening these hairs and carefully brushing them with vigor, he just does not feel the need to scratch like so many other dogs. After doing both sides of his neck and face, I elevate his chin and brush down his throat and chest. From there I go to his front shoulders and legs. Jamie then turns sideways to me and I brush long strokes from front to back. All this time I remain comfortably seated.

At first my dog would never appreciate me holding and brushing his tail, but he now knows that this is entirely normal. So we finish by me holding his tail and taking long brush strokes along the top of his back to the tip of his tail. Then we end by brushing the underside of his tail as well. Jamie loves it. Immediately he turns to face me and snorts for his collar. He knows he is not dressed until I slip his collar back on. One final event remains to complete his grooming and for that Jamie places both his front paws back on my chair seat again. This is to receive a big hug which is part of our ritual!

Jamie's veterinarian, Dr. Jean Cotton, tells me Jamie has perhaps the best coat of all the dogs she sees. I can't help but feel that his daily grooming certainly contributes to his excellent condition. Everyone tells me how shiny and handsome he is and it really makes me want to be able to see him for myself. However, I don't dwell on that. In my mind I feel I know exactly how he looks.

Ordinarily when Jamie and I go walking here at the ranch, we follow the roads. It is easier for me and I don't have to use my Braille compass and speculate where I am. But when I am hiking with another person, I love to go cross-country with Jamie. After these several years I am still amazed at how carefully he steers me around places that even a sighted person would find awkward. My friend, John Gramlich, has been hiking with me about once each week. John is in training for backpacking later this summer. John tells me how great a job Jamie consistently does for me.

Here is an invitation for the reader to spend a typical Thursday with Jamie and me. Although this account was written in 1990, I hope you find it interesting.

Every Thursday we leave home about seven-twenty in the morning. Since I am on the Board of the Wyoming National Bank of Cheyenne, I am expected to be at the weekly meeting, which commences at eight o'clock. As soon as I arise, so does Jamie. He has been sleeping right beside my bed all night. I slip my finger in the ring of his collar and say, "Find the drawer! I need clean shorts."

He walks to the correct dresser drawer with his cold nose pointing to the drawer handle. As soon as I pick up my clean shorts, he does an about-face and takes me to the shower.

Once out of the shower and dressed, it is now Jamie's turn to get all the attention. I don't even have to give him a command. He stands patiently while I fasten his leash and say, "Forward!"

Jamie leads me to his place in the breakfast room where he lies down against the wall. I unsnap his leash and then pick up his stainless steel bowl. I enter the pantry as he waits for me to put a scant two cups of Iams dog food in his dish. Then I add one heartworm pill, which he receives daily. Almost every morning I also open the refrigerator and remove the plain yogurt and add a dollop of yogurt to his dog food. I am a believer that this gives him much nicer breath than if he does without it.

Finally, I place his dish on the floor in the kitchen and then I sit down on a stool to talk with Jamie. You might think this odd when most dogs would be excited about getting their morning meal. Well, Jamie is also excited, but I have him lie there for several seconds, then after a few words I say, "Okay!"

Jamie scrambles for his dish and within a minute has licked it clean. Then he comes to me and I fasten his leash once more. "Find the closet!"

Jamie takes me to the coat closet and after donning my wraps, we go to the outside door. Here at the ranch we walk to the garage so Jamie can take care of his potty needs. We actually walk up the inclined cement driveway and he stops at the right hand edge. This makes it a bit like a curb and when I extend his leash, he steps off.

Jamie gets plenty of praise after he finishes his morning business and we return with his tail wagging. Jamie always gets a small treat when we return to the house. He expects it and loves it!

Usually, I then pour a cup of coffee and Jamie takes me to the table for my breakfast. Then comes his grooming. If there is still enough time, Jamie then takes me to the piano. I practice a bit, until Mary calls, "Ready!"

Jamie then bounds in to get me. After fastening his leash, my command to him is,

"Find the harness door!" This is the door leading down to the basement and on the back side of this door hangs his harness and leashes. With the harness in hand, I tell Jamie to, "Find the door outside," and once out he then hears, "Find the car." Jamie always takes me to the passenger side, but first he puts his nose by the rear-door handle. This is his door and after it is opened and his leash unsnapped, I say, "In the car!"

Jamie settles down on the backseat and usually begins gnawing on his nylon bone. He is an excellent traveler. Much of the time he merely sleeps peacefully stretched out on the backseat. However, at times, he sits up like an ordinary passenger and gazes out the window. Oftentimes, when passing livestock close by or when sighting another dog, he growls or sometimes gives a small bark. Otherwise, he is very quiet and unobtrusive.

Mary pulls along the curb at Seventeenth and Capitol in Cheyenne to drop us off. Jamie and I get out and harness up. "Find the door inside!" At hearing this Jamie takes me to the door of the bank and in we go. Jamie always receives a few nice compliments from the employees as we pass. His command upon entering the bank is, "Find the elevator."

Jamie stops so that I only have to put my hand on the wall where elevator buttons wait to be pushed. We go to the third floor and it does not take a command from me other than "Forward." Jamie not only takes me to the board room, but also to my chair. One time he nudged me for a treat after doing this and I gave in to his request. Because of that, I must always now give him a small treat after we get to my seat in the board room. That dog never forgets!

Normally, Jamie sleeps through the meetings, but occasionally he makes appropriate comments. Invariably, when a discussion has worn itself out, Jamie has demonstrated perfect timing with a long groan and moan. The members around the table break up with laughter.

When the meeting concludes, I often give Jamie a command, "Find the bathroom!"

Jamie is brilliant for knowing where most of the public rest rooms are located in Cheyenne. Wherever we are, I can count on Jamie to come through on that request.

Back on Capitol Avenue again, we head north toward the State Capitol building. Oftentimes, we stop to visit with friends along the way, but usually we proceed briskly up the Avenue for about six blocks. We are heading for the Hathaway Building, a State office building. Jamie and I go to the cafeteria where we meet with a group of longtime friends who are mostly retired.

These friends include people such as Bob Fleming, Bus Hacker, Bob Skyles, Jack O'Brien, Tom Morris, Rich Hillman, John Harper, Barry Cowing, Dick Hall, and Jerry McCune. We have coffee and tell a few stories before adjourning.

Sometimes, on the way to the Hathaway Building, we stop at the Federal Building. When we enter there, we must undergo security search and this is normally done by walking through the same kind of gate which is used at airports. However, since Jamie's harness will set off the alarm, they usually check me with a hand-held wand. The security guard marvels at how Jamie takes me to the elevator on entering and back outside when we depart. Often I have heard him comment, "That dog is smarter than I am!" I carefully refuse to comment on the point!

Our normal Thursday routine is to go to the home of my retired friend, Dick Hall. By this time Jamie is usually ready for another drink of water and he really expects it at Dick's. He is never disappointed. We drive to lunch at Poor Richard's Restaurant where Mary usually joins us. Bob and Louise Skyles also meet with us for lunch and we have fun talking and telling stories. Following lunch, unless I have an appointment with a doctor, lawyer, or others, Mary drives us back to the ranch. We like getting back early enough to take a good walk for exercise, which Jamie and I both need and enjoy.

The two of us receive many requests from schools to do programs for the children. Usually they include classes from the third grade through the fifth. These students have been reading about blind people and how they learn to move in this world. It is most helpful to Jamie and me whenever they also have read about guide dogs.

We demonstrate how Jamie takes me about and we show the kids how Jamie responds to various commands. The kids love it! And Jamie and I do also!

Following our demonstrations, Jamie and I sit down and we volunteer to take questions from the students. I let them know up front they can ask any question they choose to. This includes about me being blind or questions about Jamie. I tell the kids I will interpret Jamie's answers for them. They are enthusiastic with their questions and they come up with about everything.

Oftentimes after doing a program at one of the schools, we get fan mail. The letters from the kids are priceless! Teacher Kathy Ellis even had her class make an audiotape for me. Each student spoke into the microphone and told me what they learned from our visit to their class. I have played it many times and still never tire of it. This audiotape, plus the letters I receive, will bring tears to your eyes!

When leaving a classroom I usually tell the kids, "Wherever you are and you see Jamie and me walking along, please say 'Hello, Mr. Ostlund, and Hello, Jamie!"

I explained that they should say this to me because I could not see them, of course. The first time this happened to us we were walking toward the Little America Restaurant and Motel complex. I heard a small boy's voice call out, "Hello Mr. Ostlund and Jamie!"

Immediately, in more hushed tones, I heard a mother admonish the boy that he should not do that. So I called out, "That's all right, lady, I asked the children to do that whenever they see us!"

During the summer Jamie gets a very special treat. We hike about half a mile to our lake. We used to go there and then rest and relax. I love to listen to the bird sounds as well as all the sounds of nature. But Jamie gets his treat when I first slip off his harness and then his collar. I bring out a special canvas float made for training retrievers and Jamie is in heaven! He never seems to tire as I fling his float far out in the water. Time after time, he retrieves it for me and is always anxious to go again. I am the one who tires first. Jamie is such a strong swimmer and I know the exercise is wonderful for him.

We attend Cheyenne Rotary Club at noon on Wednesday. Usually I like to get there about eleven thirty because it gives me a better opportunity to visit with members as they arrive. Sometimes I take advantage of being there early and use the telephone. Jamie knows how to take me to the public phone and will wait patiently if it is already in use. Sometimes some humorous things happen when we go to Rotary.

One day, arriving early for Rotary, I told Jamie, "Find the bathroom!" He did just that. The men's room is down the hall from the Rotary meeting room and although it is not large, it has two lavatories, two wall-hung fixtures, and two toilet stalls. When we entered, hearing no other sounds, I felt we were probably the only ones in the room. Jamie took me straight to one of the wall-hung fixtures. Brushing my hand on the wall, I knew I was also standing close to a stall door. Just then, to my surprise, a male voice asked, "Does your dog bite?"

Not choosing to respond with either a yes or no, I countered with, "Please don't try to pet him!"

"Oh, I'm not trying to pet him! I'm just trying to get out of this stall!"

With that I moved Jamie to the next fixture which was away from the stall and the fellow, without further comment, beat a hasty retreat out the exit!

Another Rotary meeting demonstrated the rather subtle way that Jamie was getting away with a bit of mischief that I had been completely unaware of. Again, arriving early at the meeting, Jamie had already taken me to a seat at the table and he was properly under the table as required. Then I heard one of the waitresses speaking to another and she said, "You really have to watch that black dog when he comes in because he likes to snatch a salad off the serving cart!"

I was shocked to hear this and responded, "Are you speaking about my dog, Jamie?"

"Yes, I am, Mr. Ostlund, he does that quite often on his way to your table!"

I found that hard to believe and reached under the table to place my hand on his mouth. Imagine my surprise when I discovered a big lettuce leaf protruding out of both sides of his face!

Usually, as Jamie and I walk through public areas, I hear remarks made by passers-by about Jamie. Usually these comments are quite similar and most often are, "Oh! What a beautiful dog!"

However one day while we were in the mall, I must have passed by a couple of teenagers. I heard one remark to the other with admiration in his voice, "Man! What a bad-ass dog!"

I smile to myself as I wonder, "What next?"

I have absolute confidence when traveling with my dog. For example, I had arranged to meet Mary in Denver at the Sheraton Hotel. My friend, Dick Hall, dropped me off at the airport in Cheyenne where Jamie and I boarded a United Express flight to Denver Stapleton Airport.

Arriving in Denver, we proceeded to the lower level with our suitcase and took a taxi. I gave the driver the address of the Sheraton Hotel at the Denver Tech Center and asked about the fare. I do this because I have found just a very few drivers who will overstate the meter on arrival. Most do not, but it only takes once or twice to learn to be cautious.

Satisfied with his response, we relaxed during the twenty-minute ride to the hotel. Jamie and I enjoy being independent and after paying cabdriver we proceeded to the front desk. I displayed my credit card and checked in. I always asked for the same room I had last time, if it is available. This makes it much easier for Jamie to remember the correct room. Usually, a bellman who has never worked with a blind person before shows some hesitation about how to proceed. I break this ice by shaking hands with him and asking his name. Then I say to Jamie, "Follow Fred!" And off we go.

Once in the room we first made a tour. Jamie showed me the bed, the desk chair, and the telephone. We also checked out the bathroom. By then it was time for Jamie to enjoy his favorite pastime and eat his evening meal! Having pre-packed his meal portions, we proceeded with his supper. Then we took the elevator to the ground floor again and Jamie went out for his break. Returning to the correct room for the first time is the critical test, which he usually passed. Back in the room, I listened to news on either the TV or radio and thought about my own dinner. I don't usually give Jamie a drink until perhaps thirty minutes after he eats, unless we are short of time. He drinks better and is more ready for his 9:00 P.M. break when that arrives.

At last it was dinnertime for John, so out we went! There are two restaurants in this hotel. One is Italian and the other features a pianist, whom I particularly enjoy. We headed for the main dining room. At the lobby area I told Jamie, "Find the eating place!" Jamie can smell food a block away, so we had no problem locating the dining room. As always, Jamie was remembered from previous visits. For the benefit of the reader I will suggest that if you want to be remembered when you travel, just get a great looking black Labrador retriever that you groom to a shiny finish.

When Mary arrived from New York later that evening, she found Jamie and me still in the restaurant where we had been joined by other friends. I appreciate and marvel at our independence. When I first became blind, I thought I had totally lost that independence forever. I will be eternally grateful to the Guide Dog Foundation for the Blind, Inc., for restoring that wonderful sense of confidence to me!

This confidence is completely supported by the ever presence of the greatest benefactor I ever had since my blindness, my pal Jamie! I cannot imagine that any man ever loved his dog more than I do! I pray that we have many, many more wonderful years together!

John and Jamie negotiating a cattle guard at Remount.

Epilogue

Tomorrow is May 17, 1993, and Jamie celebrates his eighth birthday! It is difficult to believe that Jamie and I have been together for over six years. We have been through so many adventures together and traveled so many places. For me, it has been six wonderful and fulfilling years.

However, I am also learning that there is a good deal of stress put upon guide dogs. After six years of Jamie worrying about me, signs of that stress are beginning to show. Early this year I spoke with my friend, John Biegel, about these signs, and he recommended we retire Jamie. That jolted me into reality! When I don't see into a mirror, or see Jamie's black hairs turning to white, I easily forget we are both aging.

After conferring with John Biegel, and examining my own conscience, I came to an inescapable conclusion. For all this dog has done for me, the very least I can do for him is to allow him to enjoy his retirement.

During the time for Jamie's regular health checkup and shots, I mentioned Jamie's coming retirement to Jean Cotton, Jamie's doctor. I told Jean it was recommended that I retire Jamie and I wanted to find a nice retirement home for him.

Jean said, "I think I know a good place where the folks would just love to have Jamie!"

"You do?" I said, "Is it near Cheyenne?"

"Yes, in fact it is right on the edge of Cheyenne," Jean answered.

I asked further, "Would I know these people?"

Jean responded by tapping me on the shoulder and stating, "Yes, you know them all right! It's me!"

I experienced an immediate sense of relief. Jean Cotton loves animals from the very nature of her profession. She has tended Jamie for these several years and Jamie likes her dearly. What a wonderful gift for Jamie to be invited to spend his retirement with this nice lady. Jean lives on five acres of land east of Cheyenne. The land is well-fenced and Jamie should live a grand life.

I gave it much thought, but always came back to the same conclusion: give Jamie to Jean Cotton.

I gave the Guide Dog Foundation my request to be enrolled in their June class for training with a new guide dog. They in turn sent adoption papers to Jean Cotton. Now, this coming Wednesday, May 19, 1993, I am taking Jamie to Jean Cotton's house and saying good-bye! It will not be easy for me. I am continuing to try to look on the bright side which tells me Jamie will soon learn to love the Cotton family. Within a few months, he will build a new bond with them. For me, I plan to never see Jamie again because I do not want to disrupt the bonding of Jamie with Jean. In three weeks I shall be returning to Smithtown to receive a new dog. Within six months, I hope my new dog and I have bonded for keeps. At my age, soon to be sixty-six, this will undoubtedly be my last time to attend guide dog school. For the first time, I am beginning to feel my age. I am not as aggressive or as busy as I was six years ago.

It seemed important to me for Jamie to formally resign his membership in both the Cheyenne Young Men's Literary Club and also the Cheyenne Rotary Club. I have to be guilty of having too much sentimentality. However, rather than explain to each member of each club about Jamie retiring, I chose to let his letters of resignation do the talking for me.

On the following pages are separate letters which speak for themselves.

May 15, 1993
Young Men's Literary Club
Cheyenne, WY 82001

Gentlemen:
Each time I have attempted to write this letter I have been filled with considerable emotions. Hopefully, with the assistance of John Ostlund, I may be able to bring this sorrowful matter to a close.

Never shall I ever forget your thoughtfulness in accepting me as an honorary member. Coming from New York as I did, I was frankly amazed at your warmth and kindness. My friends and family in New York could hardly believe my good fortune to become accepted as an honorary member and associated with such a fine group of men!

Now, at the age of eight years, I am being "turned out to pasture." It is not my idea and for that reason I am particularly sad. In my retirement, I will be living with Jean Cotton and her family. Jean has been my veterinarian for these past years and I do like her a lot. However, I like you fellows a lot also and I feel very sad at the thought of leaving all of you!

I do hope John Ostlund will be lucky enough to find a new guide as good as I am. I know that will be very difficult. Frankly speaking, I don't believe he can discover another guide with the same talent, love, and dedication I have shown him. But then, the decision has evidently been made and I understand it to be irreversible. John might soon be learning the truth of my predictions.

Hopefully, you will not think of me as talking sour apples about my replacement. For his or her sake I do hope you will accept John's new guide in the same way you accepted me. That would be generous and loving of you, the way I know you all to be!

I close this letter with the hope that you will continue to think kindly of me. I will be thinking of all of you the same way. I shall miss you!

With love from,
Jamie Ostlund

May 13, 1993
John J. Metzke
Hirst & Applegate
PO Box 1083
Cheyenne, WY 82003

Dear John:

You are already aware that I get terribly sentimental about my dog. Of course this is especially true as it becomes time to give him away.

Included with this letter is a separate communication I helped Jamie write to the members of the Cheyenne Rotary Club. You see, Jamie is just as sentimental as I am sometimes.

I have chosen not be at Rotary on Wednesday, May 19. However I was hoping, in my absence, to have Jamie's letter of resignation read. Now comes my purpose in writing you.

Not having your home address, would you please pass his letter on to Dana? As a member of Rotary, and a good friend of Jamie, I would appreciate Dana reading this to the Rotary Club for both Jamie and me.

Of course, Dana, if your schedule prevents you from doing this, I shall endeavor to find someone else. By having the letter read during my absence, it could be much easier on me to not have to explain my being at Rotary for a meeting or two without Jamie.

On June 7, Mary and I are flying to New York to install me at the Guide Dog Foundation for the Blind once again. Although Mary will be returning in a week, my new dog and I shall not return until July 2.

Dana, we shall really appreciate you doing this for us if it works within your schedule.

With warmest regards to you both,
Sincerely,
John and Jamie

May 15, 1993
Cheyenne Rotary Club
Cheyenne, WY 82001

Dear Fellow Rotarians:

For my part, it is with a great deal of sadness that I must submit my resignation as an honorary member of the Cheyenne Rotary Club. I do want you to realize it is not my idea! However, I seem to have little choice in this kind of decision. How unfortunate for me.

Here I am at the age of eight years, and, as you say, being turned out to pasture. I really don't want to retire but the decision has been made by others. I suppose I am expected to "keep a stiff upper lip" as the British say. But with the size of my lips that would hardly be considered in good form. Instead I shall do my best to keep them from quivering as I say good-bye!

With the help of my partner, I am attempting to write this letter to you wonderful men and women who have accepted me with your kindness and love. The friends and family I left back in New York believe I am the luckiest fellow they know! And they are correct! I have been so proud to wear my Rotary badge with my name imprinted. My good feelings even carried over to join in with your singing at times. You never seemed to mind and I thank you.

My partner probably thinks it will be easy to replace me. I hardly think so. He may find another guide, but how could he ever find a guide with the same devotion, love, and wisdom I have shown to him. You probably think I am talking sour apples, but that is how I feel.

Since I am being retired, I am very happy my partner has shown the good sense to place me with my friend, Jean Cotton. She has doctored me these several years and I know I will have a fine home with Jean and her family.

However, I shall miss seeing each one of you and joining in your songs and fellowship. Please try and give me a good thought from time to time. I will be doing the same with each of you. Oh! I almost forgot! Just for me, please do what you can to make my replacement feel as welcome as you did for me!

With my love to all you wonderful people, from
Jamie Ostlund

(A letter from Dana Metzke to Jamie)
May 19, 1993

Dear Jamie:

I thought you might like to know how sorry your fellow Rotarians are to learn of your resignation from the Cheyenne Rotary Club. They understand that retirement must come to all of us one day and we all hope that when that day comes we will welcome it.

First, though, you must know how honored I am to have been you and your partner's choice to deliver your resignation message. I have to tell you honestly, though, that is wasn't easy to read your parting words which left all of us knowing we no longer will greet you each Wednesday as you stop for your membership badge then make your familiar way to your chosen seat. Your fellow Rotarians listened raptly to your every word. As I finished your message, there was a moment of silent thoughtfulness and expressions of regret that you won't be at future meetings. They were so moved by your letter that they are having it printed in the COG newsletter so those members who couldn't be at today's meeting will receive your message as well. They are extremely proud to have been associated with you and found sharing membership with you very special.

Now that you are opening a new chapter in your life with a new family, I know it only will be chance if I see you again. That thought takes me back several years to when I first saw you with your partner. I don't think you had been in Cheyenne very long. You didn't know me then and I didn't tell anyone how I felt about you that day.

I was outside the Wyoming State Capitol Building. You and your partner walked through the tall, wooden Capitol doors and paused at the top of the landing. I was frightened for you and your partner with all the people rushing by and the steep, concrete steps waiting for your descent. You looked up at your partner, waiting for instruction. He spoke to you. You looked down the towering elevation before you, lowered your head and took a careful, slow step. Step after step, you guided your partner, concentrating only on him as he corrrectly placed one foot after the other until the mountain of steps was behind you. I never again was frightened for you.

Some people feel badly because you retired early. I feel differently. By our human standards, you are only eight years old and have been with your partner only six years. But by your canine standards, you worked for forty-two years at your partner's side. Certainly you have earned your rest. The difficulty for us is that we tend to judge others' lives by our own, and even though we know better, we seem to expect that someone as remarkable as you always will be with us in the same capacity we have always known. We need to accept that we only have you for the duration of your life and that your partner can only have you for as long as you are able. How many of us can say that we performed our jobs as well as you for so long?

We also feel sad that your family cannot keep you as well as your successor. I think your partner is sad that you will feel abandoned. That's because right now your partner is your life. When I was in grade school, my family adopted a Shetland sheepdog from a family moving away from Cheyenne. Laddie came to our home terribly confused, dejected and looking in every room for a former family member. He wouldn't play with us. He didn't want our hugs. He kept watching the door for the right face to walk through it. It never did.

Two days later, his tail wagged. The next day he watched me get off my school bus. I gave him a treat saved from my lunch box. My brother showed him a new game and he loved it. One week later, he ran barking to my bus to greet me and receive his treat. He decided it was okay to love his new family. You will too. And then we won't feel guilty anymore.

I will miss petting your sleek, shiny blackness, your head cuddled up to my feet at Norwest Bank meetings, your robust yawns, your rendition of "Happy Birthday," your excitment at the possibility of a swim, your requirement of a handshake as the proper password, and your endless appreciation of fine food.

If you hadn't been a guide dog, we wouldn't be losing you now. But we wouldn't ever have known you at all. And to not have known you at all truly would be the saddest ending.

Jamie, you know that your partner, the one you guided, guarded, protected and loved, is going to be just fine.

Love,
Dana

Wednesday, April 15, 1998: Dr. Jean Cotton phoned me to inform me that Jamie had died at eleven o'clock this morning. At this time next month, Jamie would have been thirteen years old.

Fortunately for this fine fellow, he was never sick a day, but instead lived happily each day right up to the end. Jean told me he ate his usual breakfast and then went to the huge yard to do his morning inspections. His new friend, a retired greyhound, did this ritual along with Jamie each day. The greyhound would run laps around the yard while Jamie stood in the middle jumping up and down and barking encouragement to the racer.

However, by eleven o'clock, she found Jamie dead. He died peacefully which is a wonderful way to go. Hope I can be that lucky!

23

My Experience
with *WE* Magazine

RETURNING FROM DENVER EARLY IN NOVEMBER OF 1998, AS USUAL, WE listened to our phone messages. What a surprise it was to hear the voice of a lady named Fran Adhers, Managing Editor of *We* Magazine, calling from New York.

Evidently the magazine had come across the newspaper of the Rotary District Governor written in January of 1994. The story was actually written by Dana Metzke of Cheyenne, at the request of the District Governor, telling about each of my two guide dogs, and how they brought me to Rotary each week. Dana recalled my black Labrador named Jamie, who retired in 1993, as well as his replacement, blond Russ.

Fran Adhers believed this subject would make an interesting story for her magazine, for a special section called Animations. So she actually offered to pay me for a 600-word story if it proved to be acceptable. I agreed to do it.

Within ten days, and after several drafts, I had written a story, but of course it was difficult to tell if it fit properly within the 600-word boundary. Consequently, I sent her about a 900-word story, knowing full well they would edit it to fit their format.

Fran seemed pleased with the story and asked for pictures. Mary sent ten photographs to New York for their examination. I then was told that the story would appear in *We* Magazine in their January-February 1999 issue.

From the sample magazines they sent to us, Mary was impressed with the quality. By the time the issue was printed, Fran Adhers and I had several pleasant conversations by phone, as well as the exchange of correspondence. When I asked if we might get a couple dozen copies sent to us, she merely replied that we could have all we wanted. However, when they arrived I was delighted to receive two separate boxes, which totaled sixty copies, of the issue containing my story, "Blind Trust."

We gave them to our family and friends and it was nice to be able to pass them out so freely.

Since the magazine deals primarily with people of various handicaps, Fran Adhers also was quite interested in a visit Russ and I had made to the Triumph High School in Cheyenne. People with various handicaps had been invited to meet with different groups of students and talk openly about their handicaps. Fran Adhers thought we must have a school board with unusual enlightenment. I am hopeful that this story of the school makes an upcoming issue of *We* magazine. Judy Kallal, a teacher, is the contact I gave to Fran Adhers.

Responding to my request, *We* Magazine has given permission for me to replicate the exact "Blind Trust" story in this book. For this I especially thank both Charles Reilly and also Fran Adhers.

Animation

Blind Trust

A rugged rancher who can no longer distinguish his cows from his horses enlists a splendid dog *by John C. Ostlund*

First love, a black labrador, receives high honor and brings laughs at the Rotary Club, and frees a businessman.

It was one of those gorgeous summer days in July. My dog and I were enjoying the lake in the shade of a huge granite rock. A breeze now and then rustled through the ponderosa pines. Birds sang and rainbow trout broke water to snatch a stray gnat and beavers fussed at their dam.

"Jamie," I said, giving him a pat, "back to work!"

Since late 1984, at age 57, I had been totally blind as a result of diabetic retinopathy. While at the lake, I had been thinking that for all the years when I had had my eyesight, I could never have identified all the myriad sounds there.

My wife and I owned a grand ranch in the mountains west of Cheyenne. After blindness came, I began to get depressed. What I could not cope with was my absolute and total loss of independence. Most of my time found me thinking of no longer driving, no way to look at livestock, no way to handle accounts, no reading. On and on, negatives piled on. Every Thursday morning I was in the habit of driving to Cheyenne where I served on the board of directors of a bank. With sadness, I told myself I should resign.

Then something simple happened that more than shifted my attitude—it caused a positive, optimistic turnabout in me. That something was a black lab guide dog.

When a friend came out to the ranch and made the suggestion of a guide dog I not only showed no interest, I would not give it consideration. Finally, after he had brought me information from The Guide Dog Foundation for the Blind in Smithtown, New York, and I learned that the training program included country walks, I phoned them. "Do you think a guide dog learn to walk me around my ranch?" I asked.

The response came back, "I don't know why not."

I processed the paperwork at once, and, funnily, right away began looking forward with hope that I would be accepted.

Entering class in March 1987, I soon was assigned a dog, Jamie. The first time I ever walked with my dog in harness returned all the good feelings as I strode along the street. Had I been granted a magic carpet to take me where I wished, I could not have felt better than I did. The previous two years of shuffling along blindly, then with a white cane, had caused me to forget the barely discernible yet vivid pleasure of a swift walk by myself.

I recall the words of my instructor when Jamie and I were in training. "You will soon be thinking that you and your dog are really working well together," he said. "Later you will discover it takes six to twelve months before you two fully bond." It proved true. Two creatures working was transforming, and in any situation whatsoever, I had the untroubled assurance of blind trust. We were a terrific team, my partner and my pal, and me. He gave me back the independence I felt I had lost forever.

As Jamie carefully guided me around the ranch, we added a smattering of new words to his vocabulary, such as corral, creek, auto gate, tack shed, barn, cows and horses. For me, I began to feel there was hardly any limit to what I could do

if I put my mind to it. What's more, we were having fun.

On Thursday mornings, I still headed to the bank for meetings, now escorted there by Jamie who soon had the hang of whisking me to the elevator and to the third floor, then on to my seat in the board room, where he settled silently under the table. When a discussion dwelled too long on a particular subject, Jamie yawned loudly, evoking laughter from those seated and speeding up the conclusion to the talk.

At the Cheyenne Rotary Club, my dog's conduct was observed by members such as past president Fred Baggs who felt Jamie's character traits were the very ones championed by Rotary International. Baggs said was well-behaved, showed responsibility and exemplified service above self. After four years of faithfully attending meetings with me, Jamie was recognized as the first, as far as anyone knows, honorary Rotarian and was presented with his own badge: JAMIE, Classification, Guide Dog. One night, Jamie contributed his impressive baritone vocal accompaniment to

the solo cello performance of David Lockington, visiting conductor of the Cheyenne Symphony Orchestra, and though he usually sat quietly during the speakers' presentations, on occasion Jamie might yawn or snore. Once some rascal claimed he moved about under the table trying to eat off the chewing gum. In fact, he was a member in good standing. Tip: If you like being popular, get yourself a good-looking dog.

People who had become acquainted with Jamie began to marvel at his surprising talents. At dinner in Denver with another couple one evening, I admit I bragged about Jamie's ability to find our car in a large parking lot. With no fewer than 100 automobiles in rows outside, my friend wanted to wager the price of the dinner that Jamie could not find our vehicle on the first try. Hands down, we won the bet. "How?" he said, baffled. Without thinking I said, "He memorized the license plate."

When Jamie was due for

retirement, the parting was an emotional time for me. This fellow had given me a new life and a new outlook, but he had more than earned his right to retire. So back to school for me in Smithtown, where I was to meet and partner up with a new blond fellow named Russ.

Russ quickly learned ranch routine, but we decided to sell and move into the capital of Cheyenne. Now, at the age of 71, I am still busy each day going about my new life with my new dog. Russ is also an honorary member of the Rotary Club and the Young Men's Literary Club. He takes me to board meetings at the Old West Museum and all the other places I need to go. Not that long ago, I had been in a tight race for govenor of the state, but Russ is probably better known in this town than I am!

Both Jamie and Russ have been lifesavers. Of course, guide dogs are highly protective of their partner's every safe step, but it's the freedom they provide to go places, to be able to meet, greet, visit and accomplish work that I prize, the liberty of independence. Best of all, Jamie and Russ lavish me with unconditional love. Who could ask for more?

And a little over a decade ago I had hoped a guide dog might walk me around the ranch. WE

Russ, who is nicknamed the Blond Bombshell for his appeal to strangers, on alert as his partner sits for a last picture at the ranch.

Back in school the writer and new family member at The Guide Dog Foundation for the Blind. There the theme might be "Getting To Know You," a first step to bonding.

The Guide Dog
Foundation for the Blind
371 East Jericho Turnpike
Smithtown, NY 11787-2976
(516) 265 2121
(800) 548 4337
(outside New York)

24

Thoughts About Life and Death

SEPTEMBER 25, 1985—ON THIS FIFTY-EIGHTH BIRTHDAY I FIND MYSELF reflecting on life as I have known it for these fifty-eight years. I decided to put a few of my thoughts to print.

This is the first birthday I have had since I became totally blind. Having been forced to change my activities and lifestyle, I sometimes seem to spend a little more time reflecting on life and death than I formerly did.

As a child, I can barely recall my first contact with death. My grandmother, Elizabeth Spence Roberts, died at Newcastle, Wyoming, when I was not quite three years old. To my best recollection, I was puzzled by the sadness and also by why my grandmother was lying in the casket.

When the United States was brought into World War II, I was fourteen years old. A world at war is a world full of violent and sudden death. The newsreels of 1939 and 1940 showed the horror of war. By December 7, 1941, although shocked by the attack on Pearl Harbor, all of us in America knew what events we now had to face. What I was not prepared for was the sudden loss of friends and classmates. Or sometimes, even though a person's life was spared, the person might be mutilated by wounds. Was it just a matter of luck?

As time went on, I lived while two of my former roommates at the Naval Academy died. One of them was killed while serving as an instructor on a dive-bombing run off the coast of Florida. His name was Lt. Commander Dick Mergl. Dave Gunkel died of a heart attack while he was serving as a Navy commander in Washington, D.C.

The longer I live and the more I witness life, the more I attempt to discover the peace and harmony that some people seem to possess. I am also more aware of the fragility of life in all forms. I have now been a diabetic since leaving the Navy in 1950 and, coincidental with that, I am now blind.

All about me in this world are billions of people and, either on the surface or deep down, you eventually find they all have some burden to bear. I have yet to meet a person who does not carry extra loads. These millstones come in different sizes and weights and may be from heartbreak, drugs or addictions, emotions, character flaws, family or marital troubles, disease, abuses, stroke, blindness, birth defects, or a thousand other causes. People the world over are constantly seeking relief from these problems and anxieties. And I believe this is the destiny of all people. Probably this is the reality in the design of life.

Sometimes I try to come to grips with the passage of time. A few years ago there was a geology professor here at Remount Ranch who told me about the formation of this area. Originally, this was an island volcano site surrounded by an ocean and later the continent collided with it. The volcano site then became surrounded by land instead of water. To my question of how long ago this happened, he replied that this took place about 1.7 billion years ago. To contemplate the short span of one human life, whether it lasts for only a few hours, or goes on for a hundred years, is comparatively like a single grain of sand in a vast ocean.

To me, I find great comfort in adopting my own philosophy of life. I have no sense of having plowed new ground, or made any new discoveries in attempting to state my own personal beliefs. It matters not how others may view my thoughts. What is important is the strength I feel from having something solid to guide my actions and my daily living. I truly have come to believe that each of us is destined to carry some kind of burden in life. After all, God never promised us a rose garden on earth. Instead, he reserved that in a place called Heaven. I do feel each one of us is being tested and, to me, the important part is just how we each cope with the burdens we are given to carry.

My thoughts and conclusions have all been developed with a belief in God. And that is such an important consideration. Through my life I have witnessed both the calm which can come when faced with adversity, accompanied with a belief in God. Also I have witnessed the sheer terror brought by some incident of adversity when God is not present in that person's life. Only through a belief in God can real comfort come to the dying as well as to those who mourn the passing of another. And why would it not be so? A true believer knows from the Lord's Prayer and Apostles Creed that life in Heaven will go on forever, while to the agnostic, the brevity and fragility of life must be somewhat worrisome.

If I had to capsulate my feelings, I would begin with the marvelous Serenity Prayer: God grant me the serenity to accept the things I cannot change, the courage to change the things I can, and the wisdom to know the difference.

To myself I have pledged to carry my burdens gracefully and always endeavor to be a better person; to never allow the destructive force of fear to invade my thoughts or disturb my life; to maintain my peace and serenity by loving God; and strive to practice the teachings of his son, Jesus Christ.

At my death, I fully expect Heaven to raise the question, "How has John Ostlund handled his burdens?" Hopefully the response will echo loudly and clearly, "He passed the tests!"

While I was a midshipman at the Naval Academy, I enjoyed a course in classical literature. One assignment was to memorize the final verse from *Thanatopsis* by William Cullen Bryant. These thoughtful lines have remained with me through life and are especially comforting upon the contemplation of the death that faces each of us in turn.

So live that when thy summons comes to join
The innumerable caravan that moves
To that mysterious realm, where each shall take
His chamber in the silent halls of death,
Thou go not, like the quarry-slave at night,
Scourged to his dungeon, but, sustained and soothed
By an unfaltering trust, approach thy grave
Like one who wraps the drapery of his couch
About him, and lies down to pleasant dreams.

25

Glimpses

ON THIS FALL AFTERNOON, I REFLECT ON THE FACT I HAVE NOT ADDED ANY new writing to my autobiography for many months. Perhaps it is time to bring this book to a close. As I say this, I am also painfully aware of the several topics which have occurred to me from time to time and then I neglected to put those thoughts on paper. Now it is timely to wrap up a few of those topics which still seem to be hanging around and place them in a final chapter. With this thought in mind I begin this chapter I have chosen to call "GLIMPSES."

MARVELOUS MARY

Several times during these years of writing I have wanted to dedicate a chapter just to my wife, Mary. From the first day I met this wonderful lady she has continued to bring joy to my heart! By the way, the first day was November 4, 1949. I was temporarily living at St. Alban's Naval Hospital in SOQ #108. Mary was a Navy nurse given duty on #108 that day. Five months later I left the naval hospital to head west. However, I departed with both love in my heart and Mary constantly on my mind. Previously I have written some things of our courtship and marriage. I shall not be repetitious.

In this reflection, I would like to tell the reader of the mutual love and respect we have always carried for each other. Looking back to times now past, I am sometimes pained by the amount of time I spent away from home. I led an involved life and worked hard. But Mary worked even harder and at a job much more demanding, challenging, important, and difficult. She bore our eight lovely children, gave us all a beautiful home in which to live, cooked our meals, washed and ironed our clothes, shopped for our family, listened to our problems, eased our pains, loved us—the litany could go on and on. She accomplished all this with love, patience, and understanding.

I have often thought of Mary as a miracle worker, or at the very least a true wonder woman! Actually, I am too inept with words to do justice to my feelings. Each day I look forward to the opportunity to do things together. This makes for a beautiful life!

Now, December 1994, having reached sixty-seven years of age, I am so happy to be leading a more quiet life. Our days spent living here at Remount Ranch are the best years yet. We have more quiet time and time to spend with each other. What a joy!

Instead of writing about Mary's parents, her grandparents, and days growing up, I shall leave that for Mary. Besides, she will do a better job of writing her own story. My reflection is only meant to express how this lovely wife, mother, grandmother, and one day great-grandmother, has made my life complete and totally meaningful because she chose to share her life with me. To me, this successful sharing may be one of the mysteries of life. Unfortunately, fewer and fewer people seem to get to experience this very natural wonder the way I have been so fortunate to enjoy!

"Marvelous" Mary, 1999.

OSTLUND FOR GOVERNOR

A few times in my book I have mentioned my choosing to run for Governor of Wyoming. This happened in 1978. Somehow I have never undertaken to write that chapter and now I ponder, why not? It could possibly be not wanting to relive the pain of losing—thus the reason why I have found it easier to write about something else.

By now, 1994, we are in the midst of another campaign, which is very reminiscent of my experience sixteen years ago. I do hope this one has a better ending for Jim Geringer, the Republican nominee. It has now been twenty years since we last had a Republican governor in Wyoming. And here we are, presumably a predominantly Republican state.

Mary and I had talked about my entering the campaign and we included talking it over with our children, as well. It was certainly a family decision. However, my reason for running was quite clear to me.

Of course my reasons for running for State Senator were equally clear in my mind. At that time I felt we were on the verge of more mineral development due to the national need for Wyoming coal. I worked hard in the Senate to help prepare Wyoming to respond to this impact. And respond we did!

As I observed the style of Ed Herschler as governor, following his election in 1974, I thought I could do a much better job than Ed. I also thought Wyoming deserved better. After all, if I had not felt this way, then I certainly should not have been running for the office.

The primary race was a tough one. Gus Fleischli was my primary opposition and he not only ran a tough race, but also a campaign which proved very expensive for both of us. The primary did not fall until September, which was a disastrous legislative move. By the time the primary was over, I found myself low on money and facing the need for new radio and TV advertising. Meanwhile my Democratic opponent had everything ready to go. As an incumbent, Ed Herschler was unopposed in his primary campaign. In September, I was leading in the polls. My team seemed to feel the election was in the bag. This was very unfortunate. Instead, Ed Herschler kept climbing in the polls and, we, because of the expense, were no longer polling frequently. Ed Herschler peaked at just the right time and I had peaked too early. Ed Herschler won the final outcome with a plurality of 2,377 votes.

Of course I was disappointed and not just for myself. I felt as though I had let down both my family and also my friends. There were so many wonderful people dedicated to my race! But in truth, does that not happen in every election? Of course it does. There can only be one winner and I was simply not that person.

There is a bright side to the race of 1978, though. Mary and I have never regretted entering the race. We traveled this beautiful state so diligently and met the most wonderful people on earth. I always remembered the words of Rudy Anselmi of Rock Springs. At one time Rudy was properly called the Dean of the Senate. Rudy ran for Governor many years before I did. He walked out of the Capitol building with me one day as I was leaving the Senate. He knew I was contemplating a run. He put his arm on my shoulder and reflected, "Even though I lost, it was the greatest experience of my life! I am so glad I ran the race!"

And I feel the same way as Rudy Anselmi. If I had not run the race, I would have forever thought I should have. I conclude by saying, it is better to have run and lost than never to have run at all!

John and Mary campaigning, 1978.

John, Mary, and son, John, behind them, on the campaign trail, 1978.

Ostlund for Governor—a family affair, 1978.

THE CAT HOUSE RAIDER

Living on a ranch, as we do at Remount, is a truly peaceful life. However, even the best of all worlds can have moments which break into the tranquility. Recently one of those rare moments came to us.

At our ranch we have a small shed which is generally known as the cat house. This is because our three cats named Bat, Sam, and Zorro, live in this shed.

When Mary goes to the feed store, she personally buys feed for wild birds, our horses, burros, dog, and, of course, the three cats. I feed the dog, Jesse Howlett feeds the horses, and Mary personally feeds the birds and also the three cats. The cats are actually great hunters, but in the event hunting is lean, they appreciate a good meal in their bowl in the cat house. Consequently, Mary makes sure the cats have feed in their bowl. The cats are neat and generally run a proper cat house.

With the foregoing necessary background information—I shall proceed to relate the recent breech in tranquility.

Mary informed me of something mysterious going on in the cat house. She related, "Our cats do not spill their food on the floor! This morning their dish was spilled over and the main can of cat food was turned over on its side! And more than that, even the trash can by the incinerator looks as though something made a hole in the plastic bag containing garbage!"

"Must be some kind of night raider!" I mused. "Could be a fox, or maybe a possum, or even a coon!"

Mary continued to be puzzled each morning and her determination grew as she plotted to catch this raider. Mary called the animal control to ask for a trap. She figured if she put food in this trap and placed it inside the cat house, the raider would be caught and thus identified. Mary put her cats in another shed each night until her plan was successful. However no trap was available. She was told, "It would be at least two weeks before we could have one for you."

Undaunted and unwilling to delay, Mary bought her own trap. She caught the three cats and placed them in another building for the night. Using her powerful flashlight, she checked out the cat house before placing the trap inside. When Mary opened the door of the cat house and shined her light inside, looking back at Mary eye-to-eye was a large skunk!

It would be difficult to judge which was more surprised, Mary or the skunk! However Mary was the first to act. She slammed the door shut and hurried to the house to tell me of her discovery.

Meanwhile, back at the cat house, the skunk merely used the same small door to escape as he was now accustomed to do. This only-for-cats-door could not accommodate a dog, but it certainly was not skunk proof. Now the plot thickened.

Mary developed a very proper strategy for skunk removal. She stationed our care-taker, Jesse Howlett, in the Jeep armed with his shotgun. Mary knew this hungry skunk would certainly return for the supper he was quite accustomed to be receiving each night. And return he did!

It was past nine o'clock in the evening and I was already getting ready for bed. Just as I was brushing my teeth, we heard the shotgun fire! Mary quickly grabbed her jacket and rushed to the scene. Minutes later I heard a second sound of a shotgun! I began to wonder what was keeping Mary from returning. Just then I heard the sound of the kitchen door opening.

"We think we got him!" Mary called out. As she stepped into the bedroom, I wailed, "Mary! Your fragrance is awful! The skunk got you!"

"Maybe I should jump into bed with you!" she teased.

"Please back out of here, Sweetheart!" I implored. "That smell will get into the carpet and the bedding!"

Mary stopped teasing me and graciously backed into the kitchen. She turned off the lights and stood by the washing machine. There she stripped off all her clothes, including her tennis shoes, and dropped them all into the washer. As the machine began the thankless job of flushing skunk odor down the drain, Mary stepped into the shower. Following two shampoos and a scrub down, she came to bed to tell me the story.

Jesse missed the skunk with his first shot and the skunk took off through the culvert under the driveway. He was next spotted by Mary with her flashlight heading up the hill through the trees. Jesse discharged another twelve-gauge at him and they hoped they got him. Instead, the skunk had gotten both Mary and Jesse!

We went off to Annapolis on Thursday of that week and Mary did not get to check on her raider until we returned home. It was soon evidenced that either the same skunk or his brother was still sharing our cat's supper.

Meanwhile Mary had learned a lot about skunks. Mary does great research! She discovered skunks just love cat food, a fact she already had reason to believe. She also learned that skunks just hate mothballs. Mary, being a most merciful person, reasoned that if she only fed her cats during the day and refused to place cat food in the cat house overnight, and then placed mothballs in the cat house, any normal skunk would stop coming, and look elsewhere for sustenance.

Adopting this plan, Mary immediately put it into effect. She is one smart lady! Her plan has worked and no more skunk! The skunk still lives somewhere, but it no longer is eating Remount cat food. And the cats have returned to their own cat house. Tranquility prevails once more at Remount Ranch!

ANNAPOLIS REUNIONS

Just last week, on October 20, 1994, Mary and I, along with Russ, flew to Baltimore, Maryland, to attend my forty-fifth class reunion at Annapolis. We do this every five years. We enjoyed perfect weather and the entire trip was most pleasant. However, my reason for bringing this up was the opportunity to reflect on my remembrances, which now go back to a time that begins in 1944.

Since I have already written several chapters on this period of my life, I shall not be repetitive. However, I do wish to add some reflections.

The expansion of capital facilities seems to continue being both practical and beneficial for the mission of the Naval Academy. Mary tells me of the architectural beauty, which is also to be expected. Recently Mary read to me of some of the history of buildings at the Academy. It came as a great surprise to me to learn about the Naval Academy Chapel. I was unaware that the plan for construction was conceived in 1902 and finally finished in 1908. The surprise came when I realized the chapel was only thirty-seven years of age when I first entered the Academy.

Attendance at chapel was an integral part of the program. The midshipmen could choose the Jewish or Catholic service, if they preferred that over the regular chapel service, which was Protestant. I am disappointed to learn this attendance is now optional. This liberal trend reaches everyone in this country, but I will never approve of carrying on the separation of church and state to this extent. We have only to view the decline of both moral and family values to make this judgment.

These young midshipmen are in their most formative years. I say this from my own experience. I attended regular chapel services each Sunday without question, just as I attended every other class on my schedule. I shall always value everything I learned at the Academy, including chapel services.

The Academy is there to develop and provide this country with able military leadership. Living the Academy life for four years can place a future military leader under some stress. Good! Our country needs to know ahead of time how a future officer can handle stress. This can be the stress of battle, the stress of negotiations, the stress placed on people under their command and supervision, or even the stress of survival as prisoners of war. To me, somehow that stress can be easier to handle quietly and coolly with the additional education you acquire in the beautiful Naval Academy Chapel.

Mary and I were invited to partake of lunch in King Hall at noon following noon meal formation at Bancroft. Our friend, Stephen Bocanegra, a midshipman from Cheyenne, will be graduating May 31, 1995. I enjoyed having lunch at Steve's table. While we were standing awaiting the word to be seated, I whispered to Mary, "I don't remember it being this noisy when I was here!"

Mary whispered back, "That is just because you are now older!" Another reminder of just how wise my Mary is!

On Sunday afternoon while we were having lunch with Steve Bocanegra and Meredith Rathbone, I asked Steve about the voluntary attendance at chapel. He felt that most of the plebes and third classmen attend, but the two final years witness a decline in chapel attendance by the upper classes.

The addition of so many academic disciplines serves to keep the Academy out in front in properly training young Americans for leadership. They not only become the tops in their fields academically, but also develop a sense of patriotism unequaled anywhere.

Over these many years, while attending reunions every five years since 1969, I continuously reinforce my previous conclusions I came to at graduation in 1949. There is no institution which turns out more qualified people who can better represent this country in both times of peace and times of war. The young men and women graduating from the Naval Academy still carry with them the highest traditional sense of duty, honor, and country. Ever since the birth date of this nation, we have had to fight to preserve our freedoms. All those who would rather spend our taxes on welfare and other perceived social needs must not be allowed to weaken our defense position. Only through strength can America hope to maintain a world at peace! And only through the professional training provided by the service Academies can we thus maintain the lifeblood of our military services. Then we can depend upon America to remain strong, vigorous, and free!

USNA 40th Class Reunion, Tecumseh, 1994.

ABOUT TECHNOLOGY

How fortunate I have been in my lifetime to see such tremendous advances in all fields of endeavor. In the air, I have witnessed the advances in flying from the two-wing, fabric-covered, single-engine airplanes, to men orbiting and landing on the moon. I have flown in the giant Boeing 747 planes nonstop across the Pacific to Tokyo and Mary and I have flown the thousands of miles from New York to South Africa. Boeing is now preparing a new giant aircraft to be called the 777, which will soon be in daily use.

Mary and I have flown at Mach 2 on both the British Concorde as well as the French Concorde. On Scott's nineteenth birthday he flew with me from Paris to New York on the French Concorde. It was impressive to fly at an altitude which enabled a passenger to actually see the curvature of the earth. Of course my own offspring and grandchildren will travel on aircraft which are unknown today, and this is as it should be. We must keep advancing, improving, and meeting the new challenges which also give us new opportunities.

On our recent trip to Annapolis (1994), I spoke with former classmates about the technology of today's Navy. Chuck Swanson commanded a nuclear submarine, as did Shepard Jenks. Shepard navigated the first nuclear submarine, *Nautilus*, to cross the North Pole beneath the ice pack. And that was now many years ago.

It is the field of technology in which I have been a most impressed and ardent consumer. Before I lost my eyesight I had begun to use a computer. This was fortunate for me. At the present time I am using my fourth computer. With the talking program I am totally at ease while inputting data or writing. My talking calculator gets daily workouts and my talking wristwatch is a wonderful technological advantage for a blind person. In just a few days I am due to get delivery on a new product which I have been contemplating for several years. This is the latest version of Xerox's Reading Edge.

This new machine was demonstrated for me over two weeks ago. I ordered one on the basis I could return it within thirty days if not completely satisfied. The demonstration was good; I highly doubt I will return it. Frankly, I am most anxious for UPS to make delivery of my new equipment. This machine will also be connected to my computer. I shall be able to transfer written material loaded into my Reading Edge to a file in my computer, or vice versa. The Reading Edge can read anything printed. I am excited about the new advantages this equipment brings. Sometimes I do get just a tiny bit jealous of the folks who are able to use Windows and desktop publishing. But I really put that aside and am thankful for what I do have and am able to use.

In about two weeks, Karin will be with me at Remount. She has just returned from her new home in Siberia. This week Karin is in Palm Springs enjoying the sun. Next week she must be in Houston for AMOCO, but then she will be here at the ranch. Karin is bringing and installing a new modem and fax for our computer. We will have CompuServe, which will send electronic mail to Siberia or elsewhere. I also plan to use CompuServe to update our securities in our Pulse Portfolio program.

We maintain our check register on a computer database and also write most of our checks with the computer. We also keep our own monthly accounts. With my new Reading Edge I shall be able to do even more without bothering others to read for me. Technology can be terrific!

ABOUT DOGS AND KIDS

Following my loss of eyesight and since learning to use a guide dog, I have led a more active and certainly more interesting life. This began in 1987 when Jamie and I returned from the Guide Dog Foundation for the Blind. Following Jamie's retirement, I have had Russ since June of 1993. The fun and activities continue.

First of all, I look forward to hiking each day. A person who gets out and walks daily just naturally feels better about himself and about life. Without my guide dog I recall the boring days of walking on a treadmill. That was no fun at all.

With my dog we both enjoy exploring and listening to all the many sounds of life. Walking with Russ gives me an opportunity to talk with such a close pal. In his own way he answers back, so it is not strictly a one-way conversation. I usually can tell when he sights a rabbit or another animal. I just can't guess what species it is—I only know Russ sees it.

John, with his dog Russ, talking with teacher, Kathy Ellis, and her class about blindness and guide dogs, 2000.

For more than seven years now, my dogs and I have given demonstrations to school kids. In the past couple of weeks we have visited three third grades, all at Pioneer Park School. Jenny Olson, a third-grade teacher, first called and wanted to bring her class to the ranch. We agreed and set the date. Unfortunately the chosen Monday morning turned out to be rainy and very foggy. Jenny was disappointed to cancel and so was I. We scheduled it again and Russ and I went to her school about two weeks ago. Her kids had read about Helen Keller and also about guide dogs. These bright children make it so much fun to be together. Russ and I do demonstrations and then we answer questions. That is the best part of all.

"How does it feel to be blind? How long have you been blind? How does Russ take you to places? Do you feel badly to be blind? How old is Russ? How do you decide what clothes to put on? How do you cook your dinner?"

Jenny Olson sent me a tape following our visit. It was beautifully done. The tape opened with sounds from the outdoors. A bird was heard to sing, a bee was heard to buzz, soft music began to play, and with that opening Jenny Olson introduced her class. Each child spoke their name and then told me what they learned from our visit. As I listened to each voice the tears formed in my eyes and both cheeks became wet with happiness.

After returning from our visit to Annapolis, another teacher, Kelly Johnson, phoned me. She and Mrs. Larson invited Russ and me to visit their third grades last Wednesday morning. Again it was another fun and interesting adventure for Russ and me. Our programs are usually the same, but because of the kids, no two visits are alike. The kids seem to enjoy our coming, but no more than Russ and I enjoy being asked.

Every year we are also invited to visit the third grade taught by Kathy Ellis. Her kids have found wonderful ways to say their thanks to me. It warms my heart, and I hope they keep asking us.

RETIREMENT, IT CAN SNEAK UP ON YOU!

During my lifetime I don't recall ever seriously contemplating retiring. I always enjoyed doing business and, besides, retirement was for old people! Now at sixty-seven years, I have decided retirement just sneaked into my life. I did not make the decision, but it happened anyway.

Probably, if I still had my sight, it might be different. That is not worth thinking about. If I allowed myself to dream of being sighted again, I would first renew my driver's license. Behind the wheel of a vehicle I would probably make plans to go somewhere and undoubtedly get involved with something. It is better not to dream of that which is no longer possible. Besides, I have too many other things to enjoy as I am presently doing.

My wife just phoned me from her car with her cellular telephone. What a terrific device to have. In fact, I had phoned her earlier. She told me her phone showed a call when she returned to the car. I did not know that about cellular phones. There are so many interesting things to learn about each day. I love just the involvement I presently enjoy!

My happiness comes from Mary and our children and grandchildren. Mary and I are so very proud and thankful for each of our four sons, John, Tom, Pat, and Scott; and our four daughters, Peg, Nancy, Karin, and Jane. In the very same way we are also thankful for our two fine sons-in-law, Jim Essery and Gregg Gebhart. And no family ever could boast of grandchildren so bright, active, and loving. For all of this, we are especially gratified as well as appreciative.

John and Mary at Halloween, 1999.

John and "Dinger" enjoying Rockies baseball, 1998.

John and Mary's four sons and four daughters. Left to right: Scott, Patrick, Tom, John, Peg, Nancy, Karin, and Jane, 1995.

Grandsons Jason Patrick (left) and Jordan Thomas Ostlund (right), 2000.

Grandson Michael John Elmore learning to tie the reverse Windsor, 1995.

Grandson Patrick Joseph Ostlund, Jr., 2000.

Grandson and baseball player, Andrew Chapman Gebhart, 2000.

Grandson Chad Marshall Essery playing John's piano, 2000.

Granddaughter Megan Elizabeth Gebhart reading My Friend Flicka, 2000.

WE LEAVE REMOUNT FOR THE CITY!

During August of 1995 there were three different parties wanting to purchase our Remount Ranch. Two of them waited too long to act and Steve and Bonnie Bangert went ahead and made their offer. We liked this couple and their four children. Their terms were exactly as we had wanted and they were willing to close within thirty days. Additionally, they offered for us to remain at Remount until November 3. We decided to accept their offer and did so!

Mary was given the opportunity to look at the Mildred Smith home at 318 West Second Avenue in Cheyenne. After looking it over with Peg and Tom, she called me to say she thought it was perfect for us! So she bought it!

Suddenly our lives were changed and we actually began preparing to move into town.

Time seemed to fly by, once we had accepted their offer. Earlier we had discussed how we would be leaving the ranch. We had decided to hold a series of dinners at Remount with our friends. As it turned out, we never even got close to sending invitations. The job of sorting, packaging, and preparing to evacuate the ranch was enormous. And since I was no help at all, it was an enormous job for Mary. But as Mary always does, she handled it beautifully. Our children pitched in also. At the end, Peg and John Jr. worked with Mary for several days and their assistance was incredible. We were so happy for their help.

Each night, rather than cooking a dinner at the ranch, we drove to Little America dining room for dinner. The quiet and relaxing atmosphere was perfect to match the great food offerings. The piano music of John Brown was also rewarding for a group who had worked so hard each day.

We took advantage of an apartment that came available at the Hitching Post. We had previously leased one of these for most of 1993. Russ and I knew our way around and we again rented one of their nice furnished apartments. At first we thought we might only be there for about two weeks. Since we closed on our new house October 6, Mary felt we could be moved in by November 15. As it turned out, we found it desirable to also renovate the kitchen and utility rooms of our new house. This was an additional major undertaking in our renovation. Consequently, we did not get to actually reside in our new home until January 14, 1996. But the delay was certainly worth it. We love our new home, as well as liking the convenience of living in the city. We also feel good about having the Bangerts as the new owners of Remount Ranch. I have a feeling Steve Bangert is probably the same age I was when we bought the Remount in 1970.

Mary has carefully made our new house a lovely home. I have a nice office with all my equipment set in a way which seems most convenient for my needs. I have acquired two luxuries of my own. The first is a Bose Lifestyle Five sound system. I have it connected to cable DMX music, radio stations, and compact disc music, all in the famous Bose Acoustic Wave quality.

The second luxury is the acquisition of a rebuilt 1888 Steinway Grand Piano. It is a seven-and-a-half-foot model C and it is beautiful; and, of course, it has an incredible sound. Steve Westfahl in Laramie had this old piano in his warehouse. When I expressed my interest to Ray Citak, they decided to work on it and completely rebuilt it. All the hardware was refinished like new. The actual mahogany wood cabinet was taken to Denver for refinishing. Just as the original was prepared, it now has seven coats of black lacquer, which has been hand-rubbed to a high-gloss finish. The original black ebony keys are still on the piano and the white ivory keys have been recovered. New strings and pads have made this a truly unique and wonderful piano once more. Steve Westfahl and Ray Citak did an incredible job and they are certified by Steinway to perform these overhauls. I am so proud to have it. I play it every day with joy!

Karin has accepted my old piano, which was owned by my mother since before she was married. Steve Westfahl has taken that piano to Laramie for refinishing. Karin decided to upgrade it and then move it into her house in Denver. She will love having it.

We are expecting to receive most of our furniture for the living room and dining room by early March. Everything else is finished. Even Russ thinks this is the way to live! When everyone is happy, how can you beat it!

Best of all, we have the nicest neighbors here on the Avenues. So many folks have stopped by and some have even brought small welcoming gifts. I believe we are the luckiest folks around to have what we have, and that is so many, many wonderful friends and family members!

USS *CHEYENNE* SSN #773

Roger Shriner, Chairman of the USS *Cheyenne* Committee, asked if Mary and I would act as honorary chairs of this committee. This happened in 1994 and we were pleased to do so.

While the submarine was still under construction, we had the opportunity to meet the skipper, Commander Pete Ozimek, and his wife, Kathy, who was a Lt. Commander. Both were graduates of the Naval Academy.

One time when just a few of the crew were visiting here, we invited them for brunch at Remount Ranch. Following their visit, they went on to Laramie to attend a Wyoming Cowboy football game and, as honored guests, they were introduced to the spectators at halftime. During that same visit Commander Ozimek presented me with a "plank owner" cap bearing the name and number of the submarine.

Mary and I made a gift to the USS *Cheyenne* which was a beautiful western sculpture done by Herb Mignery. The large original has been prominently placed outdoors at the Cheyenne Frontier Days Old West Museum. One of the twenty smaller versions is now displayed aboard the submarine. The attached brass plate shows it to be a gift of Mary and me, USNA Class of 1949.

We went to Norfolk for the commissioning of the *Cheyenne* and what a great time that was! We stayed busy for all of the three days.

Our ultimate trip came when we were aboard the sub and spent the day cruising on and under the Pacific Ocean. This happened on February 13, 1998. We flew to San Diego and with our grandson, Chad Essery, went aboard the *Cheyenne* about seven o'clock in the morning. We were treated to both breakfast and lunch at sea and enjoyed our day of cruising beneath the Pacific Ocean.

We were part of a Cheyenne group who were invited to participate in this exciting adventure. This Los Angeles class submarine is about the same length of a football field with both end zones included. Of course it is nuclear-powered.

During our very complete tour of the sub, while we were underway, it would be difficult to say what features were the most memorable. Perhaps our grandson might best remember being invited topside to the bridge prior to diving. The ocean had some rather large waves and one broke over the bridge, soaking all who were there. At that time our grandson was to have his fifthteenth birthday just sixteen days after this cruise. It will certainly live long in his memory!

John at the USS Cheyenne, 1998.

WYOMING'S SETTING SONS!

About the first of August 1998, I received a call from Judge Jim Barrett. He and former Governor Stan Hathaway were inviting a few of their good friends to join them for lunch on August 5, at Little America. The instigation of this invitation was brought about by our friend, Jim Griffith, who lately has been residing in Arizona. Jim gave the group the name of Wyoming's Setting Sons.

Nine of us assembled at Little America on the appointed day and the picture shown identifies each one. This is a group of fellows, all of similar age, all of whom served in the military during wartime. Several had received awards for their distinguished courage and valor. All had given so much to their state and nation. It was most memorable and we all hoped we would again have the same opportunity another year. Some of these gentlemen traveled long distances to be present. For me, I not only appreciated being with them, but was also gratified for the opportunity.

Wyoming's Setting Sons
Back row: Jim Finchum, Colonel Ed Witzenburger, Jerry Hollon, Harry Roberts, and Ken Sturman.
Front row: Governor Stan Hathaway, Jim Griffith, John Ostlund, and Judge Jim Barrett.

LOOKING FORWARD!

For the past many years I have been reviewing and editing all of the chapters of my book. Admittedly, I have to laugh at myself for constantly trying to improve them. More than once I have declared the end of this endeavor and here at this date I am still fussing with it. The next millennium will soon be upon us. My original intentions were to enable our grandchildren to have better knowledge of their ancestors and an appreciation of their heritage. With these writings I am hopeful my goal has been accomplished.

Years ago I made my decision to live my life in Wyoming. For me, it was the right choice. Wherever one decides to reside, it is my hope that you will live with high values, strong morals, and a willingness to love and help your neighbor, your community, your state, and your nation. This also means taking part in the politics of your area, even if it is only to at least vote. Throughout our history so many people before you gave their lives that we may live and enjoy freedom and opportunity. The future of our precious freedom and abundant opportunity is in your hands.

With those thoughts I can only wish our children, our grandchildren, and their children yet unborn, to know that I close these writings with my love to you, my respect for you, and with my warmest and best wishes for a happy, healthy, well-lived life.

John C. Ostlund, 1999

26

Words from Others

Ostlund rally draws 1,000

By PHIL McAULEY
Managing Editor

GILLETTE — More than a thousand turned out in this booming resources center Tuesday night to wish native son John Ostlund well in his campaign for governor.

The 50-year-old Republican candidate was visibly moved by the crowd which jammed the Campbell County Fairgrounds Building for an old-time political rally and the announcement of his candidacy

The band of young musicians made the walls resound with music. The walls were covered with hand-made posters. One read: "John Ostlund is honest, John Ostlund is sincere." Another: "Let's help John Ostlund become governor."

The crowd munched hot dogs as Ostlund greeted at the door every person who attended.

The former state senator's wife, Mary, and their eight children and daughter-in-law also circulated, greeting the townspeople.

"These are my people ... these are the people who put me in the Senate," Ostlund said.

"I am so touched and pleased." He pledged to "campaign on my record from the day I was born."

Ostlund, who is a rancher and a businessman, singled out bad leadership and impact as reasons he decided to seek the governorship. He said the state's people need to be more involved in future decisions concerning the state.

He said the state needs to be more responsive to the effects of impact, to increase its educational opportunities, to develop its water for "her own people" and to assume less dependence upon the federal government.

Before resigning his Senate seat last Saturday to run for governor, Ostlund chaired the powerful Senate Committee on Mines, Minerals and Industrial Development. He was also one of four legislators from the 13 western states serving on a committee to explore the future of the Western Interstate Commission on Higher Education and served on the governing board of the Council of State Governments.

"We must get our collective house in order and have valid, realistic priorities. We must have care and concern in our government," he said.

"Our offices must listen, not simply dictate," added Ostlund.

He served on then-Gov. Hansen's first committee on mental health, as finance chairman for the Wyoming Boy Schouts, as director of the Wyoming Heart Association and on the board of trustees of the University of Wyoming.

John announces that he will seek the Republican gubernatorial nomination, Gillette, Wyoming, May 1978.

The Casper Star-Tribune
Casper, Wyoming
May 10, 1978

The News Record
Gillette, Wyoming
November 9, 1978

Editorial

It was a good race!

What happened? What went wrong?

These questions and others will be asked and answered in many different ways about John Ostlund's campaign with Gov. Ed Herschler for the governorship.

The race has been run and Campbell County came close to having its first governor from Gillette and this county through an election. One other man from here, Alonzo Clark, was elected secretary of state in 1927 and later served as governor when Gov. Frank Emerson died in office.

Campbell County can be proud of the candidacy of John Ostlund. His knowledge of Wyoming came from living all of his life in this state. His awareness of its problems came from having served not only in the state legislature, but also from unselfish service on state boards, charitable boards, regional committees and national groups.

In all cases the man applied himself and his knowledge to each job with an effort to make conditions better when he was finished than when he arrived. Where there were problems, his approach was to assess them and to seek solutions.

Such were the attributes John Ostlund offered. Such was the impression he made on many people about the state. And when the votes were counted on Tuesday night it became apparent that many people who did not know him before, were convinced of his qualities. Many could see that he would make a good governor.

This is what made the race close and Campbell County — as well as John himself and his family — may well be proud of the final results in light of this being his initial effort for a state office.

We are well aware that today is too close following a long and grueling campaign to think about the future. But it is sufficient to say with all sincerity, we hope that John Ostlund does not eliminate from his thoughts of again seeking a public office. He has too much to offer Wyoming for this great state to lose him.

JKN

Page 10 The News-Record, Gillette, Wyoming, Sunday, January 22, 1984

John Ostlund

**The News Record
Gillette, Wyoming
January 22, 1984**

John and Mary Ostlund (above left) met while both were serving in the Navy. They've been married over 30 years and are the parents of eight children. Above is a 1934 Ostlund family photo. From left are Bob, Axel, Polly and John (age 7).

**Text By
Jeff Davison**

One of Gillette's most influential men charts new course

John Ostlund. The man is tied to Gillette in so many ways. Through real estate, through oil, through politics, construction, banking, business, service groups, fund drives, ranching — the list is nearly endless.

If you wanted to pick the person who has had the most impact on Campbell County in the last 20 years, John Ostlund might be a leading candidate. His influence has been felt in many arenas, from launching a wide variety of business ventures to steering major legislation during six years in the state Senate to running for governor.

But, sometime soon, Ostlund will leave Gillette. He and his wife, Mary, are already shipping items to the Remount Ranch in Laramie County. By March they hope to be settled on the 1,800-acre spread, which lies between Laramie and Cheyenne. The move, which will allow Ostlund to slow down a little and to be closer to the doctors in Denver who are struggling to save his eyesight, will end 34 years of his being among Gillette's leading citizens.

Ostlund and his brother Bob are entrepeneurs. Much of what they accomplished they did together and with other investors. But John, because of his legislative service, 1978 race for governor and generally high profile, is the one who's most often been in the public eye.

"I don't know of any organization that he didn't belong to at one time or another," says Sam Ratcliff, a Gillette businessman and former county Republican Party chairman. "And he gave his all to it at the time he was doing it."

That's not too much of an exageration. Ostlund has been everything from a Chamber of Commerce director to finance officer for the Boy Scouts; from president of the Rotary Club to president of the Wyoming Industrial Development Organization; from a member of the Elks and the American Legion to a member of the University of Wyoming Board of Trustees. And that's only scratching the surface.

"A person has to be involved in an endeavor to try to make a better place to live," Ostlund says of his joining nature. "That's really the motivating force."

Ostlund grew up in Gillette. His father, Axel Ostlund, also wore many hats — plumber, businessman, rancher and mayor of Gillette for two years in the early 1950s.

John, born in 1927, graduated from Campbell County High School in 1944 and spent a year at Kemper Military School in Booneville, Mo., before winning an appointment to the U.S. Naval Academy. He graduated from Annapolis in 1949 and served as an ensign on a destroyer in the Mediterranean fleet.

"I was really planning to become a career Naval officer," he recalls. But then a medical problem — diabetes — arose "and abruptly I was looking for a new career."

So he returned to Gillette in 1950. Bob, who's about 1½ years older, came home around the same time, after serving in the Air Corps and earning a civil engineering degree at the University of Wyoming.

They went into partnership with their father in Ostlunds Inc. "We were in the plumbing, heating, sheet metal and John Deere (tractor) business," Bob Ostlund recalls. But it wasn't long before they started branching out.

Their first venture, John said, was to go together with Jerry Jasper in the Gillette Gas Co. — which later became Petrolane's first Wyoming acquisition.

The brothers "felt tourism was going to be important to Wyoming's economy," John recalls, so they went in with James R. Daly and Toots Marquis to build the Sands Restaurant, in 1961. In 1963, they added the original wing of the Sands Motel, John says and in 1964 he left the family business to run that operation. They bought the Gay 90's restaurant a year later, built the motel which is now the Ramada in 1969 and sold both motels in 1971.

Ratcliff worked "on and off" as a bartender at the Sands for several years in the '60s. "He was probably one of the nicest men I ever worked for," Ratcliff says of John. "He'd get right in behind the bar if you were busy and help wash glasses . . ."I don't ever remember John raising his voice in a mad way or anything else."

Things were also happening on other fronts. In 1970, they were part of a group that formed a holding company and bought Wyoming National Bank of Casper. That company now controls eight banks, including Wyoming National of Gillette, of which John is board chairman. They were in a group which bought a part of the Keeline Ranch (their portion, which they now lease out, is the Black Thunder Ranch). Ostlund Investments, formed "about 1959," John says, has been involved in such things as property development and rental and mineral leasing and exploration.

The list of business deals could go on forever. But also worth noting are the founding of the Century 21 Sun Agency, Bob's founding of Remax and the 1976 acquisition of Western Manufacturing, the parent company of Western Oil Tool and Manufacturing of Casper, which is a major manufacturing operation. Bob is president of Western Manufacturing.

"We've been partners all these years, up until about six months ago, I guess," Bob says. When John prepared to move, they dissolved most of their associations.

"We're just plain, simple farmers who wanted to work hard," Bob adds. "There's still a lot of people who want to work."

But Bob also notes that their success has caused resentment. "You know how that works," he says, "people say 'born with a silver spoon' and all that."

So John Ostlund has made money. But, he says, "I don't know how to measure success. Sometimes I think that to be a success is to be a good husband and a good father, and if I do those things, I've been successful."

John and Mary Ostlund (they met while he was in the Navy and she was in the Navy Nurse Corps) have raised eight children. Tom is vice president of Century 21, where John Jr. also works after recently returning from Los Angeles. Patrick is a swabbing unit operator in the oil field. Scott is a junior at UW. Daughter Peg is married to Mike Elmore. Nancy, also married, lives in San Diego. Karin is a UW business graduate and works for Amoco in Powell. Jane married Greg Gebhart on Dec. 29 and is attending UW with her

husband. The Ostlunds have two grandchildren and expect two more soon.

"We have a very close family," John says. "We're very family oriented. It's been just a tremendously important part of our lives."

Politics also has been an important part of his life. His father was a Republican official for many years, but John says that's not what led him into it.

Instead, shortly after returning from the Navy, he was invited to a Republican Central Committee meeting.

"What he didn't tell me," John recalls, "was that there was kind of a split in the Republican Party. About half of them wanted the old chairman and about half of them wanted a new one. So you know what happened — I got elected chairman."

He was county chairman from 1951 to 1959, then a state committeeman until 1974.

In 1972, he was elected to the state Senate, and was re-elected in 1976. He resigned after the 1978 session to run for governor. The race against Gov. Ed Herschler turned into a heated and often bitter battle. It ended with Ostlund carrying 12 of the 23 counties but Herschler winning 51 percent of the vote. The final margin was 2,377 votes out of 137,567 cast — one of the closest gubernatorial races in the state's history.

Although Ostlund is proud of his legislative record, that 1978 campaign gave him a chance to see how many people didn't like it. He was attacked for "promoting mining interests in the Legislature," for "being the biggest spokesman for the mineral industry in the state Senate," for opposing Herschler's severance tax proposal and was called an inappropriate candidate because some of his land holdings included mineable coal deposits.

In fact, since Ostlund has been involved in minerals, banking, manufacturing, real estate and other ventures, it's hard to find an area of public life in which he wouldn't have a conflict of interest. Those charges arose again when he testified in behalf of the Hampshire Energy synthetic fuels project. Also, Ostlund helped clear the way for conversion of the old University of

The News-Record, Gillette, Wyoming, Sunday, January 22, 1984 Page 11

Two views of the young John Ostlund: the one on the left was taken in 1944. The one on the right, taken in 1947, shows Ostlund in his Midshipman's uniform. He graduated from the United States Naval Academy in 1949.

John Ostlund is shown above in 1978, announcing his campaign for the Republican nomination for governor. Ostlund won the nomination but lost the general election to Gov. Ed Herschler. It was one of the closest races in Wyoming history. Below are John (right) and his brother, Bob, in a photo from a family album. The brothers were partners in a wide variety of ventures over the years.

Wyoming Experimental Farm into a regional park and until recently chaired the board overseeing its development. That brought rumors that development of the park would enhance the value of some of his property.

Despite those old charges of conflicts and of aiding industry rather than people, Ostlund feels he served Wyoming well in his six years as senator. Certainly, the legislation he spearheaded has been instrumental in shaping the state's course.

In 1974, he was appointed to an interim committee which was charged with planning legislation to help ease the impact of industrial development. The committee chairman resigned and Ostlund took over.

That committee produced a package of bills which resulted in the founding of the Wyoming Community Development Authority (which provides low-interest home loans); the joint powers act (which allows for such joint city-county projects as development of the former University of Wyoming Experimental Farm into a park here); the Emergency School Loan Fund; doubling of the state sales and use tax return to local governments; removal of the use tax exemption (Ostlund says too many large industries, such as railroads, were exempt from the tax) and the coal tax for impact assistance (which created the funds which the Farm Loan Board now allocates to help with such city and county projects as streets and sewers).

"We presented them as a package — as a solution to a problem that begged answers," Ostlund says. "...I think it's worked very well. I don't know how we could have provided housing for so many Wyoming people without the Wyoming Community Development Authority and the coal tax for impact assistance has been invaluable."

The bills passed the 1975 Legislature, with Ostlund doing much of the steering in the Senate. "It was quite a tussle," he says. "I remember all the days of standing there and debating. But I enjoyed it."

Ostlund's also proud of the school capital construction bill (known as the Ostlund bill).

He recalls his biggest Senate defeat came in 1978, when it was widely known he planned to run for governor. The WCDA act had been declared unconstitutional the day before the session opened. Ostlund sought a constitutional amendment to legalize it. But, he says, "on third reading, every Democrat in the Senate voted against it." A bill salvaging the home loan section finally cleared. But the other WCDA section, providing low-interest loans to local governments, was never resurrected.

The Ostlunds plan to move to Remount Ranch as soon as remodeling of the house there is completed. "I keep postponing it," he says. "This summer, I thought we'd be moved by fall." Now, he says, the move probably won't be made before March — if the house is ready then.

He has installed a computer at the ranch that is linked to the markets and will allow him to run Ostlund Investments from there. He tentatively plans to move out of his current office at 304 Douglas Highway by the end of the month, although he plans to keep an office at the Sun Agency and visit Gillette once or twice per month.

The News Record
Gillette, Wyoming
August 18, 1985

Ostlund didn't see Cam-plex

By KEVIN DOLL

Cam-plex is a sight to behold, a massive $11-million facility destined to be the home of everything from horse racing to theatre in Campbell County.

But one of the men most responsible for its existence will probably never see it.

John Ostlund is blind.

The popular 57-year-old businessman and former state senator was on hand Wednesday evening to speak at the complex's dedication.

He talked with pride of what had been accomplished by various individuals and groups working together. And, as he has done so often over the years, he offered leadership, this time in the form of advice. The county commissioners, he said, should leave the running of Cam-plex to the people who have guided its development, the Public Land Board. They shouldn't try to oversee it themselves.

Carbon-Coated

A Gillette native and community leader for years, Ostlund now lives on the famous Remount Ranch near Laramie with his wife Mary. They moved there last year so he could slow down a little and be closer to the Denver doctors who are helping him fight for his eyesight.

"I'm blind — but I feel good." Ostlund said in between greeting a steady stream of well wishers. A diabetic, 36 years of insulin had caused him to gradually lose his eyesight.

"It's been a little tough for him." said his son, Tom, explaining his father can see some images, but for the most part, just light and dark.

"He knows so many people and it's hard for him because he can't tell who they are when they come up to greet him," Tom said. John's eyesight had been gradually improving last year until deteriorating in December. Surgery in March helped temporarily.

Ostlund hasn't given up — he has a doctor's appointment this week — but he realizes that the odds of regaining his vision aren't good.

Yet the 1978 Republican gubernatorial nominee is keeping busy. He serves on a bank board in Laramie and is active in the Rotary Club there. He and Mary periodically make it back to Gillette to visit family and friends.

Wednesday's ceremonies brought back memories of 1980

when the University of Wyoming put its 740-acre experimental farm (today's Cam-plex) up for sale and Ostlund led the effort to secure it for public use. A bond issue was passed to buy the land in September of 1981, and Ostlund chaired the newly formed Public Land Board as it set about seeking input on development.

There were several critical junctures, including the summer of 1983 when the Gillette City Council and County Commissioners locked horns over the issue of utilities and annexation of Cam-plex. Ostlund's cool head and moderating tone got the two sides together so development could proceed on schedule.

The 700 people attending Wednesday's dedication gave Ostlund a standing ovation. They saw what he could not, and thanked him heartily for helping make Cam-plex a reality.

Cam-plex photo, *Westwind Graphics*

The News Record
Gillette, Wyoming
September 14, 1997

September 6, 1997

John Ostlund

In appreciation for your pioneering dedication and visionary effort in the development of CAM-PLEX Multi-Event Facilities for the citizens of Campbell County

Campbell County Public Land Board

Cam-plex land man

If it weren't for **John Ostlund**, many people believe Campbell County wouldn't have Cam-plex today.

That's why the Campbell County Public Land Board honored Ostlund last weekend with a plaque for his "pioneering dedication and visionary leadership."

"We've talked about it off and on for a long time ... because John was the one originally instrumental in acquiring this land," said **Sherry McGrath**, chairwoman of the land board.

The State of Wyoming sold the land from what had been a University of Wyoming experimental farm in 1983 to a city-county joint powers board for $3.7 million. It included 740 acres. Another 200 acres was donated by Kerr-McGee

McGrath said it was Ostlund who put together the idea to buy the land and use it for the community good. "(He was) obviously dreaming a very big dream and he had the tenacity to convince people that it made sense."

Ostlund, a former state senator and the first chairman of the land board, said people wistfully spoke of buying the land in the early 1980s.

Ostlund got a commitment from the city and then approached the commissioners. "I said, 'I should know better than to volunteer, but I think it would be great if we could own that experimental farm. ... The needs of the community need to be met and there are many.' "

He talked to UW about selling the land for the appraised value. UW agreed and a bond election was scheduled for September. Then just before the election, UW discovered it didn't own the land, the state did. And because of the amount, the Legislature would have to approve selling it.

He convinced people to approve the bond issue anyway, and then sponsored a bill in the Legislature a few months later that would allow the joint powers board to buy the land — and convinced the state to give up mineral rights to the land.

But while his efforts made Camplex possible, what it has become was developed from the dreams of residents, he said.

A committee scheduled meetings with residents to hear what they wanted to put on the land. "We wanted to get a better assessment of what the people of Campbell County wanted," Ostlund said. "They came up with things I hadn't even thought about. It all went into the land planning aspect.

"I think it has worked just beautifully, as far as I know, from everyone's point of view," said Ostlund, 70, who now lives in Cheyenne. "I hope so. It's the envy of the rest of the state."

Nation crying out for more leaders, 20 new grads told

The News Record
Gillette, Wyoming
May 24, 1989

"It will only have to be that way if you let it be that way," John Ostlund told the 1989 graduates of the Gillette Area Leadership Institute (GALI) Friday.

JOHN OSTLUND
Drug abuse a growing problem

The former Gillette businessman and community leader was speaking of various problems Wyoming and the nation face, including drug abuse and a disintegration of the political process.

Twenty local residents, involved in Gillette businesses and government, received GALI diplomas at the Friday banquet after completing the nine-month, Chamber of Commerce-sponsored course designed to develop community leaders.

Ostlund was the Republican nominee for governor in 1978 and narrowly lost to Ed Herschler. He and his wife Mary moved to a ranch halfway between Laramie and Cheyenne five years ago so he could be closer to eye specialists. Ostlund lost his sight 4½ years ago due to diabetes.

With his seeing eye dog resting at his side, Ostlund told the GALI graduates that, in addition to ability and desire, leadership requires opportunity. He added, "There's a plethora of opportunity today . . . There are situations out there crying out for leadership."

Noting that the United States leads the world in the use of illegal drugs, Ostlund said, "We used to think there was no drug problem in Gillette. We were shocked to find them in the high school, then the junior highs. And now they're in every elementary school in the country."

While applauding the efforts of Congress to build more prisons and stiffen drug laws, Ostlund said, "We have to do something as parents . . . The best place to stop drugs is at the earliest age."

Ostlund said that, rather than talking to children about the penalties of being caught with illegal drugs, the emphasis should be on the positive. "We should teach them to have pride in keeping their minds and bodies healthy," he said. Ostlund added, "I'm not usually pessimistic, but we're losing (the fight against drugs) right now."

Referring to last month's congressional election in Wyoming, Ostlund said political campaigns are focusing more and more on "personal attacks rather than issues."

He said candidates no longer run on the platforms painstakingly prepared by their parties, and that the platforms themselves are becoming less and less meaningful. "Each year the platforms shrink and shrink because we're too timid to take stands on the issues," he explained.

Ostlund also bemoaned the emergence of countless one-issue groups which are only interested in their cause, rather than the overall welfare of society.

"I don't have the answer," he concluded, "but you will. Don't let it be that way. Offer your help and your ideas. If you don't get involved, there'll be a vacuum that will be filled by far-out ideas."

The graduation was the third since the GALI program began. The program is self-perpetuating in that the graduates for this year's program will plan and organize the program for next year's class whose members will be chosen this summer. The nine one-day sessions running from September to May included tours and lectures about local government and industry, sessions on leadership, and a trip to Cheyenne to learn about the Legislature and state government.